CONFESSIONS OF A BLABBERMOUTH

Published by DC Comics,

1700 Broadway,

New York, NY 10019.

Printed in Canada.

DC Comics, a Warner Bros.

Entertainment Company.

ISBN: 1-4012-1148-8

ISBN: 978-1-4012-1148-6

COVER BY AARON ALEXOVICH

confessions of a

blabbermouth

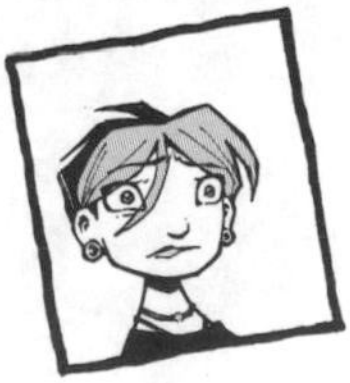

Written by Mike Carey & Louise Carey

Illustrated by Aaron Alexovich

Lettering by John J. Hill

minx

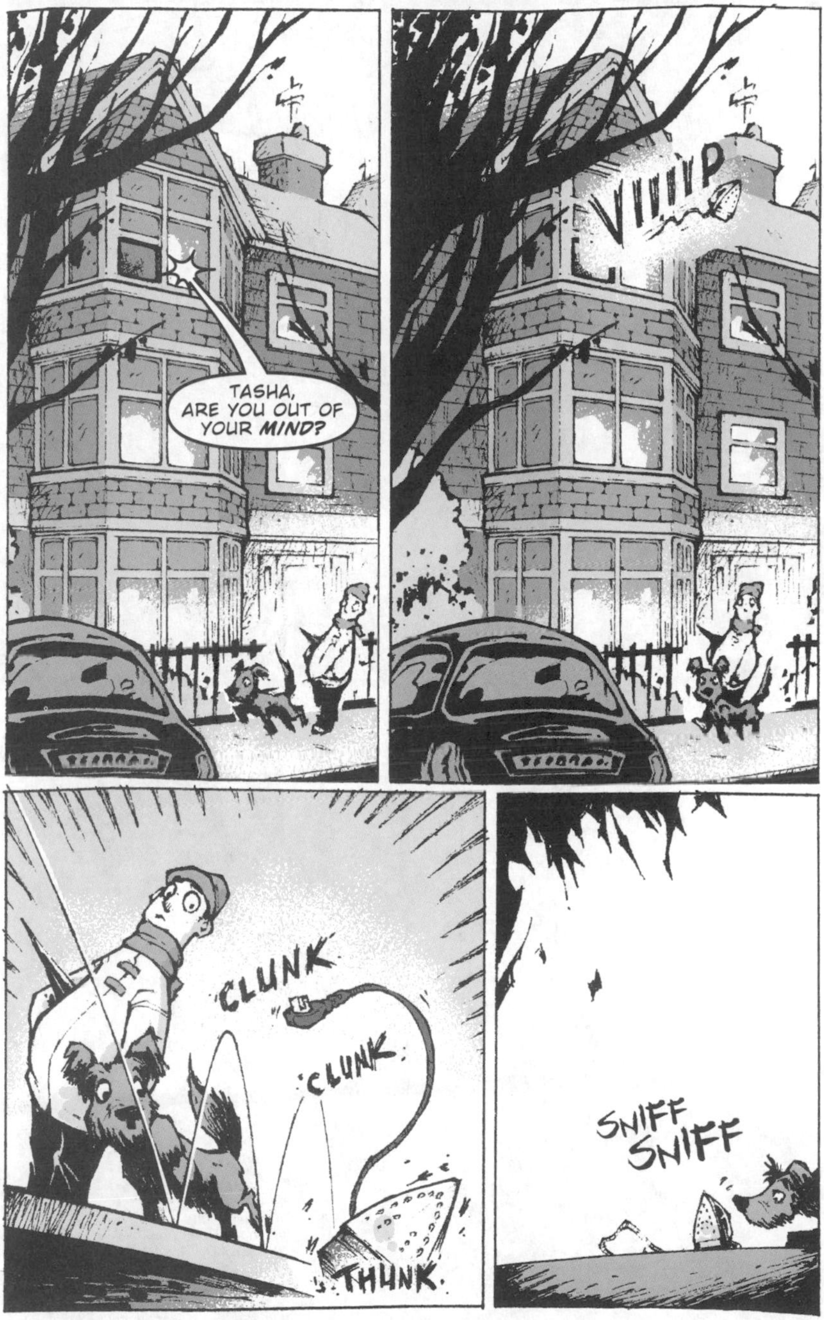
TASHA, ARE YOU OUT OF YOUR *MIND?*
VIIIIIP
CLUNK
CLUNK
THUNK
SNIFF SNIFF

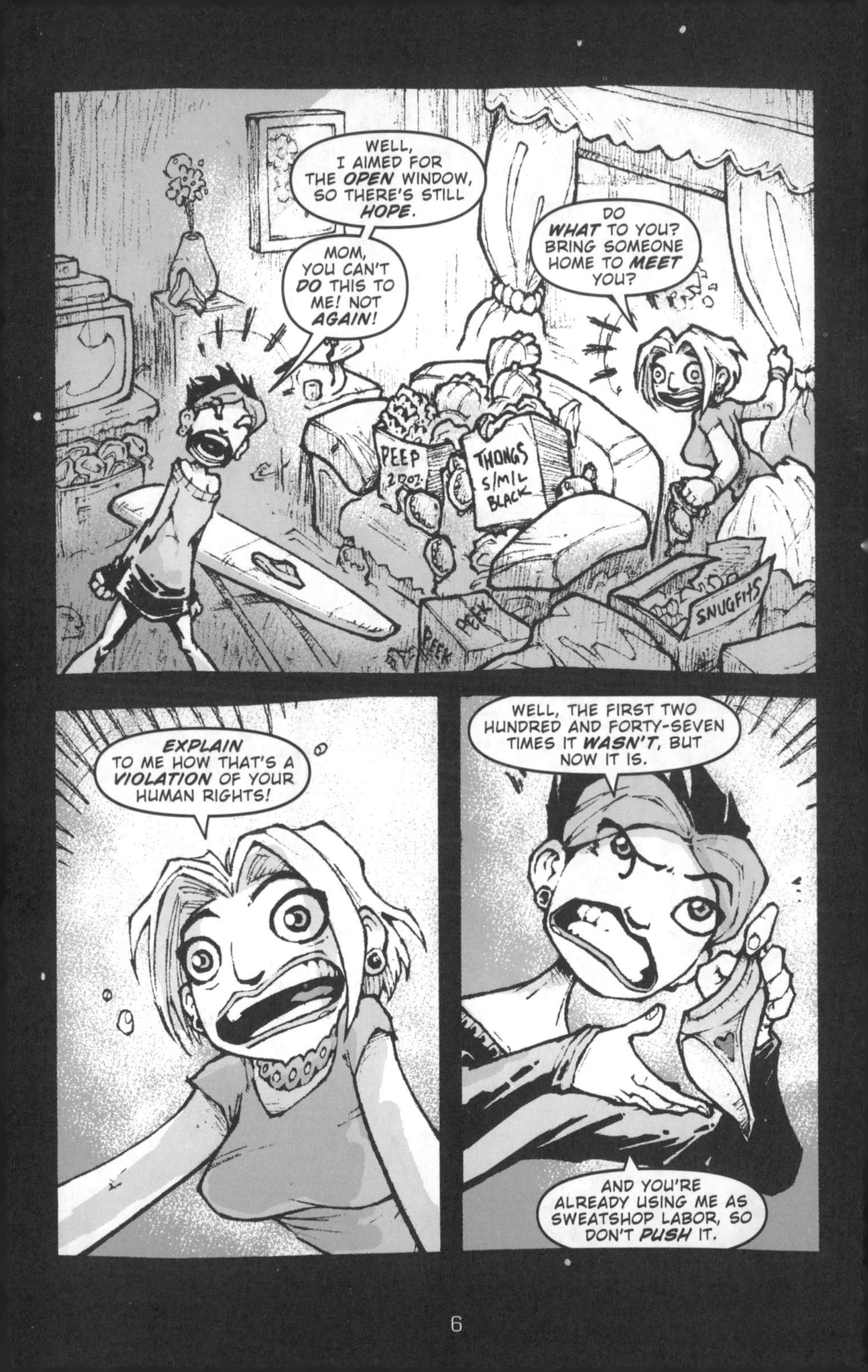
WELL, I AIMED FOR THE OPEN WINDOW, SO THERE'S STILL HOPE.
MOM, YOU CAN'T DO THIS TO ME! NOT AGAIN!
DO WHAT TO YOU? BRING SOMEONE HOME TO MEET YOU?
PEEP 2002.
THONGS S/M/L BLACK
SNUGFITS
PEEK
PEEK
EXPLAIN TO ME HOW THAT'S A VIOLATION OF YOUR HUMAN RIGHTS!
WELL, THE FIRST TWO HUNDRED AND FORTY-SEVEN TIMES IT WASN'T, BUT NOW IT IS.
AND YOU'RE ALREADY USING ME AS SWEATSHOP LABOR, SO DON'T PUSH IT.

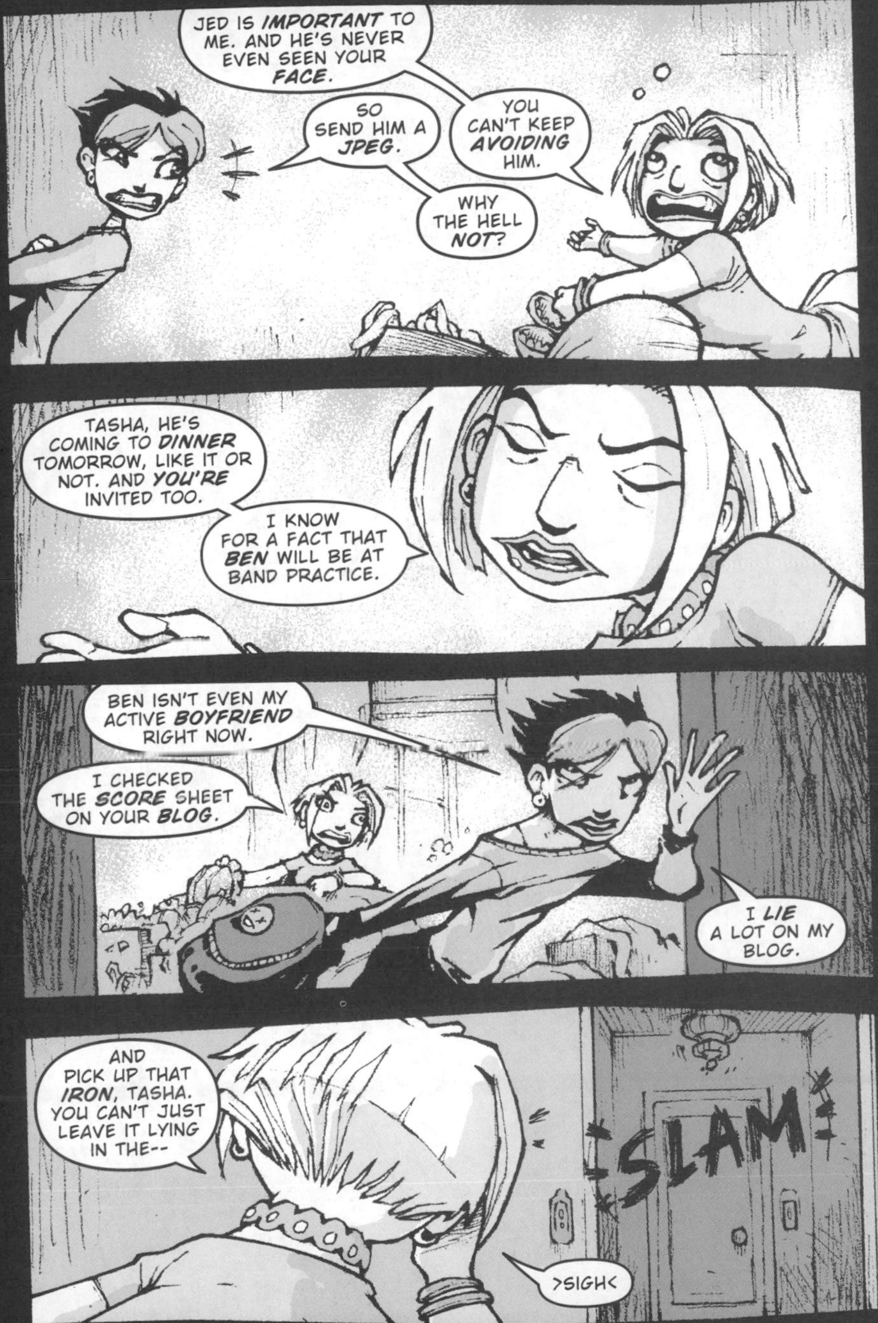
JED IS IMPORTANT TO ME. AND HE'S NEVER EVEN SEEN YOUR FACE.
SO SEND HIM A JPEG.
YOU CAN'T KEEP AVOIDING HIM.
WHY THE HELL NOT?
TASHA, HE'S COMING TO DINNER TOMORROW, LIKE IT OR NOT. AND YOU'RE INVITED TOO.
I KNOW FOR A FACT THAT BEN WILL BE AT BAND PRACTICE.
BEN ISN'T EVEN MY ACTIVE BOYFRIEND RIGHT NOW.
I CHECKED THE SCORE SHEET ON YOUR BLOG.
I LIE A LOT ON MY BLOG.
AND PICK UP THAT IRON, TASHA. YOU CAN'T JUST LEAVE IT LYING IN THE--
SLAM
>SIGH<

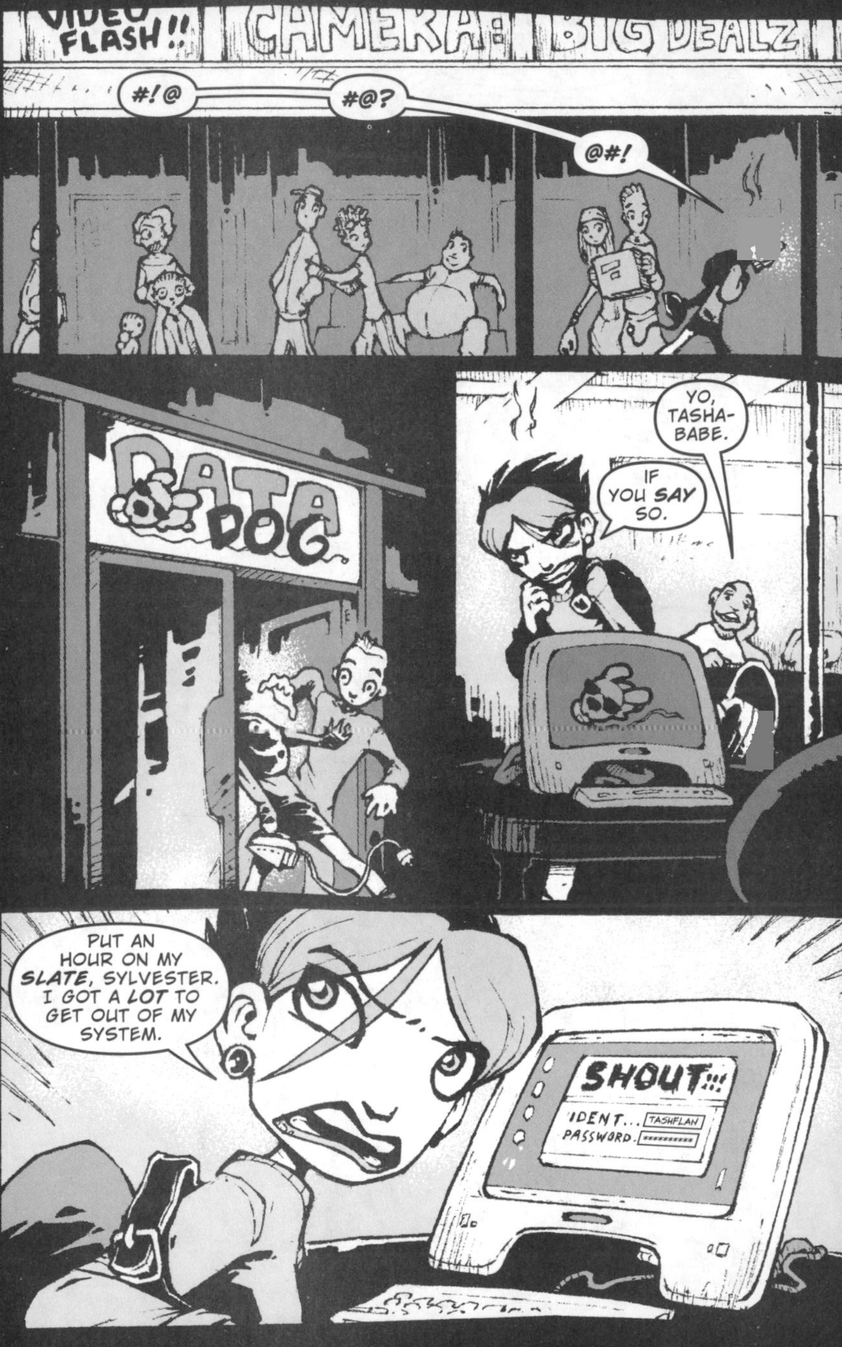
VIDEO FLASH!!
CAMERA: BIG DEALZ
#!@
#@?
@#!
DATA DOG
YO, TASHA-BABE.
IF YOU SAY SO.
PUT AN HOUR ON MY SLATE, SYLVESTER. I GOT A LOT TO GET OUT OF MY SYSTEM.
SHOUT!!!
IDENT... TASHFLAN
PASSWORD.

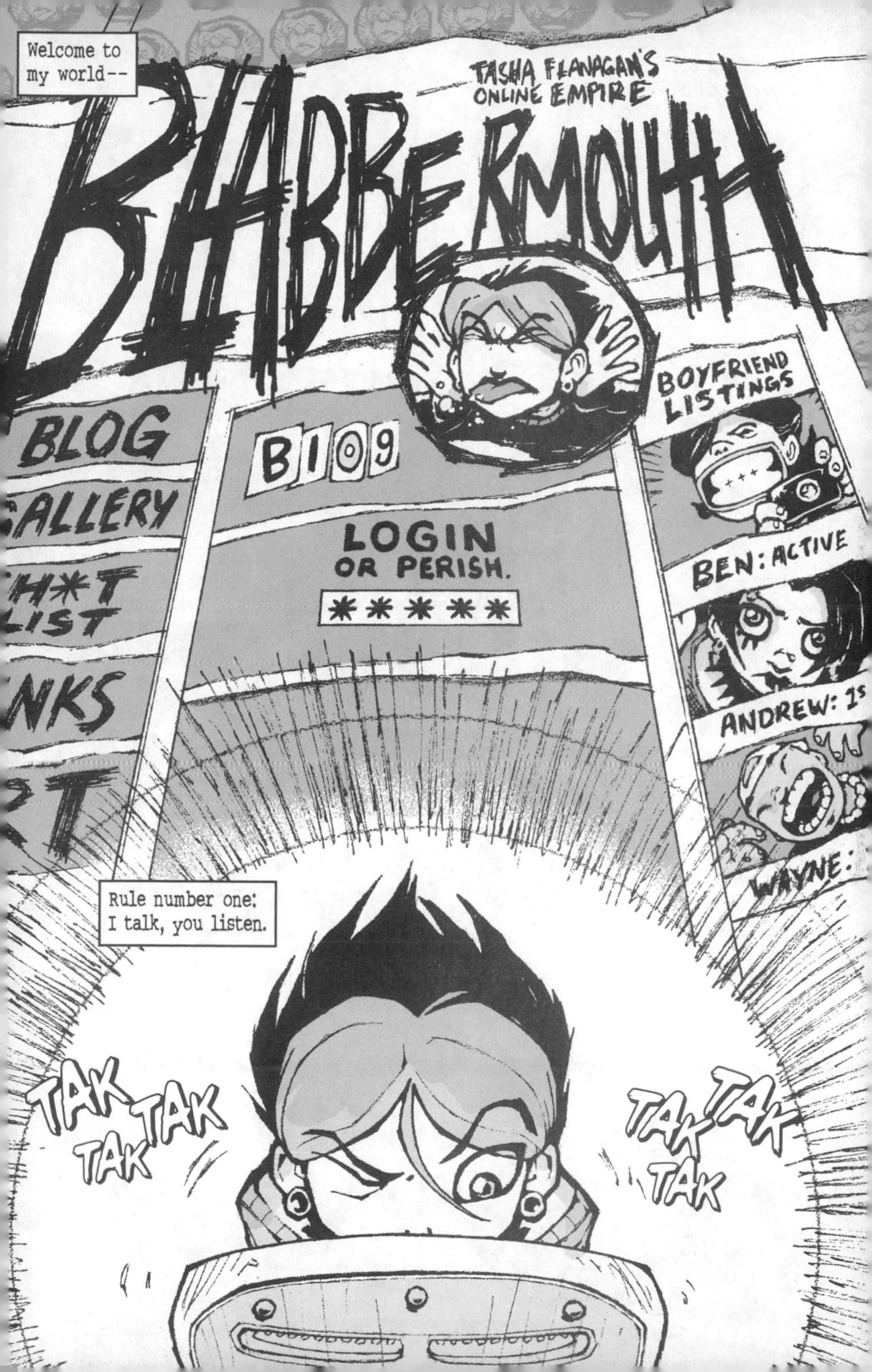

Welcome to my world--
BLABBERMOUTH
TASHA FLANAGAN'S ONLINE EMPIRE
BLOG
GALLERY
SH*T LIST
NKS
BIO
LOGIN OR PERISH.
*****
BOYFRIEND LISTINGS
BEN: ACTIVE
ANDREW: 1s
WAYNE:
Rule number one: I talk, you listen.
TAK TAK TAK
TAK TAK TAK

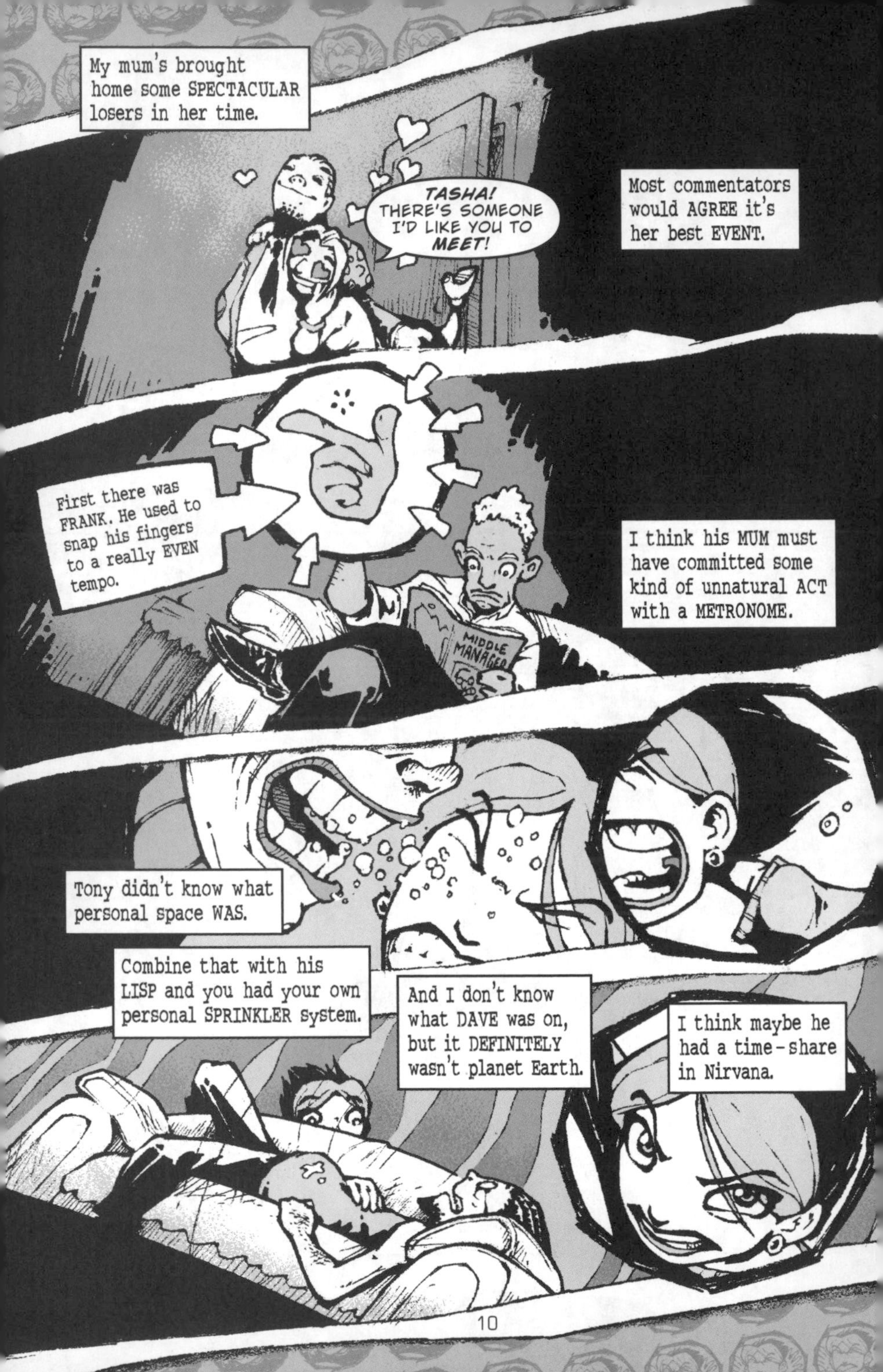
My mum's brought home some SPECTACULAR losers in her time.
TASHA! THERE'S SOMEONE I'D LIKE YOU TO MEET!
Most commentators would AGREE it's her best EVENT.
First there was FRANK. He used to snap his fingers to a really EVEN tempo.
MIDDLE MANAGER
I think his MUM must have committed some kind of unnatural ACT with a METRONOME.
Tony didn't know what personal space WAS.
Combine that with his LISP and you had your own personal SPRINKLER system.
And I don't know what DAVE was on, but it DEFINITELY wasn't planet Earth.
I think maybe he had a time-share in Nirvana.

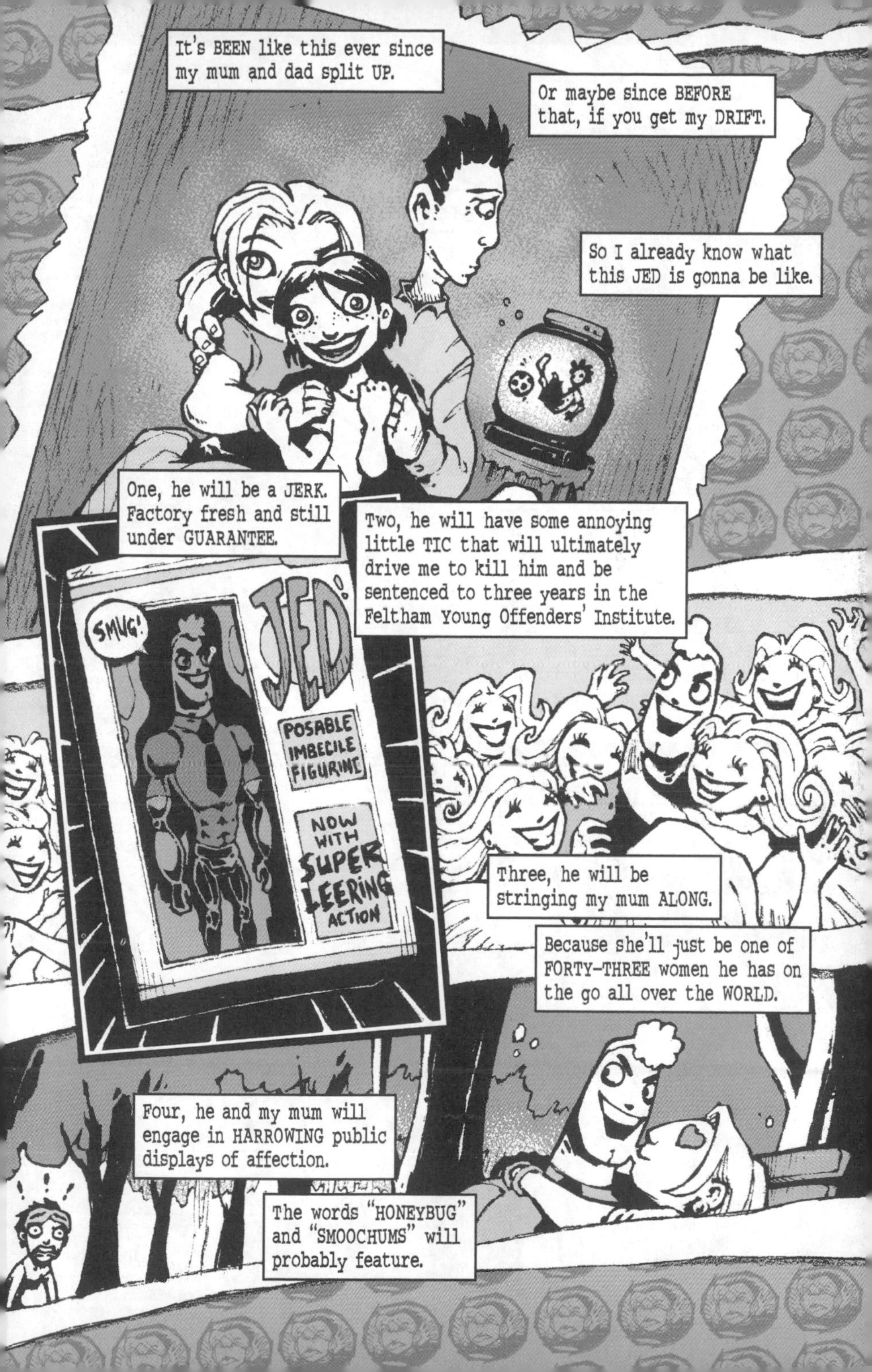

It's BEEN like this ever since my mum and dad split UP.
Or maybe since BEFORE that, if you get my DRIFT.
So I already know what this JED is gonna be like.
One, he will be a JERK. Factory fresh and still under GUARANTEE.
Two, he will have some annoying little TIC that will ultimately drive me to kill him and be sentenced to three years in the Feltham Young Offenders' Institute.
SMUG!
JED
POSABLE IMBECILE FIGURINE
NOW WITH SUPER LEERING ACTION
Three, he will be stringing my mum ALONG.
Because she'll just be one of FORTY-THREE women he has on the go all over the WORLD.
Four, he and my mum will engage in HARROWING public displays of affection.
The words "HONEYBUG" and "SMOOCHUMS" will probably feature.

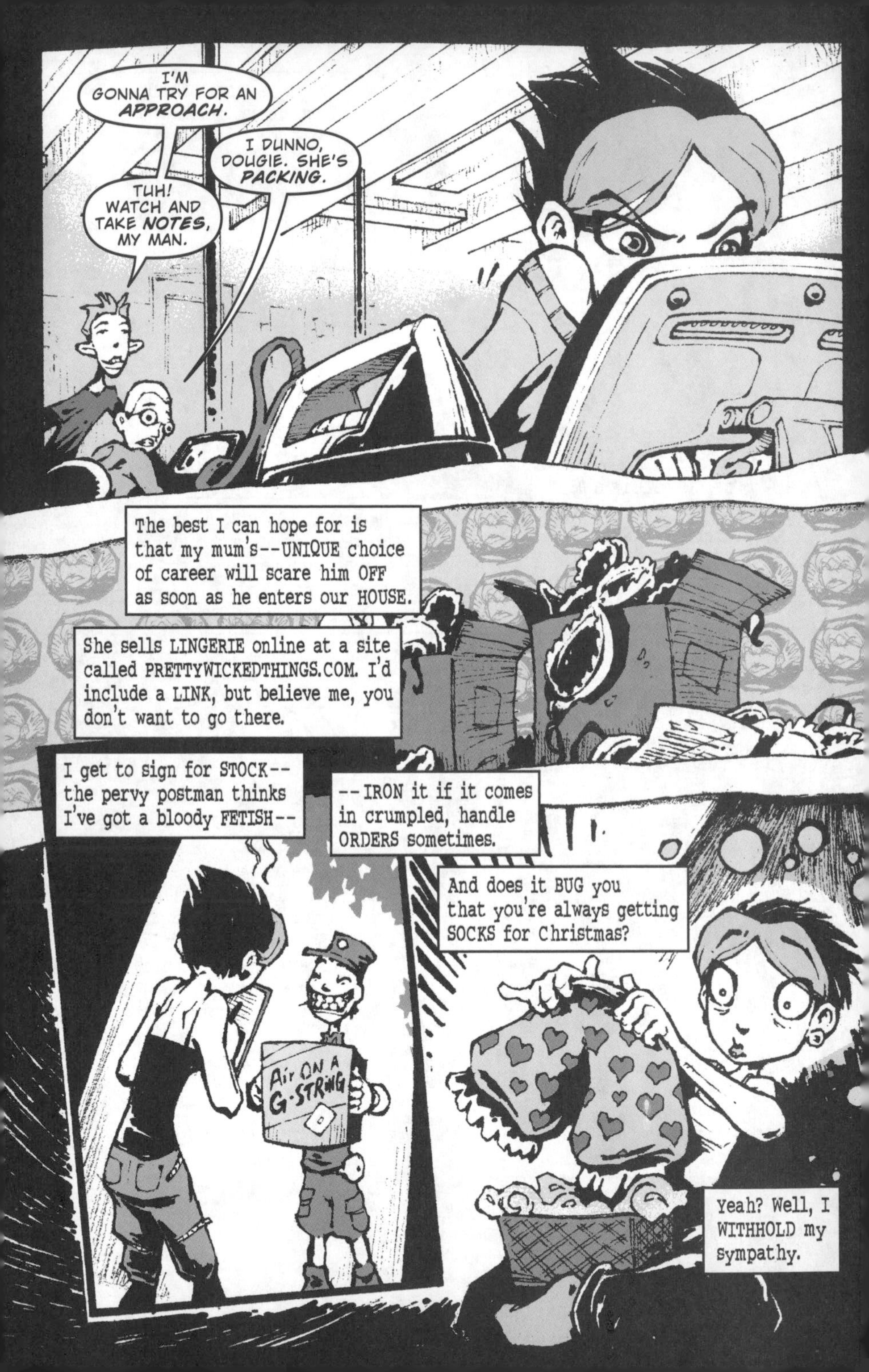
I'M GONNA TRY FOR AN APPROACH.
I DUNNO, DOUGIE. SHE'S PACKING.
TUH! WATCH AND TAKE NOTES, MY MAN.
The best I can hope for is that my mum's--UNIQUE choice of career will scare him OFF as soon as he enters our HOUSE.
She sells LINGERIE online at a site called PRETTYWICKEDTHINGS.COM. I'd include a LINK, but believe me, you don't want to go there.
I get to sign for STOCK-- the pervy postman thinks I've got a bloody FETISH--
Air ON A G-STRING
--IRON it if it comes in crumpled, handle ORDERS sometimes.
And does it BUG you that you're always getting SOCKS for Christmas?
Yeah? Well, I WITHHOLD my sympathy.

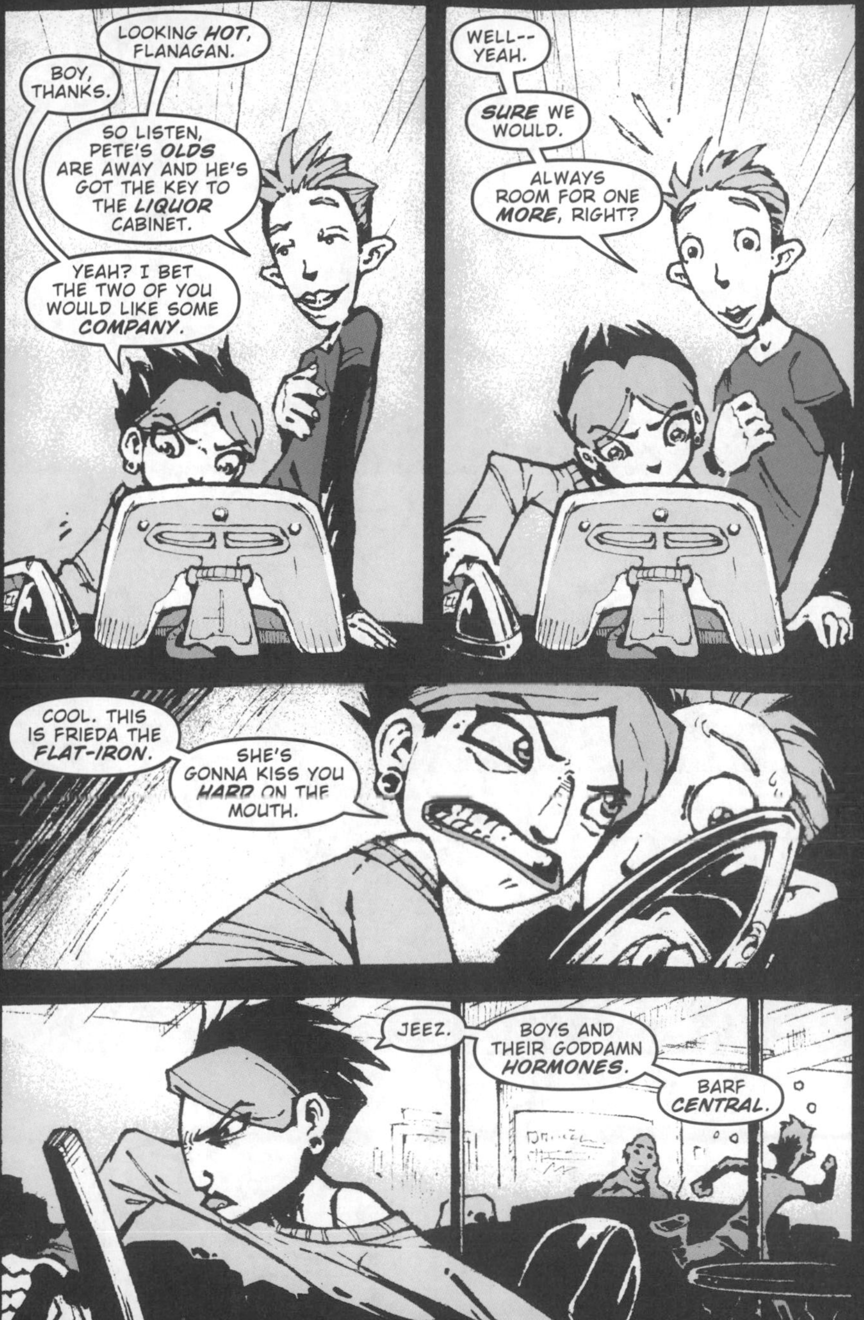
BOY, THANKS.
LOOKING HOT, FLANAGAN.
SO LISTEN, PETE'S OLDS ARE AWAY AND HE'S GOT THE KEY TO THE LIQUOR CABINET.
YEAH? I BET THE TWO OF YOU WOULD LIKE SOME COMPANY.
WELL-- YEAH.
SURE WE WOULD.
ALWAYS ROOM FOR ONE MORE, RIGHT?
COOL. THIS IS FRIEDA THE FLAT-IRON.
SHE'S GONNA KISS YOU HARD ON THE MOUTH.
JEEZ.
BOYS AND THEIR GODDAMN HORMONES.
BARF CENTRAL.

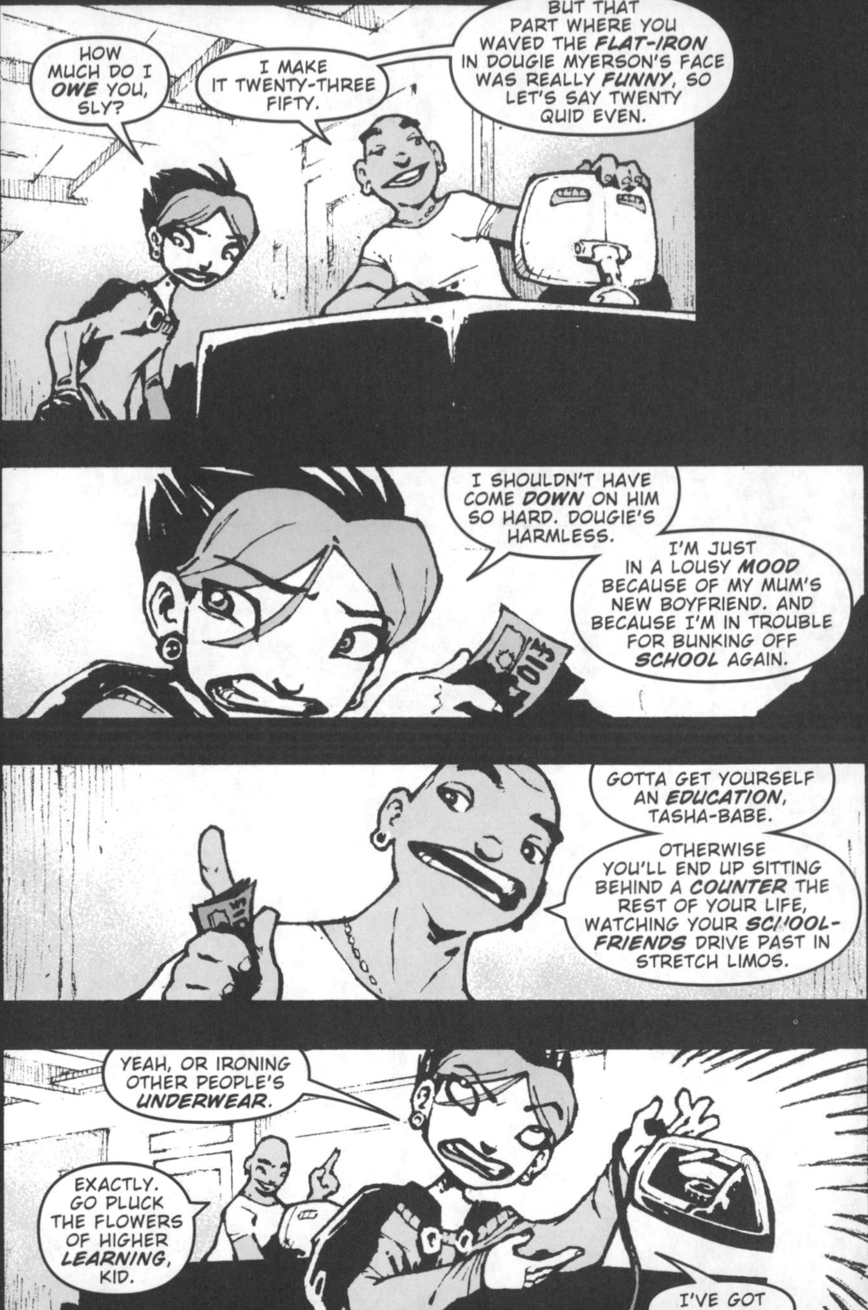
HOW MUCH DO I ***OWE*** YOU, SLY?
I MAKE IT TWENTY-THREE FIFTY.
BUT THAT PART WHERE YOU WAVED THE ***FLAT-IRON*** IN DOUGIE MYERSON'S FACE WAS REALLY ***FUNNY***, SO LET'S SAY TWENTY QUID EVEN.
I SHOULDN'T HAVE COME ***DOWN*** ON HIM SO HARD. DOUGIE'S HARMLESS.
I'M JUST IN A LOUSY ***MOOD*** BECAUSE OF MY MUM'S NEW BOYFRIEND. AND BECAUSE I'M IN TROUBLE FOR BUNKING OFF ***SCHOOL*** AGAIN.
GOTTA GET YOURSELF AN ***EDUCATION***, TASHA-BABE.
OTHERWISE YOU'LL END UP SITTING BEHIND A ***COUNTER*** THE REST OF YOUR LIFE, WATCHING YOUR ***SCHOOL-FRIENDS*** DRIVE PAST IN STRETCH LIMOS.
YEAH, OR IRONING OTHER PEOPLE'S ***UNDERWEAR***.
EXACTLY. GO PLUCK THE FLOWERS OF HIGHER ***LEARNING***, KID.
I'VE GOT HAYFEVER--

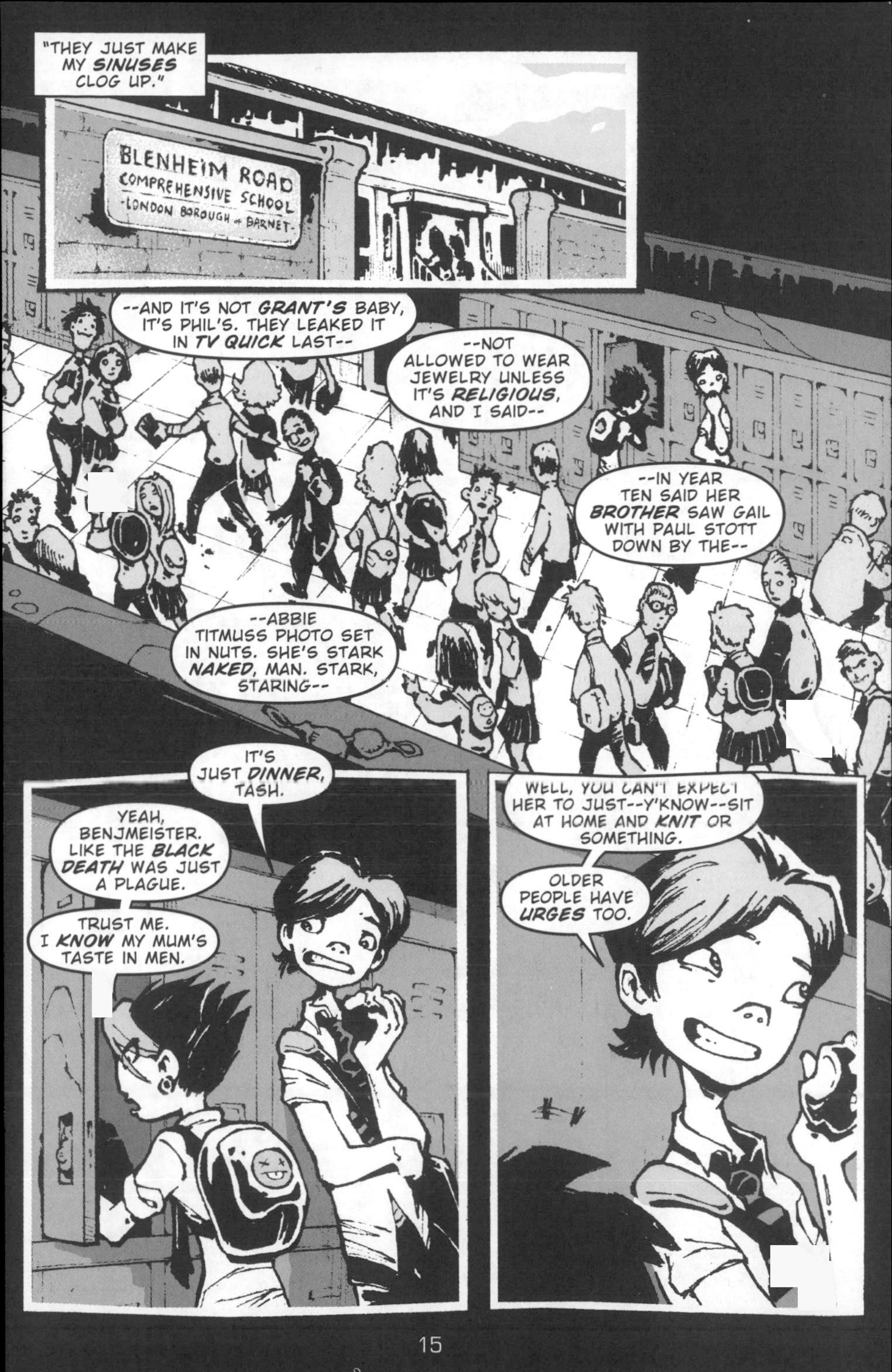
"THEY JUST MAKE MY SINUSES CLOG UP."
BLENHEIM ROAD COMPREHENSIVE SCHOOL -LONDON BOROUGH of BARNET-
--AND IT'S NOT GRANT'S BABY, IT'S PHIL'S. THEY LEAKED IT IN TV QUICK LAST--
--NOT ALLOWED TO WEAR JEWELRY UNLESS IT'S RELIGIOUS, AND I SAID--
--IN YEAR TEN SAID HER BROTHER SAW GAIL WITH PAUL STOTT DOWN BY THE--
--ABBIE TITMUSS PHOTO SET IN NUTS. SHE'S STARK NAKED, MAN. STARK, STARING--
IT'S JUST DINNER, TASH.
YEAH, BENJMEISTER. LIKE THE BLACK DEATH WAS JUST A PLAGUE.
TRUST ME. I KNOW MY MUM'S TASTE IN MEN.
WELL, YOU CAN'T EXPECT HER TO JUST--Y'KNOW--SIT AT HOME AND KNIT OR SOMETHING.
OLDER PEOPLE HAVE URGES TOO.

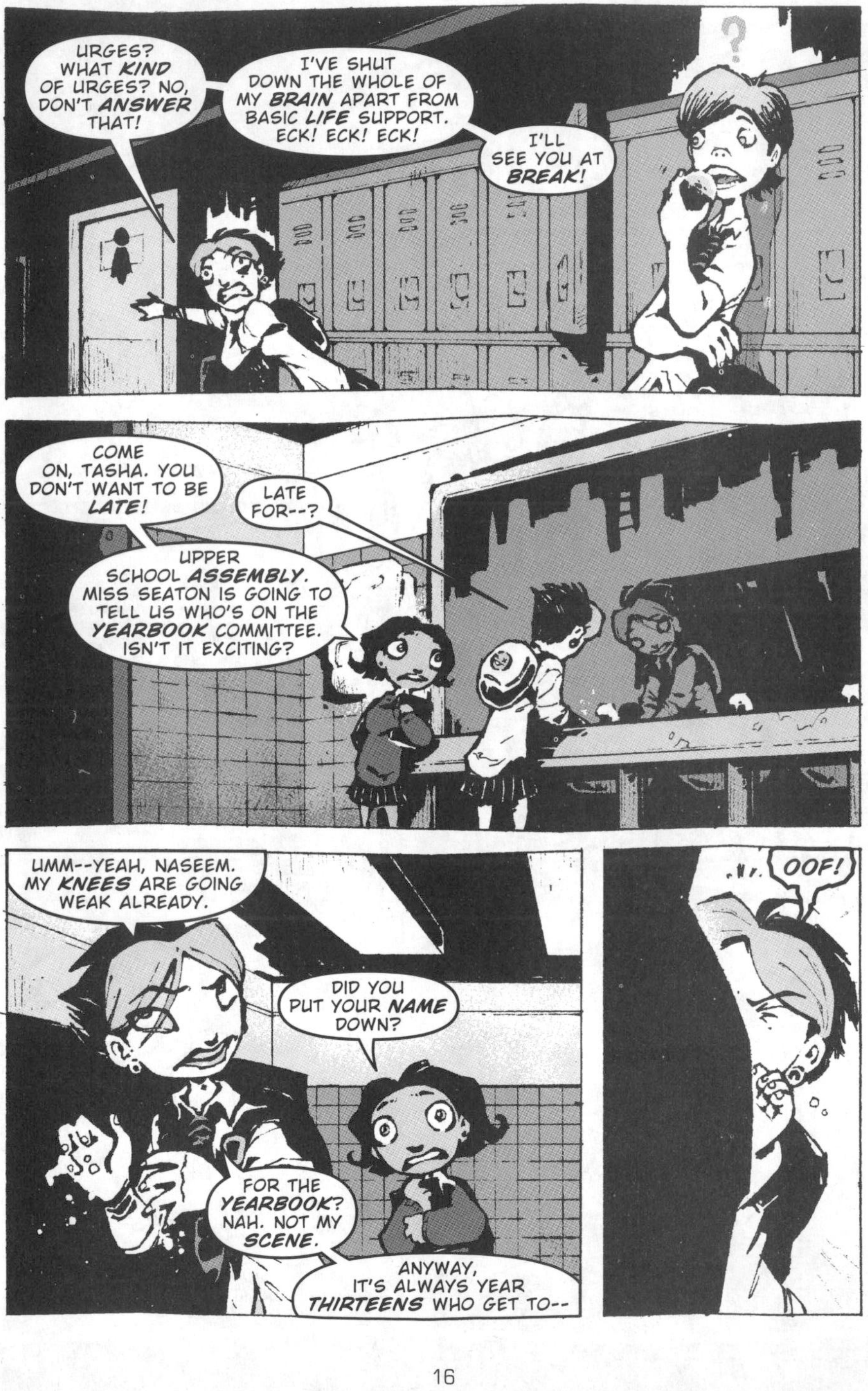

URGES? WHAT KIND OF URGES? NO, DON'T ANSWER THAT!
I'VE SHUT DOWN THE WHOLE OF MY BRAIN APART FROM BASIC LIFE SUPPORT. ECK! ECK! ECK!
?
I'LL SEE YOU AT BREAK!
COME ON, TASHA. YOU DON'T WANT TO BE LATE!
LATE FOR--?
UPPER SCHOOL ASSEMBLY. MISS SEATON IS GOING TO TELL US WHO'S ON THE YEARBOOK COMMITTEE. ISN'T IT EXCITING?
UMM--YEAH, NASEEM. MY KNEES ARE GOING WEAK ALREADY.
DID YOU PUT YOUR NAME DOWN?
FOR THE YEARBOOK? NAH. NOT MY SCENE.
ANYWAY, IT'S ALWAYS YEAR THIRTEENS WHO GET TO--
OOF!

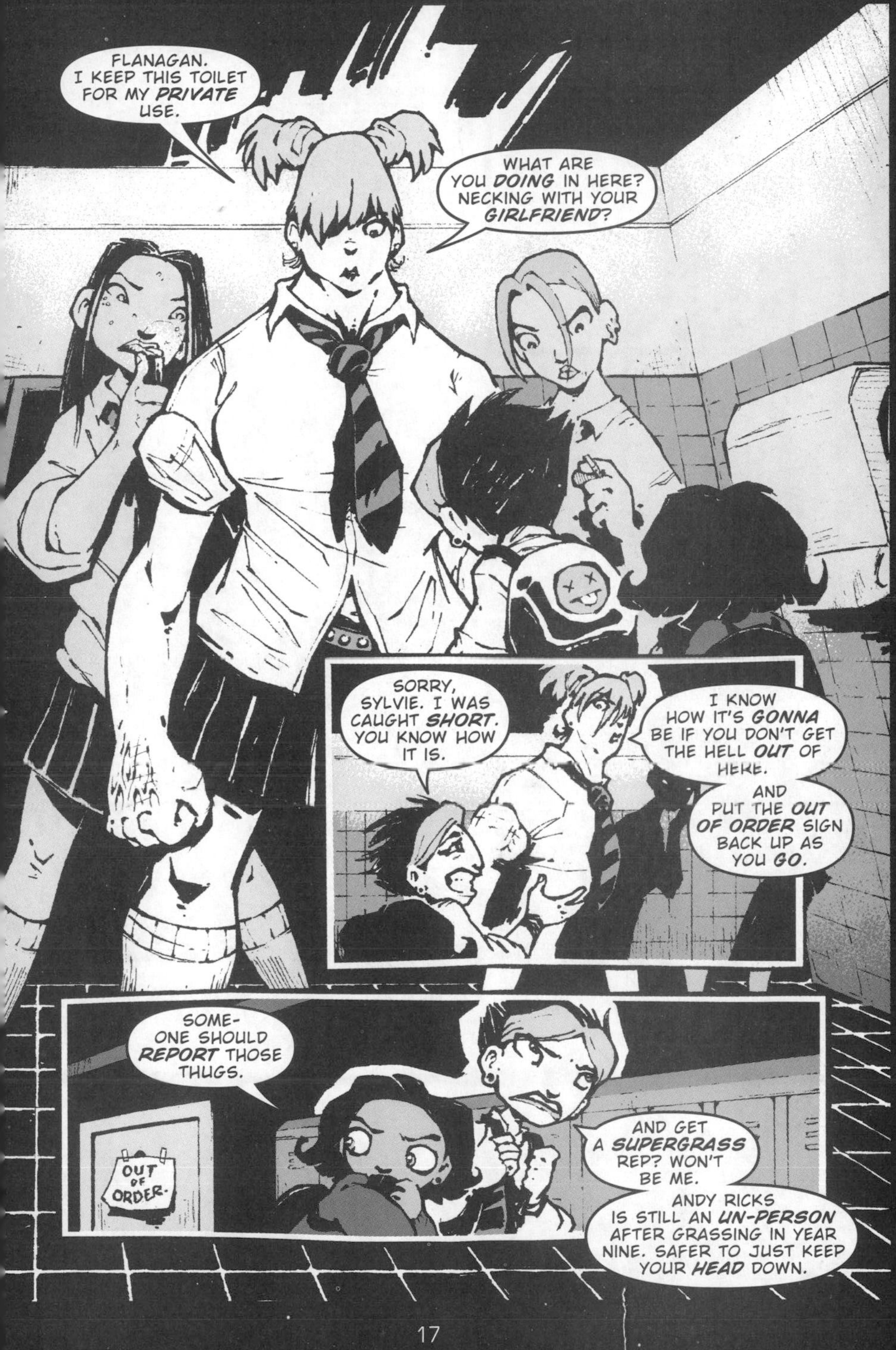
FLANAGAN. I KEEP THIS TOILET FOR MY *PRIVATE* USE.
WHAT ARE YOU *DOING* IN HERE? NECKING WITH YOUR *GIRLFRIEND*?
SORRY, SYLVIE. I WAS CAUGHT *SHORT*. YOU KNOW HOW IT IS.
I KNOW HOW IT'S *GONNA* BE IF YOU DON'T GET THE HELL *OUT* OF HERE.
AND PUT THE *OUT OF ORDER* SIGN BACK UP AS YOU *GO*.
SOME-ONE SHOULD *REPORT* THOSE THUGS.
OUT OF ORDER.
AND GET A *SUPERGRASS* REP? WON'T BE ME.
ANDY RICKS IS STILL AN *UN-PERSON* AFTER GRASSING IN YEAR NINE. SAFER TO JUST KEEP YOUR *HEAD* DOWN.

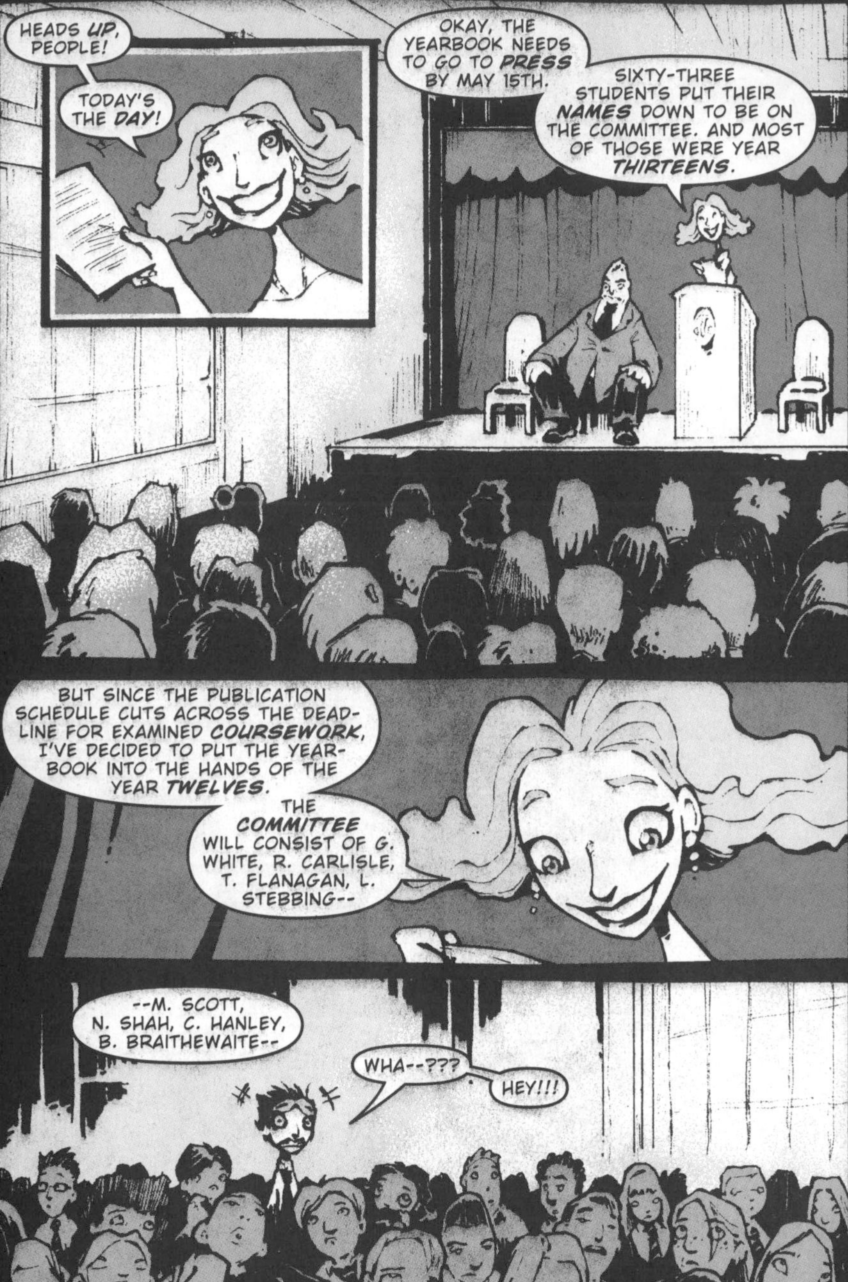
HEADS UP, PEOPLE!
TODAY'S THE DAY!
OKAY, THE YEARBOOK NEEDS TO GO TO PRESS BY MAY 15TH.
SIXTY-THREE STUDENTS PUT THEIR NAMES DOWN TO BE ON THE COMMITTEE. AND MOST OF THOSE WERE YEAR THIRTEENS.
BUT SINCE THE PUBLICATION SCHEDULE CUTS ACROSS THE DEAD-LINE FOR EXAMINED COURSEWORK, I'VE DECIDED TO PUT THE YEAR-BOOK INTO THE HANDS OF THE YEAR TWELVES.
THE COMMITTEE WILL CONSIST OF G. WHITE, R. CARLISLE, T. FLANAGAN, L. STEBBING--
--M. SCOTT, N. SHAH, C. HANLEY, B. BRAITHEWAITE--
WHA--???
HEY!!!

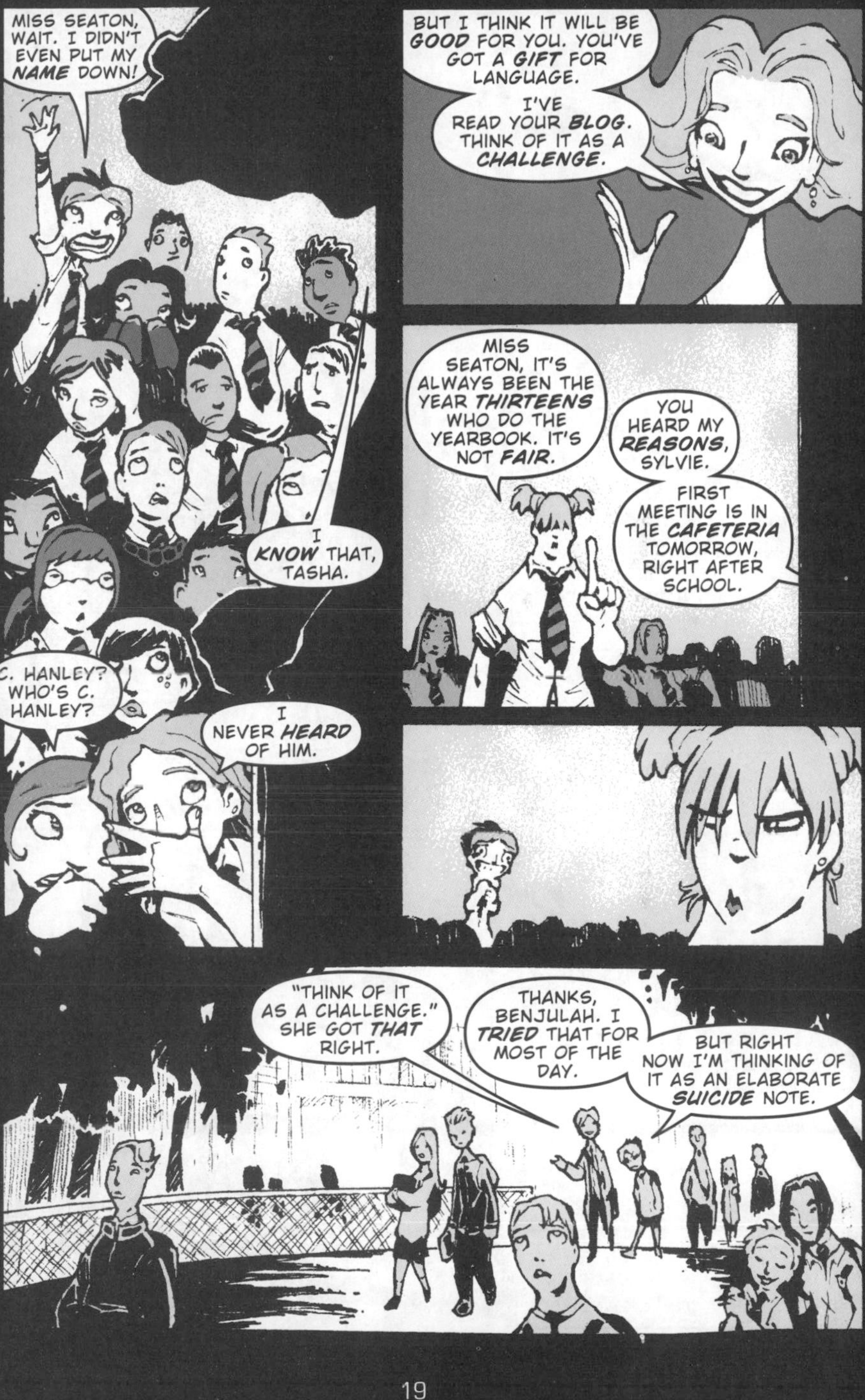
MISS SEATON, WAIT. I DIDN'T EVEN PUT MY NAME DOWN!
BUT I THINK IT WILL BE GOOD FOR YOU. YOU'VE GOT A GIFT FOR LANGUAGE.
I'VE READ YOUR BLOG. THINK OF IT AS A CHALLENGE.
I KNOW THAT, TASHA.
MISS SEATON, IT'S ALWAYS BEEN THE YEAR THIRTEENS WHO DO THE YEARBOOK. IT'S NOT FAIR.
YOU HEARD MY REASONS, SYLVIE.
FIRST MEETING IS IN THE CAFETERIA TOMORROW, RIGHT AFTER SCHOOL.
C. HANLEY? WHO'S C. HANLEY?
I NEVER HEARD OF HIM.
"THINK OF IT AS A CHALLENGE." SHE GOT THAT RIGHT.
THANKS, BENJULAH. I TRIED THAT FOR MOST OF THE DAY.
BUT RIGHT NOW I'M THINKING OF IT AS AN ELABORATE SUICIDE NOTE.

BLABBERMOUTH!!

Basically, I'm between a rock and a hard place. The rock: At school, Sylvie is going to KILL me.

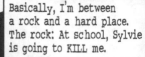

The problem with Miss Seaton's brainwave is that it operates on the basic principle that Sylvie and her gang are kind, CARING people who are HAPPY TO WORK together with the year 12's.

She's too young and innocent to realize th Sylvie and Co. aren't exactly rolling out th FRIENDSHIP wagon.

I mean, unless they're trying to mow us DOWN with it.

BLENHEIM SPECTRUM

‡SIGH‡ NO, YOU HAVE TO RUB THE STICKS *TOGETHER* TO MAKE FIRE.

The thing is, the yearbook is the sacred property of the year 13's. They're the ones leaving the school, so they're the ones who do the yearbook. It's pretty simple.

Of course, it would have to be. I mean, year 13's are NOT the world's greatest thinkers.

I bet you're wondering what the hard place is?

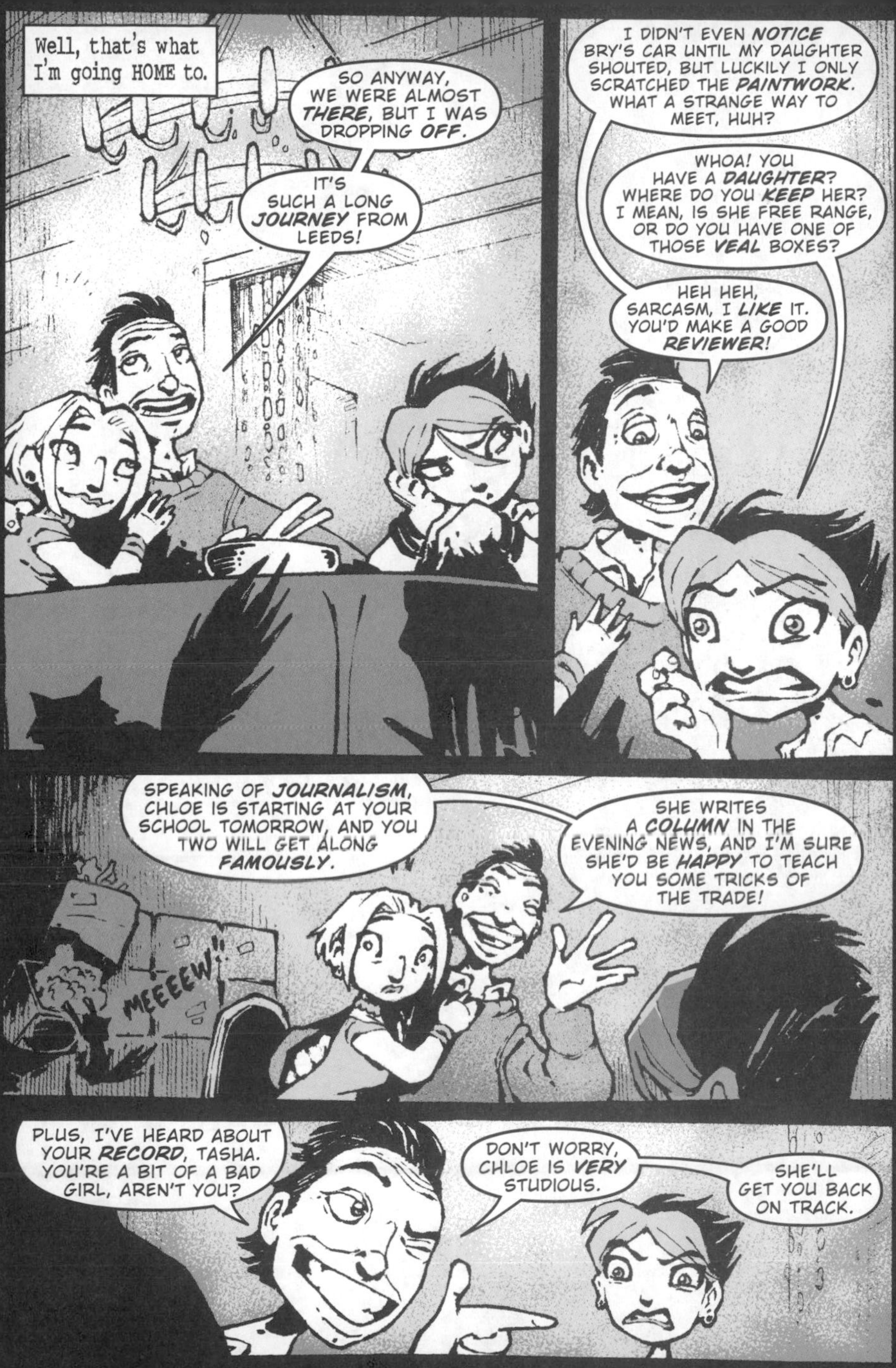
Well, that's what I'm going HOME to.
SO ANYWAY, WE WERE ALMOST THERE, BUT I WAS DROPPING OFF.
IT'S SUCH A LONG JOURNEY FROM LEEDS!
I DIDN'T EVEN NOTICE BRY'S CAR UNTIL MY DAUGHTER SHOUTED, BUT LUCKILY I ONLY SCRATCHED THE PAINTWORK. WHAT A STRANGE WAY TO MEET, HUH?
WHOA! YOU HAVE A DAUGHTER? WHERE DO YOU KEEP HER? I MEAN, IS SHE FREE RANGE, OR DO YOU HAVE ONE OF THOSE VEAL BOXES?
HEH HEH, SARCASM, I LIKE IT. YOU'D MAKE A GOOD REVIEWER!
SPEAKING OF JOURNALISM, CHLOE IS STARTING AT YOUR SCHOOL TOMORROW, AND YOU TWO WILL GET ALONG FAMOUSLY.
SHE WRITES A COLUMN IN THE EVENING NEWS, AND I'M SURE SHE'D BE HAPPY TO TEACH YOU SOME TRICKS OF THE TRADE!
MEEEEW
PLUS, I'VE HEARD ABOUT YOUR RECORD, TASHA. YOU'RE A BIT OF A BAD GIRL, AREN'T YOU?
DON'T WORRY, CHLOE IS VERY STUDIOUS.
SHE'LL GET YOU BACK ON TRACK.

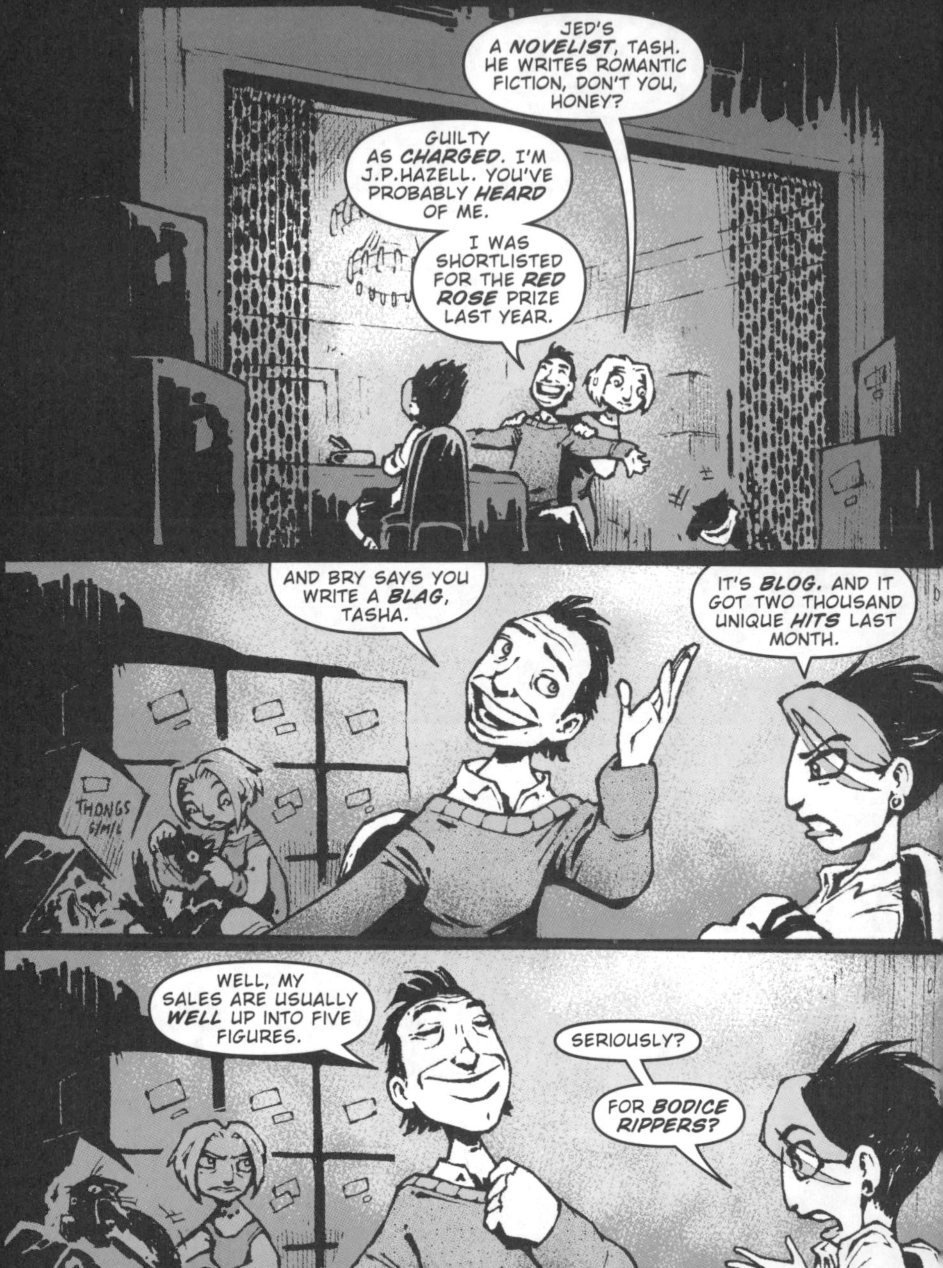
JED'S A NOVELIST, TASH. HE WRITES ROMANTIC FICTION, DON'T YOU, HONEY?
GUILTY AS CHARGED. I'M J.P.HAZELL. YOU'VE PROBABLY HEARD OF ME.
I WAS SHORTLISTED FOR THE RED ROSE PRIZE LAST YEAR.
AND BRY SAYS YOU WRITE A BLAG, TASHA.
IT'S BLOG. AND IT GOT TWO THOUSAND UNIQUE HITS LAST MONTH.
THONGS
WELL, MY SALES ARE USUALLY WELL UP INTO FIVE FIGURES.
SERIOUSLY?
FOR BODICE RIPPERS?

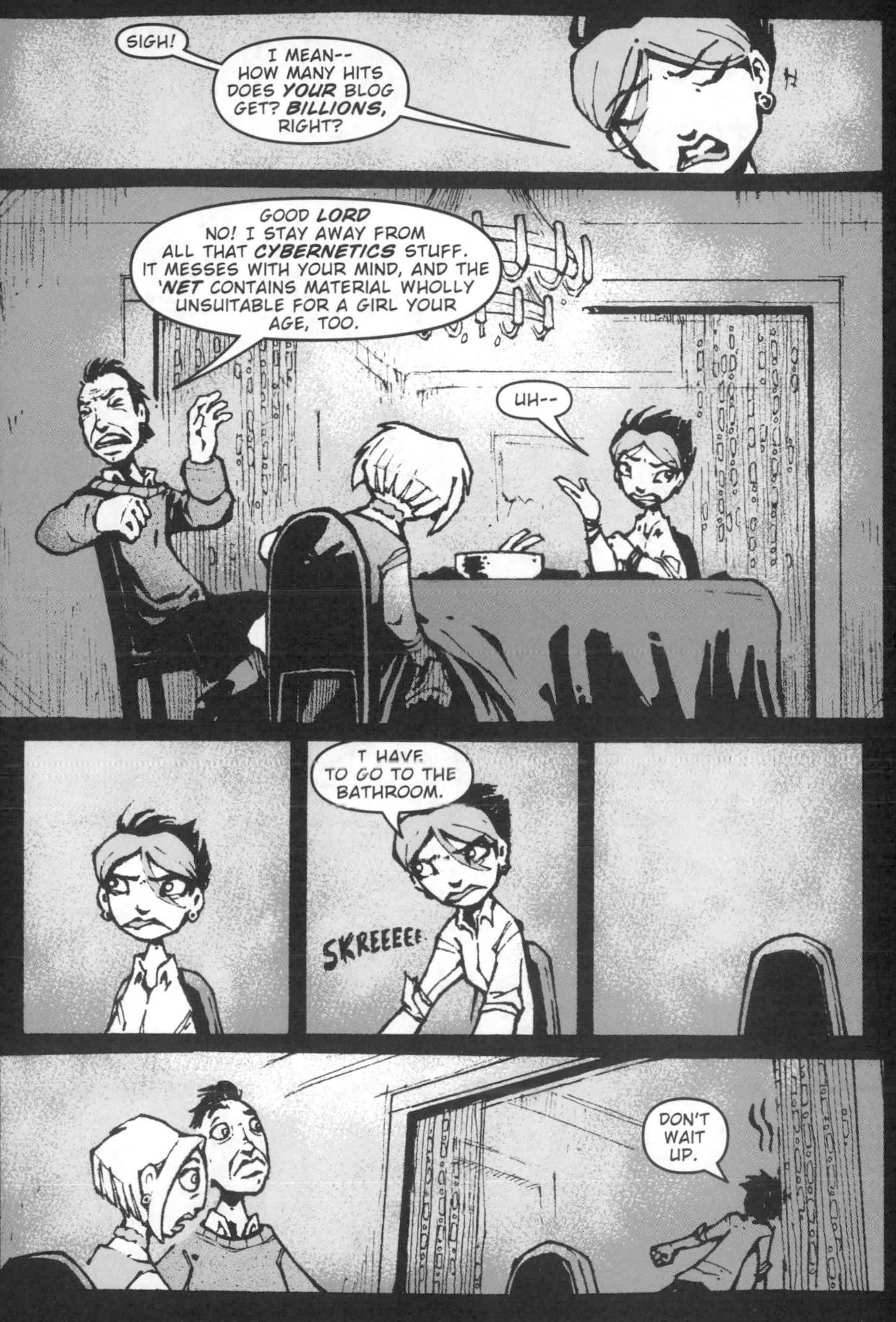
SIGH!
I MEAN-- HOW MANY HITS DOES YOUR BLOG GET? BILLIONS, RIGHT?
GOOD LORD NO! I STAY AWAY FROM ALL THAT CYBERNETICS STUFF. IT MESSES WITH YOUR MIND, AND THE 'NET CONTAINS MATERIAL WHOLLY UNSUITABLE FOR A GIRL YOUR AGE, TOO.
UH--
I HAVE TO GO TO THE BATHROOM.
SKREEEEE
DON'T WAIT UP.

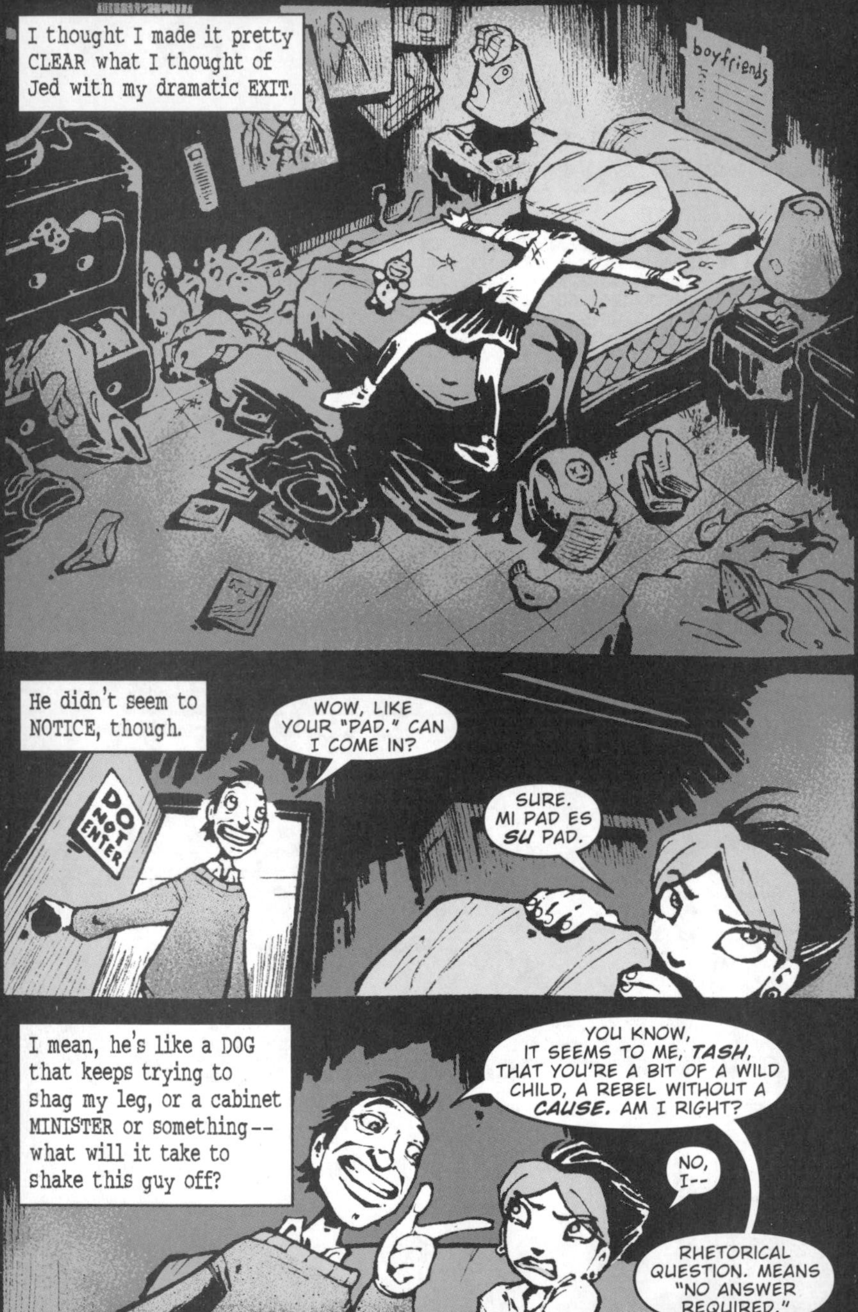
I thought I made it pretty CLEAR what I thought of Jed with my dramatic EXIT.
boyfriends
He didn't seem to NOTICE, though.
WOW, LIKE YOUR "PAD." CAN I COME IN?
DO NOT ENTER
SURE. MI PAD ES SU PAD.
I mean, he's like a DOG that keeps trying to shag my leg, or a cabinet MINISTER or something-- what will it take to shake this guy off?
YOU KNOW, IT SEEMS TO ME, TASH, THAT YOU'RE A BIT OF A WILD CHILD, A REBEL WITHOUT A CAUSE. AM I RIGHT?
NO, I--
RHETORICAL QUESTION. MEANS "NO ANSWER REQUIRED."

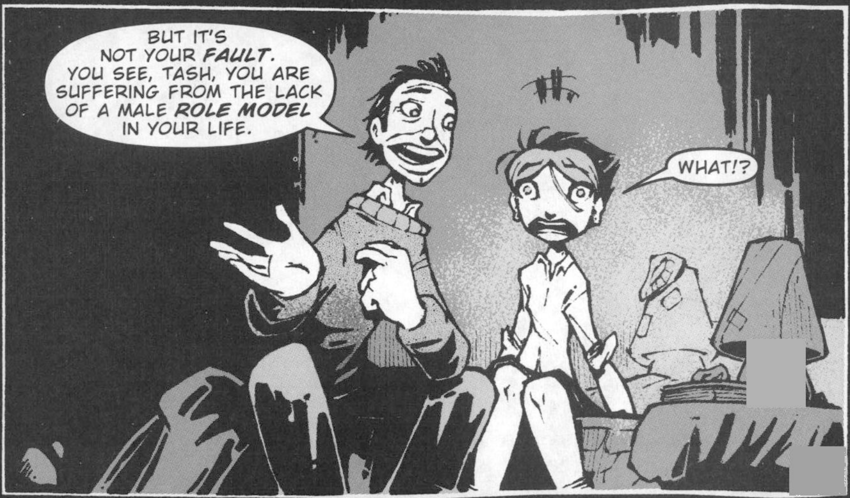
BUT IT'S NOT YOUR FAULT. YOU SEE, TASH, YOU ARE SUFFERING FROM THE LACK OF A MALE ROLE MODEL IN YOUR LIFE.
WHAT!?

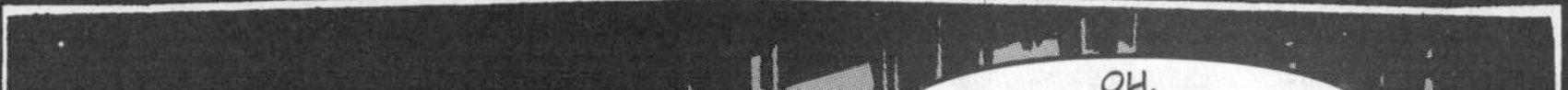
OH, YOUR MOTHER IS A FANTASTIC GIRL, I'M NOT SAYING SHE ISN'T, BUT YOU NEED A STRONG FATHER AS WELL AS A LOVING MOTHER.

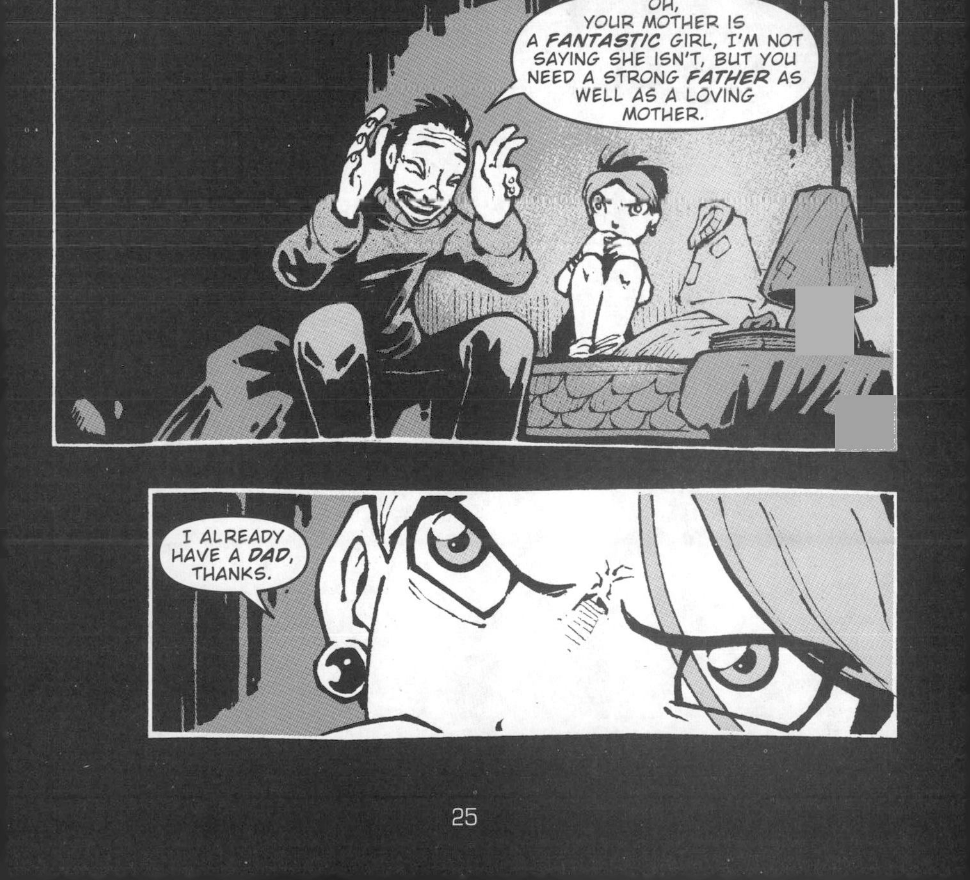
I ALREADY HAVE A DAD, THANKS.

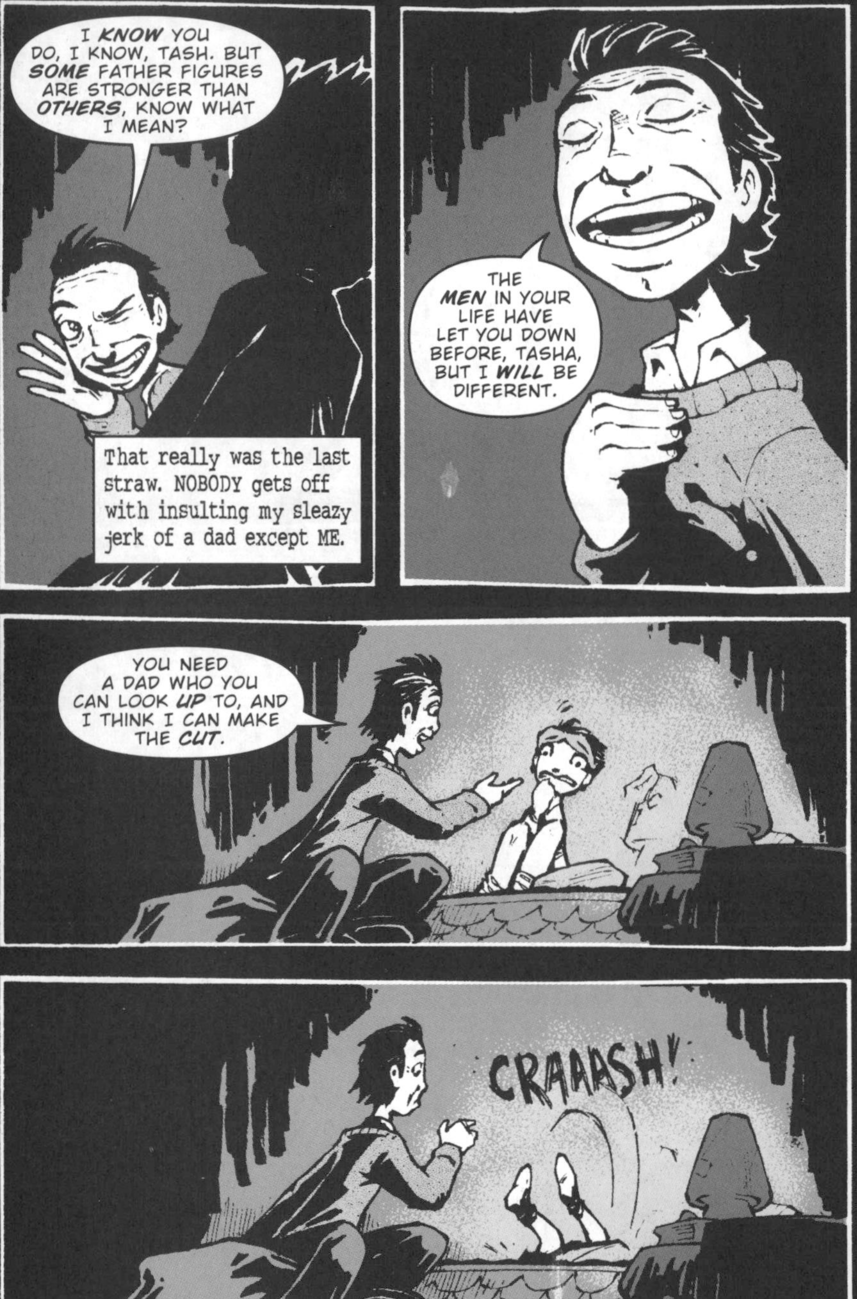
I KNOW YOU DO, I KNOW, TASH. BUT SOME FATHER FIGURES ARE STRONGER THAN OTHERS, KNOW WHAT I MEAN?
That really was the last straw. NOBODY gets off with insulting my sleazy jerk of a dad except ME.
THE MEN IN YOUR LIFE HAVE LET YOU DOWN BEFORE, TASHA, BUT I WILL BE DIFFERENT.
YOU NEED A DAD WHO YOU CAN LOOK UP TO, AND I THINK I CAN MAKE THE CUT.
CRAAASH!

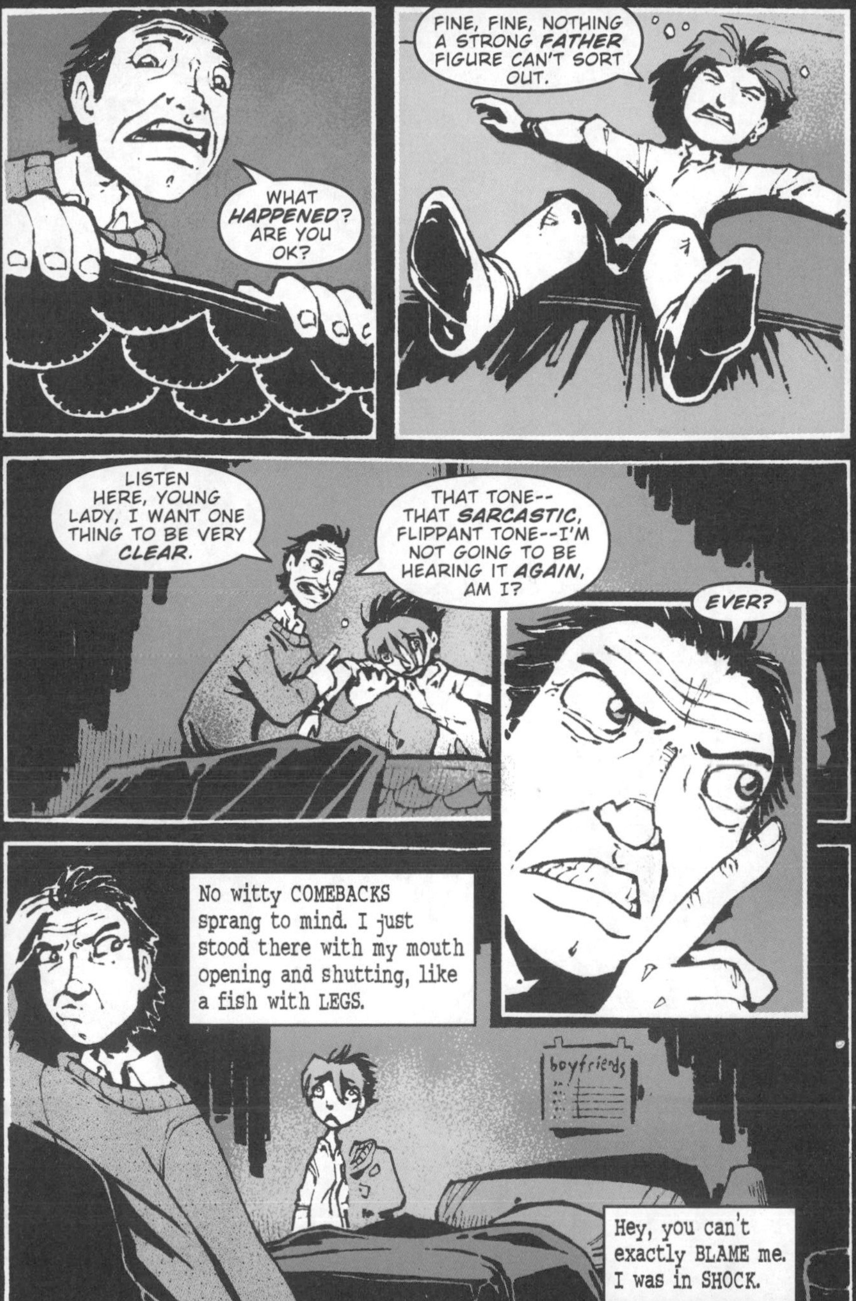
WHAT HAPPENED? ARE YOU OK?
FINE, FINE, NOTHING A STRONG FATHER FIGURE CAN'T SORT OUT.
LISTEN HERE, YOUNG LADY, I WANT ONE THING TO BE VERY CLEAR.
THAT TONE-- THAT SARCASTIC, FLIPPANT TONE--I'M NOT GOING TO BE HEARING IT AGAIN, AM I?
EVER?
No witty COMEBACKS sprang to mind. I just stood there with my mouth opening and shutting, like a fish with LEGS.
boyfriends
Hey, you can't exactly BLAME me. I was in SHOCK.

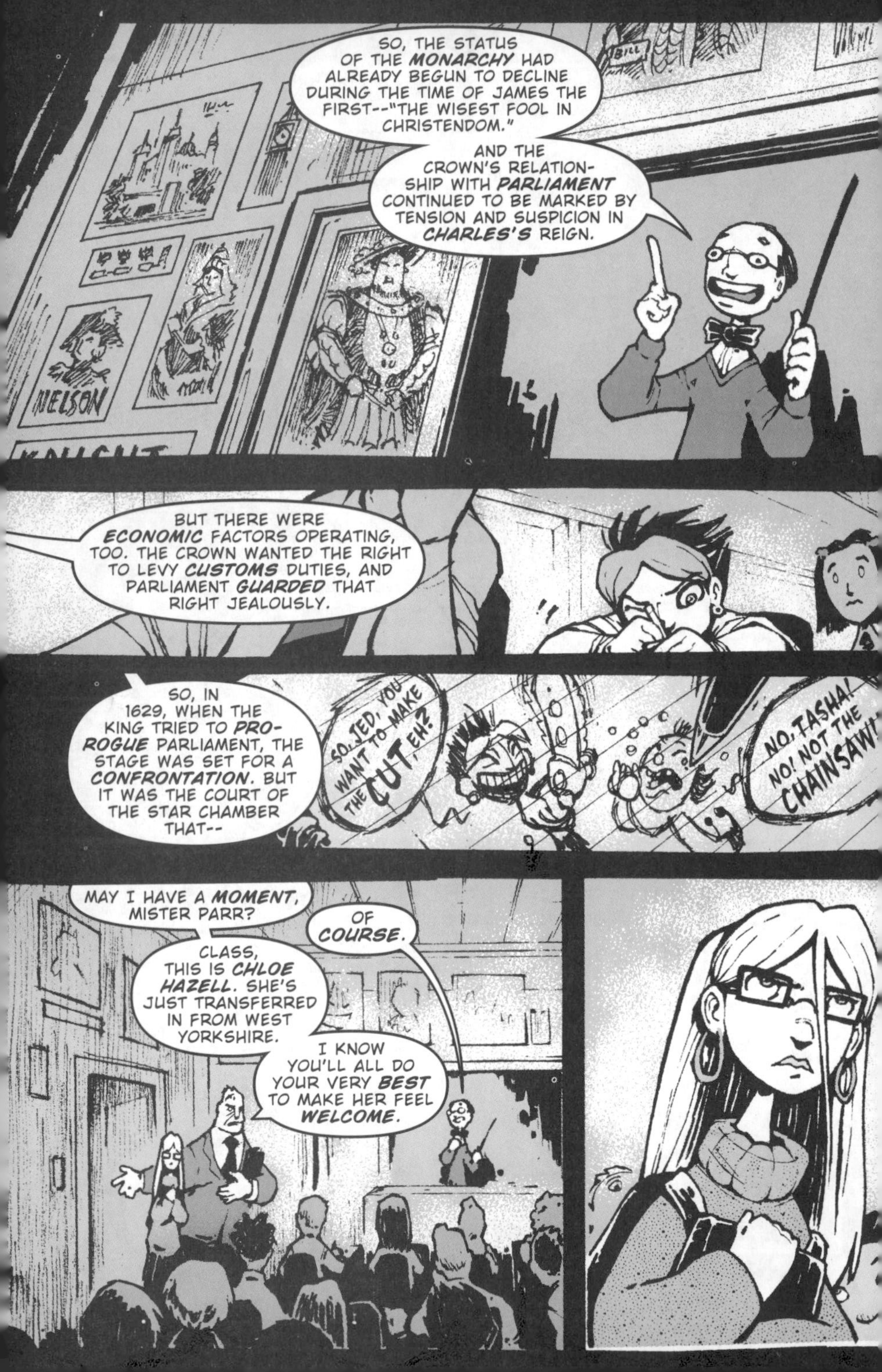

SO, THE STATUS OF THE MONARCHY HAD ALREADY BEGUN TO DECLINE DURING THE TIME OF JAMES THE FIRST--"THE WISEST FOOL IN CHRISTENDOM."
AND THE CROWN'S RELATIONSHIP WITH PARLIAMENT CONTINUED TO BE MARKED BY TENSION AND SUSPICION IN CHARLES'S REIGN.
NELSON
BILL
BUT THERE WERE ECONOMIC FACTORS OPERATING, TOO. THE CROWN WANTED THE RIGHT TO LEVY CUSTOMS DUTIES, AND PARLIAMENT GUARDED THAT RIGHT JEALOUSLY.
SO, IN 1629, WHEN THE KING TRIED TO PROROGUE PARLIAMENT, THE STAGE WAS SET FOR A CONFRONTATION. BUT IT WAS THE COURT OF THE STAR CHAMBER THAT--
SO, JED, YOU WANT TO MAKE THE CUT, EH?
NO, TASHA! NO! NOT THE CHAINSAW!
MAY I HAVE A MOMENT, MISTER PARR?
OF COURSE.
CLASS, THIS IS CHLOE HAZELL. SHE'S JUST TRANSFERRED IN FROM WEST YORKSHIRE.
I KNOW YOU'LL ALL DO YOUR VERY BEST TO MAKE HER FEEL WELCOME.

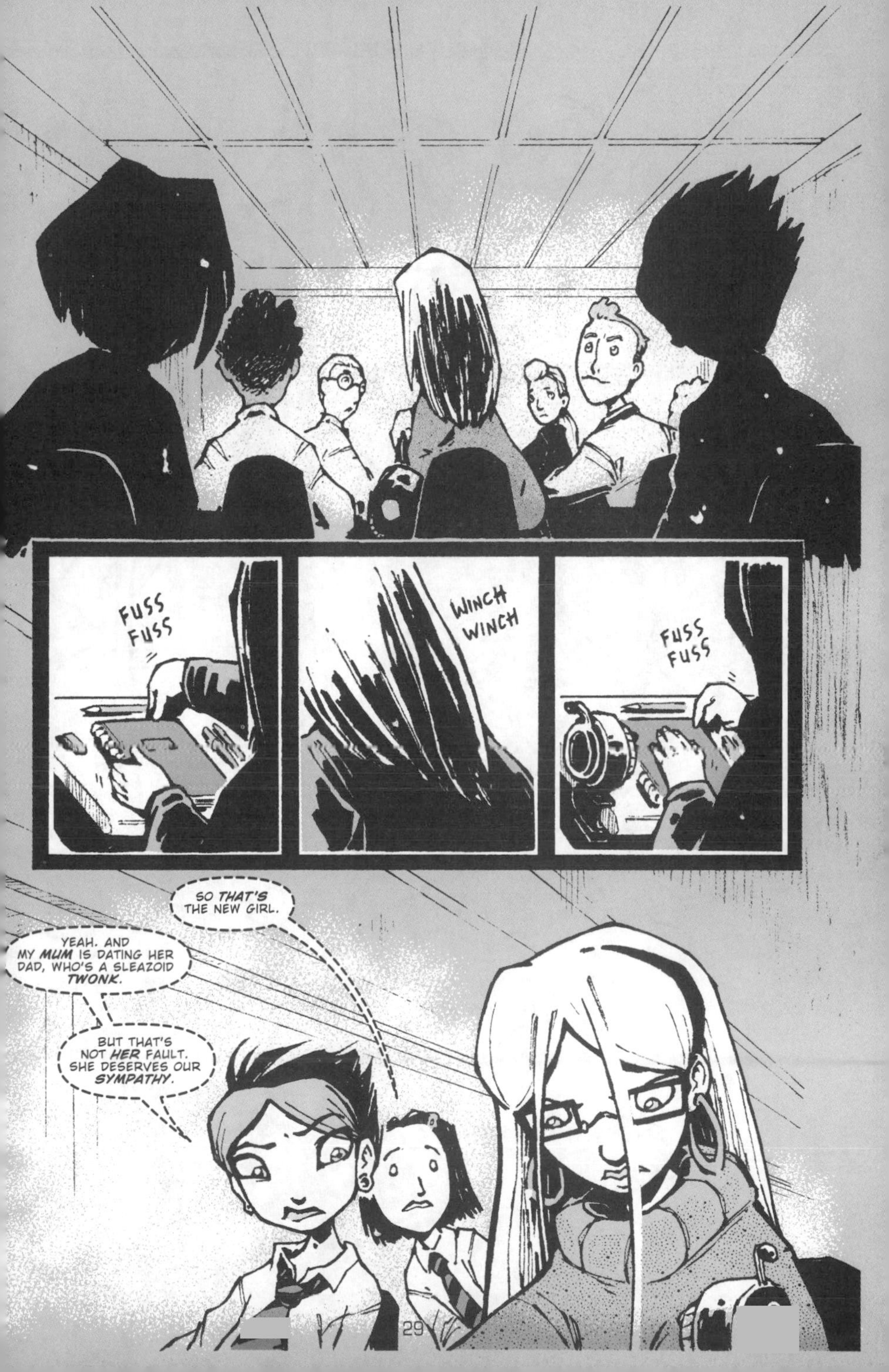
FUSS FUSS
WINCH WINCH
FUSS FUSS
SO THAT'S THE NEW GIRL.
YEAH. AND MY MUM IS DATING HER DAD, WHO'S A SLEAZOID TWONK.
BUT THAT'S NOT HER FAULT. SHE DESERVES OUR SYMPATHY.

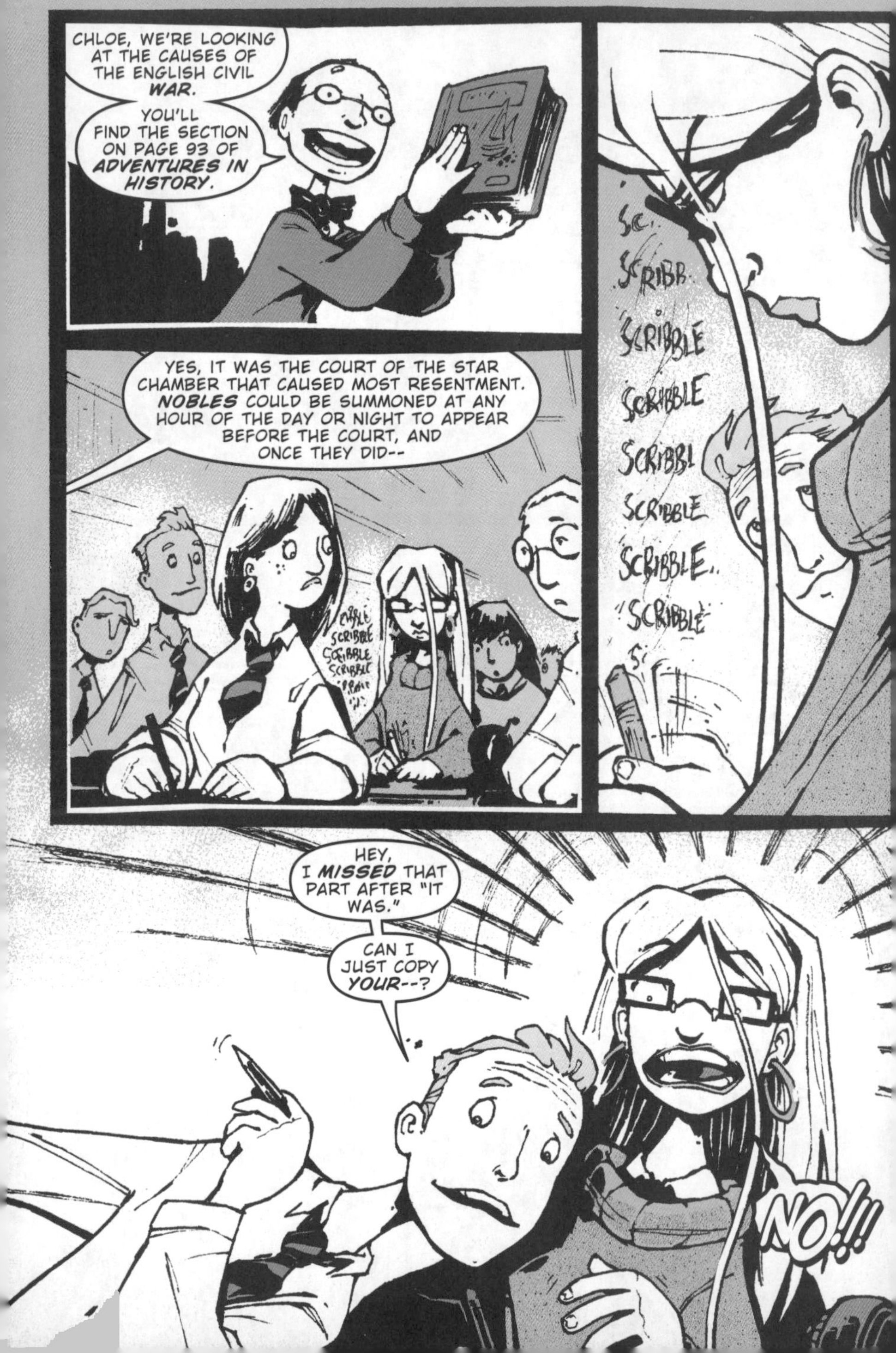
CHLOE, WE'RE LOOKING AT THE CAUSES OF THE ENGLISH CIVIL WAR.
YOU'LL FIND THE SECTION ON PAGE 93 OF ADVENTURES IN HISTORY.
YES, IT WAS THE COURT OF THE STAR CHAMBER THAT CAUSED MOST RESENTMENT. NOBLES COULD BE SUMMONED AT ANY HOUR OF THE DAY OR NIGHT TO APPEAR BEFORE THE COURT, AND ONCE THEY DID--
SCRIBBLE
SCRIBBLE
SCRIBBLE
SCRIBBLE
SCRIBBLE
SCRIBBLE
SCRIBBLE
SCRIBBLE
SCRIBBLE
HEY, I MISSED THAT PART AFTER "IT WAS."
CAN I JUST COPY YOUR--?
NO!!!

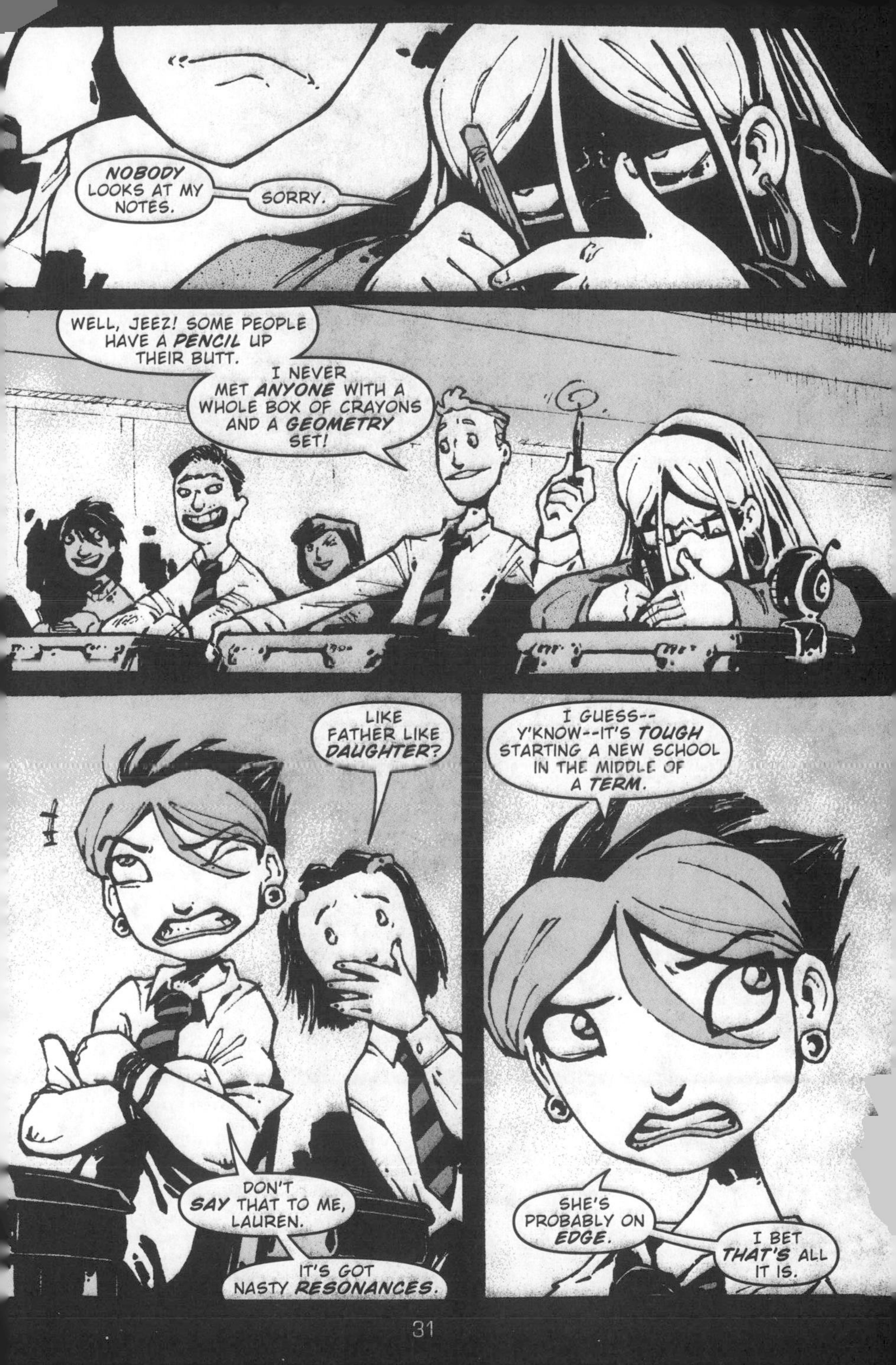
NOBODY LOOKS AT MY NOTES.
SORRY.
WELL, JEEZ! SOME PEOPLE HAVE A PENCIL UP THEIR BUTT.
I NEVER MET ANYONE WITH A WHOLE BOX OF CRAYONS AND A GEOMETRY SET!
LIKE FATHER LIKE DAUGHTER?
DON'T SAY THAT TO ME, LAUREN.
IT'S GOT NASTY RESONANCES.
I GUESS-- Y'KNOW--IT'S TOUGH STARTING A NEW SCHOOL IN THE MIDDLE OF A TERM.
SHE'S PROBABLY ON EDGE.
I BET THAT'S ALL IT IS.

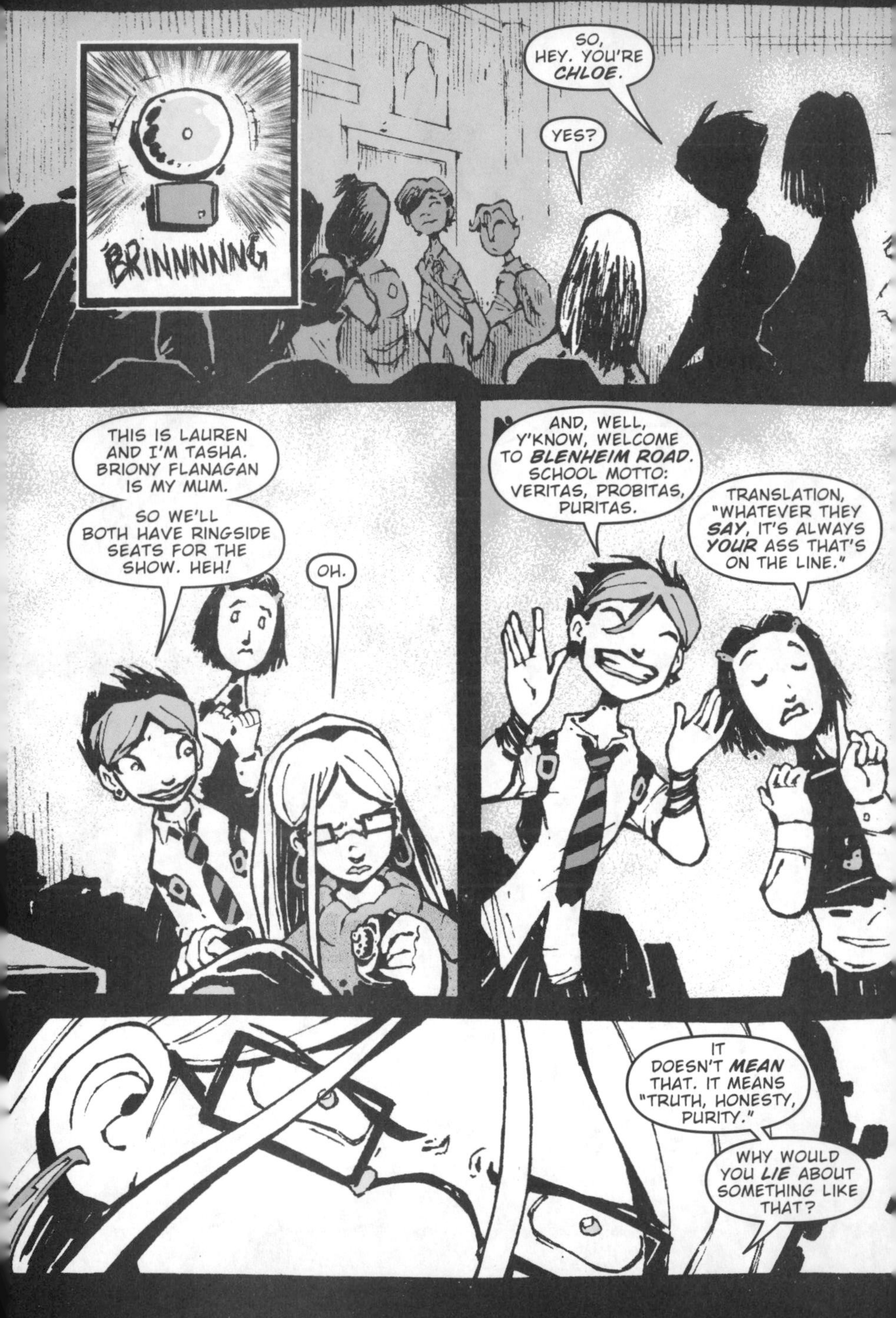
BRINNNNNG
SO, HEY. YOU'RE CHLOE.
YES?
THIS IS LAUREN AND I'M TASHA. BRIONY FLANAGAN IS MY MUM.
SO WE'LL BOTH HAVE RINGSIDE SEATS FOR THE SHOW. HEH!
OH.
AND, WELL, Y'KNOW, WELCOME TO BLENHEIM ROAD. SCHOOL MOTTO: VERITAS, PROBITAS, PURITAS.
TRANSLATION, "WHATEVER THEY SAY, IT'S ALWAYS YOUR ASS THAT'S ON THE LINE."
IT DOESN'T MEAN THAT. IT MEANS "TRUTH, HONESTY, PURITY."
WHY WOULD YOU LIE ABOUT SOMETHING LIKE THAT?

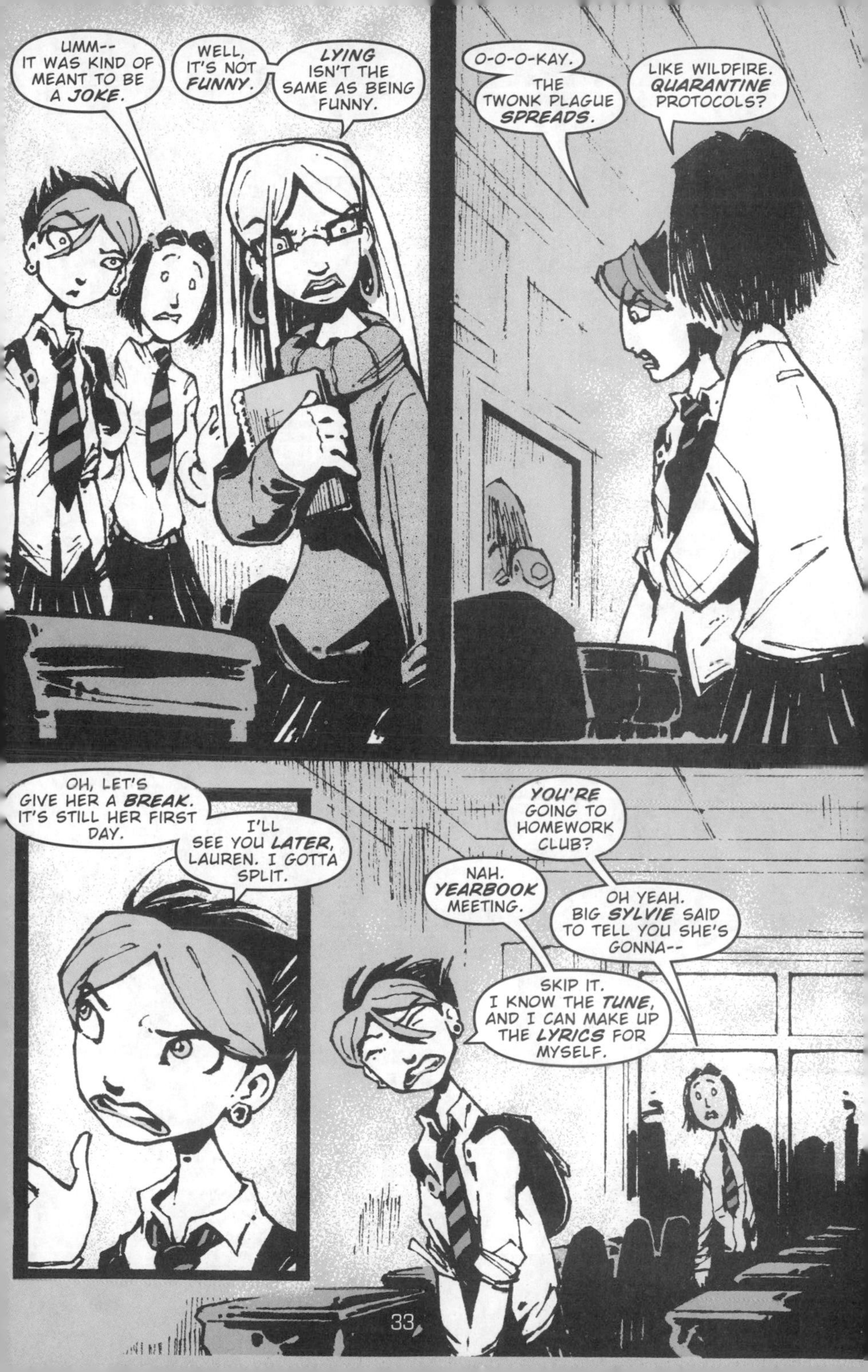
UMM-- IT WAS KIND OF MEANT TO BE A JOKE.
WELL, IT'S NOT FUNNY.
LYING ISN'T THE SAME AS BEING FUNNY.
O-O-O-KAY.
THE TWONK PLAGUE SPREADS.
LIKE WILDFIRE. QUARANTINE PROTOCOLS?
OH, LET'S GIVE HER A BREAK. IT'S STILL HER FIRST DAY.
I'LL SEE YOU LATER, LAUREN. I GOTTA SPLIT.
YOU'RE GOING TO HOMEWORK CLUB?
NAH. YEARBOOK MEETING.
OH YEAH. BIG SYLVIE SAID TO TELL YOU SHE'S GONNA--
SKIP IT. I KNOW THE TUNE, AND I CAN MAKE UP THE LYRICS FOR MYSELF.

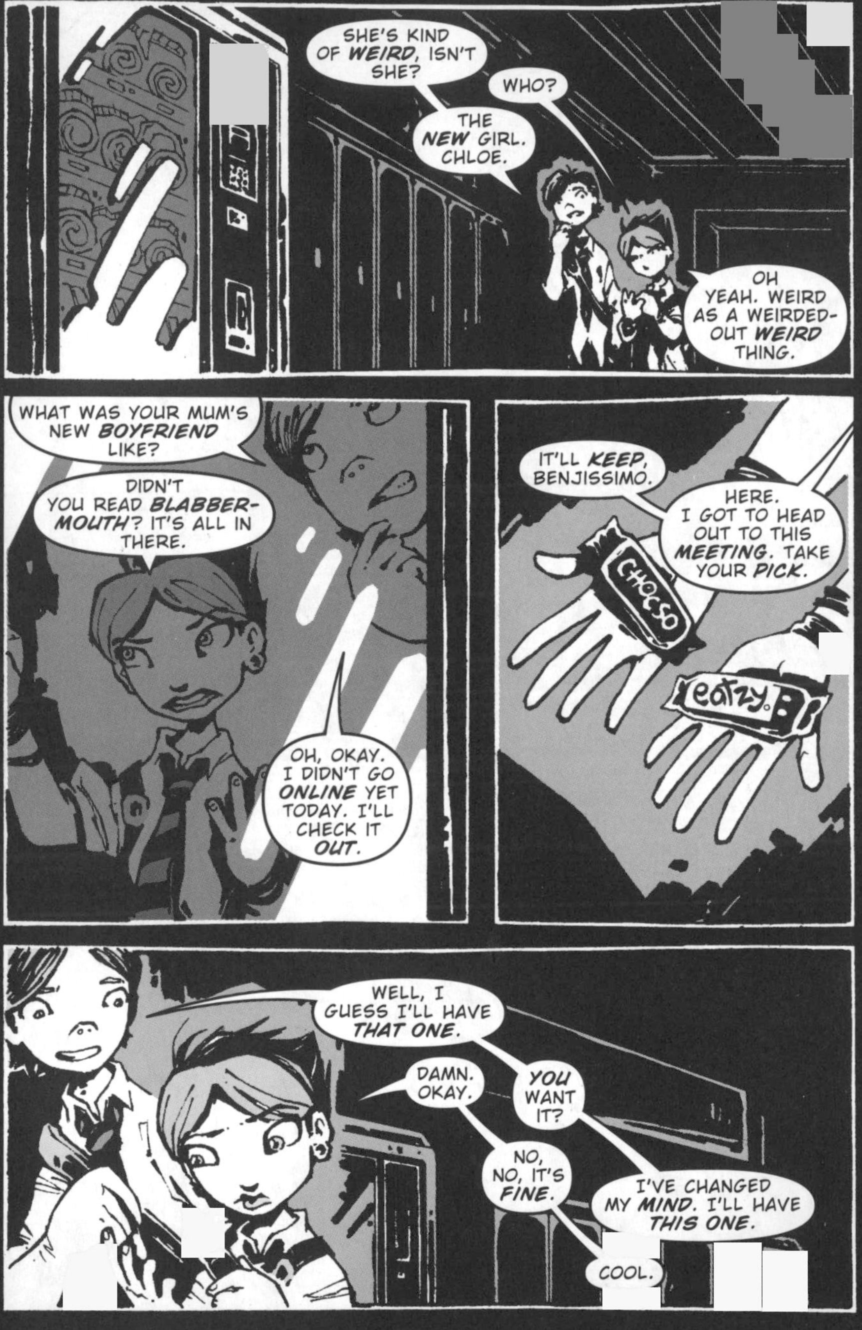

SHE'S KIND OF *WEIRD*, ISN'T SHE?
WHO?
THE *NEW* GIRL. CHLOE.
OH YEAH. WEIRD AS A WEIRDED-OUT *WEIRD* THING.
WHAT WAS YOUR MUM'S NEW *BOYFRIEND* LIKE?
DIDN'T YOU READ *BLABBER-MOUTH*? IT'S ALL IN THERE.
OH, OKAY. I DIDN'T GO *ONLINE* YET TODAY. I'LL CHECK IT *OUT*.
IT'LL *KEEP*, BENJISSIMO.
HERE. I GOT TO HEAD OUT TO THIS *MEETING*. TAKE YOUR *PICK*.
CHOCSO
eatzy.
WELL, I GUESS I'LL HAVE *THAT ONE*.
DAMN. OKAY.
YOU WANT IT?
NO, NO, IT'S *FINE*.
I'VE CHANGED MY *MIND*. I'LL HAVE *THIS ONE*.
COOL.

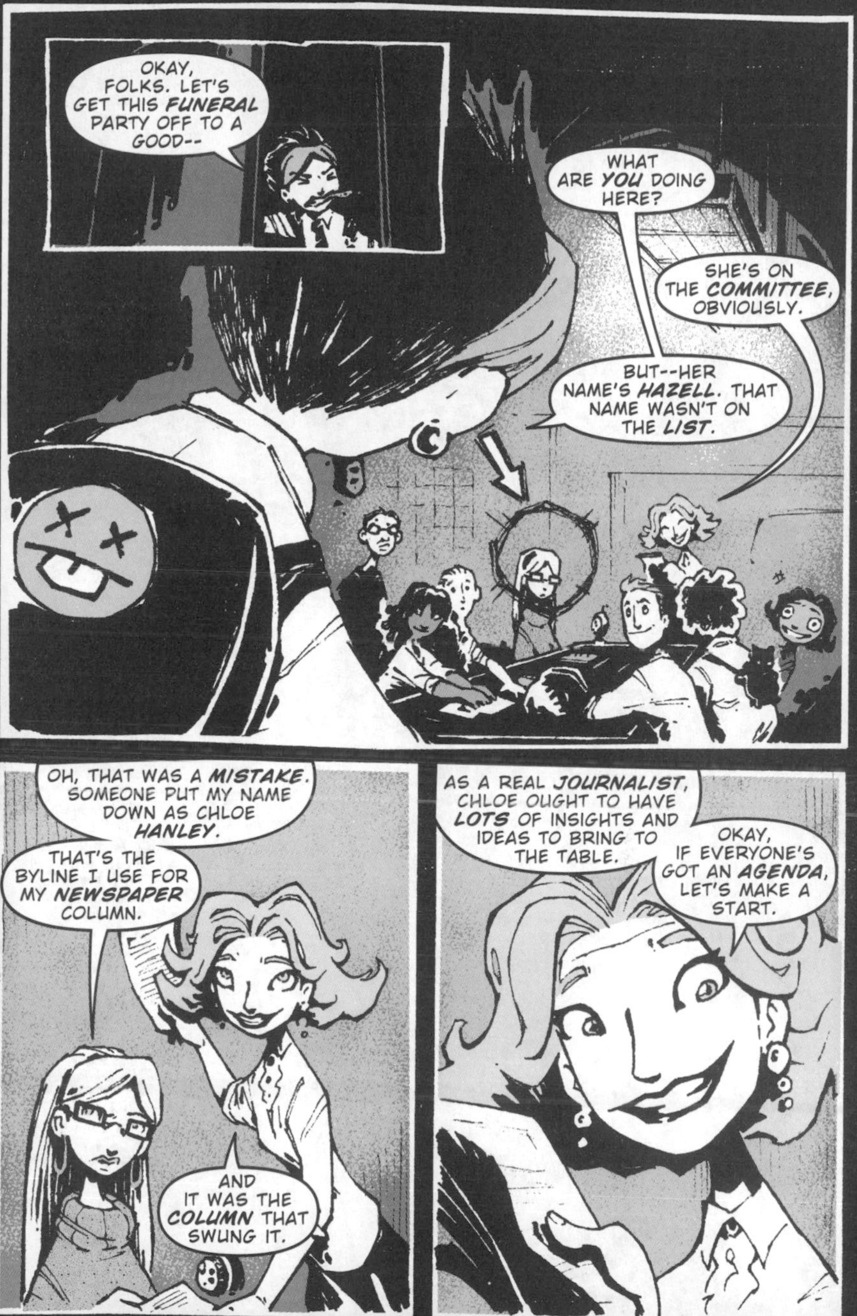
OKAY, FOLKS. LET'S GET THIS FUNERAL PARTY OFF TO A GOOD--
WHAT ARE YOU DOING HERE?
SHE'S ON THE COMMITTEE, OBVIOUSLY.
BUT--HER NAME'S HAZELL. THAT NAME WASN'T ON THE LIST.
OH, THAT WAS A MISTAKE. SOMEONE PUT MY NAME DOWN AS CHLOE HANLEY.
THAT'S THE BYLINE I USE FOR MY NEWSPAPER COLUMN.
AND IT WAS THE COLUMN THAT SWUNG IT.
AS A REAL JOURNALIST, CHLOE OUGHT TO HAVE LOTS OF INSIGHTS AND IDEAS TO BRING TO THE TABLE.
OKAY, IF EVERYONE'S GOT AN AGENDA, LET'S MAKE A START.

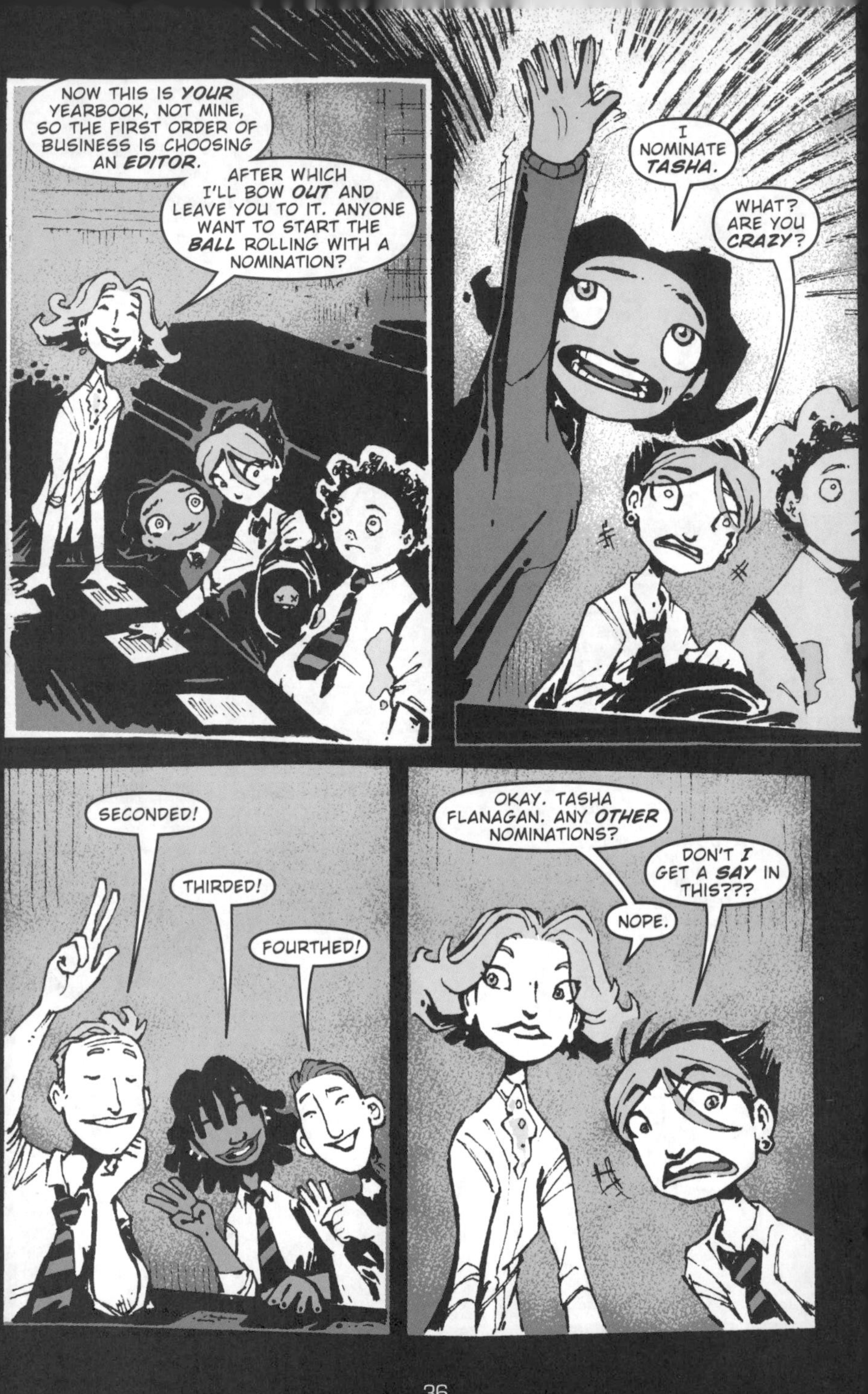
NOW THIS IS YOUR YEARBOOK, NOT MINE, SO THE FIRST ORDER OF BUSINESS IS CHOOSING AN EDITOR.
AFTER WHICH I'LL BOW OUT AND LEAVE YOU TO IT. ANYONE WANT TO START THE BALL ROLLING WITH A NOMINATION?
I NOMINATE TASHA.
WHAT? ARE YOU CRAZY?
SECONDED!
THIRDED!
FOURTHED!
OKAY. TASHA FLANAGAN. ANY OTHER NOMINATIONS?
DON'T I GET A SAY IN THIS???
NOPE.

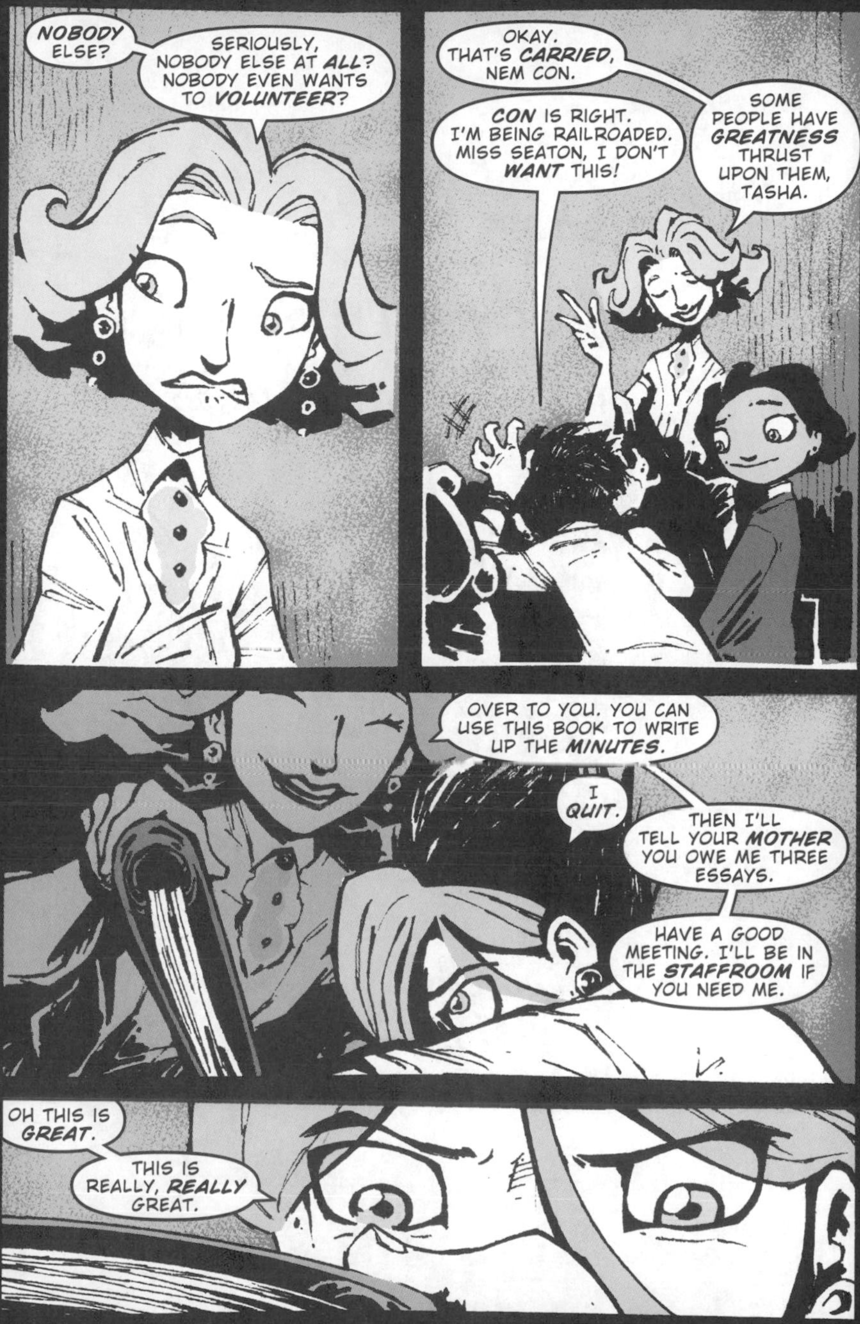
NOBODY ELSE?
SERIOUSLY, NOBODY ELSE AT ALL? NOBODY EVEN WANTS TO VOLUNTEER?
OKAY. THAT'S CARRIED, NEM CON.
CON IS RIGHT. I'M BEING RAILROADED. MISS SEATON, I DON'T WANT THIS!
SOME PEOPLE HAVE GREATNESS THRUST UPON THEM, TASHA.
OVER TO YOU. YOU CAN USE THIS BOOK TO WRITE UP THE MINUTES.
I QUIT.
THEN I'LL TELL YOUR MOTHER YOU OWE ME THREE ESSAYS.
HAVE A GOOD MEETING. I'LL BE IN THE STAFFROOM IF YOU NEED ME.
OH THIS IS GREAT.
THIS IS REALLY, REALLY GREAT.

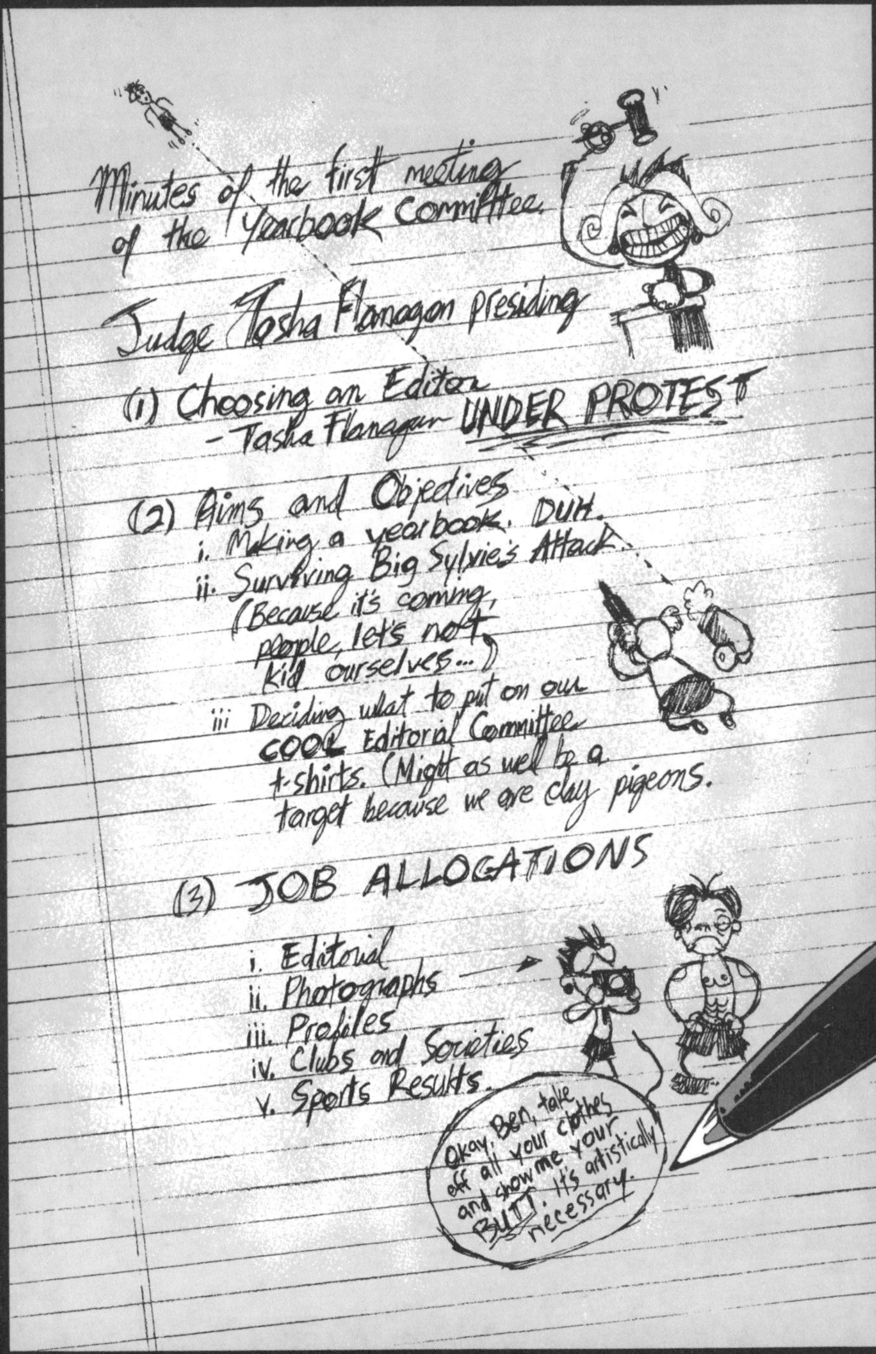
Minutes of the first meeting
of the Yearbook Committee.
Judge Tasha Flanagan presiding
(1) Choosing an Editor
- Tasha Flanagan UNDER PROTEST
(2) Aims and Objectives
i. Making a yearbook. DUH.
ii. Surviving Big Sylvie's Attack.
(Because it's coming,
people, let's not
kid ourselves...)
iii Deciding what to put on our
COOL Editorial Committee
t-shirts. (Might as well be a
target because we are clay pigeons.
(3) JOB ALLOCATIONS
i. Editorial
ii. Photographs
iii. Profiles
iv. Clubs and Societies
v. Sports Results.
Okay, Ben, take off all your clothes and show me your BUTT. It's artistically necessary.

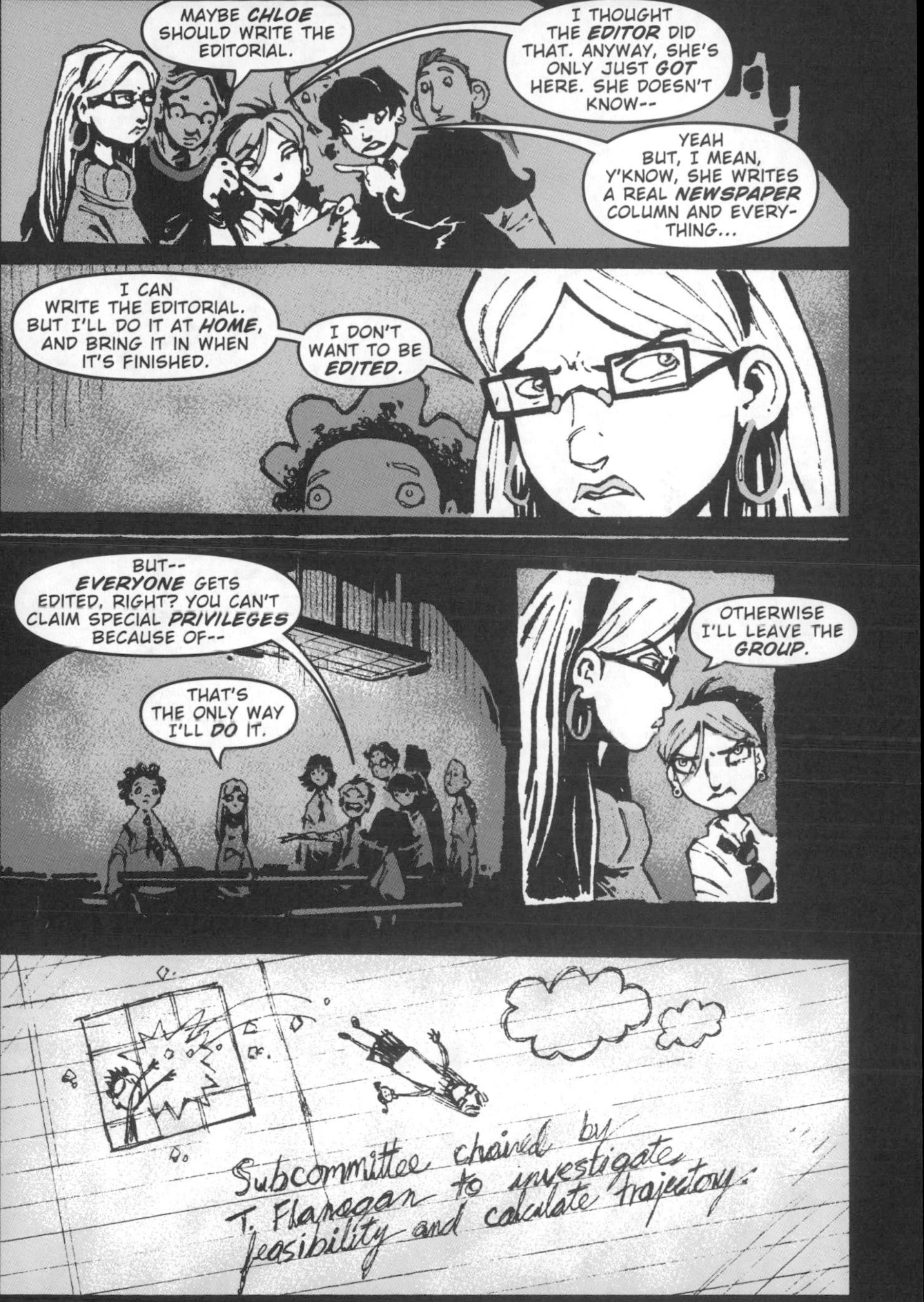
MAYBE CHLOE SHOULD WRITE THE EDITORIAL.
I THOUGHT THE EDITOR DID THAT. ANYWAY, SHE'S ONLY JUST GOT HERE. SHE DOESN'T KNOW--
YEAH BUT, I MEAN, Y'KNOW, SHE WRITES A REAL NEWSPAPER COLUMN AND EVERYTHING...
I CAN WRITE THE EDITORIAL. BUT I'LL DO IT AT HOME, AND BRING IT IN WHEN IT'S FINISHED.
I DON'T WANT TO BE EDITED.
BUT-- EVERYONE GETS EDITED, RIGHT? YOU CAN'T CLAIM SPECIAL PRIVILEGES BECAUSE OF--
THAT'S THE ONLY WAY I'LL DO IT.
OTHERWISE I'LL LEAVE THE GROUP.
Subcommittee chaired by T. Flanagan to investigate feasibility and calculate trajectory.

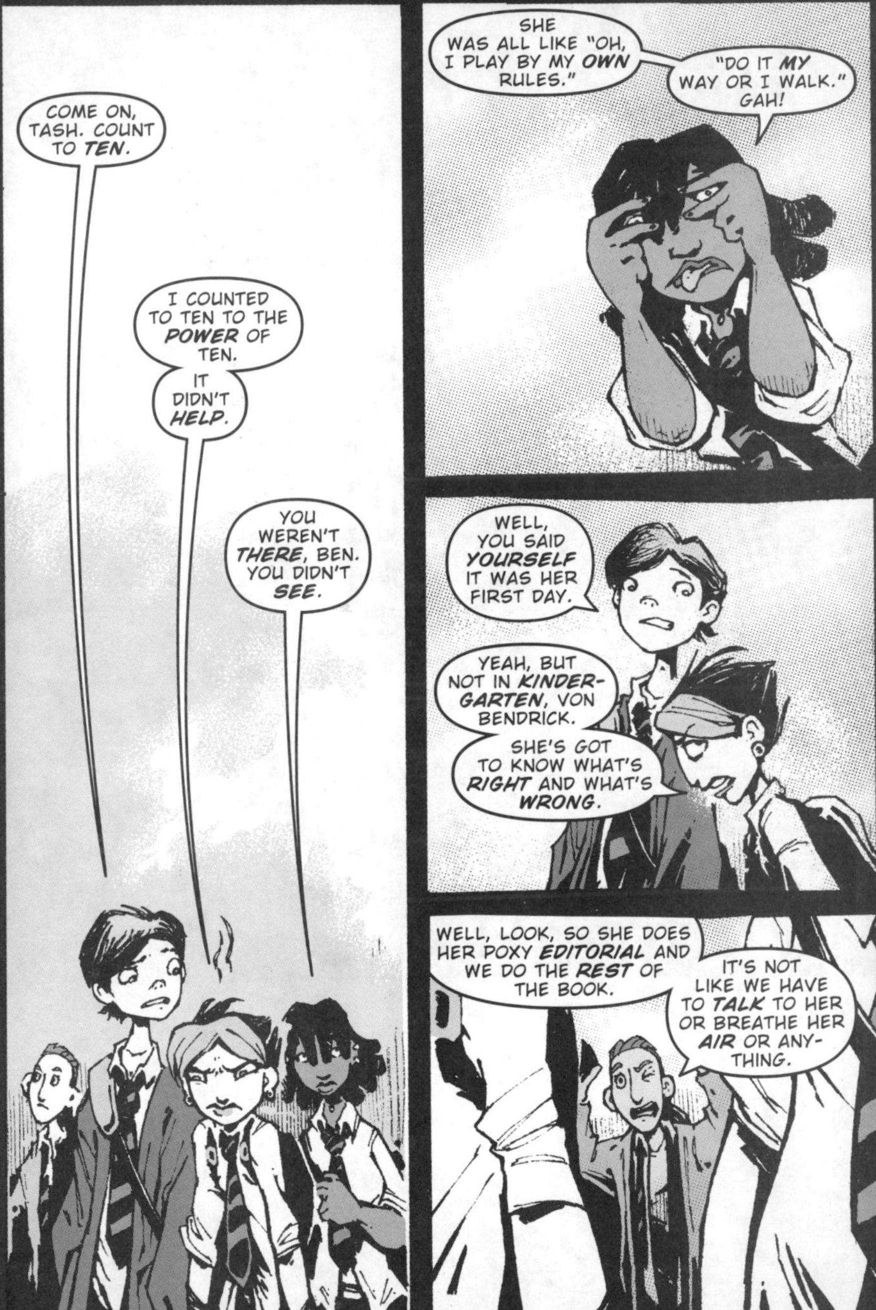
COME ON, TASH. COUNT TO TEN.
I COUNTED TO TEN TO THE POWER OF TEN.
IT DIDN'T HELP.
YOU WEREN'T THERE, BEN. YOU DIDN'T SEE.
SHE WAS ALL LIKE "OH, I PLAY BY MY OWN RULES."
"DO IT MY WAY OR I WALK." GAH!
WELL, YOU SAID YOURSELF IT WAS HER FIRST DAY.
YEAH, BUT NOT IN KINDER-GARTEN, VON BENDRICK.
SHE'S GOT TO KNOW WHAT'S RIGHT AND WHAT'S WRONG.
WELL, LOOK, SO SHE DOES HER POXY EDITORIAL AND WE DO THE REST OF THE BOOK.
IT'S NOT LIKE WE HAVE TO TALK TO HER OR BREATHE HER AIR OR ANY-THING.

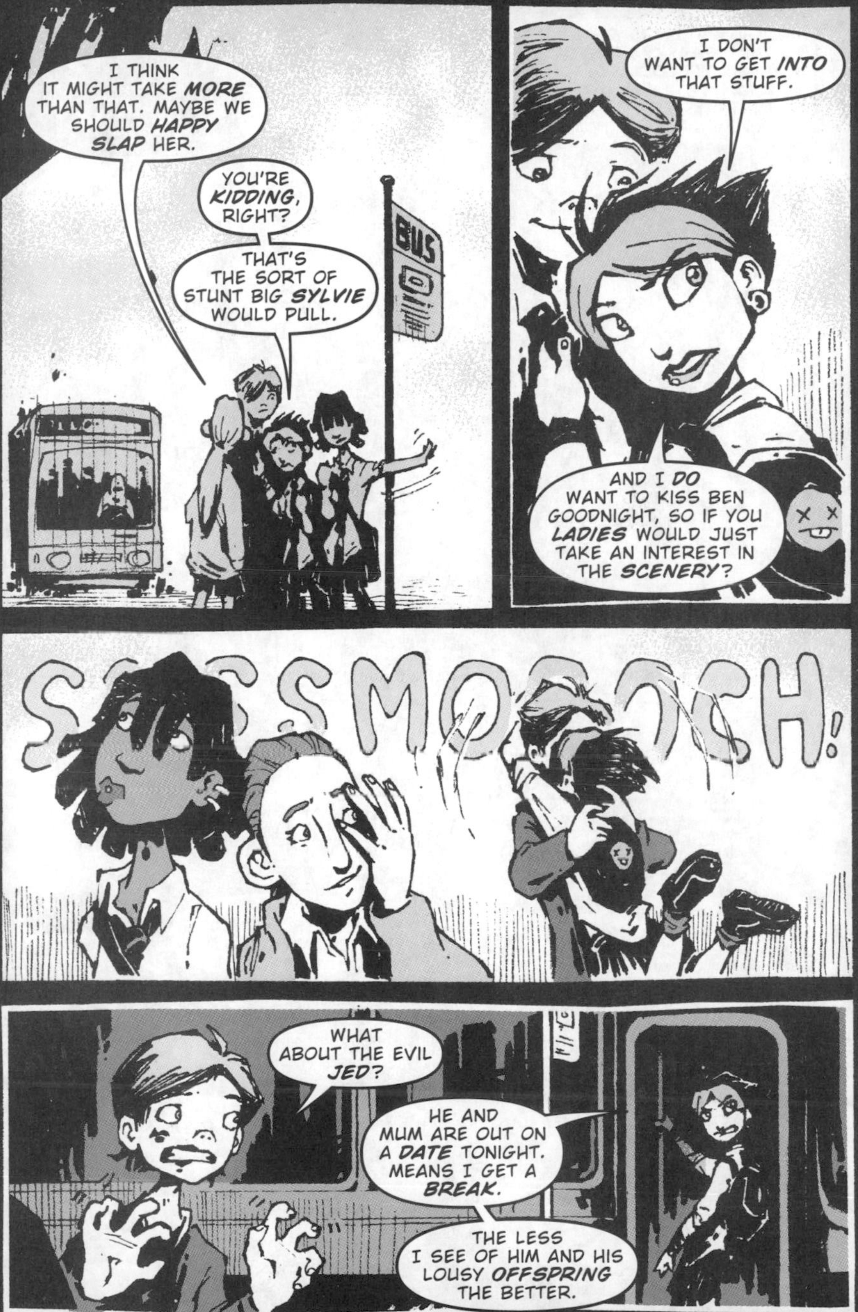
I THINK IT MIGHT TAKE MORE THAN THAT. MAYBE WE SHOULD HAPPY SLAP HER.
YOU'RE KIDDING, RIGHT?
THAT'S THE SORT OF STUNT BIG SYLVIE WOULD PULL.
BUS
I DON'T WANT TO GET INTO THAT STUFF.
AND I DO WANT TO KISS BEN GOODNIGHT, SO IF YOU LADIES WOULD JUST TAKE AN INTEREST IN THE SCENERY?
SMOOCH!
WHAT ABOUT THE EVIL JED?
HE AND MUM ARE OUT ON A DATE TONIGHT. MEANS I GET A BREAK.
THE LESS I SEE OF HIM AND HIS LOUSY OFFSPRING THE BETTER.

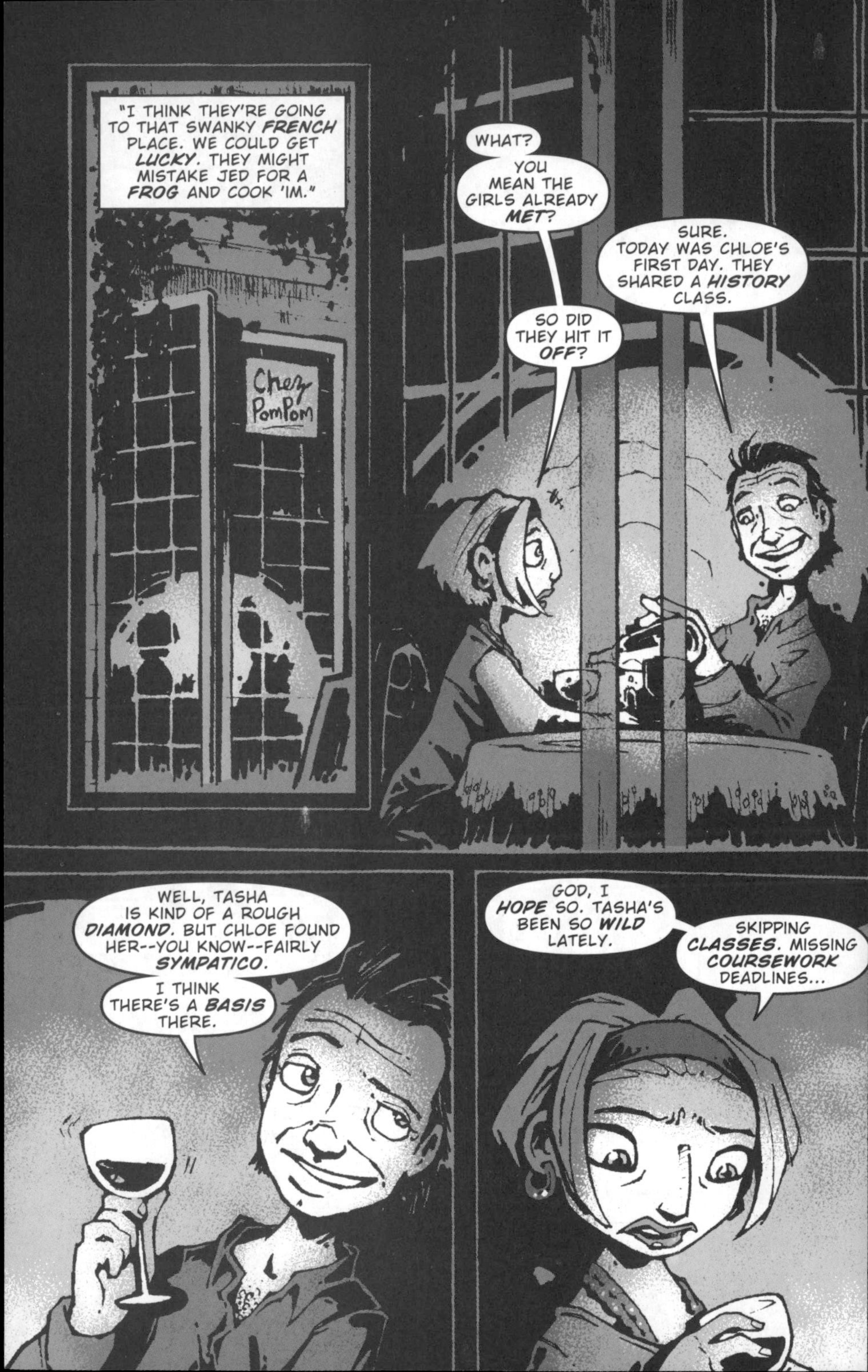
"I THINK THEY'RE GOING TO THAT SWANKY FRENCH PLACE. WE COULD GET LUCKY. THEY MIGHT MISTAKE JED FOR A FROG AND COOK 'IM."
Chez PomPom
WHAT?
YOU MEAN THE GIRLS ALREADY MET?
SURE. TODAY WAS CHLOE'S FIRST DAY. THEY SHARED A HISTORY CLASS.
SO DID THEY HIT IT OFF?
WELL, TASHA IS KIND OF A ROUGH DIAMOND. BUT CHLOE FOUND HER--YOU KNOW--FAIRLY SYMPATICO.
I THINK THERE'S A BASIS THERE.
GOD, I HOPE SO. TASHA'S BEEN SO WILD LATELY.
SKIPPING CLASSES. MISSING COURSEWORK DEADLINES...

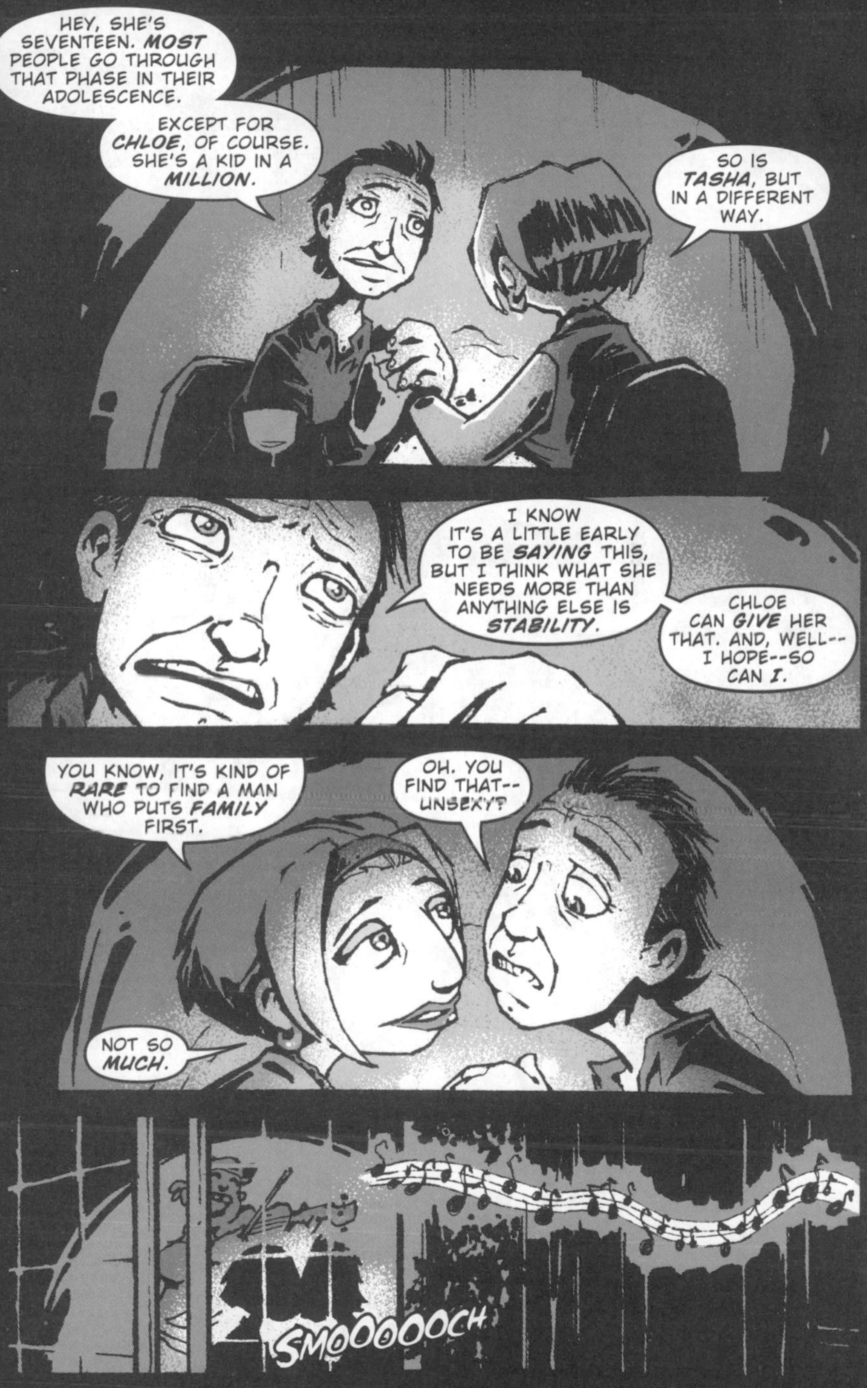
HEY, SHE'S SEVENTEEN. MOST PEOPLE GO THROUGH THAT PHASE IN THEIR ADOLESCENCE.
EXCEPT FOR CHLOE, OF COURSE. SHE'S A KID IN A MILLION.
SO IS TASHA, BUT IN A DIFFERENT WAY.
I KNOW IT'S A LITTLE EARLY TO BE SAYING THIS, BUT I THINK WHAT SHE NEEDS MORE THAN ANYTHING ELSE IS STABILITY.
CHLOE CAN GIVE HER THAT. AND, WELL-- I HOPE--SO CAN I.
YOU KNOW, IT'S KIND OF RARE TO FIND A MAN WHO PUTS FAMILY FIRST.
OH. YOU FIND THAT-- UNSEXY?
NOT SO MUCH.
SMOOOOOCH

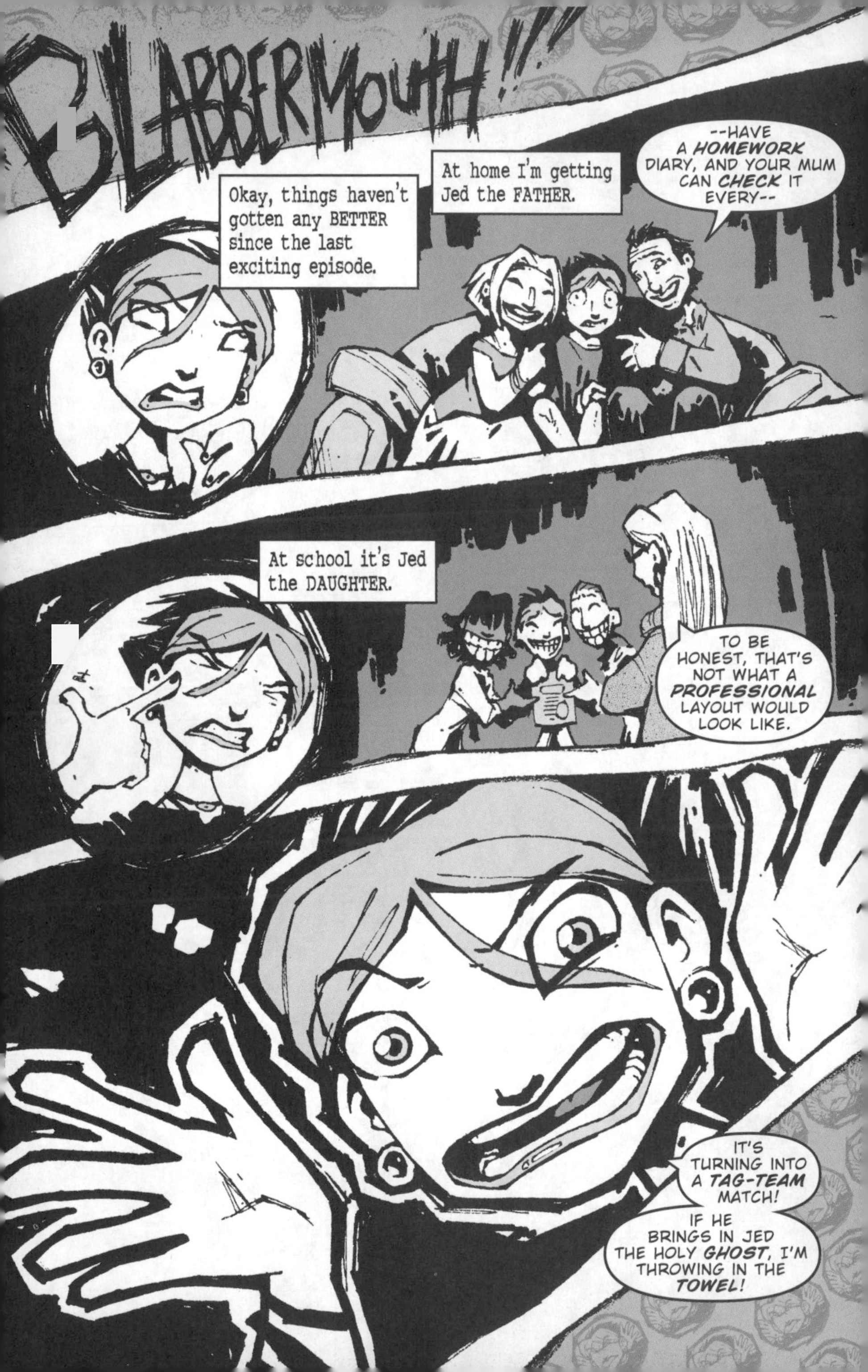
BLABBERMOUTH!!
Okay, things haven't gotten any BETTER since the last exciting episode.
At home I'm getting Jed the FATHER.
--HAVE A HOMEWORK DIARY, AND YOUR MUM CAN CHECK IT EVERY--
At school it's Jed the DAUGHTER.
TO BE HONEST, THAT'S NOT WHAT A PROFESSIONAL LAYOUT WOULD LOOK LIKE.
IT'S TURNING INTO A TAG-TEAM MATCH!
IF HE BRINGS IN JED THE HOLY GHOST, I'M THROWING IN THE TOWEL!

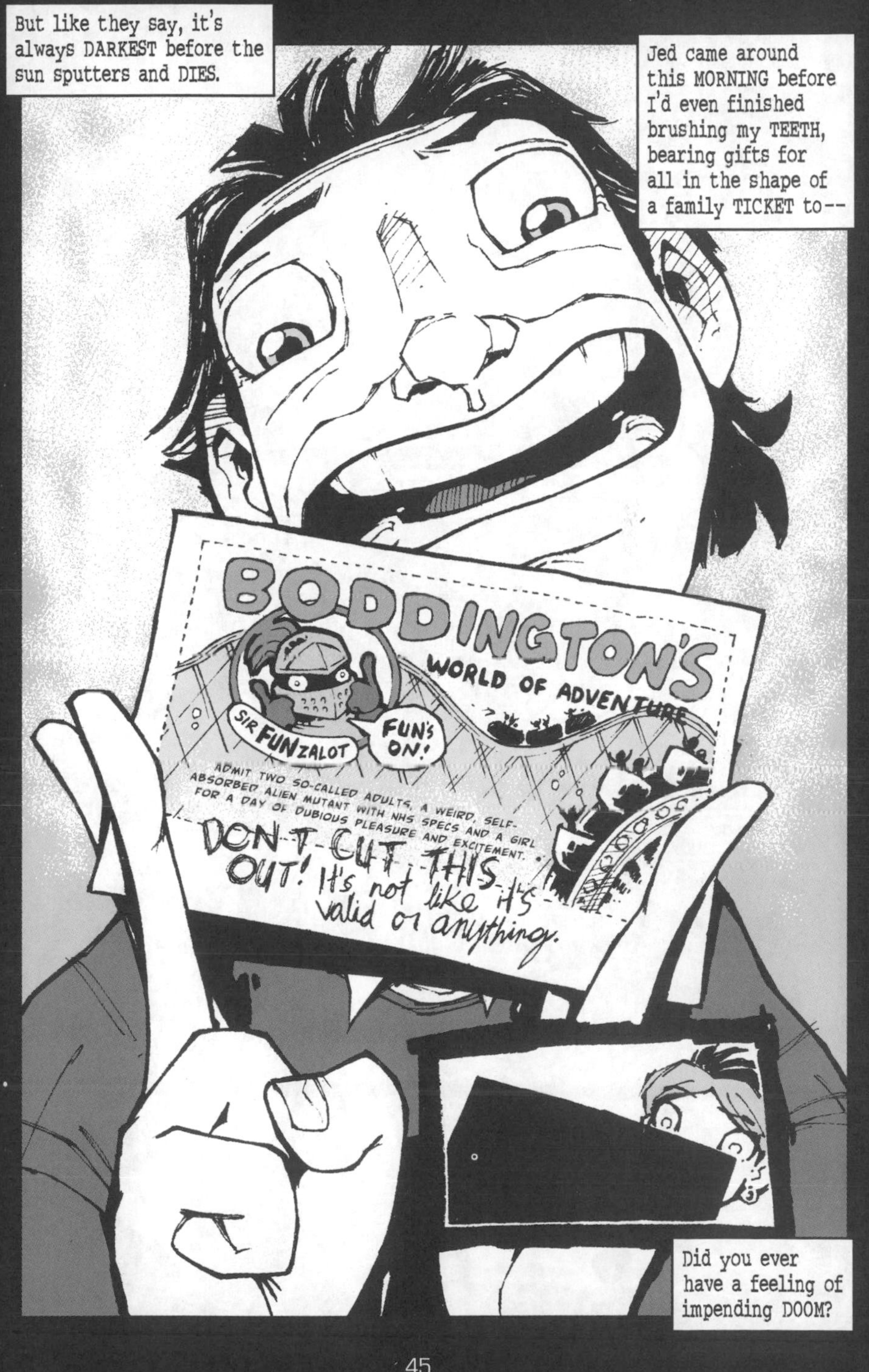

But like they say, it's always DARKEST before the sun sputters and DIES.
Jed came around this MORNING before I'd even finished brushing my TEETH, bearing gifts for all in the shape of a family TICKET to--
BODDINGTON'S WORLD OF ADVENTURE
SIR FUNZALOT
FUN'S ON!
ADMIT TWO SO-CALLED ADULTS, A WEIRD, SELF-ABSORBED ALIEN MUTANT WITH NHS SPECS AND A GIRL FOR A DAY OF DUBIOUS PLEASURE AND EXCITEMENT.
DON'T CUT THIS OUT! It's not like it's valid or anything.
Did you ever have a feeling of impending DOOM?

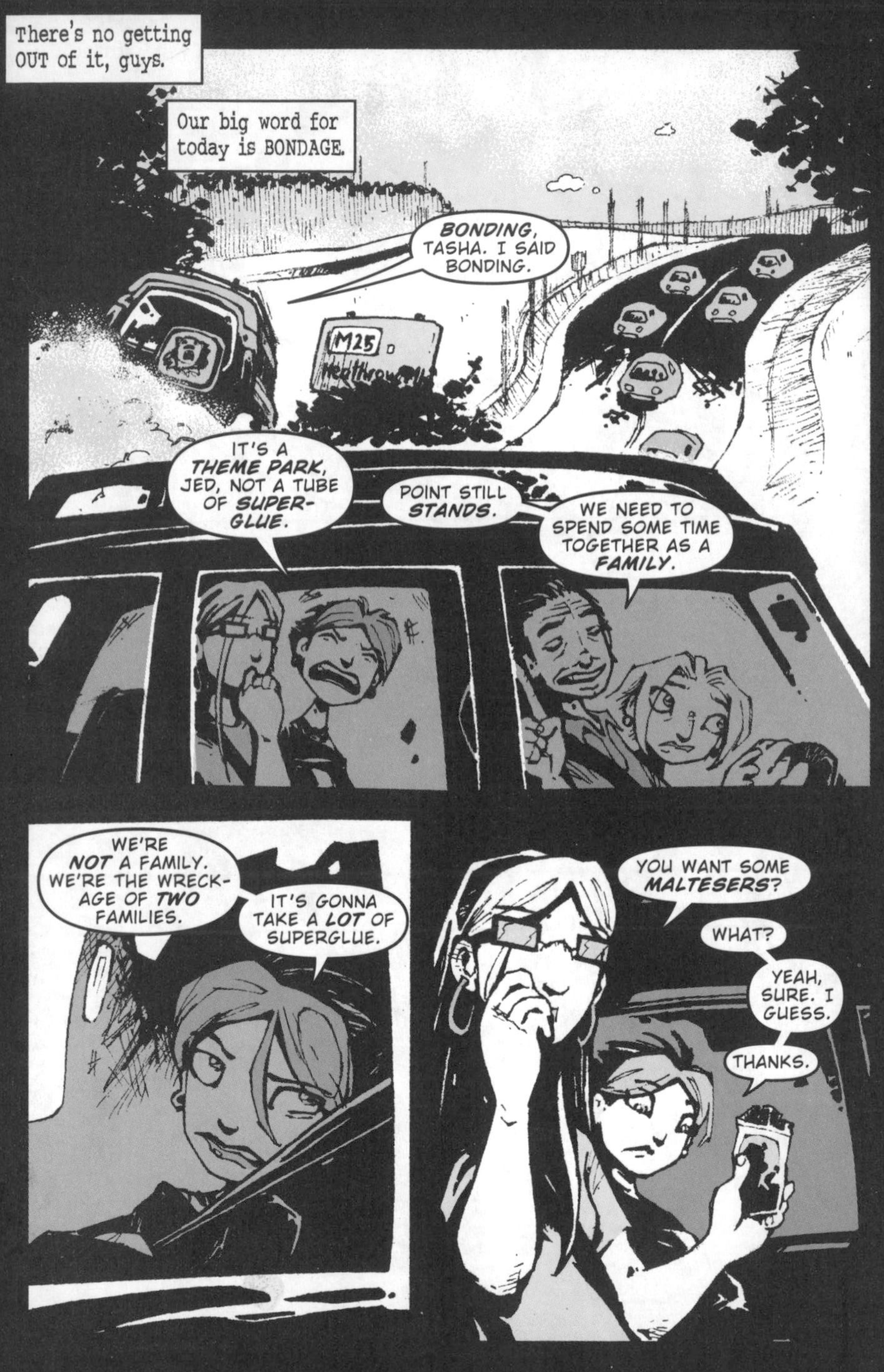

There's no getting OUT of it, guys.
Our big word for today is BONDAGE.
BONDING, TASHA. I SAID BONDING.
M25
IT'S A THEME PARK, JED, NOT A TUBE OF SUPER-GLUE.
POINT STILL STANDS.
WE NEED TO SPEND SOME TIME TOGETHER AS A FAMILY.
WE'RE NOT A FAMILY. WE'RE THE WRECK-AGE OF TWO FAMILIES.
IT'S GONNA TAKE A LOT OF SUPERGLUE.
YOU WANT SOME MALTESERS?
WHAT?
YEAH, SURE. I GUESS.
THANKS.

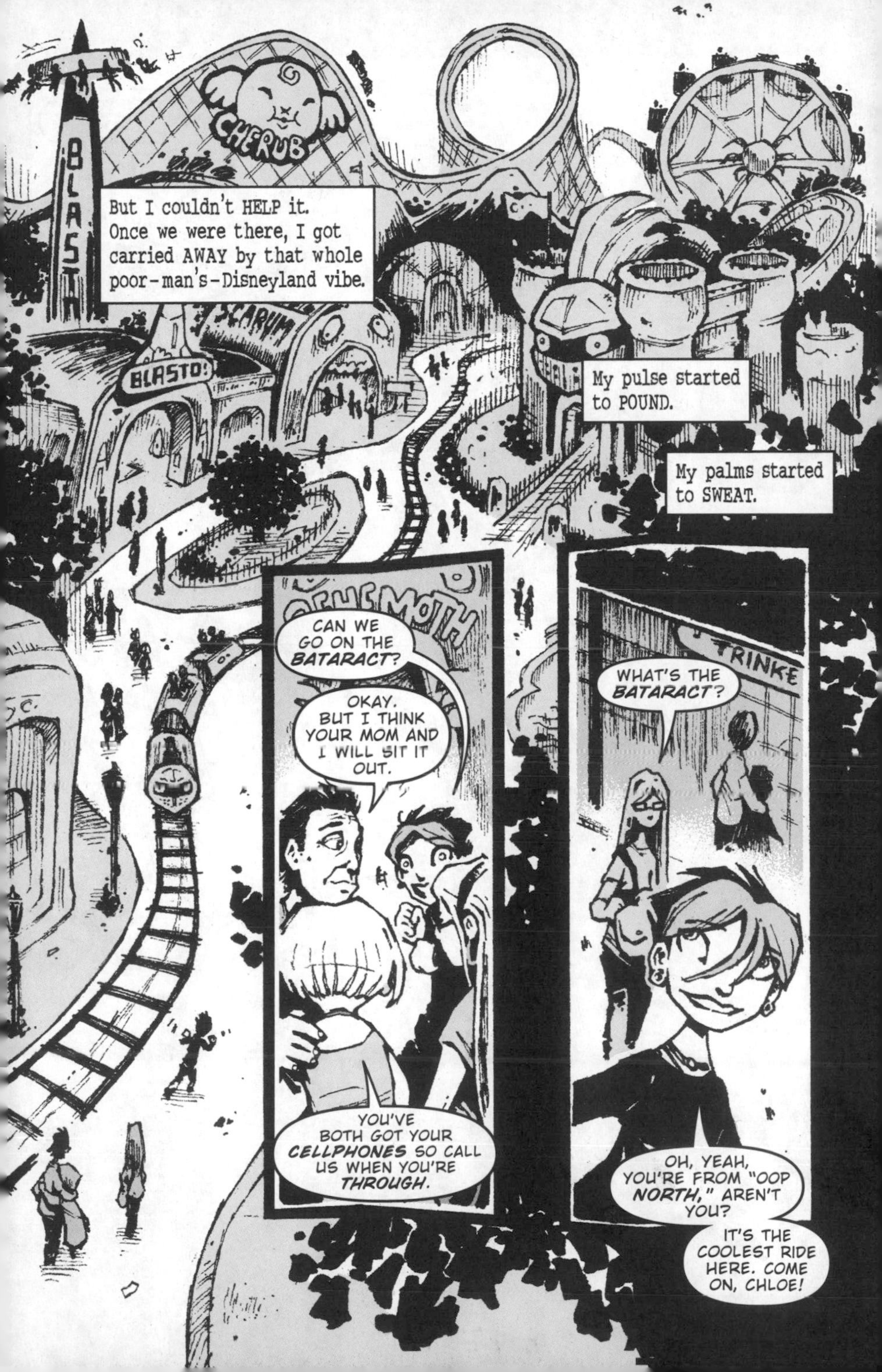
CHERUB
BLAST
But I couldn't HELP it. Once we were there, I got carried AWAY by that whole poor-man's-Disneyland vibe.
SCARUM
BLASTO!
My pulse started to POUND.
My palms started to SWEAT.
CAN WE GO ON THE BATARACT?
OKAY. BUT I THINK YOUR MOM AND I WILL SIT IT OUT.
YOU'VE BOTH GOT YOUR CELLPHONES SO CALL US WHEN YOU'RE THROUGH.
TRINKE
WHAT'S THE BATARACT?
OH, YEAH, YOU'RE FROM "OOP NORTH," AREN'T YOU?
IT'S THE COOLEST RIDE HERE. COME ON, CHLOE!

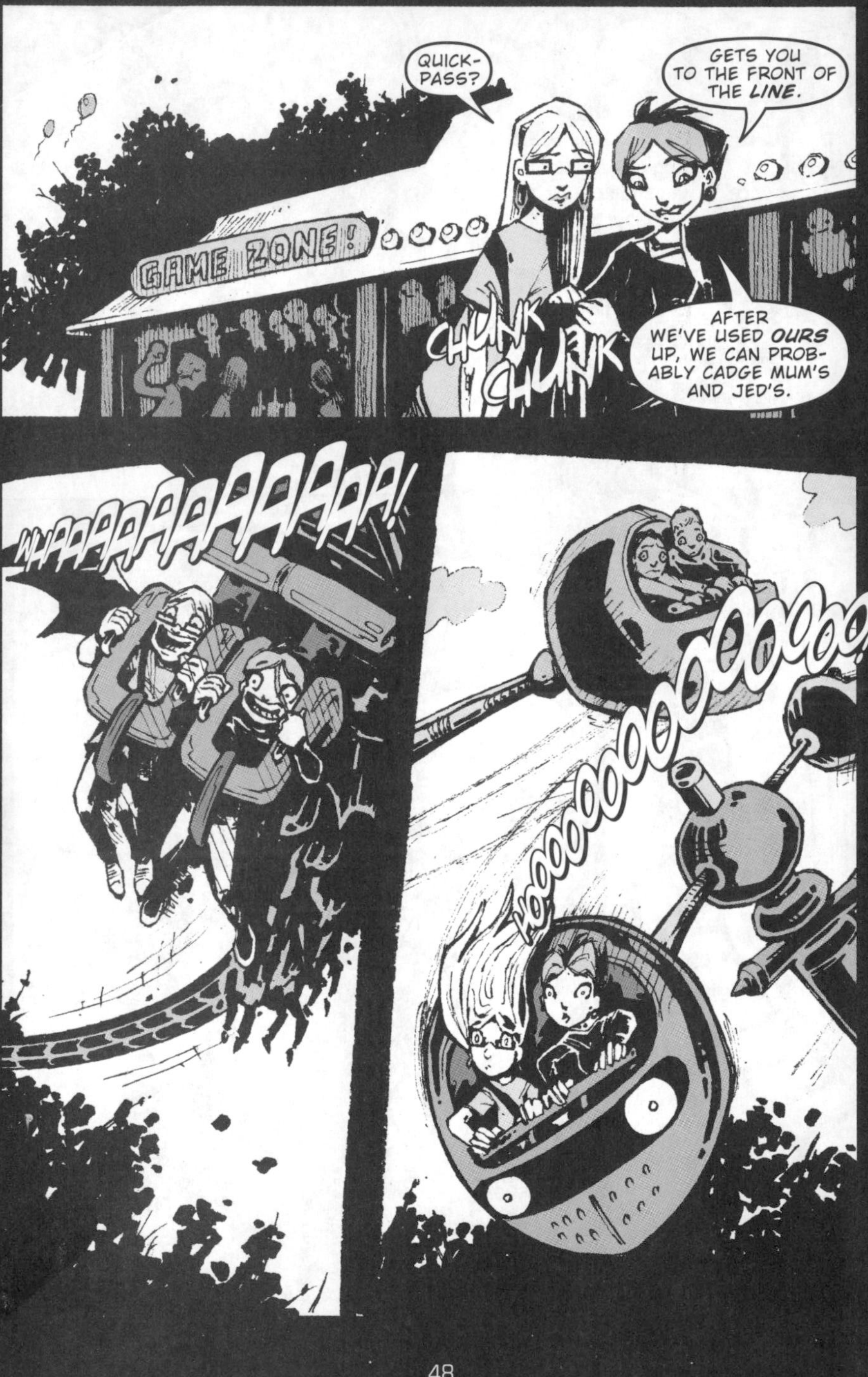
QUICK-PASS?
GETS YOU TO THE FRONT OF THE LINE.
GAME ZONE!
CHUNK CHUNK CHUNK
AFTER WE'VE USED OURS UP, WE CAN PROBABLY CADGE MUM'S AND JED'S.
WHAAAAAAAAAAAA!
WOOOOOOOOOOOOOOOOOO!

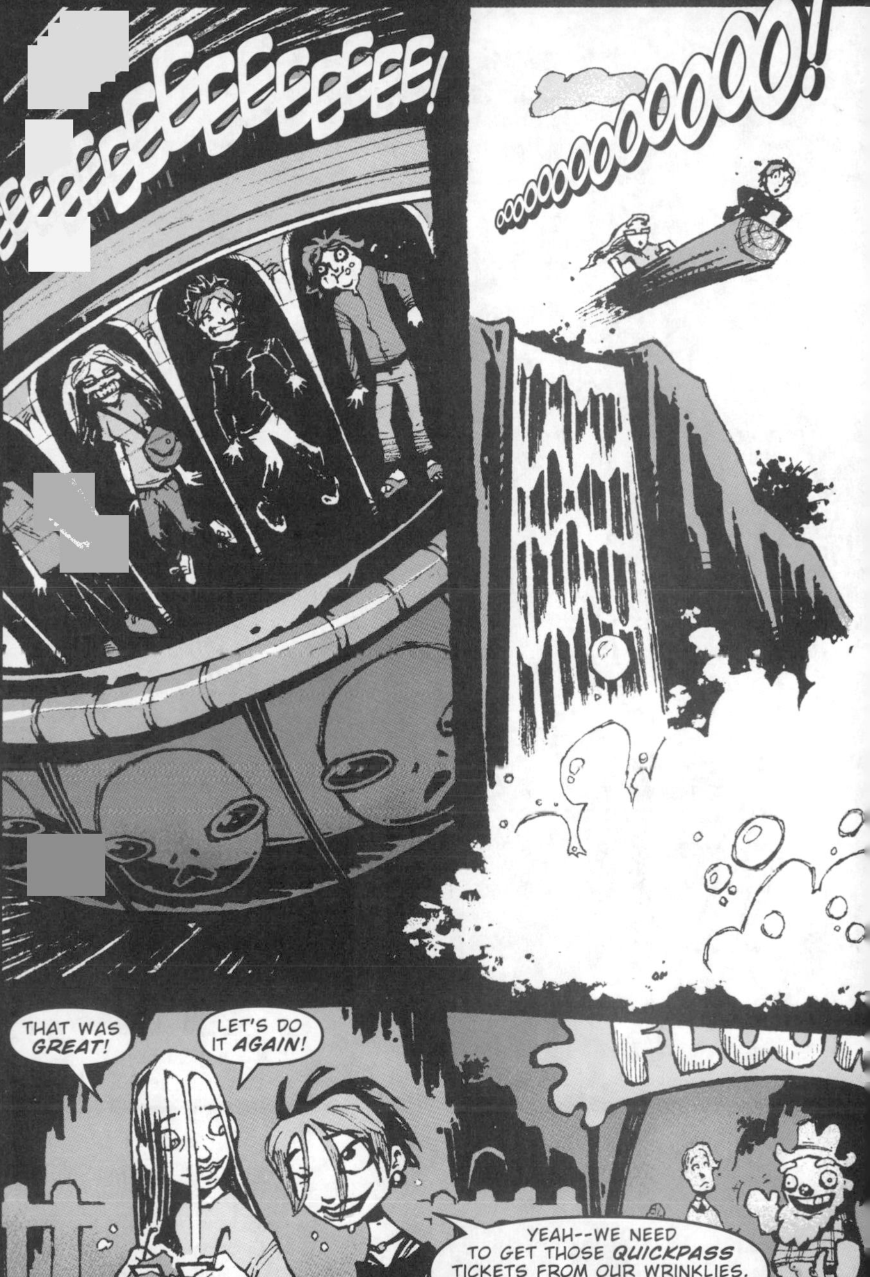
EEEEEEEEEEEEEEEEEEEEEE!
OOOOOOOOOOOOOOOOO!
THAT WAS GREAT!
LET'S DO IT AGAIN!
YEAH--WE NEED TO GET THOSE QUICKPASS TICKETS FROM OUR WRINKLIES. OTHERWISE WE'LL BE STANDING IN LINE UNTIL--

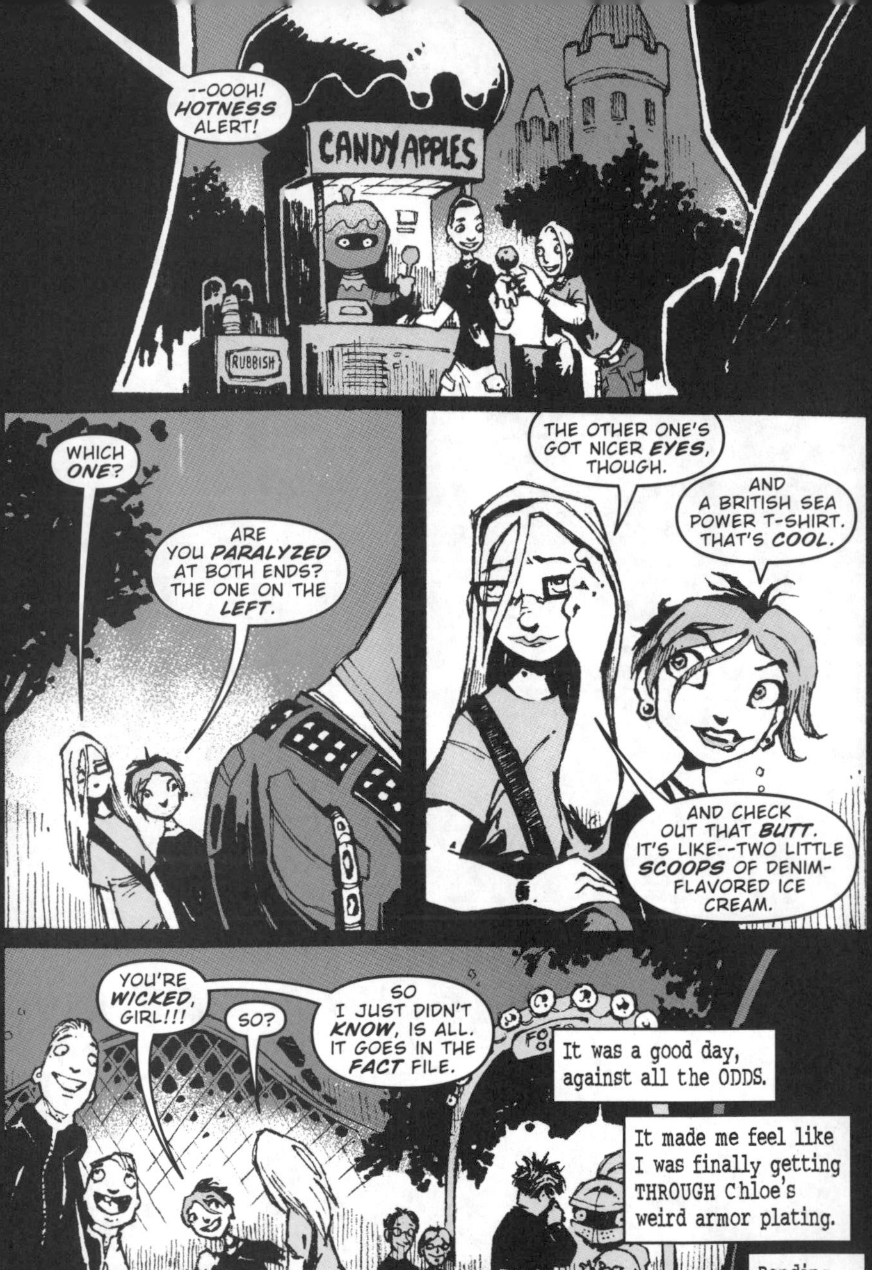

--OOOH! HOTNESS ALERT!
CANDY APPLES
RUBBISH
WHICH ONE?
ARE YOU PARALYZED AT BOTH ENDS? THE ONE ON THE LEFT.
THE OTHER ONE'S GOT NICER EYES, THOUGH.
AND A BRITISH SEA POWER T-SHIRT. THAT'S COOL.
AND CHECK OUT THAT BUTT. IT'S LIKE--TWO LITTLE SCOOPS OF DENIM-FLAVORED ICE CREAM.
YOU'RE WICKED, GIRL!!!
SO?
SO I JUST DIDN'T KNOW, IS ALL. IT GOES IN THE FACT FILE.
It was a good day, against all the ODDS.
It made me feel like I was finally getting THROUGH Chloe's weird armor plating.
Bonding. WITHOUT superglue.

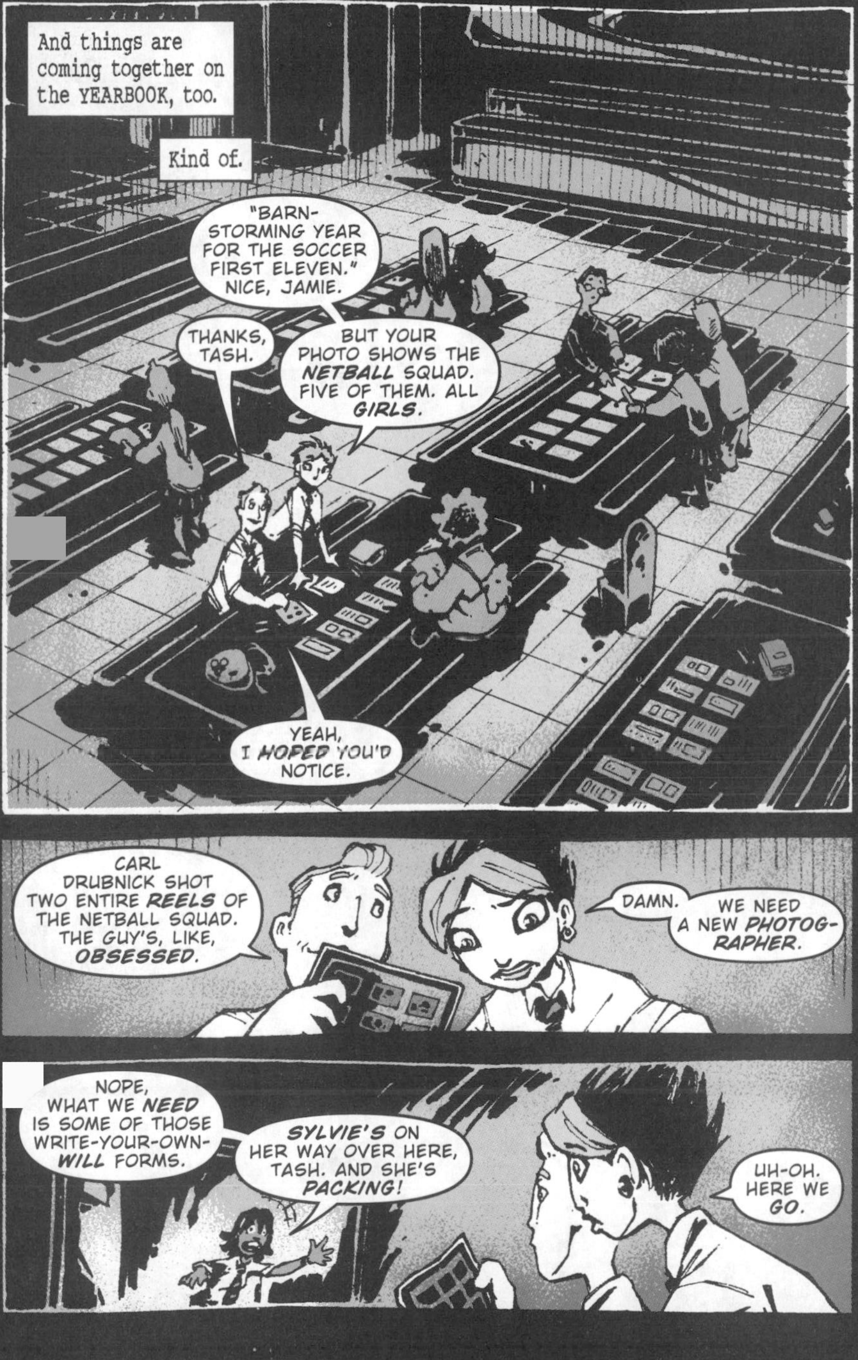
And things are coming together on the YEARBOOK, too.
Kind of.
"BARN-STORMING YEAR FOR THE SOCCER FIRST ELEVEN." NICE, JAMIE.
THANKS, TASH.
BUT YOUR PHOTO SHOWS THE NETBALL SQUAD. FIVE OF THEM. ALL GIRLS.
YEAH, I HOPED YOU'D NOTICE.
CARL DRUBNICK SHOT TWO ENTIRE REELS OF THE NETBALL SQUAD. THE GUY'S, LIKE, OBSESSED.
DAMN.
WE NEED A NEW PHOTOG-RAPHER.
NOPE, WHAT WE NEED IS SOME OF THOSE WRITE-YOUR-OWN-WILL FORMS.
SYLVIE'S ON HER WAY OVER HERE, TASH. AND SHE'S PACKING!
UH-OH. HERE WE GO.

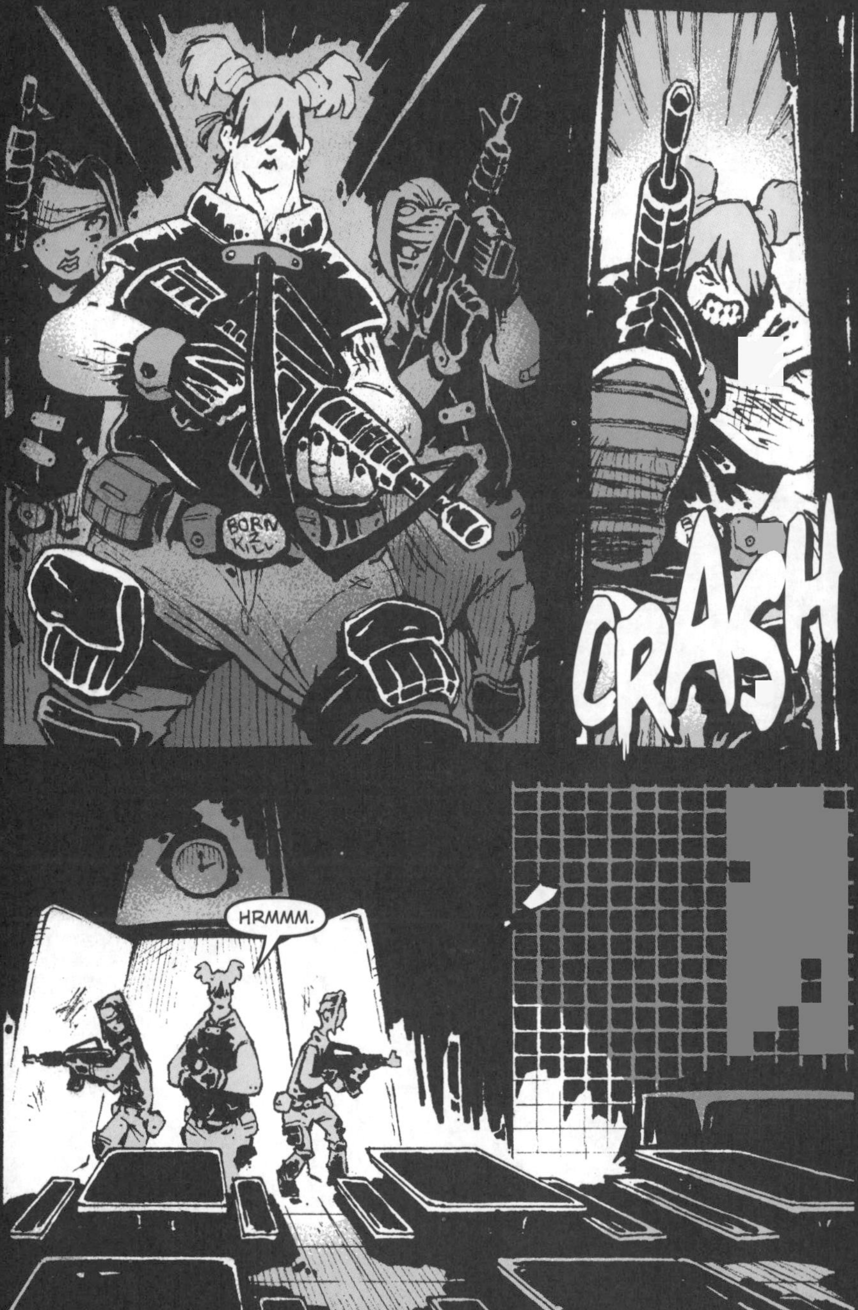
BORN 2 KILL
CRASH
HRMMM.

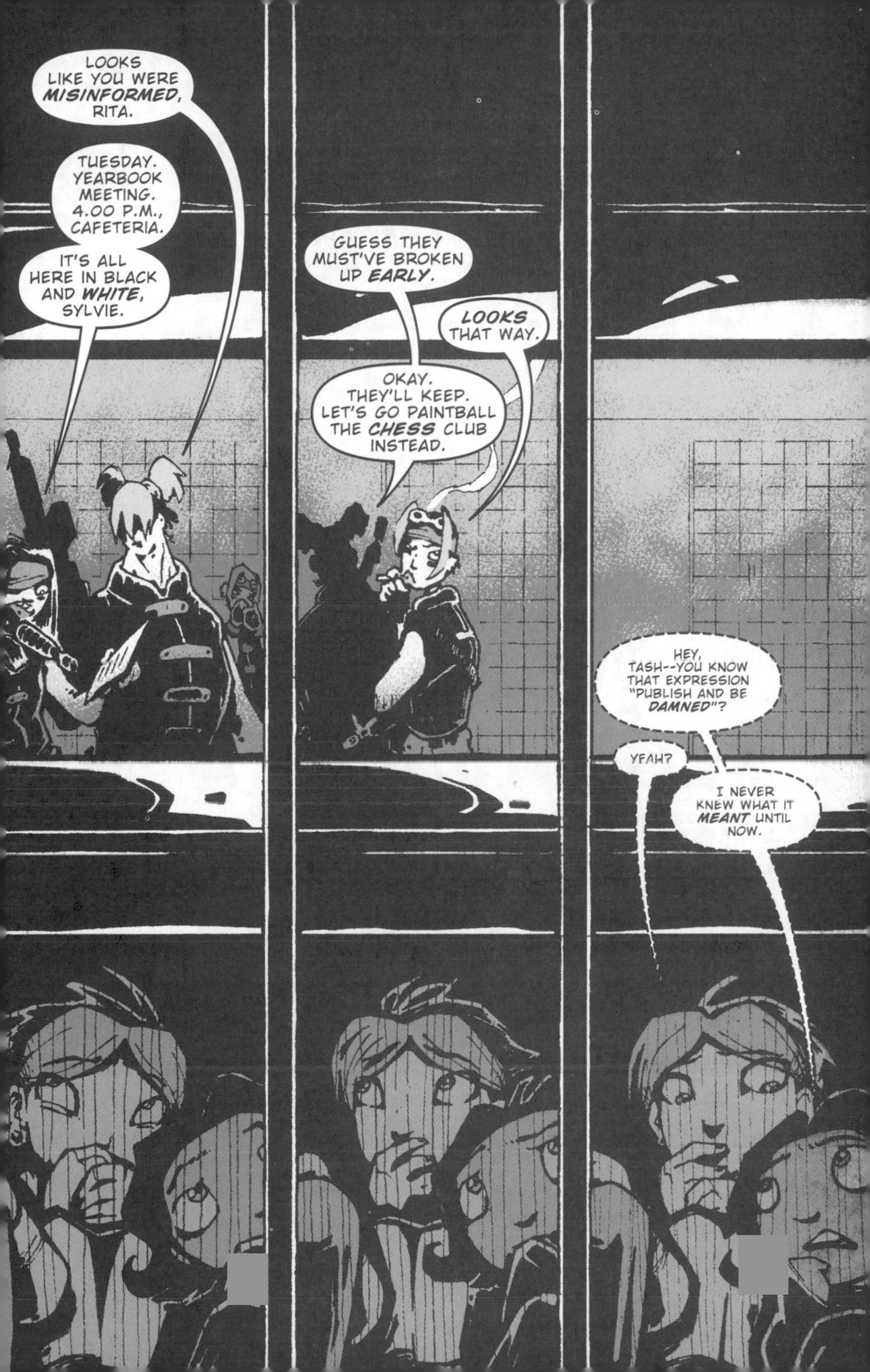
LOOKS LIKE YOU WERE MISINFORMED, RITA.
TUESDAY. YEARBOOK MEETING. 4.00 P.M., CAFETERIA.
IT'S ALL HERE IN BLACK AND WHITE, SYLVIE.
GUESS THEY MUST'VE BROKEN UP EARLY.
LOOKS THAT WAY.
OKAY. THEY'LL KEEP. LET'S GO PAINTBALL THE CHESS CLUB INSTEAD.
HEY, TASH--YOU KNOW THAT EXPRESSION "PUBLISH AND BE DAMNED"?
YEAH?
I NEVER KNEW WHAT IT MEANT UNTIL NOW.

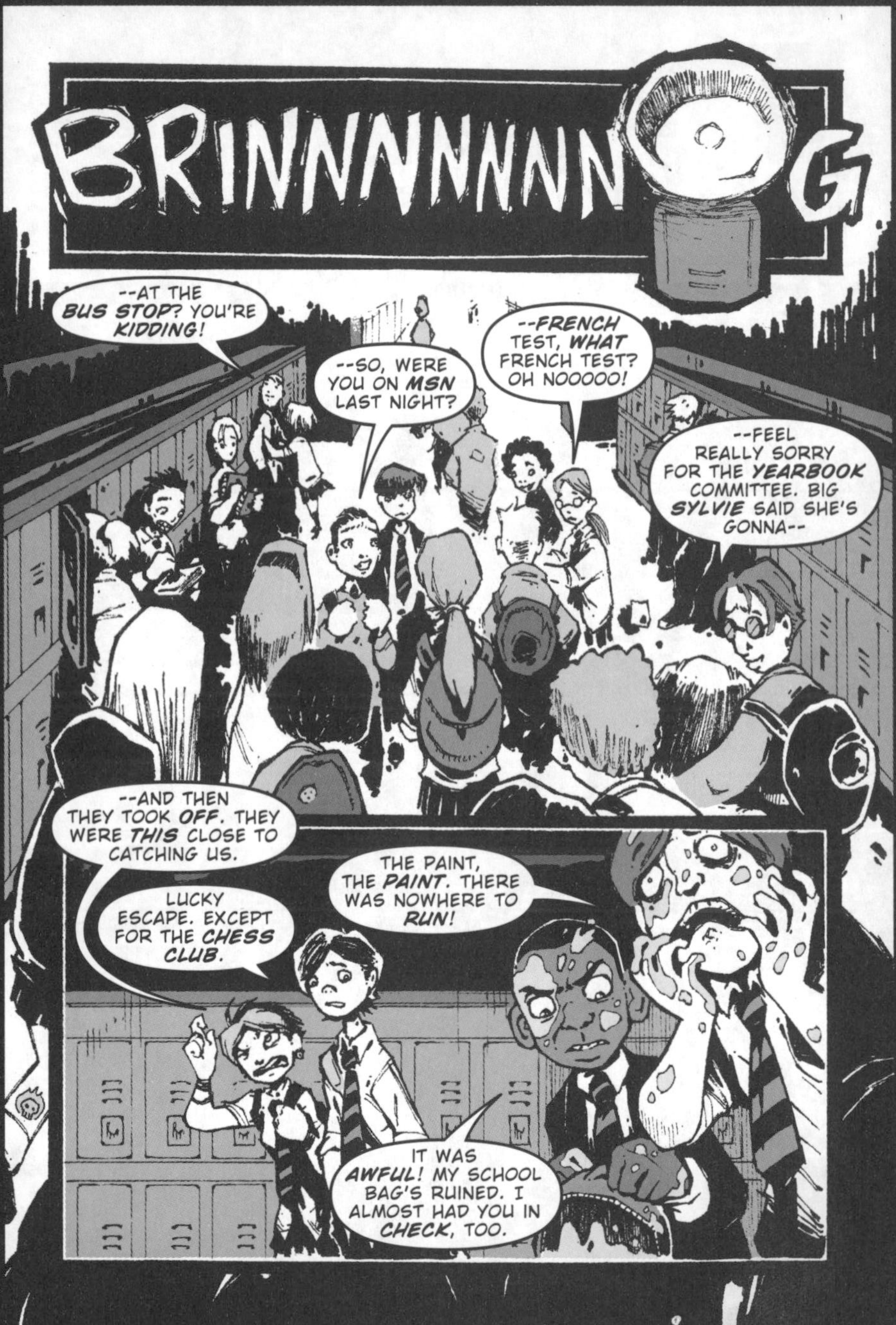
BRINNNNNNNG
--AT THE BUS STOP? YOU'RE KIDDING!
--SO, WERE YOU ON MSN LAST NIGHT?
--FRENCH TEST, WHAT FRENCH TEST? OH NOOOOO!
--FEEL REALLY SORRY FOR THE YEARBOOK COMMITTEE. BIG SYLVIE SAID SHE'S GONNA--
--AND THEN THEY TOOK OFF. THEY WERE THIS CLOSE TO CATCHING US.
LUCKY ESCAPE. EXCEPT FOR THE CHESS CLUB.
THE PAINT, THE PAINT. THERE WAS NOWHERE TO RUN!
IT WAS AWFUL! MY SCHOOL BAG'S RUINED. I ALMOST HAD YOU IN CHECK, TOO.

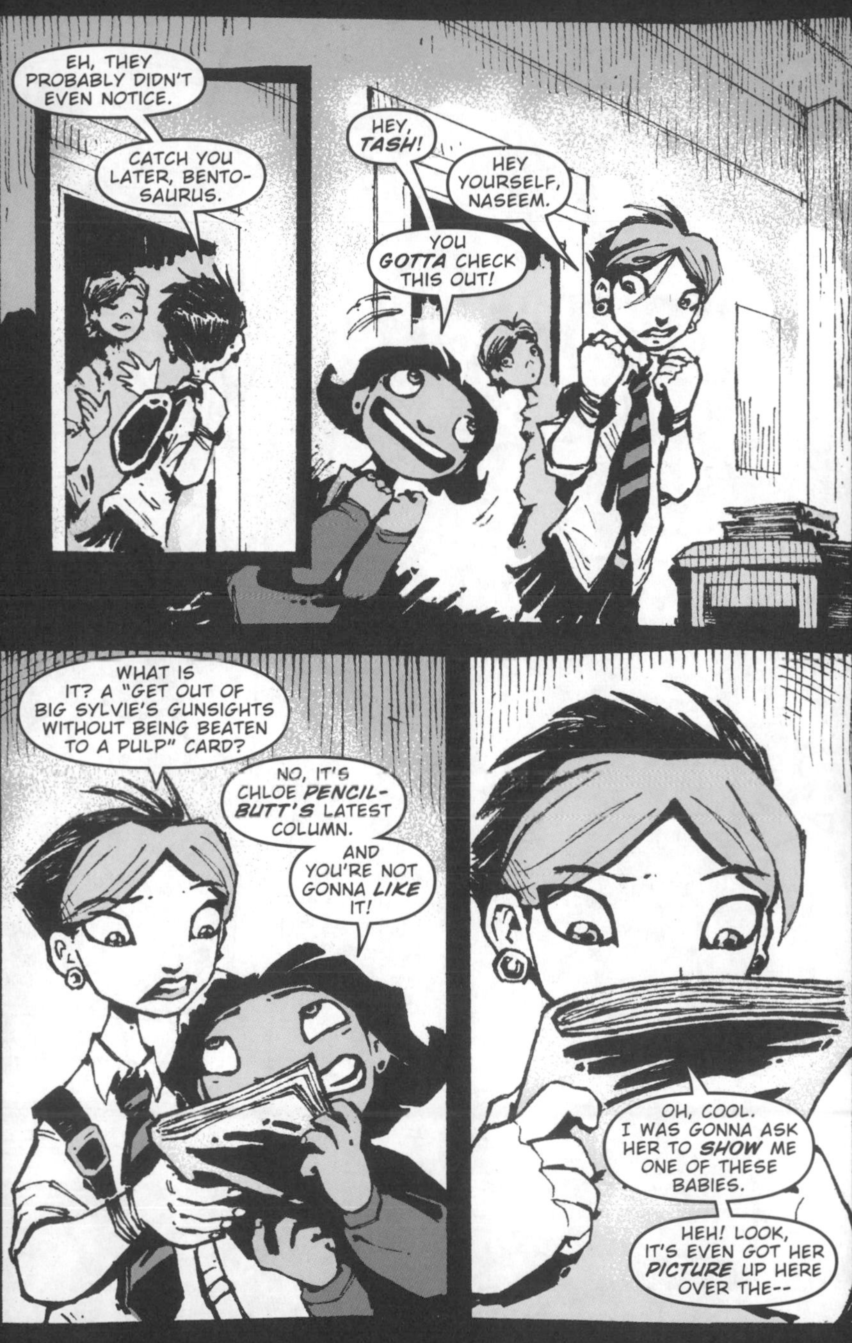
EH, THEY PROBABLY DIDN'T EVEN NOTICE.
CATCH YOU LATER, BENTO-SAURUS.
HEY, *TASH*!
HEY YOURSELF, NASEEM.
YOU *GOTTA* CHECK THIS OUT!
WHAT IS IT? A "GET OUT OF BIG SYLVIE'S GUNSIGHTS WITHOUT BEING BEATEN TO A PULP" CARD?
NO, IT'S CHLOE *PENCIL-BUTT'S* LATEST COLUMN.
AND YOU'RE NOT GONNA *LIKE* IT!
OH, COOL. I WAS GONNA ASK HER TO *SHOW* ME ONE OF THESE BABIES.
HEH! LOOK, IT'S EVEN GOT HER *PICTURE* UP HERE OVER THE--

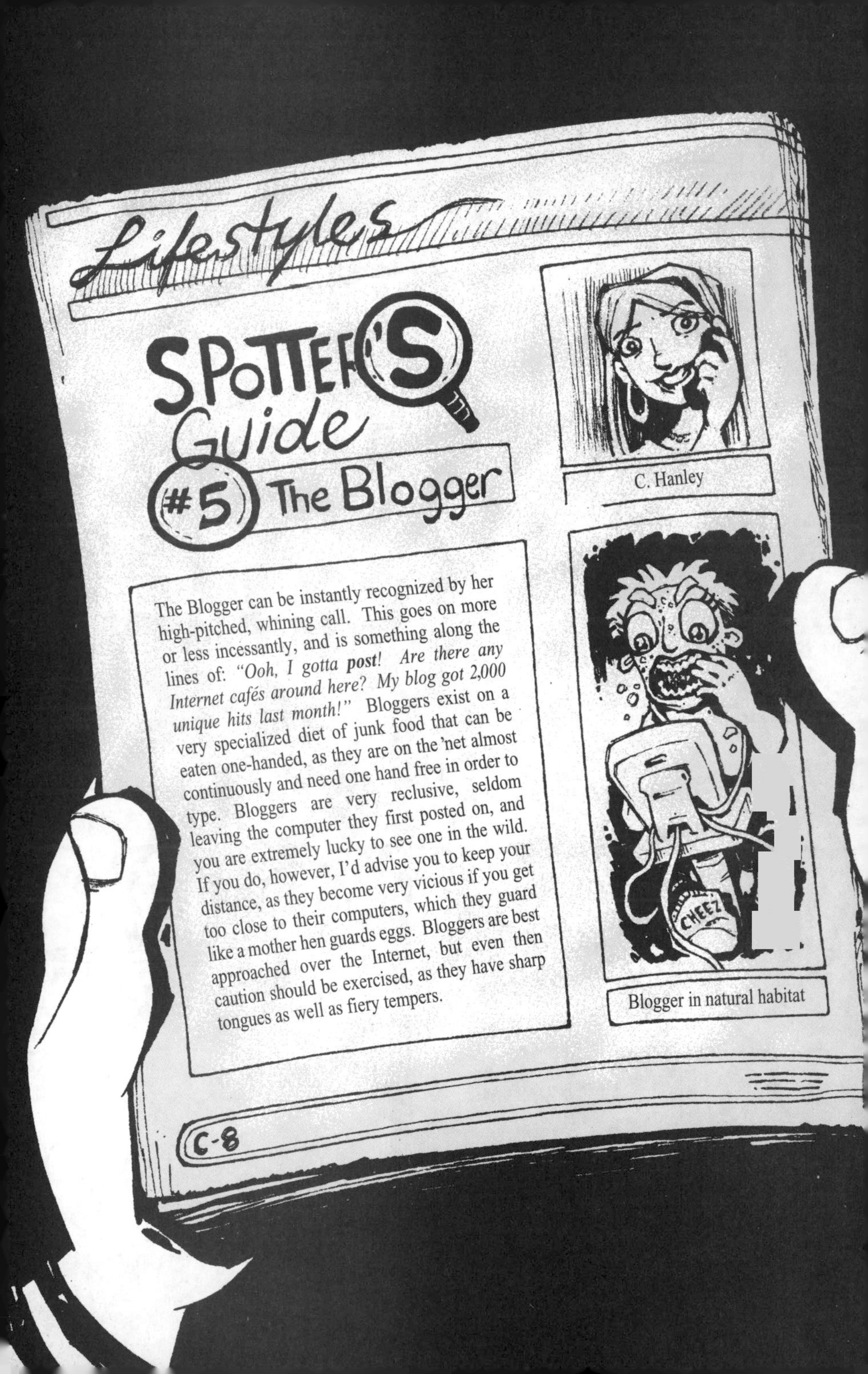
Lifestyles
SPOTTER'S Guide
#5 The Blogger
C. Hanley
The Blogger can be instantly recognized by her high-pitched, whining call. This goes on more or less incessantly, and is something along the lines of: *"Ooh, I gotta* ***post****! Are there any Internet cafés around here? My blog got 2,000 unique hits last month!"* Bloggers exist on a very specialized diet of junk food that can be eaten one-handed, as they are on the 'net almost continuously and need one hand free in order to type. Bloggers are very reclusive, seldom leaving the computer they first posted on, and you are extremely lucky to see one in the wild. If you do, however, I'd advise you to keep your distance, as they become very vicious if you get too close to their computers, which they guard like a mother hen guards eggs. Bloggers are best approached over the Internet, but even then caution should be exercised, as they have sharp tongues as well as fiery tempers.
CHEEZ
Blogger in natural habitat
C-8

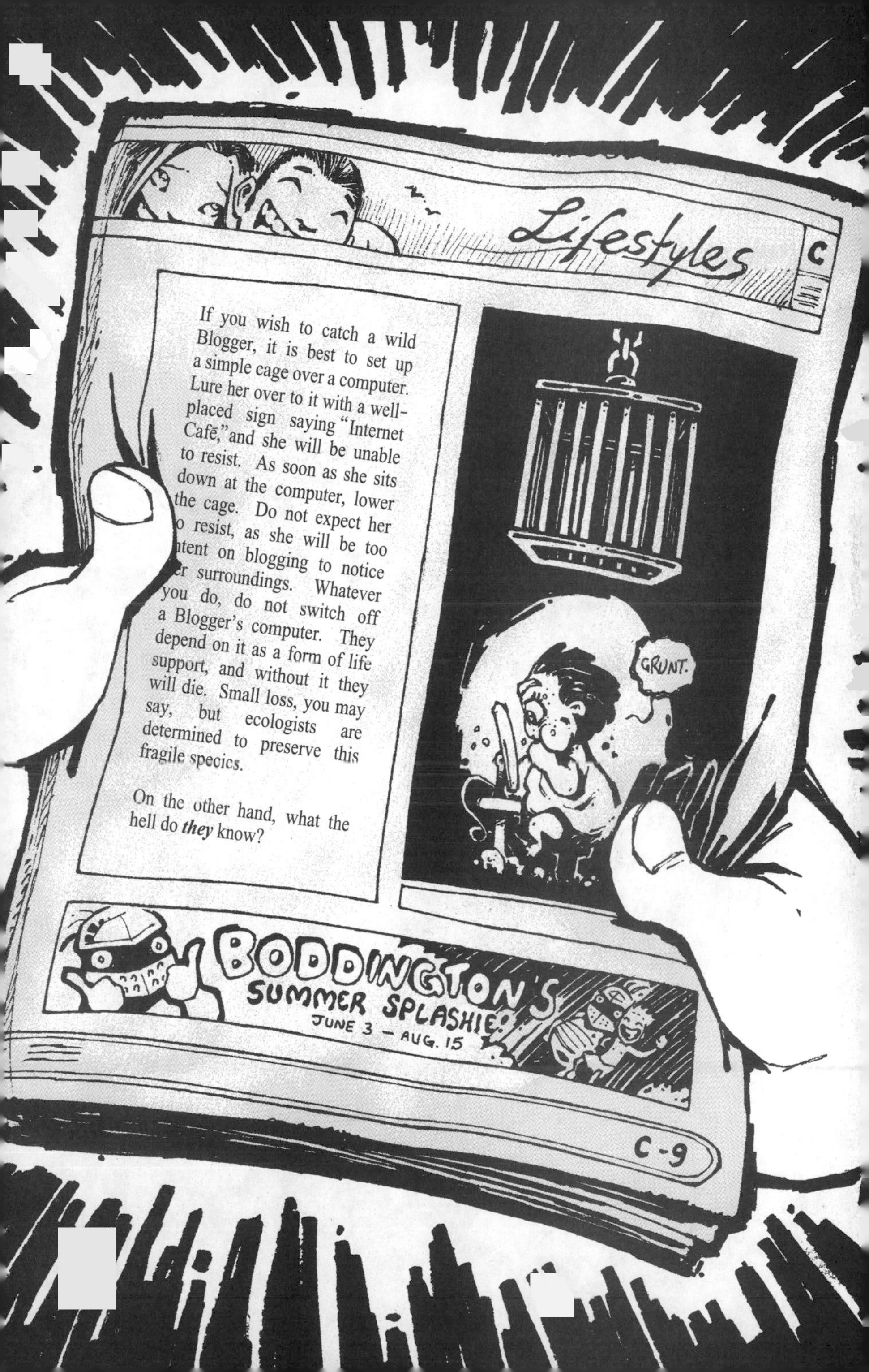
Lifestyles
C
If you wish to catch a wild Blogger, it is best to set up a simple cage over a computer. Lure her over to it with a well-placed sign saying "Internet Cafe," and she will be unable to resist. As soon as she sits down at the computer, lower the cage. Do not expect her to resist, as she will be too intent on blogging to notice her surroundings. Whatever you do, do not switch off a Blogger's computer. They depend on it as a form of life support, and without it they will die. Small loss, you may say, but ecologists are determined to preserve this fragile species.
On the other hand, what the hell do *they* know?
GRUNT.
BODDINGTON'S
SUMMER SPLASHIE!
JUNE 3 – AUG. 15
C-9

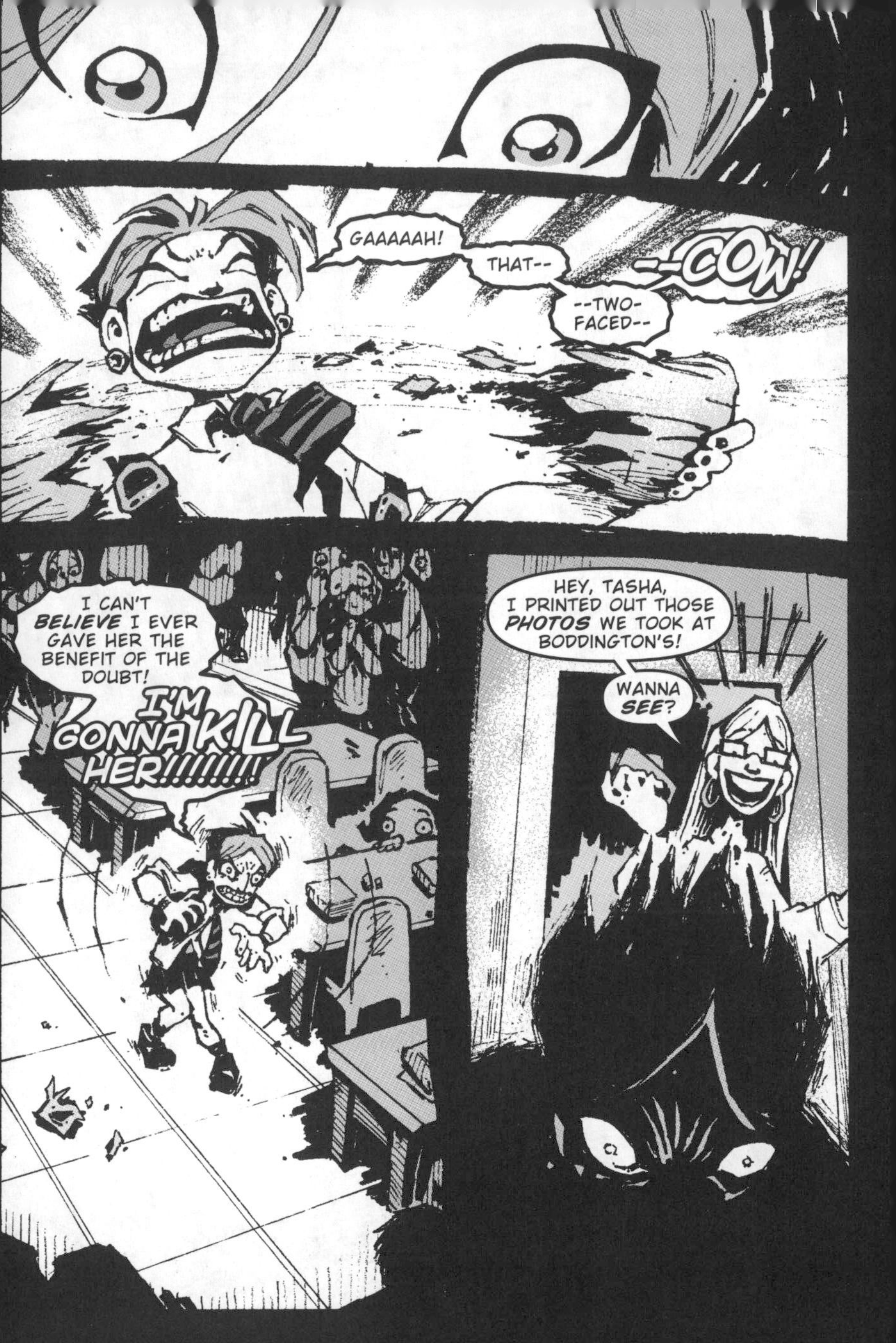
GAAAAAH!
THAT--
--TWO-FACED--
--COW!
I CAN'T BELIEVE I EVER GAVE HER THE BENEFIT OF THE DOUBT!
I'M GONNA KILL HER!!!!!!!!!
HEY, TASHA, I PRINTED OUT THOSE PHOTOS WE TOOK AT BODDINGTON'S!
WANNA SEE?

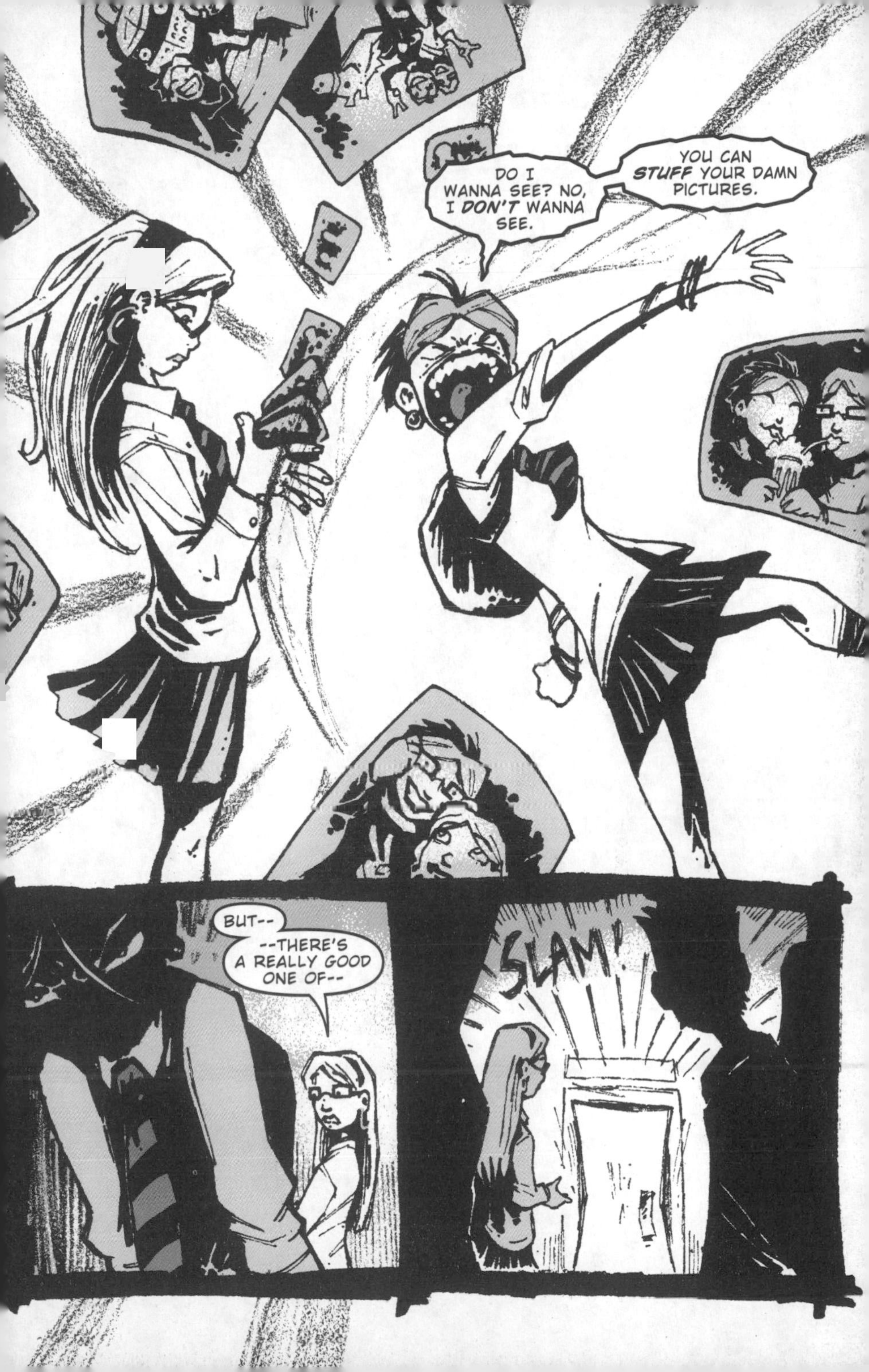
DO I WANNA SEE? NO, I DON'T WANNA SEE.
YOU CAN STUFF YOUR DAMN PICTURES.
BUT--
--THERE'S A REALLY GOOD ONE OF--
SLAM!

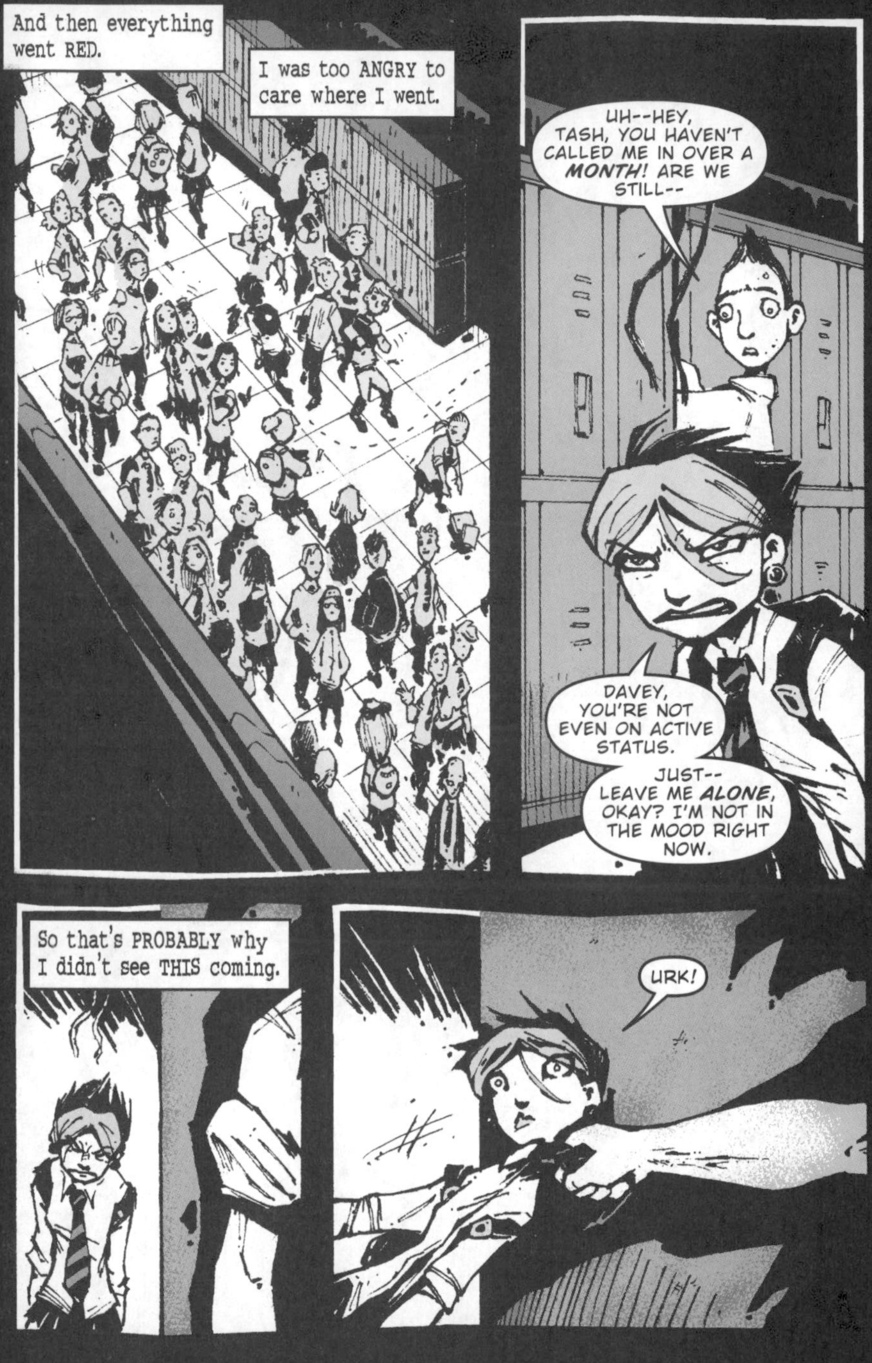
And then everything went RED.
I was too ANGRY to care where I went.
UH--HEY, TASH, YOU HAVEN'T CALLED ME IN OVER A MONTH! ARE WE STILL--
DAVEY, YOU'RE NOT EVEN ON ACTIVE STATUS.
JUST-- LEAVE ME ALONE, OKAY? I'M NOT IN THE MOOD RIGHT NOW.
So that's PROBABLY why I didn't see THIS coming.
URK!

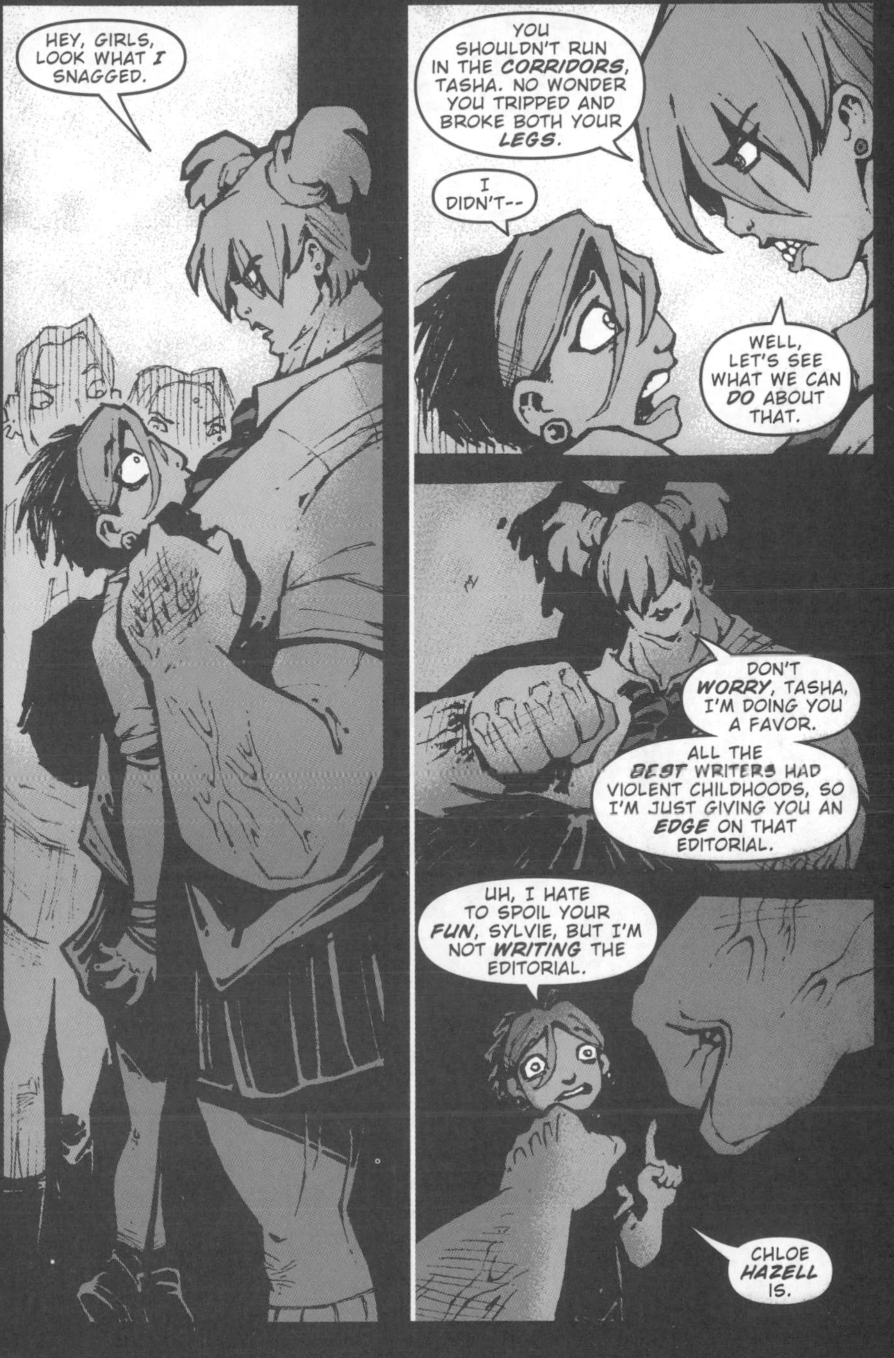
HEY, GIRLS, LOOK WHAT I SNAGGED.
YOU SHOULDN'T RUN IN THE CORRIDORS, TASHA. NO WONDER YOU TRIPPED AND BROKE BOTH YOUR LEGS.
I DIDN'T--
WELL, LET'S SEE WHAT WE CAN DO ABOUT THAT.
DON'T WORRY, TASHA, I'M DOING YOU A FAVOR.
ALL THE BEST WRITERS HAD VIOLENT CHILDHOODS, SO I'M JUST GIVING YOU AN EDGE ON THAT EDITORIAL.
UH, I HATE TO SPOIL YOUR FUN, SYLVIE, BUT I'M NOT WRITING THE EDITORIAL.
CHLOE HAZELL IS.

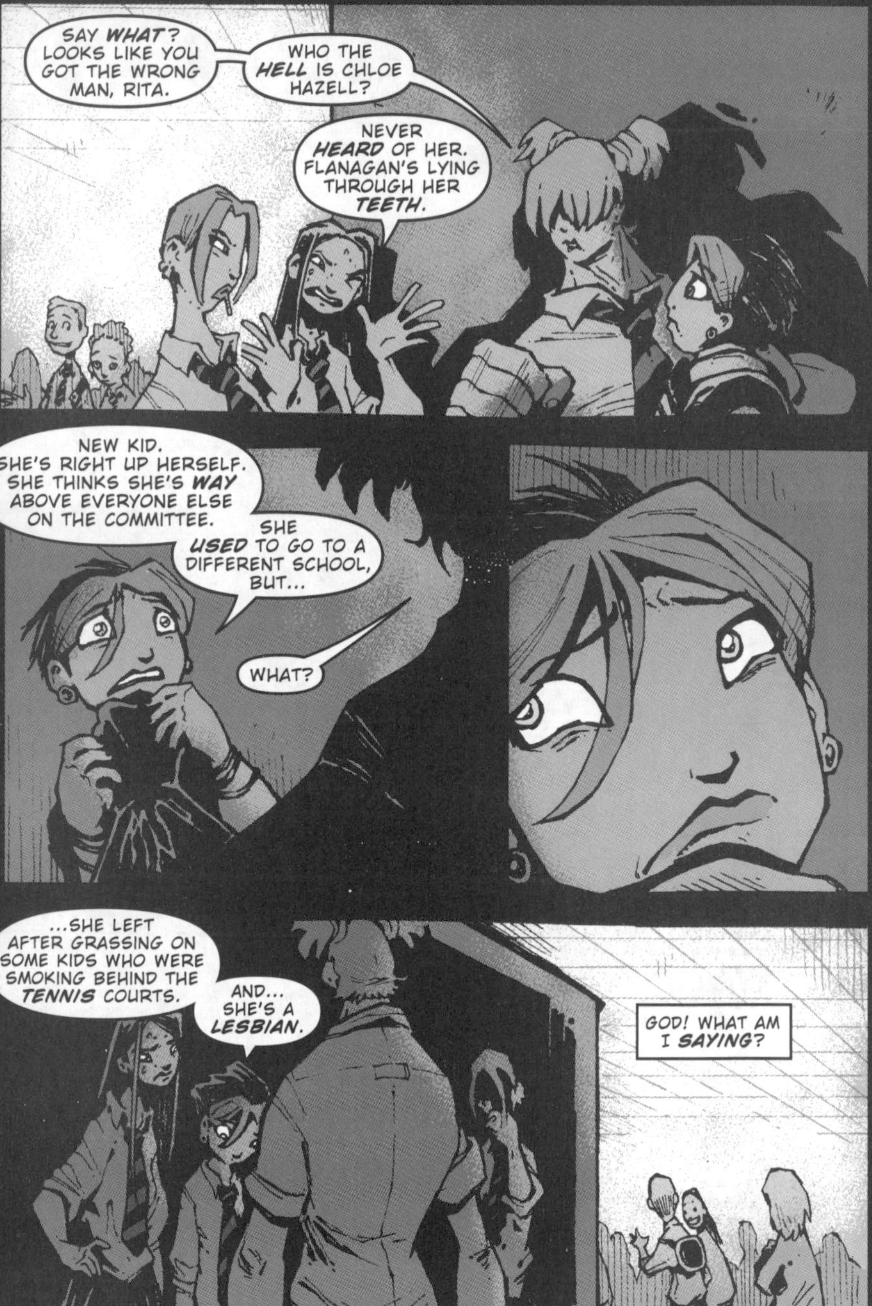
SAY *WHAT*? LOOKS LIKE YOU GOT THE WRONG MAN, RITA.
WHO THE *HELL* IS CHLOE HAZELL?
NEVER *HEARD* OF HER. FLANAGAN'S LYING THROUGH HER *TEETH*.
NEW KID. SHE'S RIGHT UP HERSELF. SHE THINKS SHE'S *WAY* ABOVE EVERYONE ELSE ON THE COMMITTEE.
SHE *USED* TO GO TO A DIFFERENT SCHOOL, BUT...
WHAT?
...SHE LEFT AFTER GRASSING ON SOME KIDS WHO WERE SMOKING BEHIND THE *TENNIS* COURTS.
AND... SHE'S A *LESBIAN*.
GOD! WHAT AM I *SAYING*?

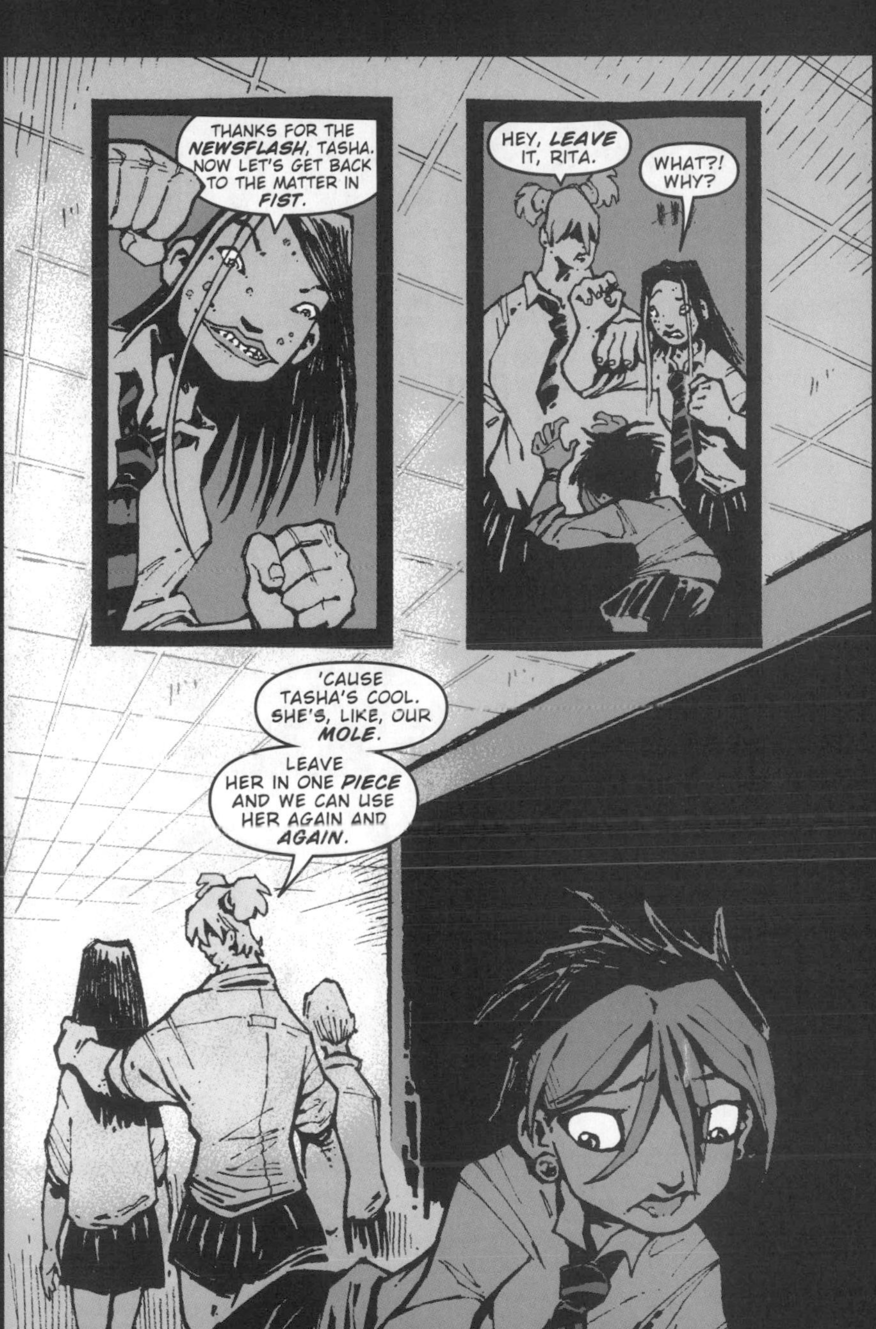
THANKS FOR THE NEWSFLASH, TASHA. NOW LET'S GET BACK TO THE MATTER IN FIST.
HEY, LEAVE IT, RITA.
WHAT?! WHY?
'CAUSE TASHA'S COOL. SHE'S, LIKE, OUR MOLE.
LEAVE HER IN ONE PIECE AND WE CAN USE HER AGAIN AND AGAIN.

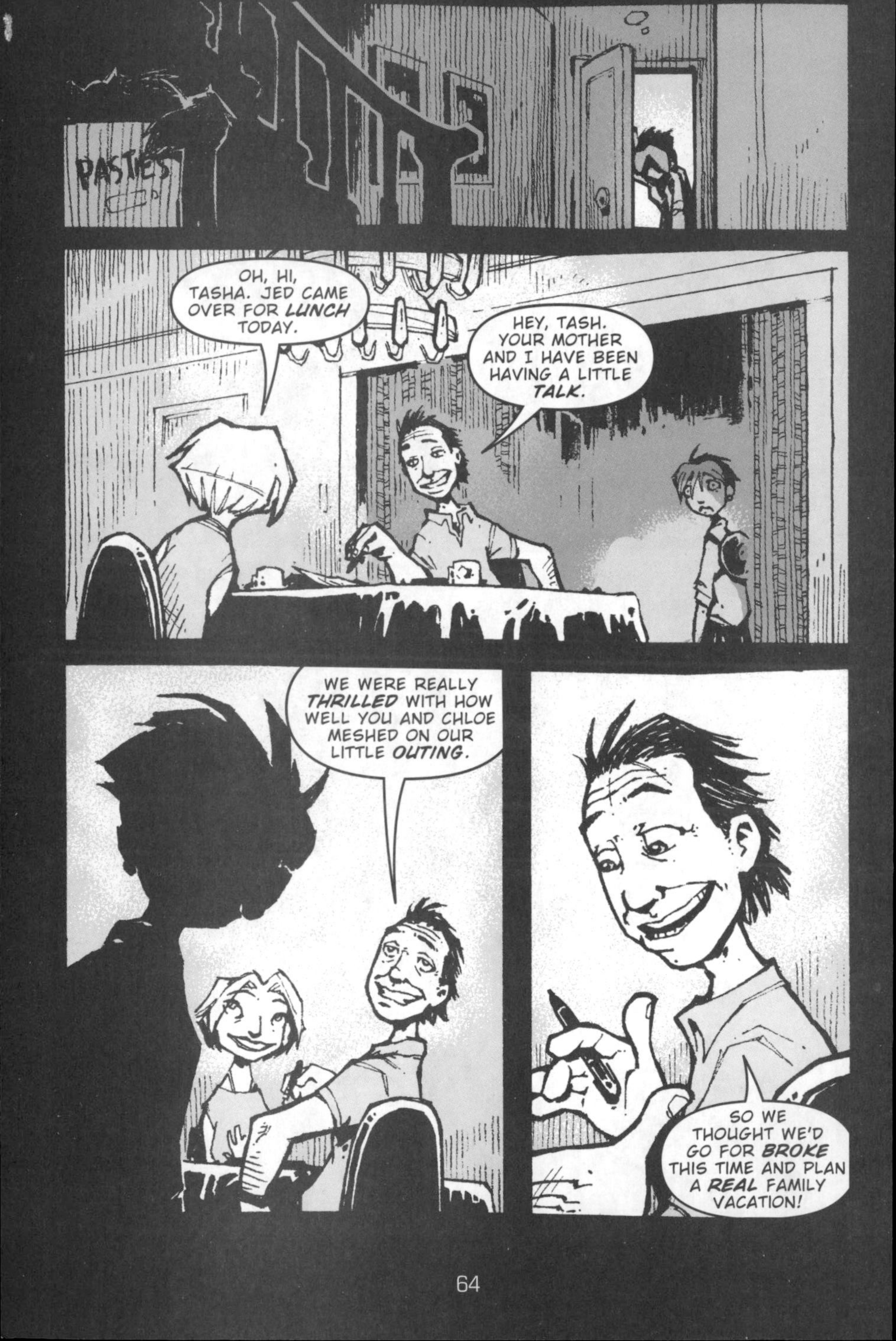
PASTIES
OH, HI, TASHA. JED CAME OVER FOR LUNCH TODAY.
HEY, TASH. YOUR MOTHER AND I HAVE BEEN HAVING A LITTLE TALK.
WE WERE REALLY THRILLED WITH HOW WELL YOU AND CHLOE MESHED ON OUR LITTLE OUTING.
SO WE THOUGHT WE'D GO FOR BROKE THIS TIME AND PLAN A REAL FAMILY VACATION!

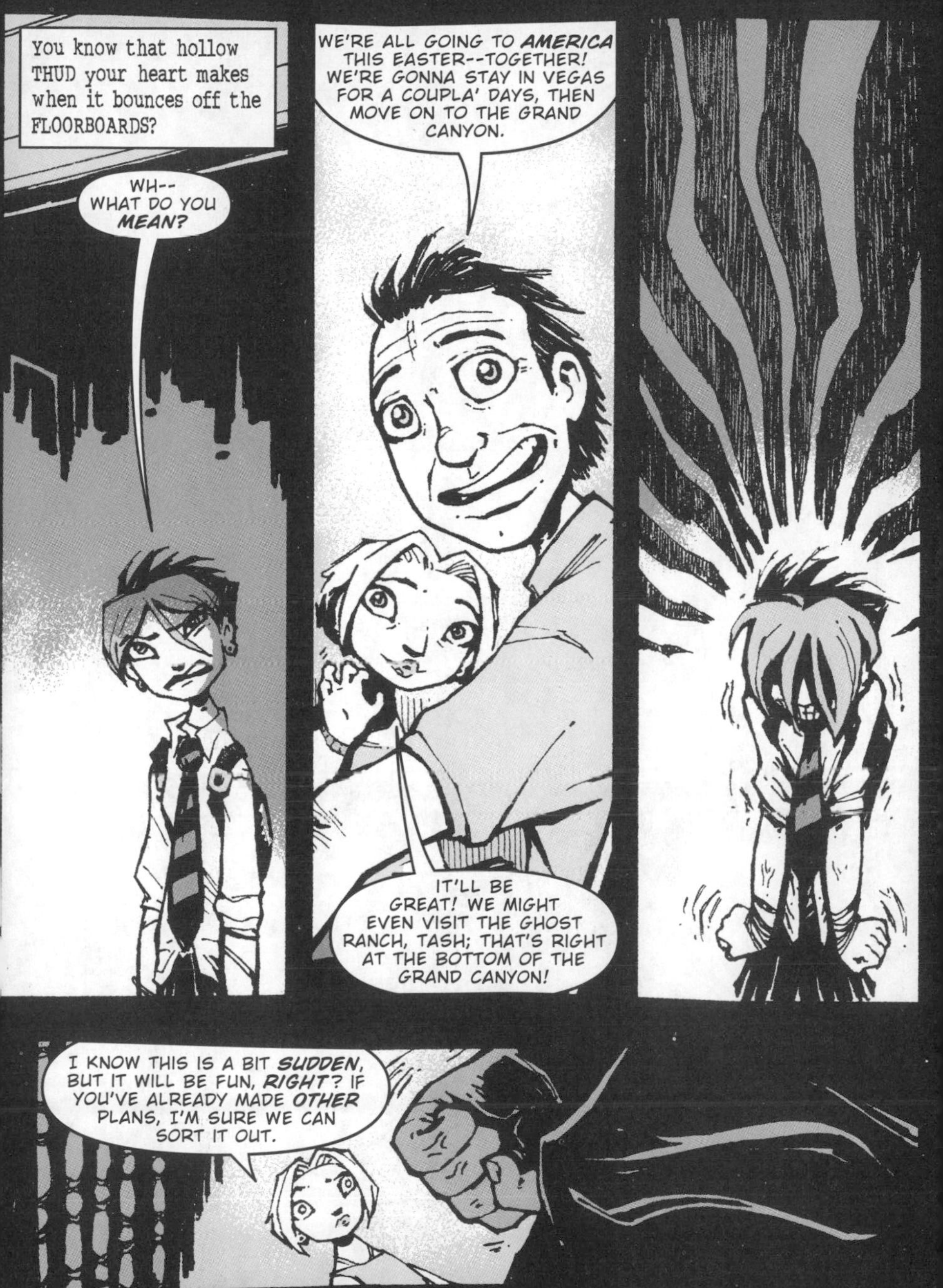
You know that hollow THUD your heart makes when it bounces off the FLOORBOARDS?
WH-- WHAT DO YOU MEAN?
WE'RE ALL GOING TO AMERICA THIS EASTER--TOGETHER! WE'RE GONNA STAY IN VEGAS FOR A COUPLA' DAYS, THEN MOVE ON TO THE GRAND CANYON.
IT'LL BE GREAT! WE MIGHT EVEN VISIT THE GHOST RANCH, TASH; THAT'S RIGHT AT THE BOTTOM OF THE GRAND CANYON!
I KNOW THIS IS A BIT SUDDEN, BUT IT WILL BE FUN, RIGHT? IF YOU'VE ALREADY MADE OTHER PLANS, I'M SURE WE CAN SORT IT OUT.

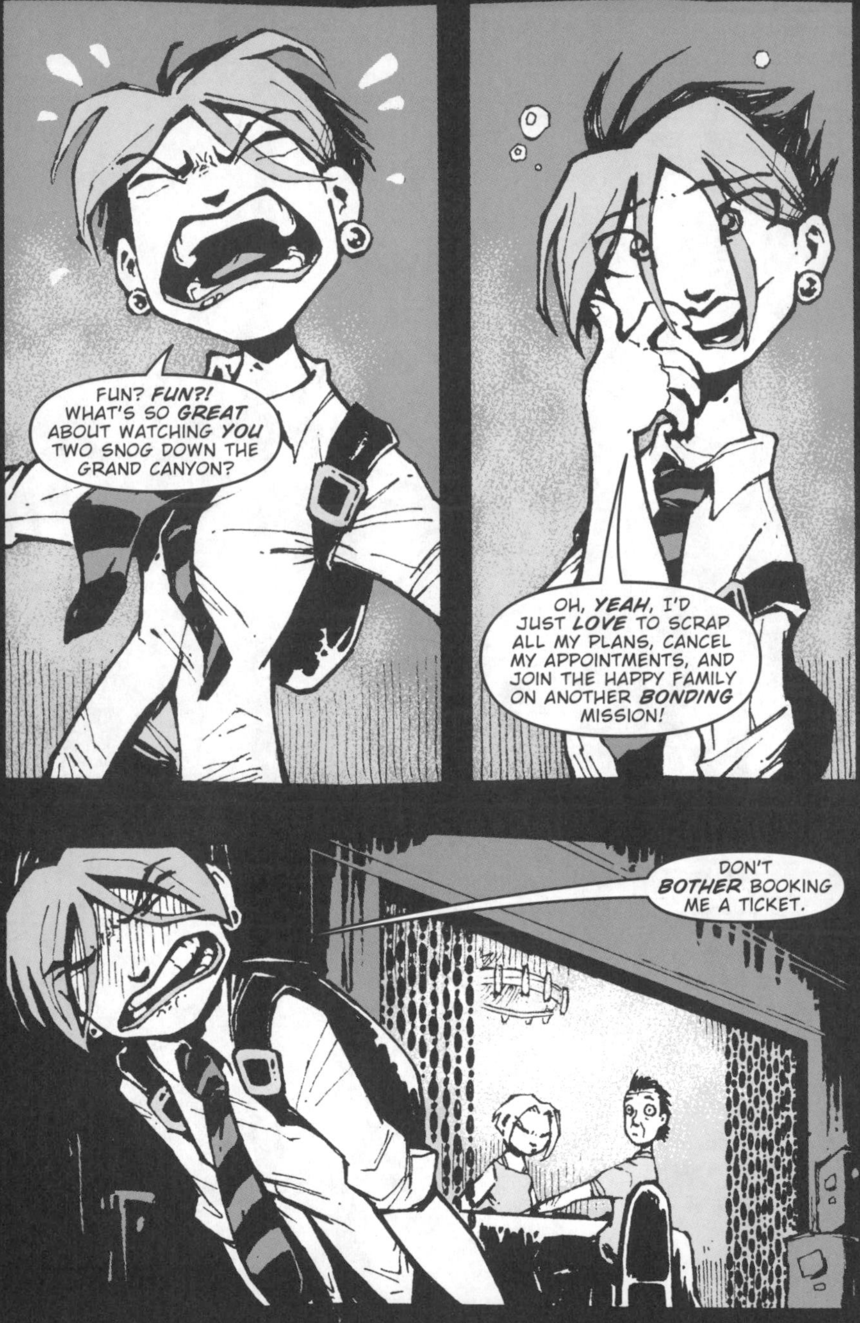
FUN? *FUN?!* WHAT'S SO *GREAT* ABOUT WATCHING *YOU* TWO SNOG DOWN THE GRAND CANYON?
OH, *YEAH*, I'D JUST *LOVE* TO SCRAP ALL MY PLANS, CANCEL MY APPOINTMENTS, AND JOIN THE HAPPY FAMILY ON ANOTHER *BONDING* MISSION!
DON'T *BOTHER* BOOKING ME A TICKET.

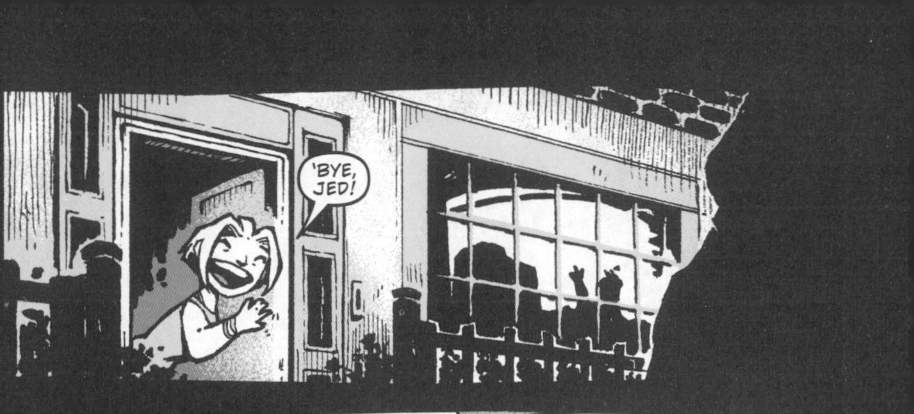
'BYE, JED!

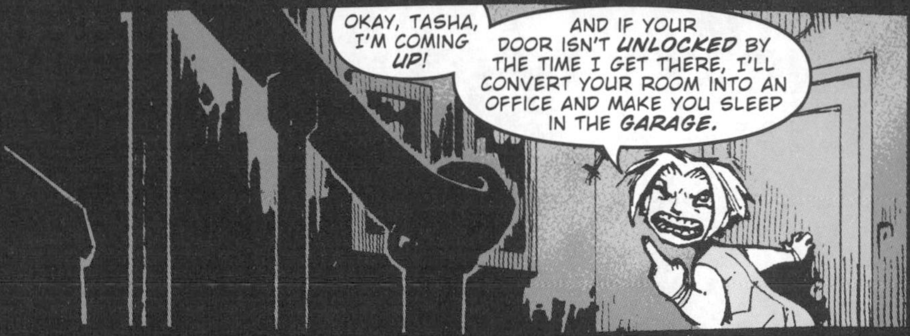
OKAY, TASHA, I'M COMING *UP*!
AND IF YOUR DOOR ISN'T *UNLOCKED* BY THE TIME I GET THERE, I'LL CONVERT YOUR ROOM INTO AN OFFICE AND MAKE YOU SLEEP IN THE *GARAGE.*

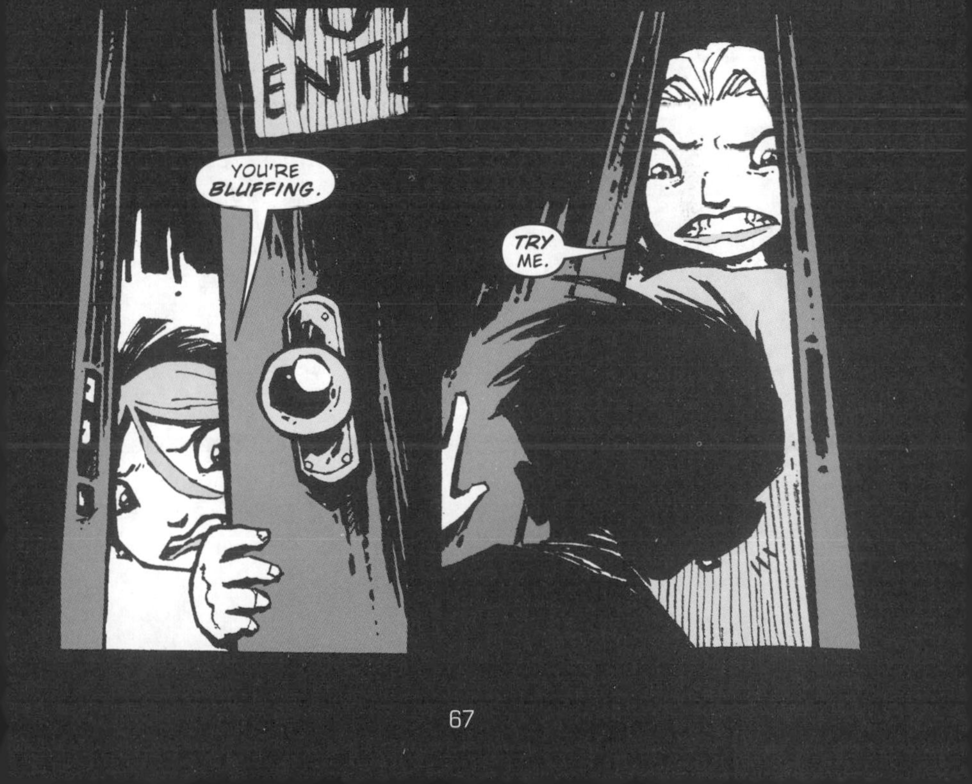
YOU'RE *BLUFFING*.
TRY ME.

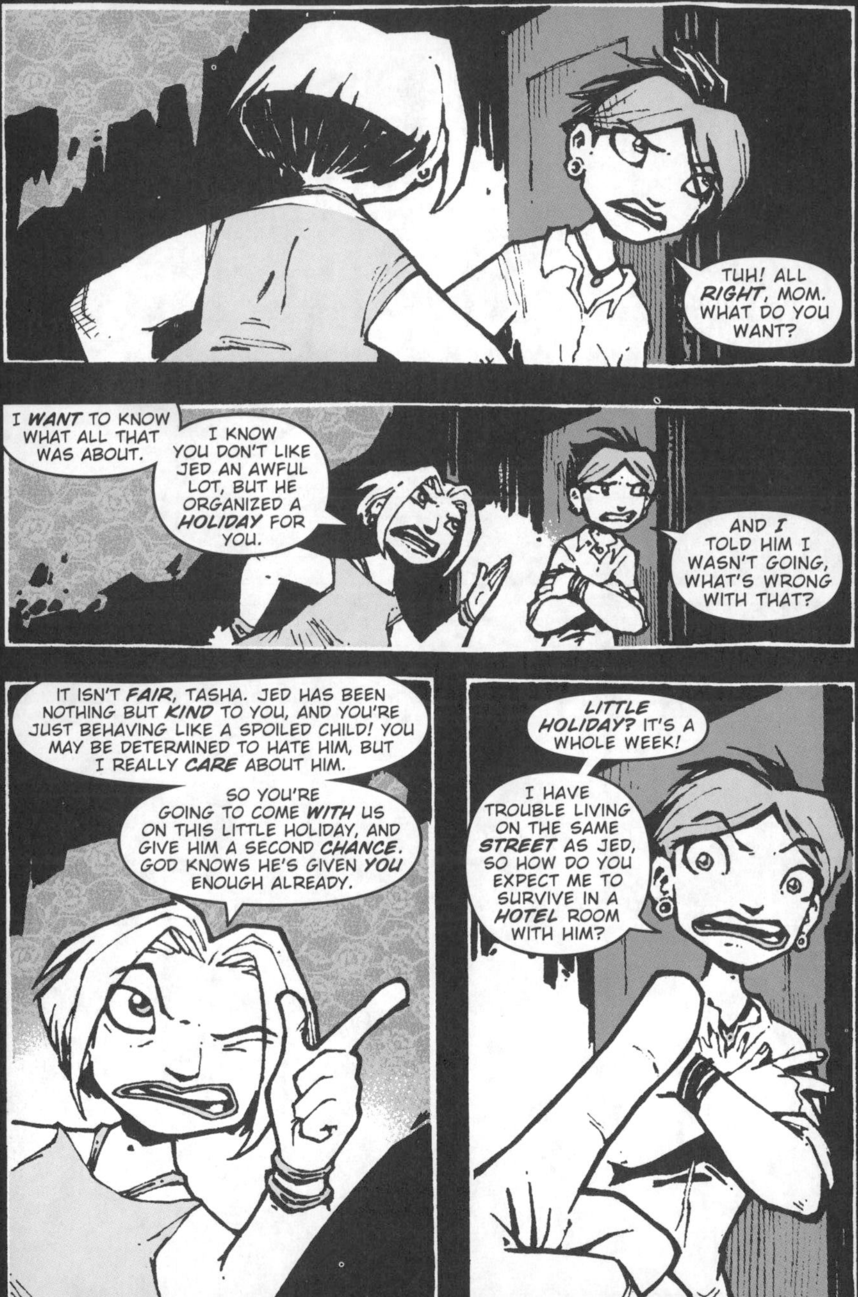
TUH! ALL RIGHT, MOM. WHAT DO YOU WANT?
I WANT TO KNOW WHAT ALL THAT WAS ABOUT.
I KNOW YOU DON'T LIKE JED AN AWFUL LOT, BUT HE ORGANIZED A HOLIDAY FOR YOU.
AND I TOLD HIM I WASN'T GOING, WHAT'S WRONG WITH THAT?
IT ISN'T FAIR, TASHA. JED HAS BEEN NOTHING BUT KIND TO YOU, AND YOU'RE JUST BEHAVING LIKE A SPOILED CHILD! YOU MAY BE DETERMINED TO HATE HIM, BUT I REALLY CARE ABOUT HIM.
SO YOU'RE GOING TO COME WITH US ON THIS LITTLE HOLIDAY, AND GIVE HIM A SECOND CHANCE. GOD KNOWS HE'S GIVEN YOU ENOUGH ALREADY.
LITTLE HOLIDAY? IT'S A WHOLE WEEK!
I HAVE TROUBLE LIVING ON THE SAME STREET AS JED, SO HOW DO YOU EXPECT ME TO SURVIVE IN A HOTEL ROOM WITH HIM?

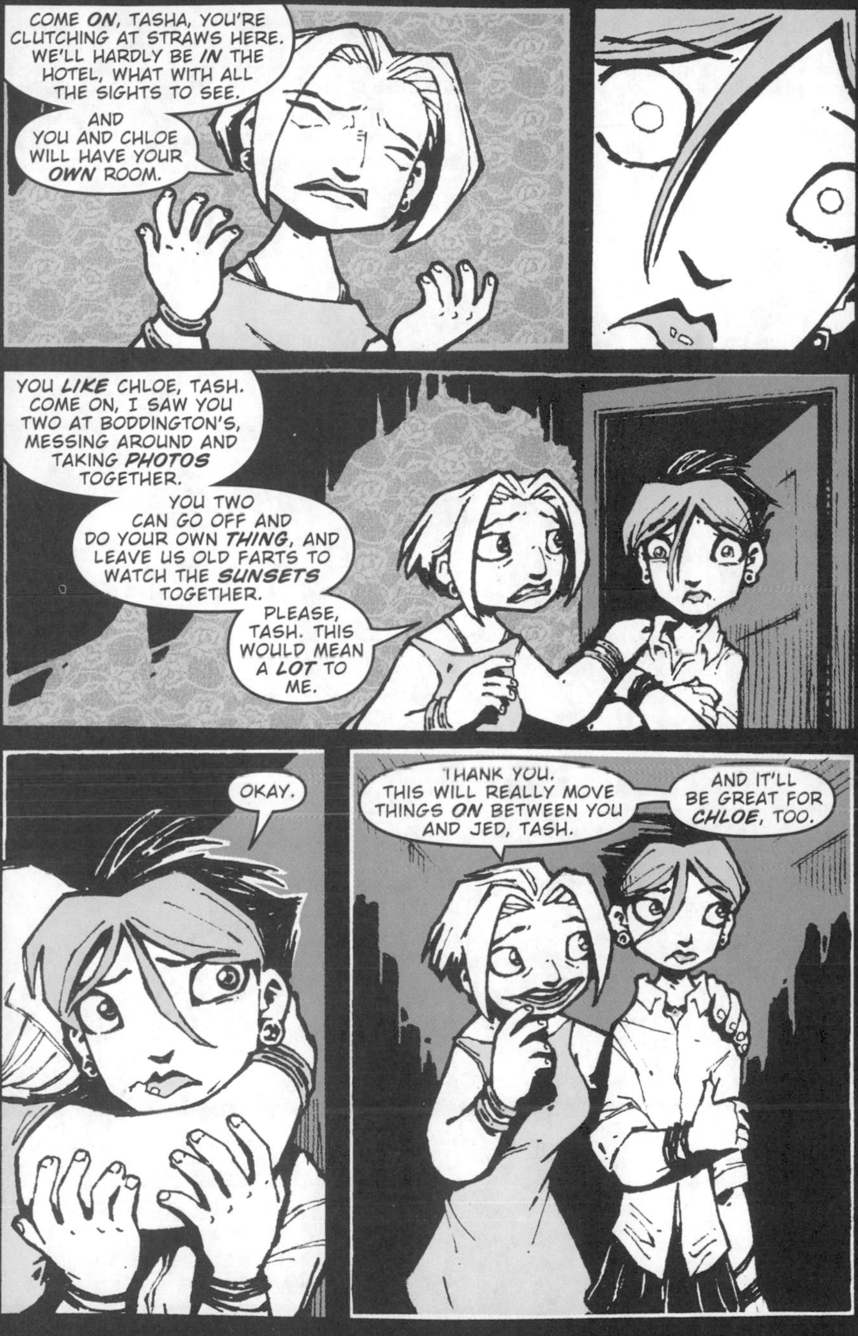
COME ON, TASHA, YOU'RE CLUTCHING AT STRAWS HERE. WE'LL HARDLY BE IN THE HOTEL, WHAT WITH ALL THE SIGHTS TO SEE.
AND YOU AND CHLOE WILL HAVE YOUR OWN ROOM.
YOU LIKE CHLOE, TASH. COME ON, I SAW YOU TWO AT BODDINGTON'S, MESSING AROUND AND TAKING PHOTOS TOGETHER.
YOU TWO CAN GO OFF AND DO YOUR OWN THING, AND LEAVE US OLD FARTS TO WATCH THE SUNSETS TOGETHER.
PLEASE, TASH. THIS WOULD MEAN A LOT TO ME.
OKAY.
THANK YOU. THIS WILL REALLY MOVE THINGS ON BETWEEN YOU AND JED, TASH.
AND IT'LL BE GREAT FOR CHLOE, TOO.

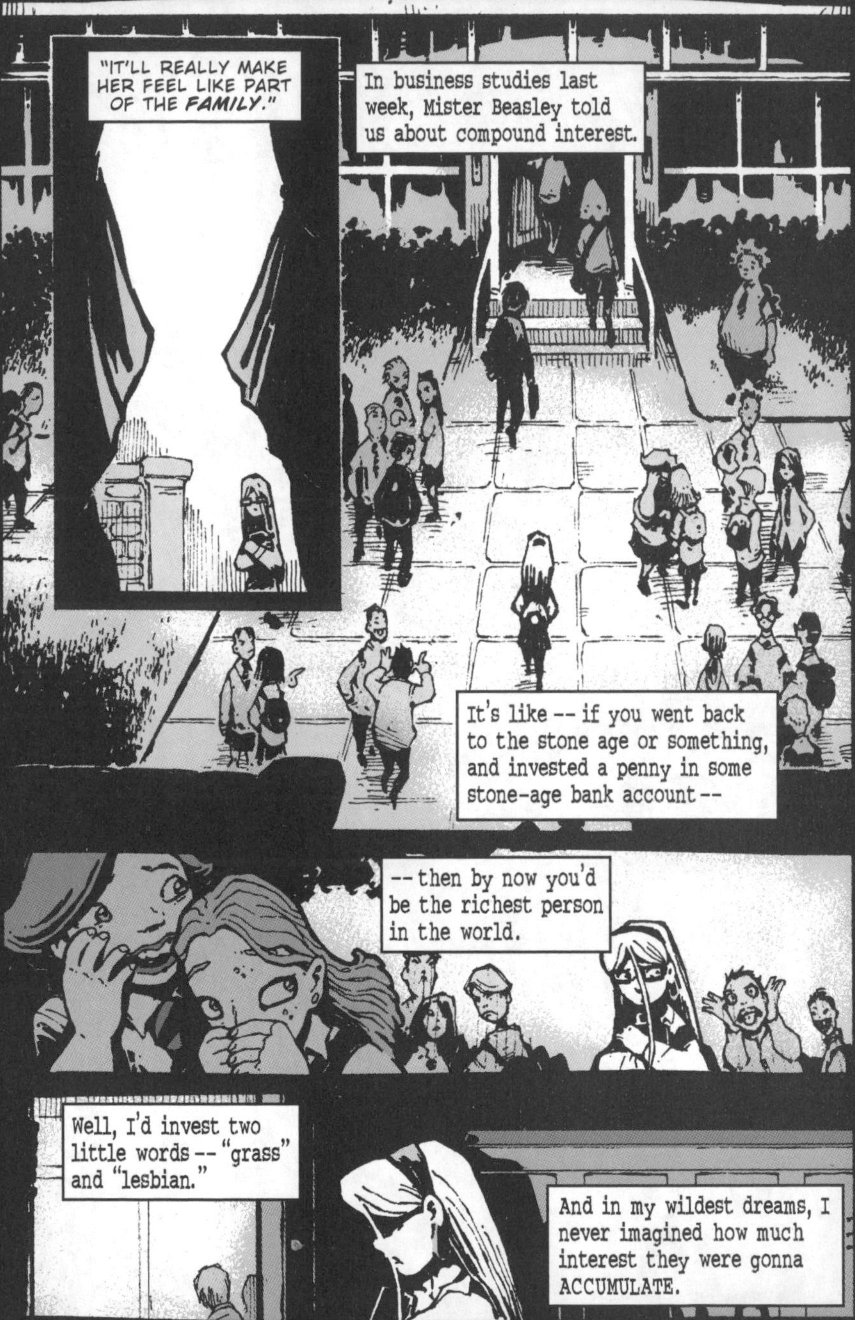
"IT'LL REALLY MAKE HER FEEL LIKE PART OF THE *FAMILY*."
In business studies last week, Mister Beasley told us about compound interest.
It's like -- if you went back to the stone age or something, and invested a penny in some stone-age bank account --
-- then by now you'd be the richest person in the world.
Well, I'd invest two little words -- "grass" and "lesbian."
And in my wildest dreams, I never imagined how much interest they were gonna ACCUMULATE.

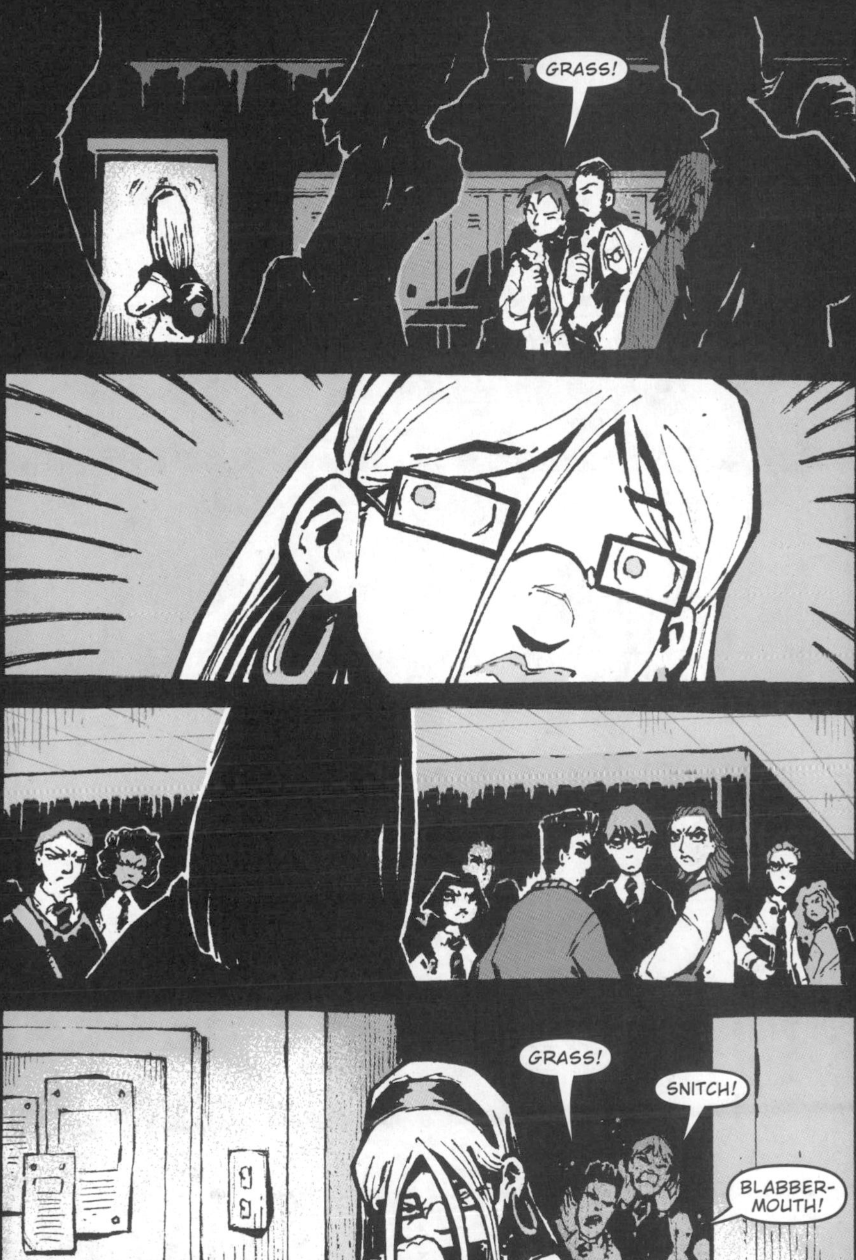
GRASS!
GRASS!
SNITCH!
BLABBER-MOUTH!

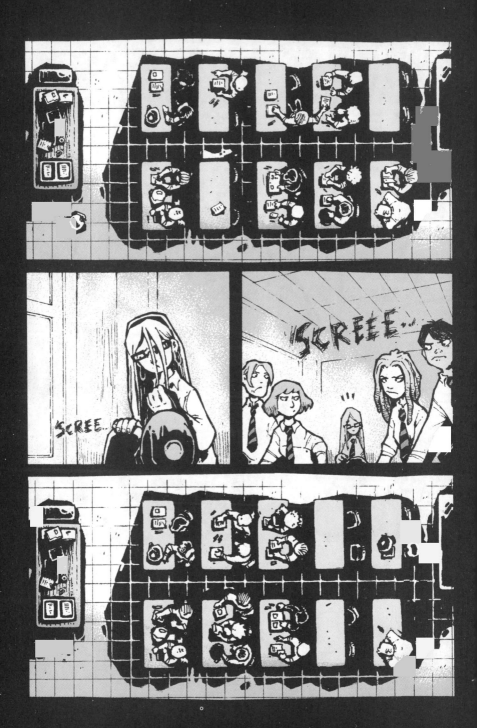

SCREEE...

SCREE...

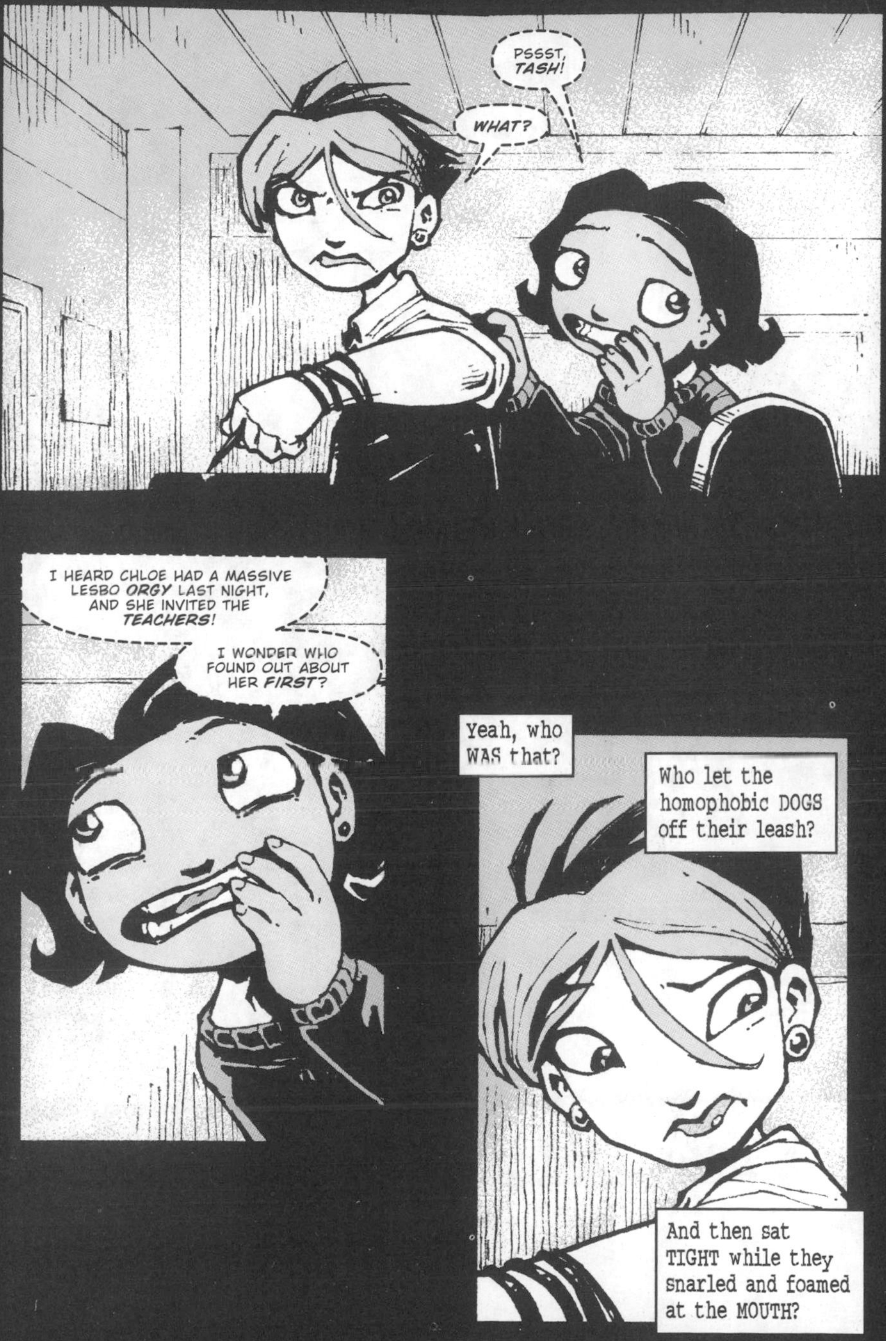
PSSST, TASH!
WHAT?
I HEARD CHLOE HAD A MASSIVE LESBO ORGY LAST NIGHT, AND SHE INVITED THE TEACHERS!
I WONDER WHO FOUND OUT ABOUT HER FIRST?
Yeah, who WAS that?
Who let the homophobic DOGS off their leash?
And then sat TIGHT while they snarled and foamed at the MOUTH?

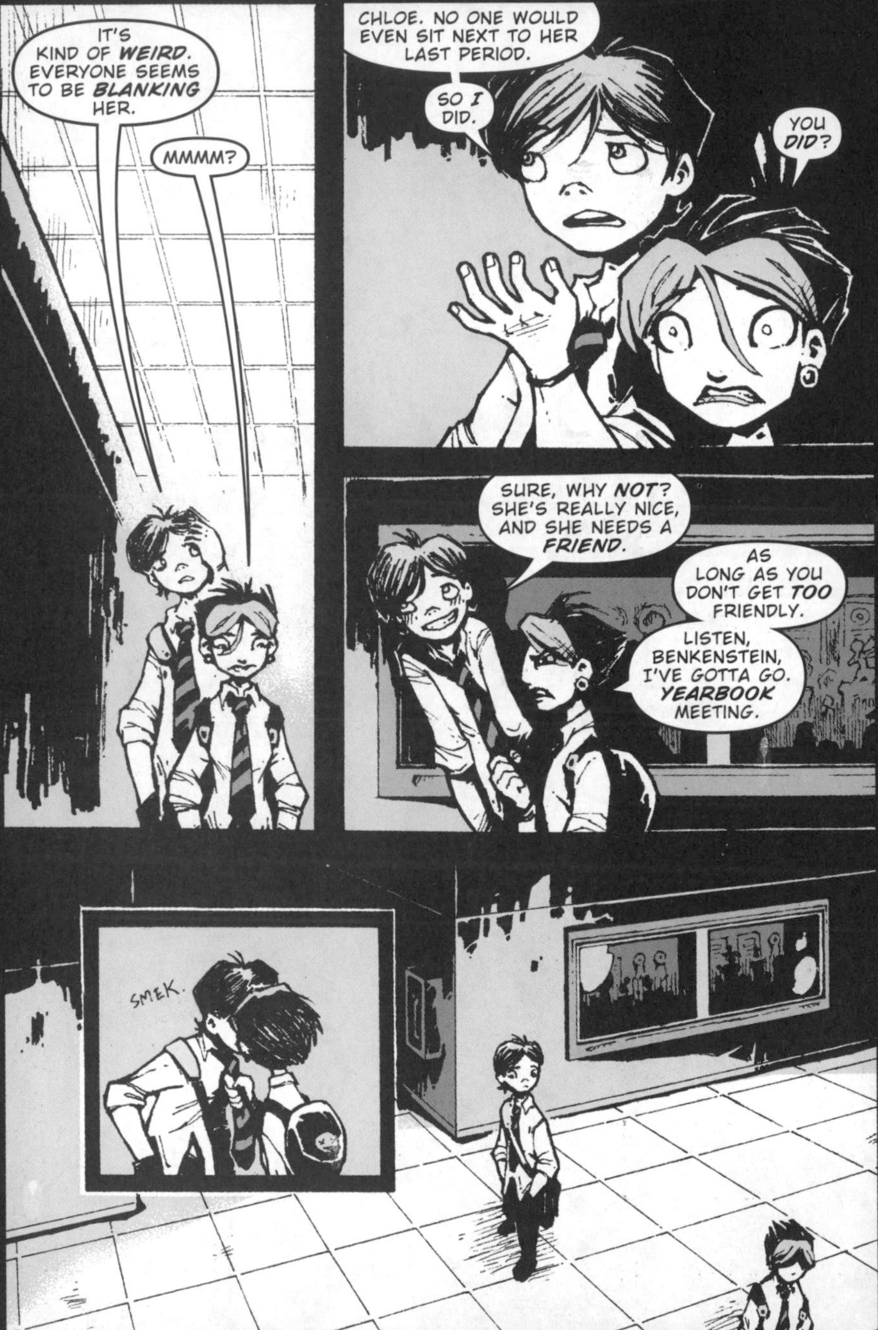
IT'S KIND OF WEIRD. EVERYONE SEEMS TO BE BLANKING HER.
MMMM?
CHLOE. NO ONE WOULD EVEN SIT NEXT TO HER LAST PERIOD.
SO I DID.
YOU DID?
SURE, WHY NOT? SHE'S REALLY NICE, AND SHE NEEDS A FRIEND.
AS LONG AS YOU DON'T GET TOO FRIENDLY.
LISTEN, BENKENSTEIN, I'VE GOTTA GO. YEARBOOK MEETING.
SMEK.

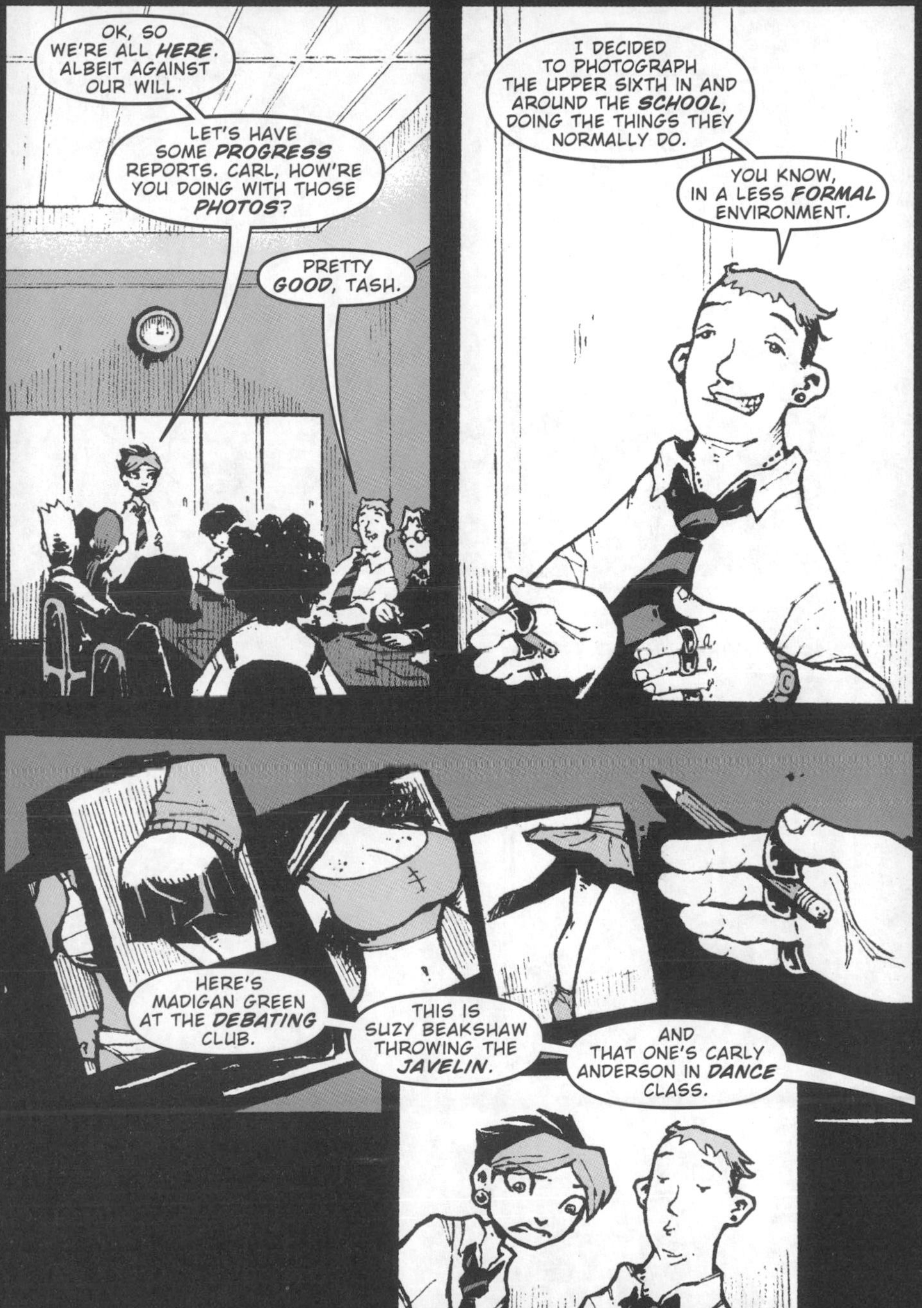
OK, SO WE'RE ALL HERE. ALBEIT AGAINST OUR WILL.
LET'S HAVE SOME PROGRESS REPORTS. CARL, HOW'RE YOU DOING WITH THOSE PHOTOS?
PRETTY GOOD, TASH.
I DECIDED TO PHOTOGRAPH THE UPPER SIXTH IN AND AROUND THE SCHOOL, DOING THE THINGS THEY NORMALLY DO.
YOU KNOW, IN A LESS FORMAL ENVIRONMENT.
HERE'S MADIGAN GREEN AT THE DEBATING CLUB.
THIS IS SUZY BEAKSHAW THROWING THE JAVELIN.
AND THAT ONE'S CARLY ANDERSON IN DANCE CLASS.

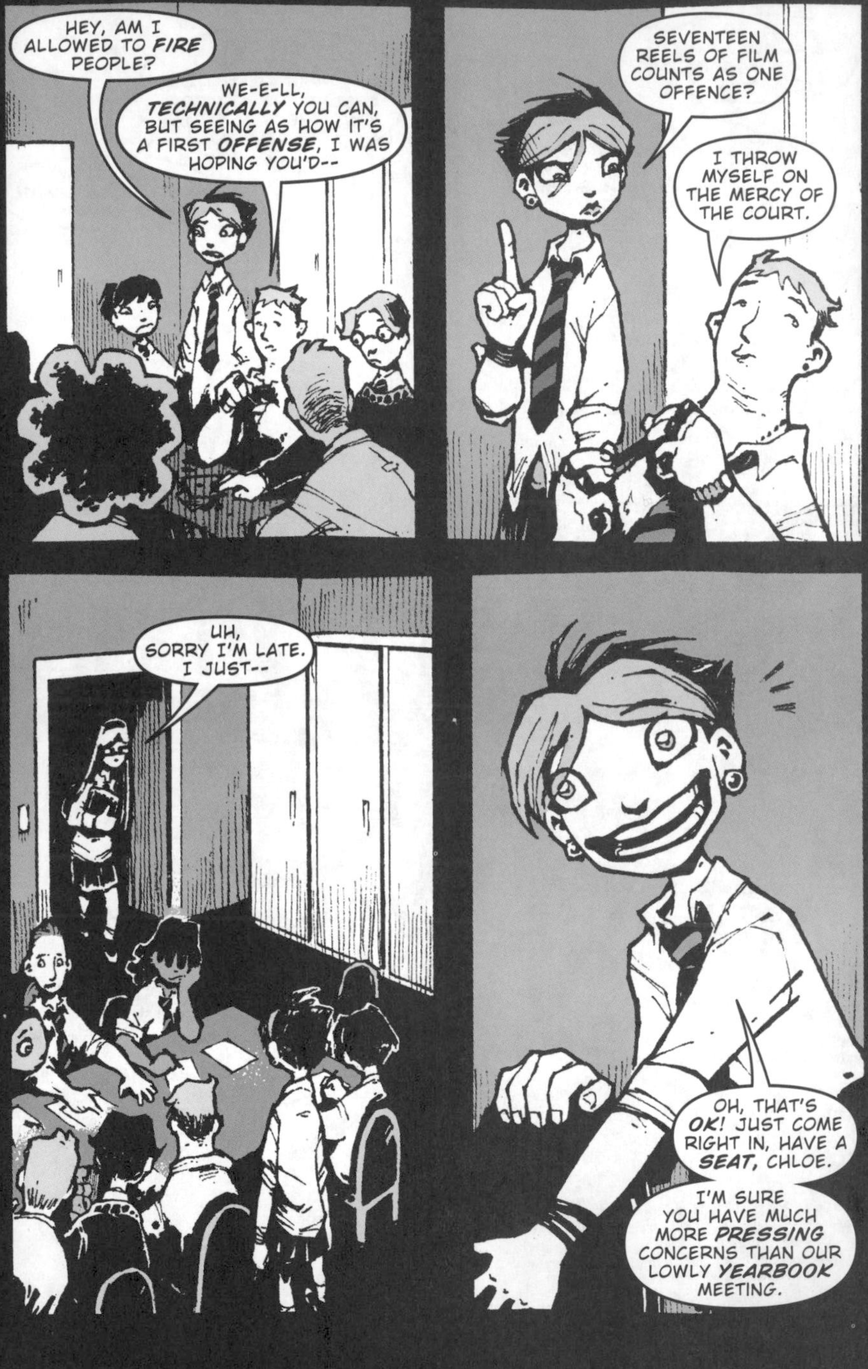
HEY, AM I ALLOWED TO FIRE PEOPLE?
WE-E-LL, TECHNICALLY YOU CAN, BUT SEEING AS HOW IT'S A FIRST OFFENSE, I WAS HOPING YOU'D--
SEVENTEEN REELS OF FILM COUNTS AS ONE OFFENCE?
I THROW MYSELF ON THE MERCY OF THE COURT.
UH, SORRY I'M LATE. I JUST--
OH, THAT'S OK! JUST COME RIGHT IN, HAVE A SEAT, CHLOE.
I'M SURE YOU HAVE MUCH MORE PRESSING CONCERNS THAN OUR LOWLY YEARBOOK MEETING.

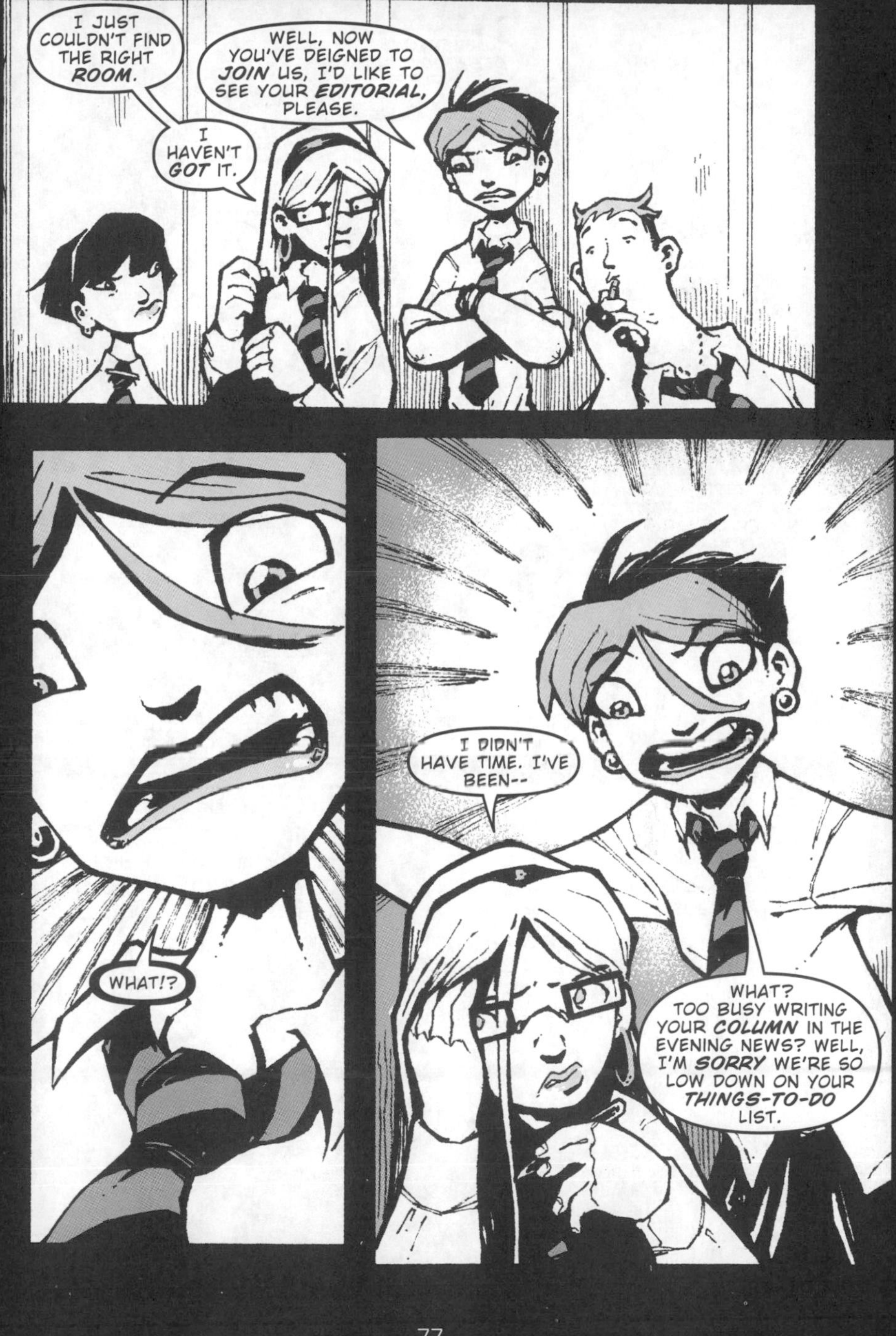
I JUST COULDN'T FIND THE RIGHT ROOM.
WELL, NOW YOU'VE DEIGNED TO JOIN US, I'D LIKE TO SEE YOUR EDITORIAL, PLEASE.
I HAVEN'T GOT IT.
WHAT!?
I DIDN'T HAVE TIME. I'VE BEEN--
WHAT? TOO BUSY WRITING YOUR COLUMN IN THE EVENING NEWS? WELL, I'M SORRY WE'RE SO LOW DOWN ON YOUR THINGS-TO-DO LIST.

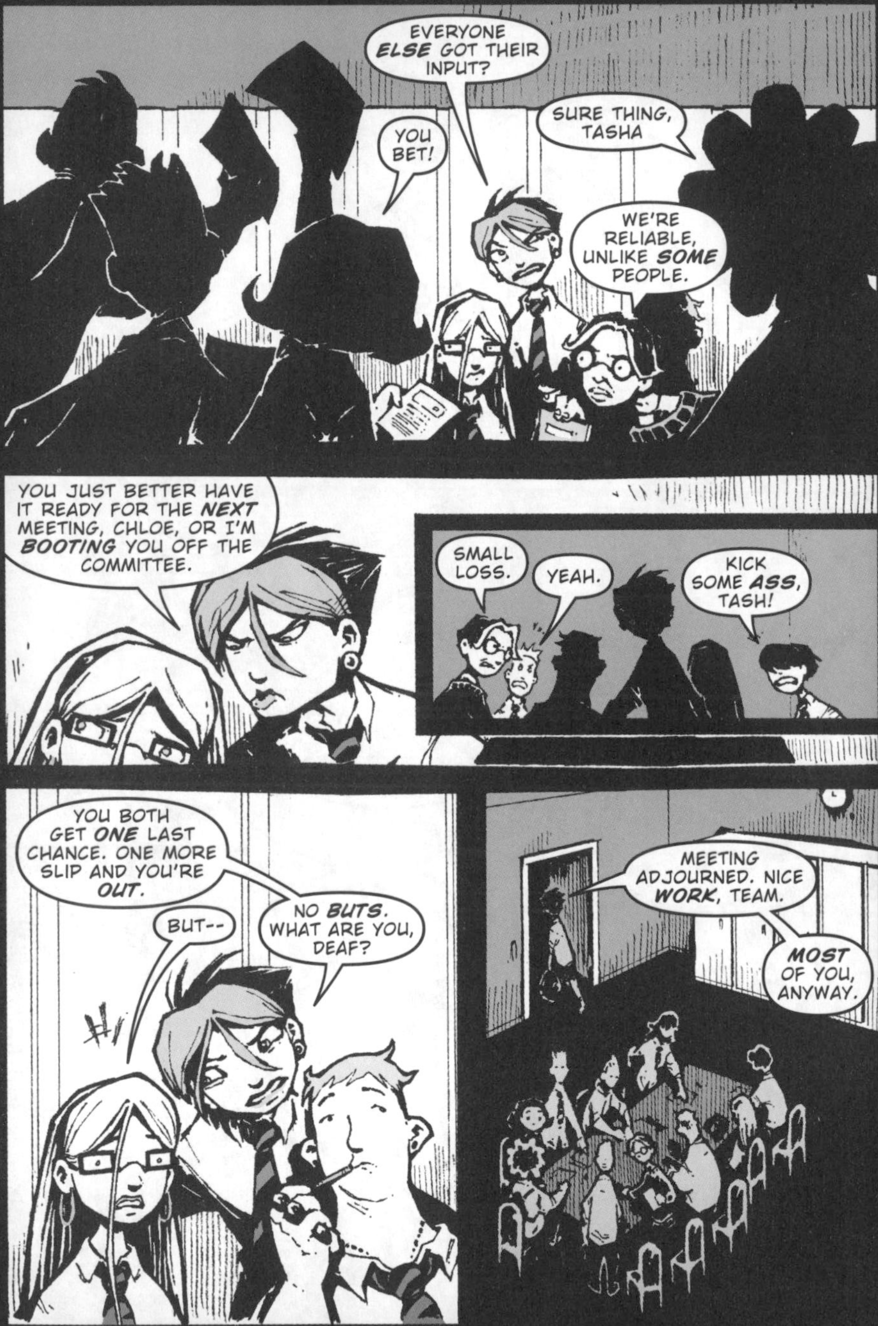
EVERYONE ELSE GOT THEIR INPUT?
YOU BET!
SURE THING, TASHA
WE'RE RELIABLE, UNLIKE SOME PEOPLE.
YOU JUST BETTER HAVE IT READY FOR THE NEXT MEETING, CHLOE, OR I'M BOOTING YOU OFF THE COMMITTEE.
SMALL LOSS.
YEAH.
KICK SOME ASS, TASH!
YOU BOTH GET ONE LAST CHANCE. ONE MORE SLIP AND YOU'RE OUT.
BUT--
NO BUTS. WHAT ARE YOU, DEAF?
MEETING ADJOURNED. NICE WORK, TEAM.
MOST OF YOU, ANYWAY.

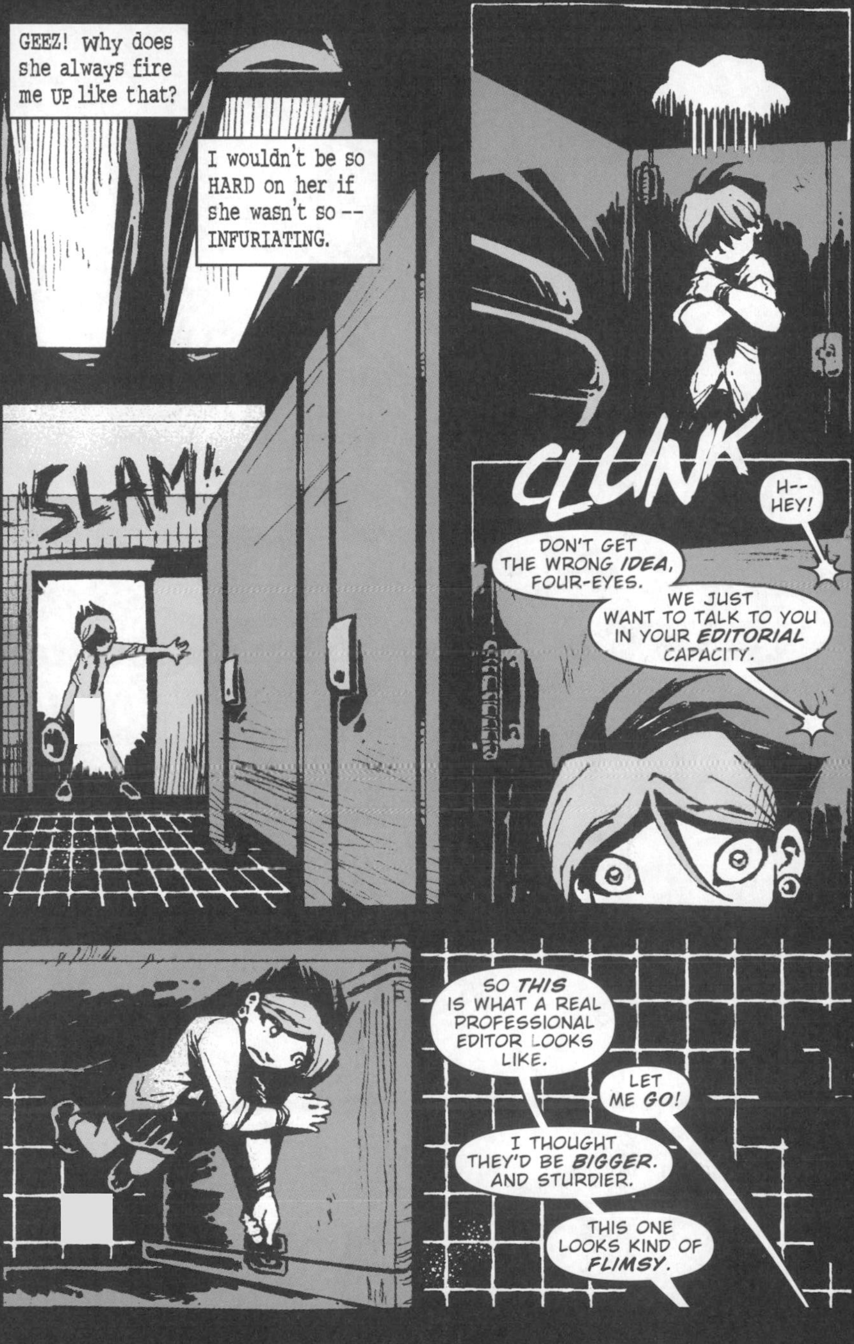

GEEZ! Why does she always fire me UP like that?
I wouldn't be so HARD on her if she wasn't so -- INFURIATING.
SLAM!
CLUNK
H-- HEY!
DON'T GET THE WRONG IDEA, FOUR-EYES.
WE JUST WANT TO TALK TO YOU IN YOUR EDITORIAL CAPACITY.
SO THIS IS WHAT A REAL PROFESSIONAL EDITOR LOOKS LIKE.
LET ME GO!
I THOUGHT THEY'D BE BIGGER. AND STURDIER.
THIS ONE LOOKS KIND OF FLIMSY.

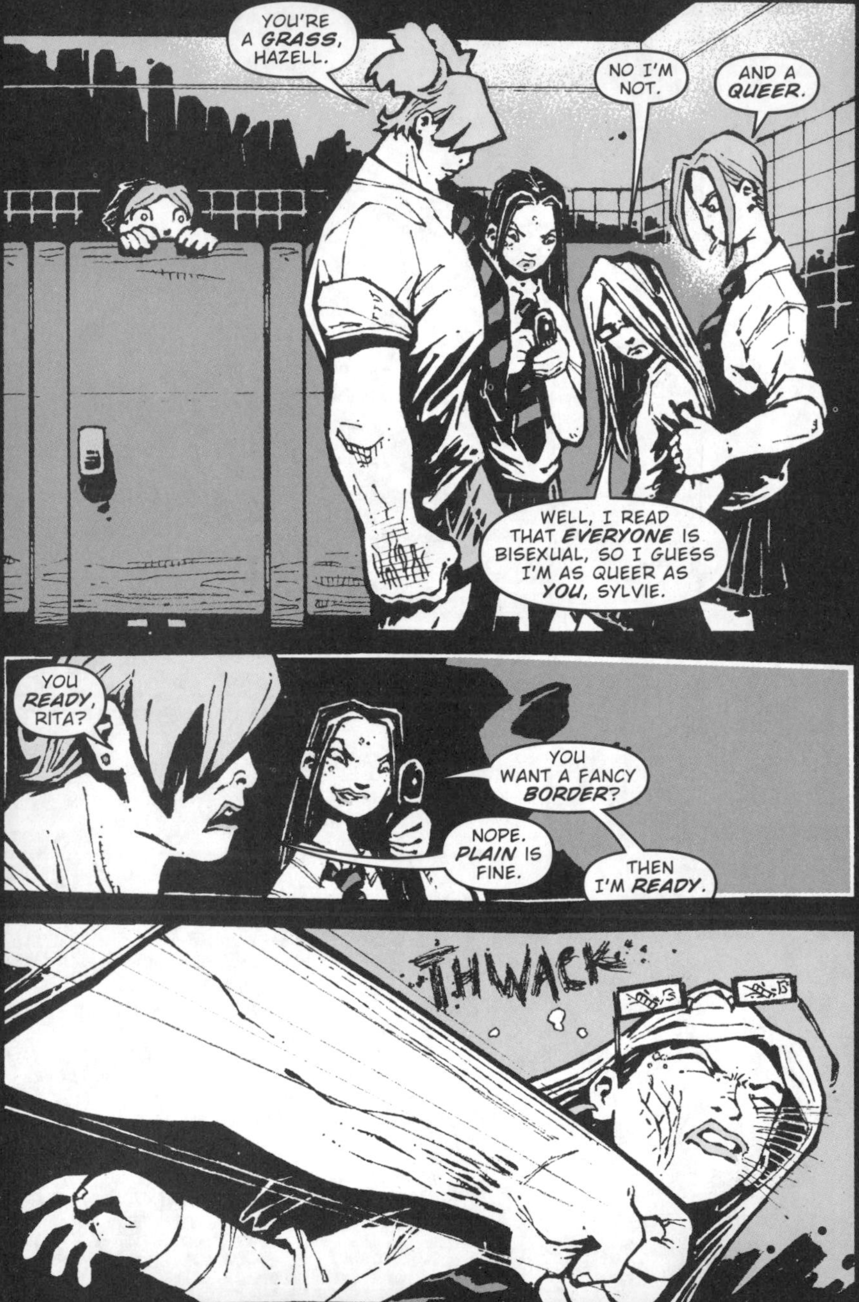
YOU'RE A GRASS, HAZELL.
NO I'M NOT.
AND A QUEER.
WELL, I READ THAT EVERYONE IS BISEXUAL, SO I GUESS I'M AS QUEER AS YOU, SYLVIE.
YOU READY, RITA?
YOU WANT A FANCY BORDER?
NOPE. PLAIN IS FINE.
THEN I'M READY.
THWACK

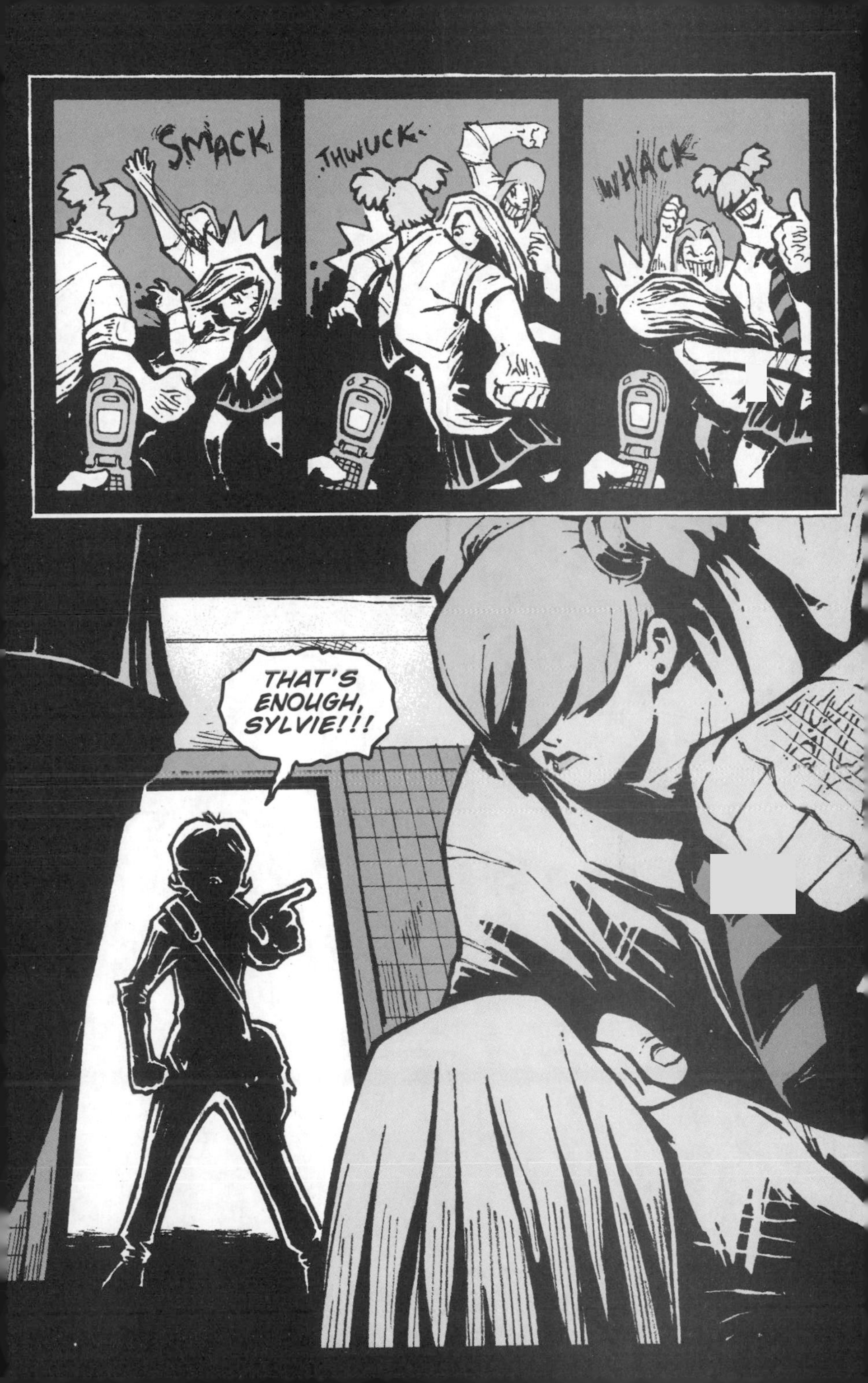
SMACK
THWUCK
WHACK
THAT'S ENOUGH, SYLVIE!!!

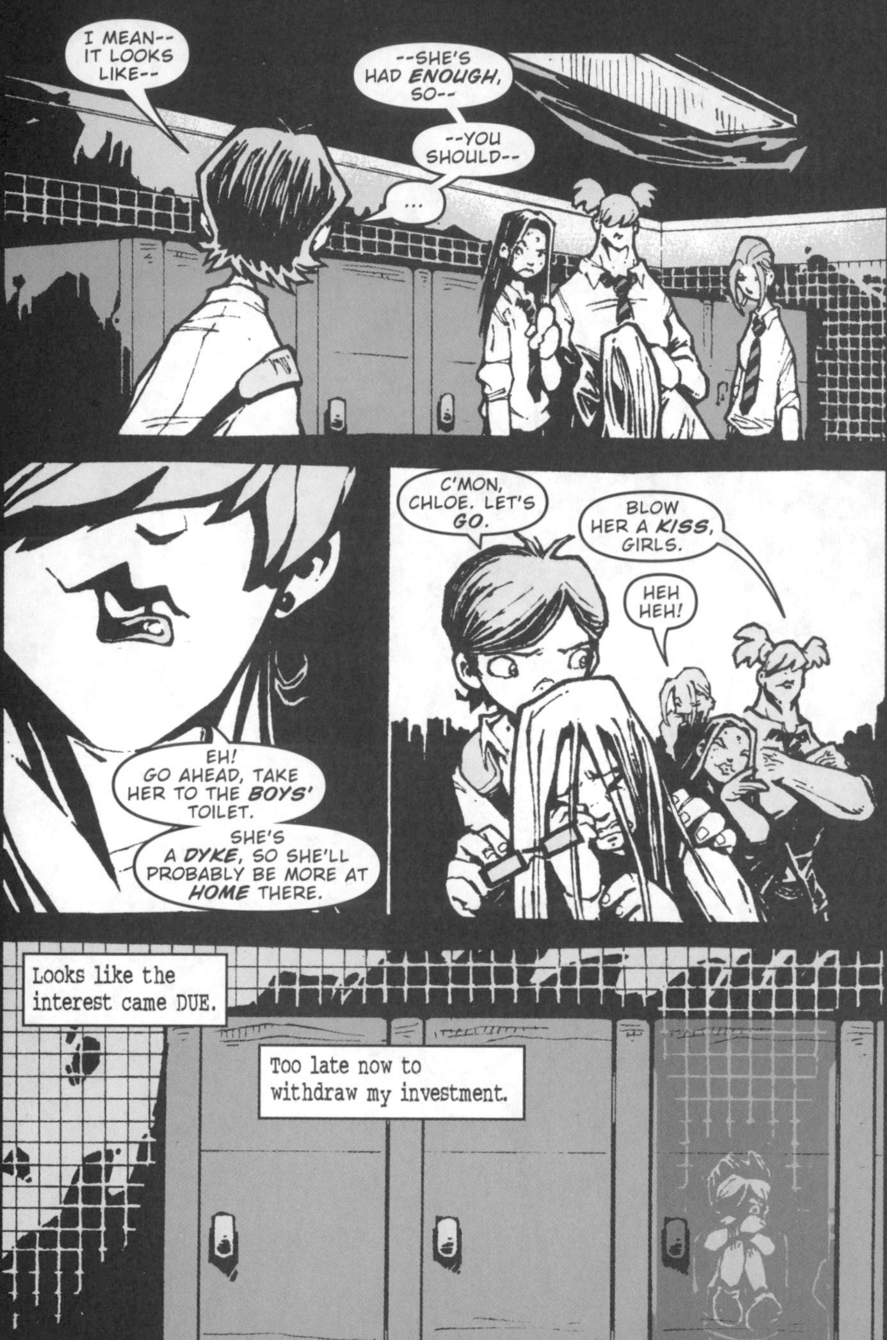
I MEAN-- IT LOOKS LIKE--
--SHE'S HAD ENOUGH, SO--
--YOU SHOULD--
...
EH! GO AHEAD, TAKE HER TO THE BOYS' TOILET.
SHE'S A DYKE, SO SHE'LL PROBABLY BE MORE AT HOME THERE.
C'MON, CHLOE. LET'S GO.
BLOW HER A KISS, GIRLS.
HEH HEH!
Looks like the interest came DUE.
Too late now to withdraw my investment.

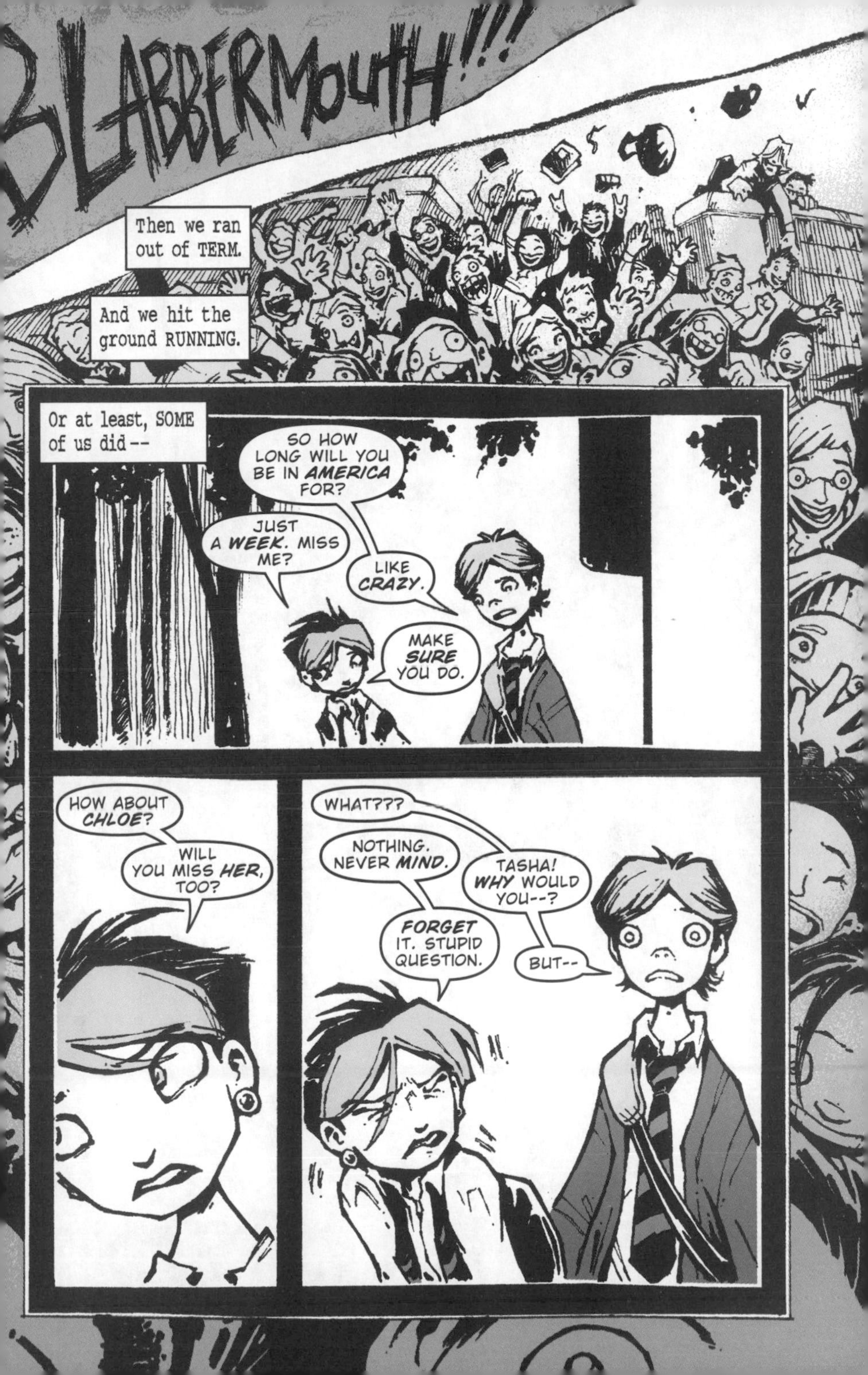
BLABBERMOUTH!!!
Then we ran out of TERM.
And we hit the ground RUNNING.
Or at least, SOME of us did --
SO HOW LONG WILL YOU BE IN AMERICA FOR?
JUST A WEEK. MISS ME?
LIKE CRAZY.
MAKE SURE YOU DO.
HOW ABOUT CHLOE?
WILL YOU MISS HER, TOO?
WHAT???
NOTHING. NEVER MIND.
FORGET IT. STUPID QUESTION.
TASHA! WHY WOULD YOU--?
BUT--

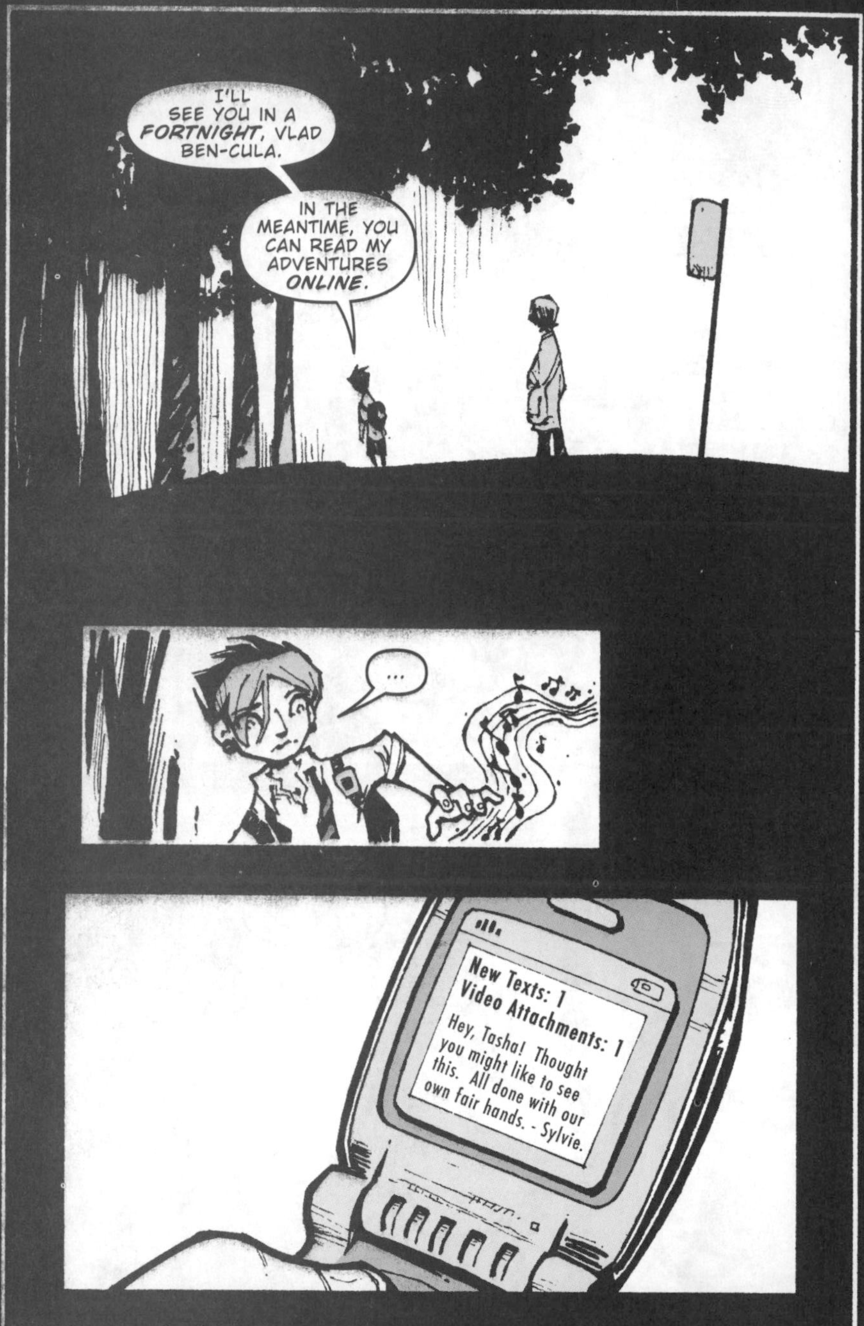
I'LL SEE YOU IN A FORTNIGHT, VLAD BEN-CULA.
IN THE MEANTIME, YOU CAN READ MY ADVENTURES ONLINE.
...
New Texts: 1
Video Attachments: 1
Hey, Tasha! Thought you might like to see this. All done with our own fair hands. - Sylvie.

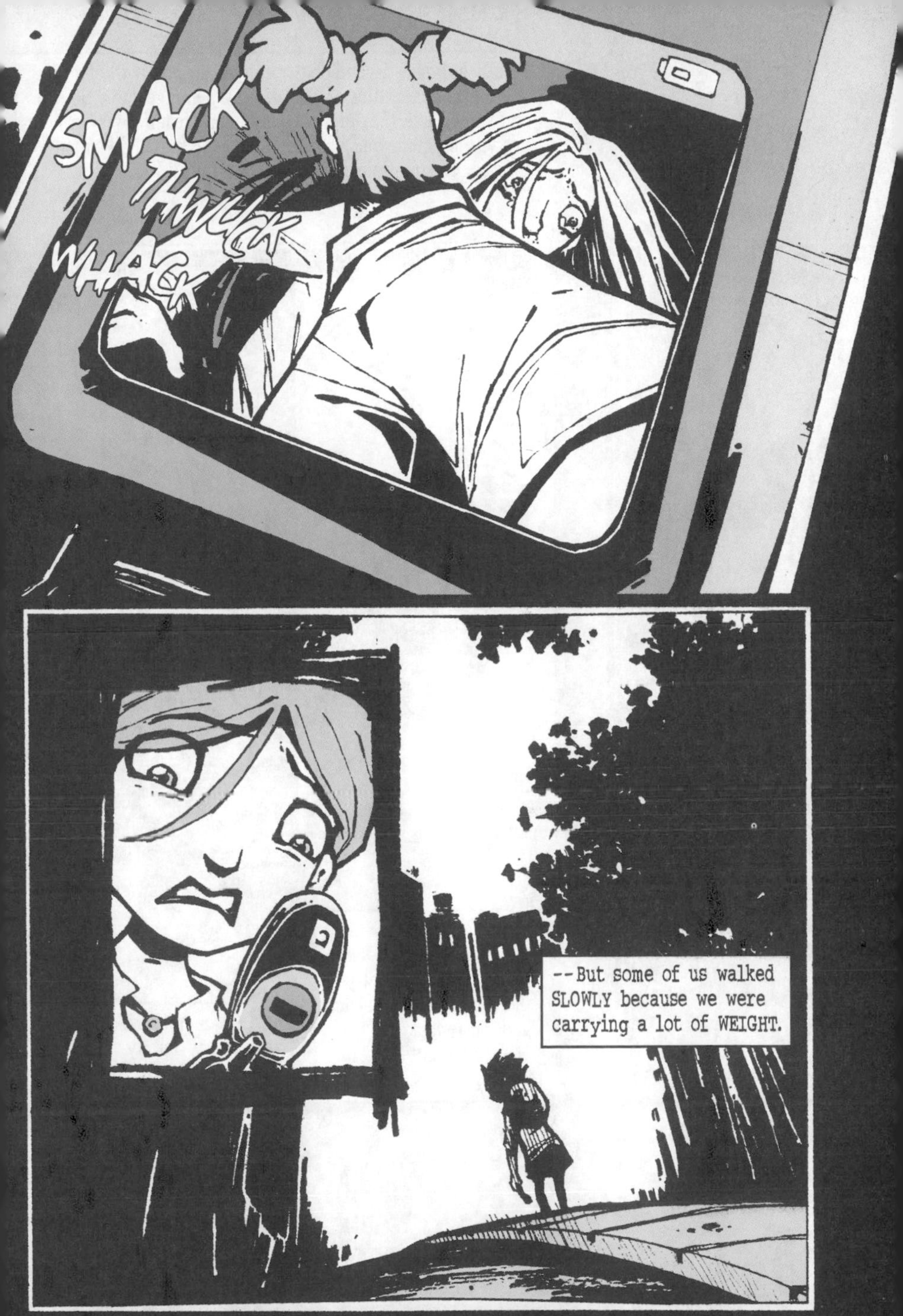
SMACK
THWUCK
WHACK
--But some of us walked SLOWLY because we were carrying a lot of WEIGHT.

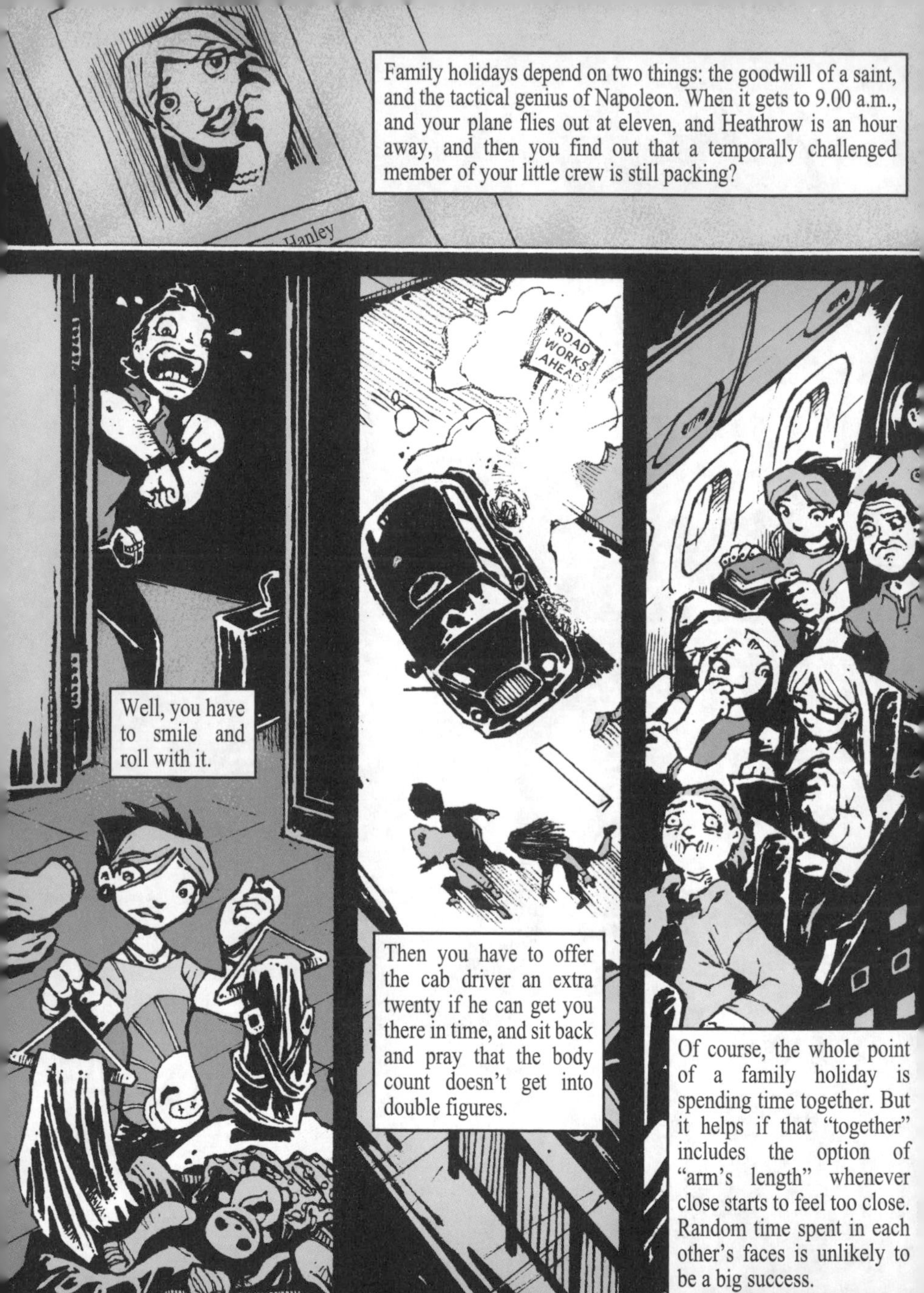
Hanley
Family holidays depend on two things: the goodwill of a saint, and the tactical genius of Napoleon. When it gets to 9.00 a.m., and your plane flies out at eleven, and Heathrow is an hour away, and then you find out that a temporally challenged member of your little crew is still packing?
Well, you have to smile and roll with it.
ROAD WORKS AHEAD
Then you have to offer the cab driver an extra twenty if he can get you there in time, and sit back and pray that the body count doesn't get into double figures.
Of course, the whole point of a family holiday is spending time together. But it helps if that "together" includes the option of "arm's length" whenever close starts to feel too close. Random time spent in each other's faces is unlikely to be a big success.

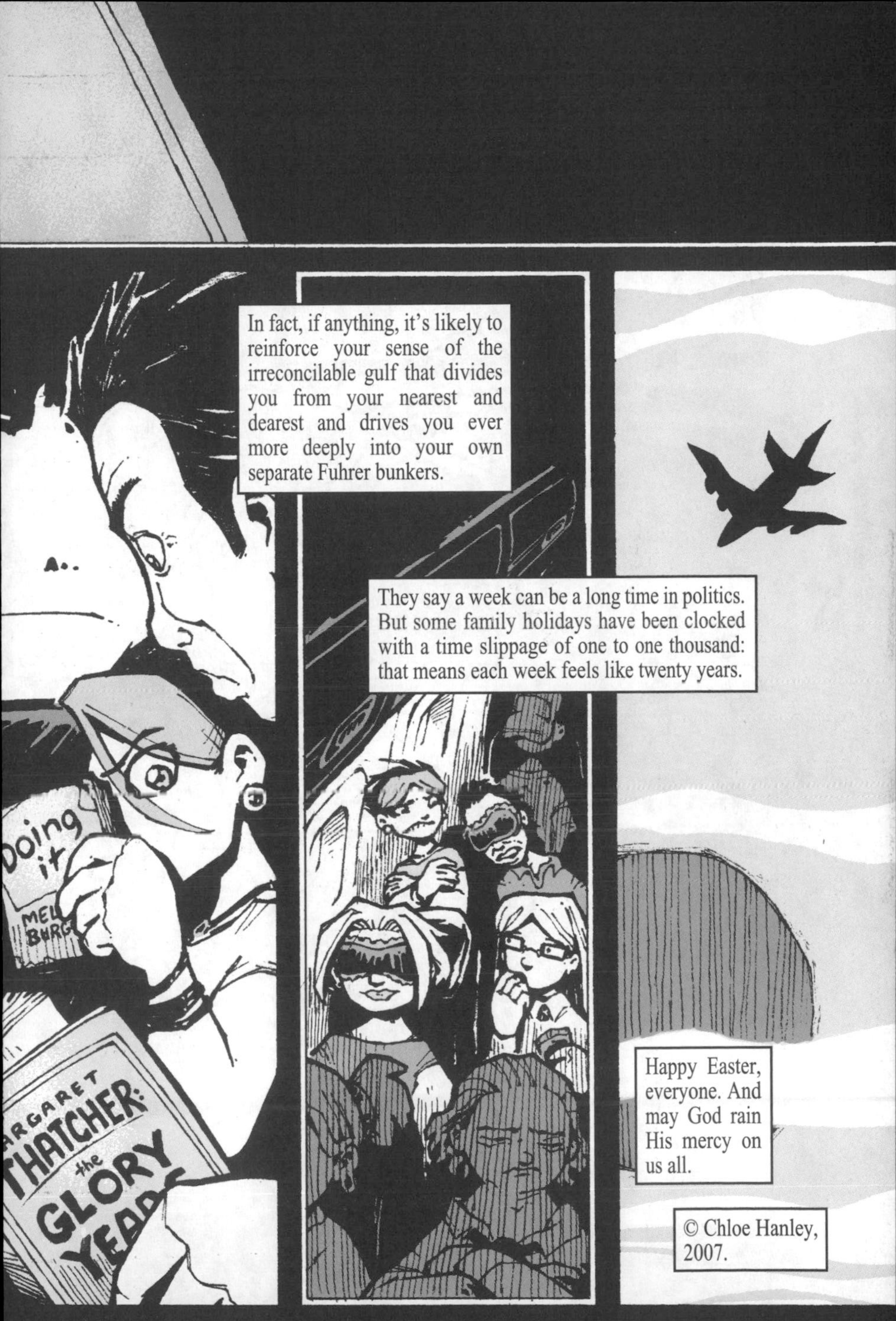
In fact, if anything, it's likely to reinforce your sense of the irreconcilable gulf that divides you from your nearest and dearest and drives you ever more deeply into your own separate Fuhrer bunkers.
Doing it
THATCHER:
the
GLORY
They say a week can be a long time in politics. But some family holidays have been clocked with a time slippage of one to one thousand: that means each week feels like twenty years.
Happy Easter, everyone. And may God rain His mercy on us all.
© Chloe Hanley, 2007.

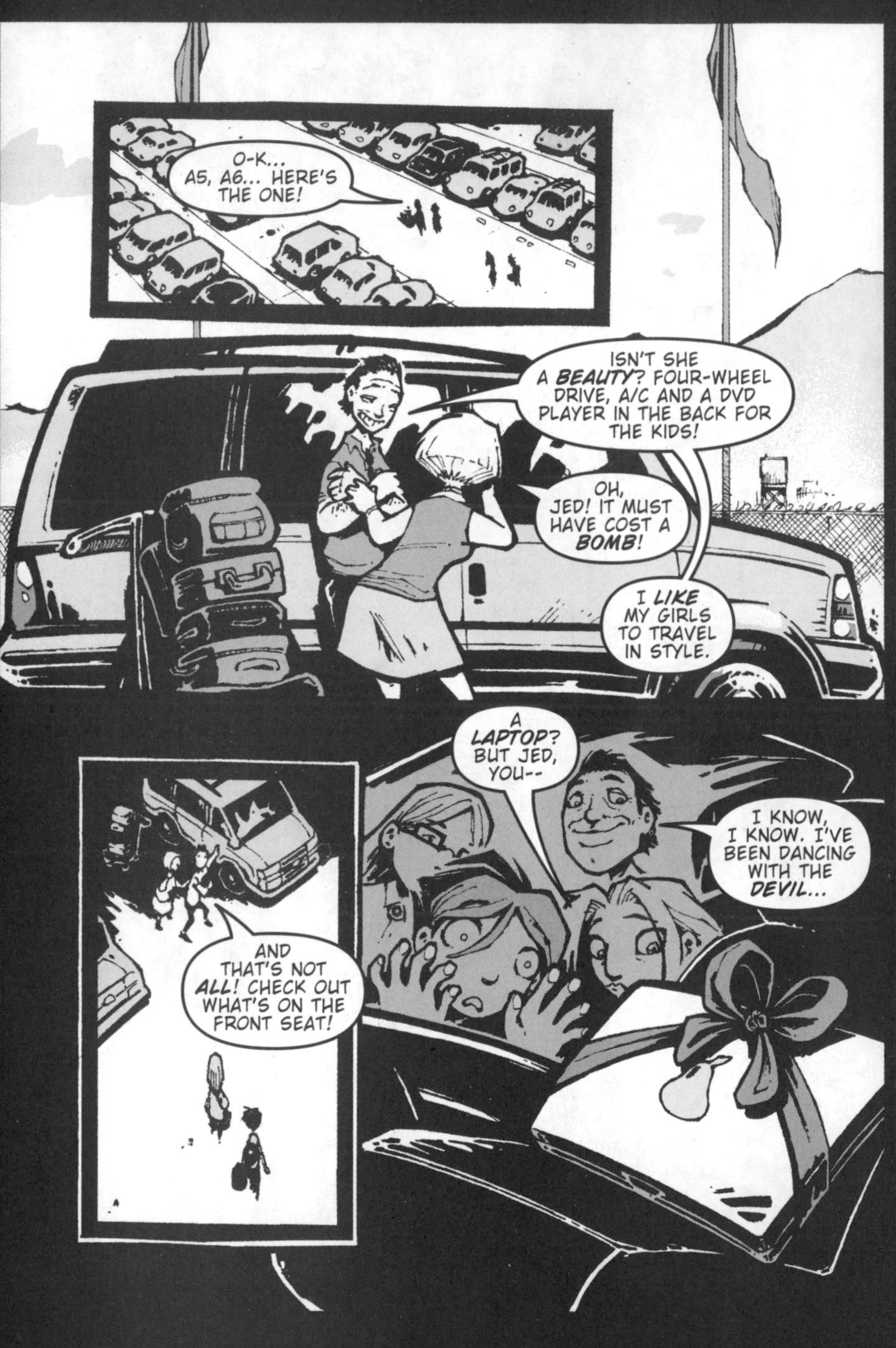
O-K...
A5, A6... HERE'S THE ONE!
ISN'T SHE A BEAUTY? FOUR-WHEEL DRIVE, A/C AND A DVD PLAYER IN THE BACK FOR THE KIDS!
OH, JED! IT MUST HAVE COST A BOMB!
I LIKE MY GIRLS TO TRAVEL IN STYLE.
AND THAT'S NOT ALL! CHECK OUT WHAT'S ON THE FRONT SEAT!
A LAPTOP? BUT JED, YOU--
I KNOW, I KNOW. I'VE BEEN DANCING WITH THE DEVIL...

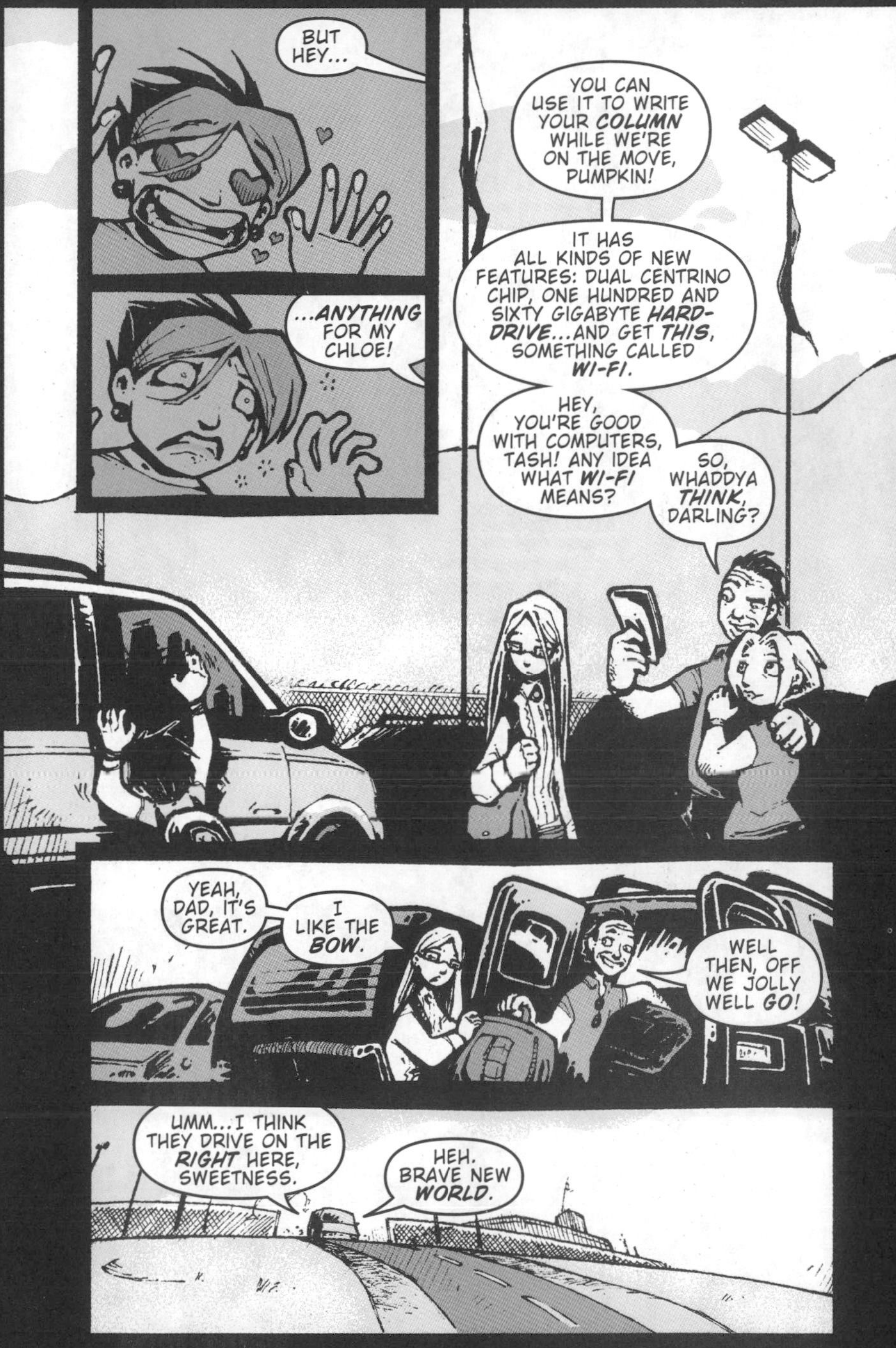
BUT HEY...
...ANYTHING FOR MY CHLOE!
YOU CAN USE IT TO WRITE YOUR COLUMN WHILE WE'RE ON THE MOVE, PUMPKIN!
IT HAS ALL KINDS OF NEW FEATURES: DUAL CENTRINO CHIP, ONE HUNDRED AND SIXTY GIGABYTE HARD-DRIVE...AND GET THIS, SOMETHING CALLED WI-FI.
HEY, YOU'RE GOOD WITH COMPUTERS, TASH! ANY IDEA WHAT WI-FI MEANS?
SO, WHADDYA THINK, DARLING?
YEAH, DAD, IT'S GREAT.
I LIKE THE BOW.
WELL THEN, OFF WE JOLLY WELL GO!
UMM...I THINK THEY DRIVE ON THE RIGHT HERE, SWEETNESS.
HEH. BRAVE NEW WORLD.

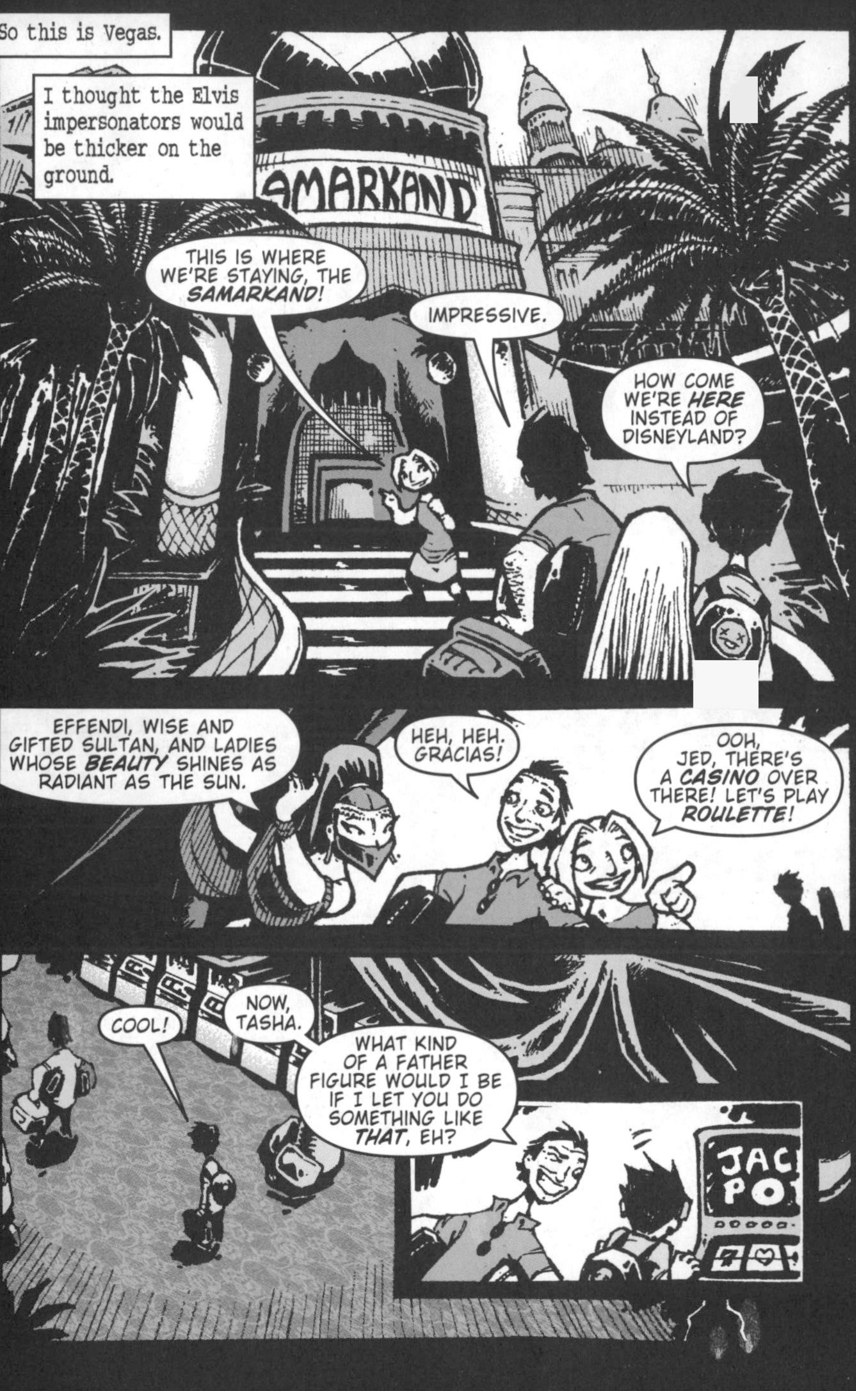
So this is Vegas.
I thought the Elvis impersonators would be thicker on the ground.
SAMARKAND
THIS IS WHERE WE'RE STAYING, THE SAMARKAND!
IMPRESSIVE.
HOW COME WE'RE HERE INSTEAD OF DISNEYLAND?
EFFENDI, WISE AND GIFTED SULTAN, AND LADIES WHOSE BEAUTY SHINES AS RADIANT AS THE SUN.
HEH, HEH. GRACIAS!
OOH, JED, THERE'S A CASINO OVER THERE! LET'S PLAY ROULETTE!
COOL!
NOW, TASHA.
WHAT KIND OF A FATHER FIGURE WOULD I BE IF I LET YOU DO SOMETHING LIKE THAT, EH?

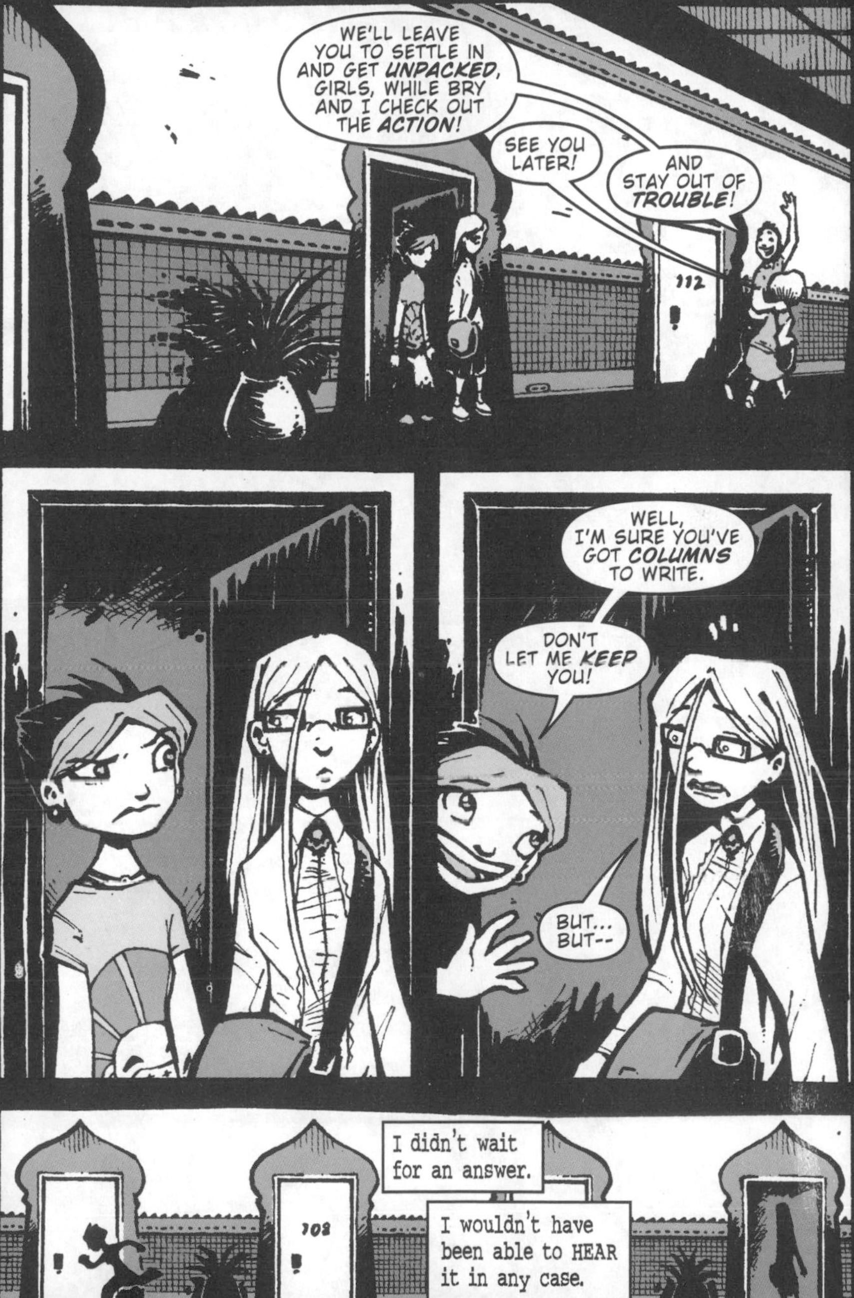
WE'LL LEAVE YOU TO SETTLE IN AND GET UNPACKED, GIRLS, WHILE BRY AND I CHECK OUT THE ACTION!
SEE YOU LATER!
AND STAY OUT OF TROUBLE!
112
WELL, I'M SURE YOU'VE GOT COLUMNS TO WRITE.
DON'T LET ME KEEP YOU!
BUT... BUT--
I didn't wait for an answer.
108
I wouldn't have been able to HEAR it in any case.

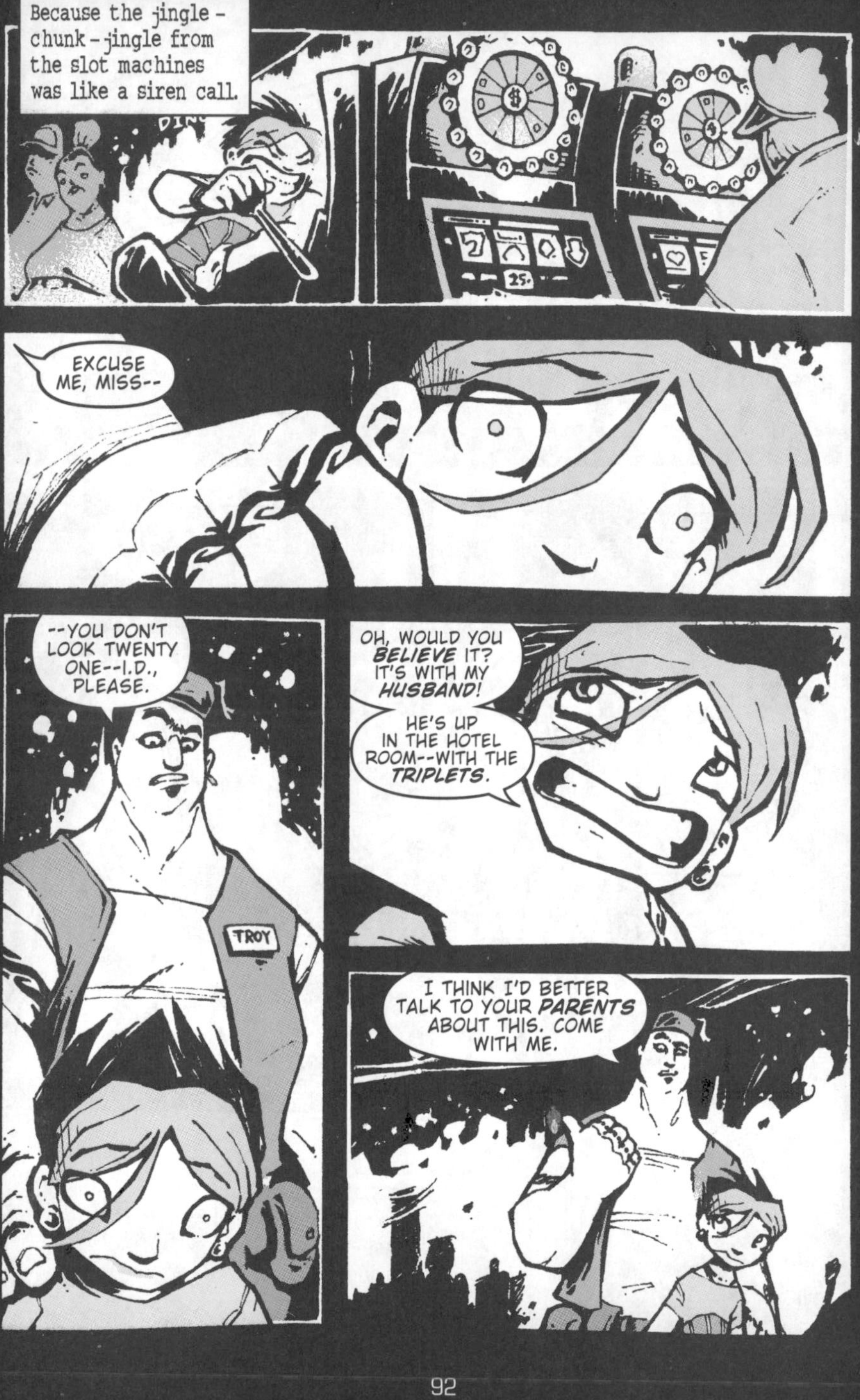
Because the jingle-chunk-jingle from the slot machines was like a siren call.
EXCUSE ME, MISS--
--YOU DON'T LOOK TWENTY ONE--I.D., PLEASE.
TROY
OH, WOULD YOU BELIEVE IT? IT'S WITH MY HUSBAND!
HE'S UP IN THE HOTEL ROOM--WITH THE TRIPLETS.
I THINK I'D BETTER TALK TO YOUR PARENTS ABOUT THIS. COME WITH ME.

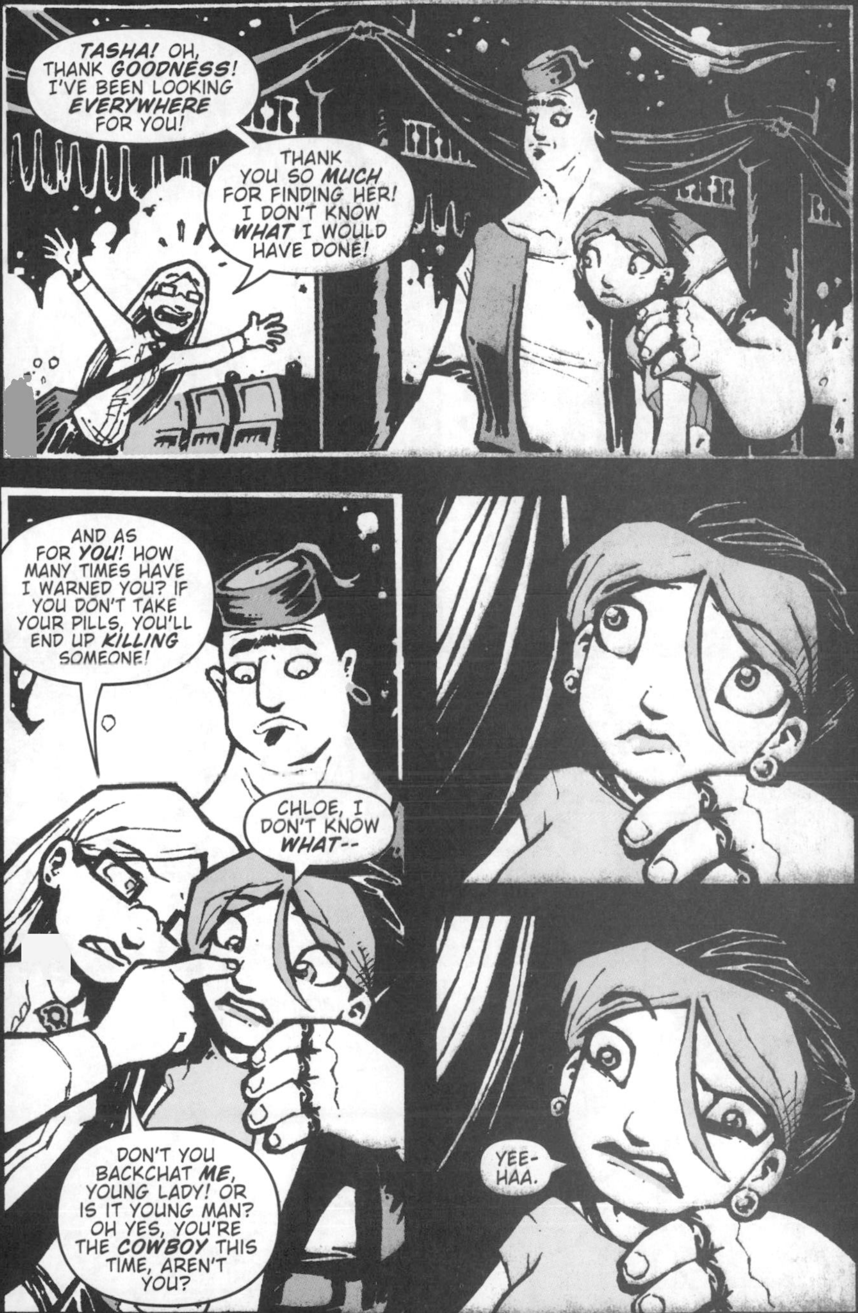
TASHA! OH, THANK GOODNESS! I'VE BEEN LOOKING EVERYWHERE FOR YOU!
THANK YOU SO MUCH FOR FINDING HER! I DON'T KNOW WHAT I WOULD HAVE DONE!
AND AS FOR YOU! HOW MANY TIMES HAVE I WARNED YOU? IF YOU DON'T TAKE YOUR PILLS, YOU'LL END UP KILLING SOMEONE!
CHLOE, I DON'T KNOW WHAT--
DON'T YOU BACKCHAT ME, YOUNG LADY! OR IS IT YOUNG MAN? OH YES, YOU'RE THE COWBOY THIS TIME, AREN'T YOU?
YEE-HAA.

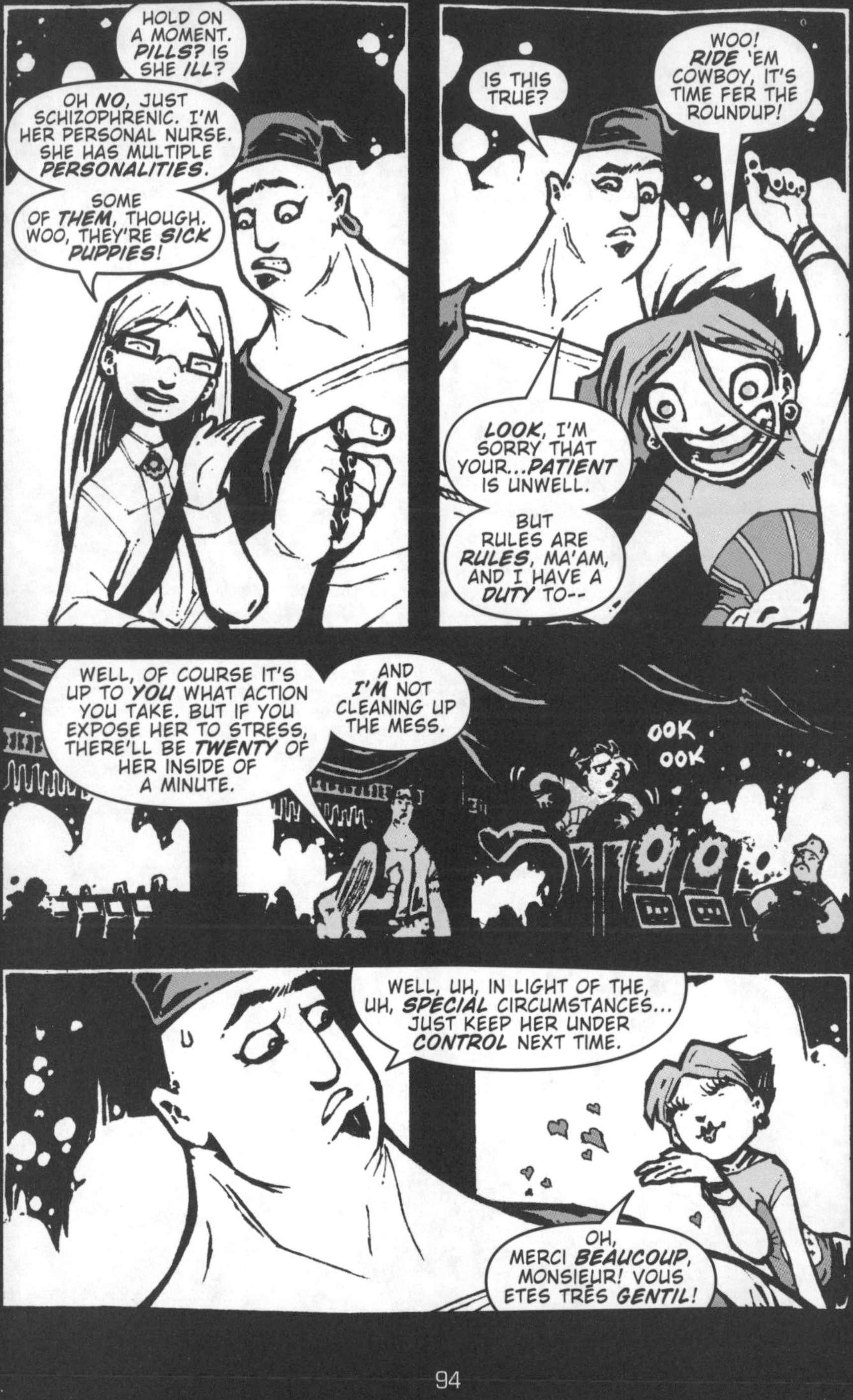
HOLD ON A MOMENT. PILLS? IS SHE ILL?
OH NO, JUST SCHIZOPHRENIC. I'M HER PERSONAL NURSE. SHE HAS MULTIPLE PERSONALITIES.
SOME OF THEM, THOUGH. WOO, THEY'RE SICK PUPPIES!
IS THIS TRUE?
WOO! RIDE 'EM COWBOY, IT'S TIME FER THE ROUNDUP!
LOOK, I'M SORRY THAT YOUR...PATIENT IS UNWELL.
BUT RULES ARE RULES, MA'AM, AND I HAVE A DUTY TO--
WELL, OF COURSE IT'S UP TO YOU WHAT ACTION YOU TAKE. BUT IF YOU EXPOSE HER TO STRESS, THERE'LL BE TWENTY OF HER INSIDE OF A MINUTE.
AND I'M NOT CLEANING UP THE MESS.
OOK OOK
WELL, UH, IN LIGHT OF THE, UH, SPECIAL CIRCUMSTANCES... JUST KEEP HER UNDER CONTROL NEXT TIME.
OH, MERCI BEAUCOUP, MONSIEUR! VOUS ETES TRÉS GENTIL!

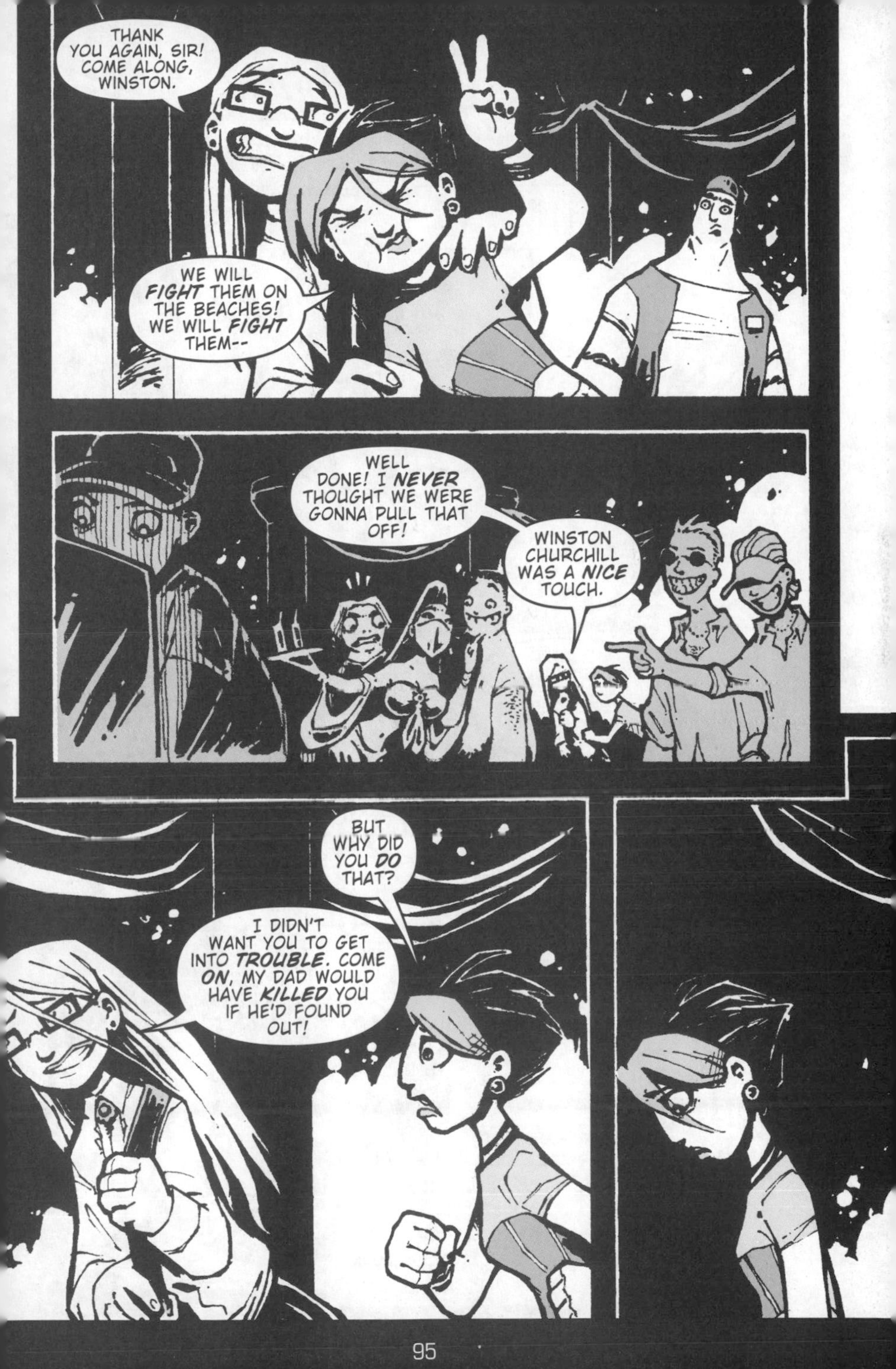
THANK YOU AGAIN, SIR! COME ALONG, WINSTON.
WE WILL **FIGHT** THEM ON THE BEACHES! WE WILL **FIGHT** THEM--
WELL DONE! I **NEVER** THOUGHT WE WERE GONNA PULL THAT OFF!
WINSTON CHURCHILL WAS A **NICE** TOUCH.
BUT WHY DID YOU **DO** THAT?
I DIDN'T WANT YOU TO GET INTO **TROUBLE**. COME **ON**, MY DAD WOULD HAVE **KILLED** YOU IF HE'D FOUND OUT!

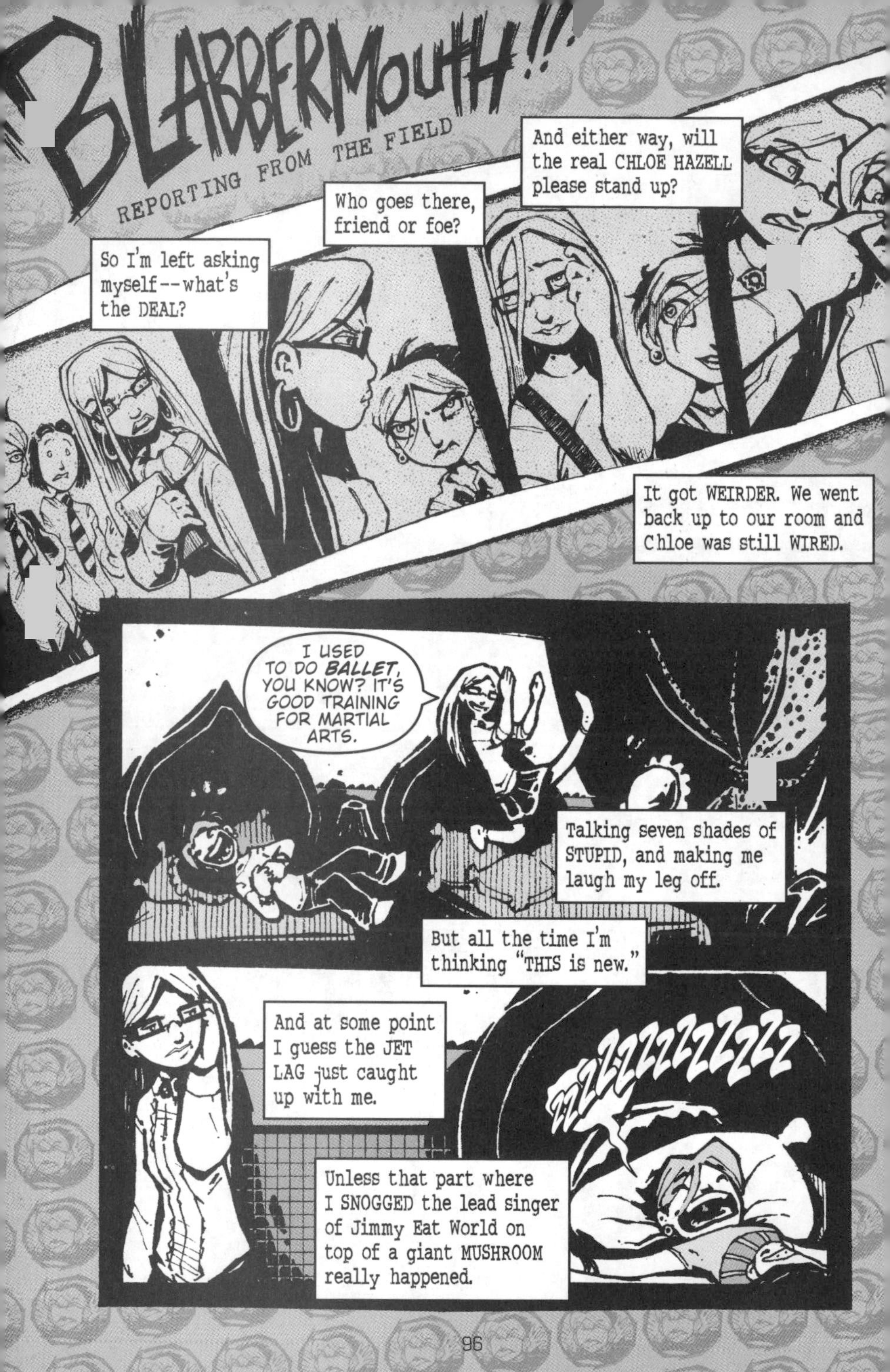
BLABBERMOUTH!!
REPORTING FROM THE FIELD
So I'm left asking myself--what's the DEAL?
Who goes there, friend or foe?
And either way, will the real CHLOE HAZELL please stand up?
It got WEIRDER. We went back up to our room and Chloe was still WIRED.
I USED TO DO BALLET, YOU KNOW? IT'S GOOD TRAINING FOR MARTIAL ARTS.
Talking seven shades of STUPID, and making me laugh my leg off.
But all the time I'm thinking "THIS is new."
And at some point I guess the JET LAG just caught up with me.
ZZZZ-ZZZZZZZZZZ
Unless that part where I SNOGGED the lead singer of Jimmy Eat World on top of a giant MUSHROOM really happened.

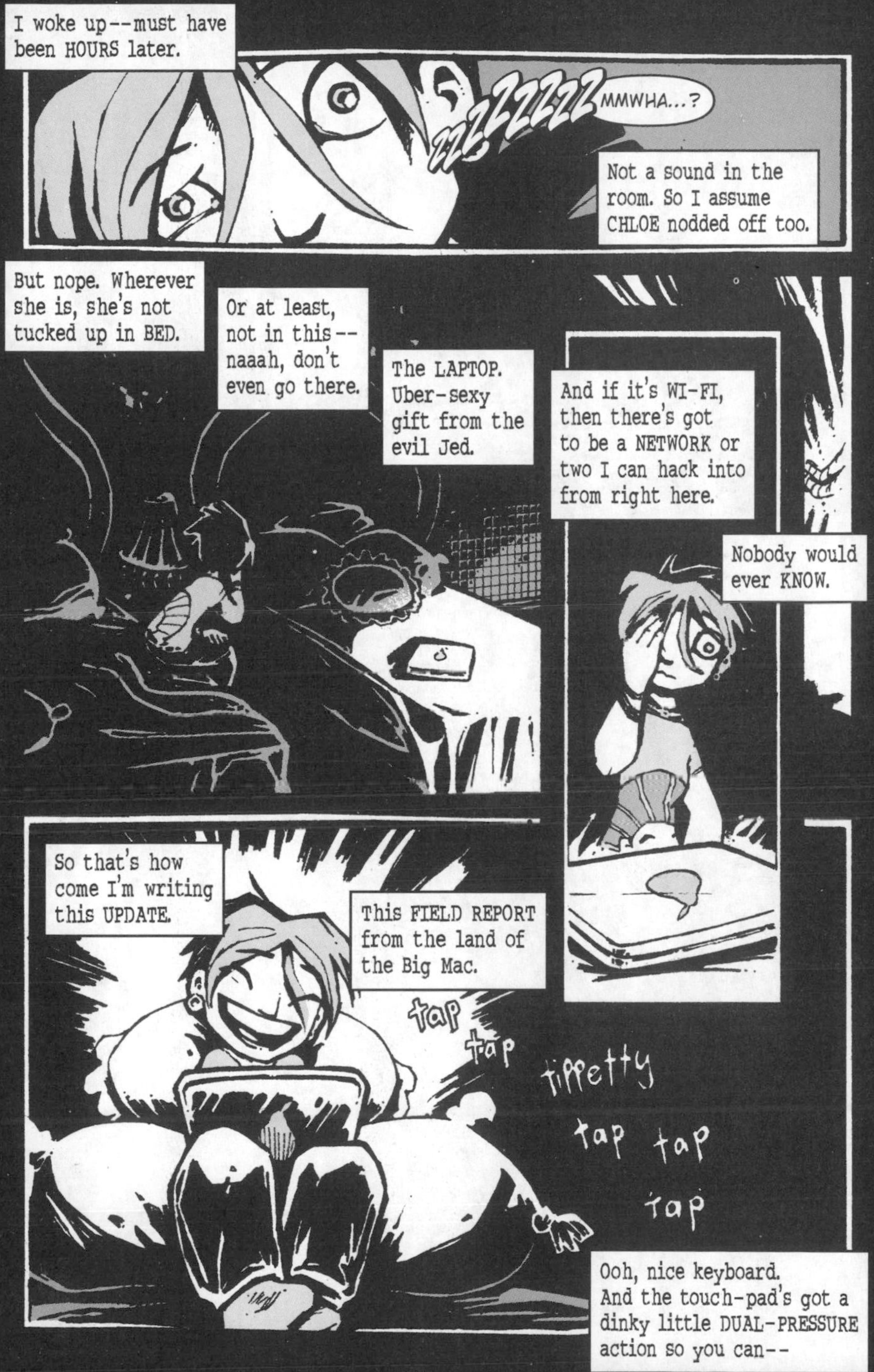
I woke up--must have been HOURS later.
ZZZZZZZZZ MMWHA...?
Not a sound in the room. So I assume CHLOE nodded off too.
But nope. Wherever she is, she's not tucked up in BED.
Or at least, not in this--naaah, don't even go there.
The LAPTOP. Uber-sexy gift from the evil Jed.
And if it's WI-FI, then there's got to be a NETWORK or two I can hack into from right here.
Nobody would ever KNOW.
So that's how come I'm writing this UPDATE.
This FIELD REPORT from the land of the Big Mac.
tap tap tippetty tap tap tap
Ooh, nice keyboard. And the touch-pad's got a dinky little DUAL-PRESSURE action so you can--

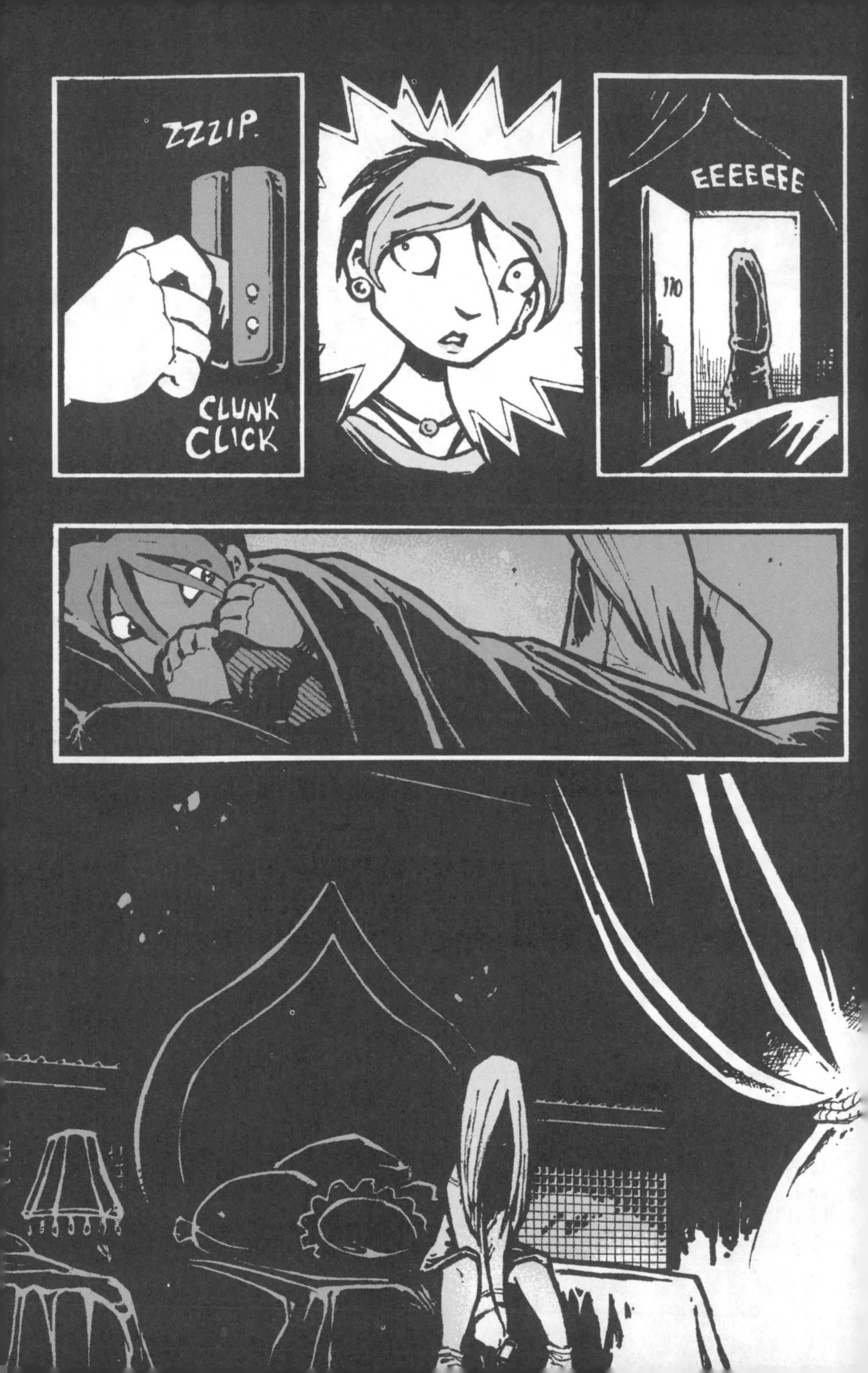
ZZZIP.
CLUNK
CLICK
EEEEEEE
110

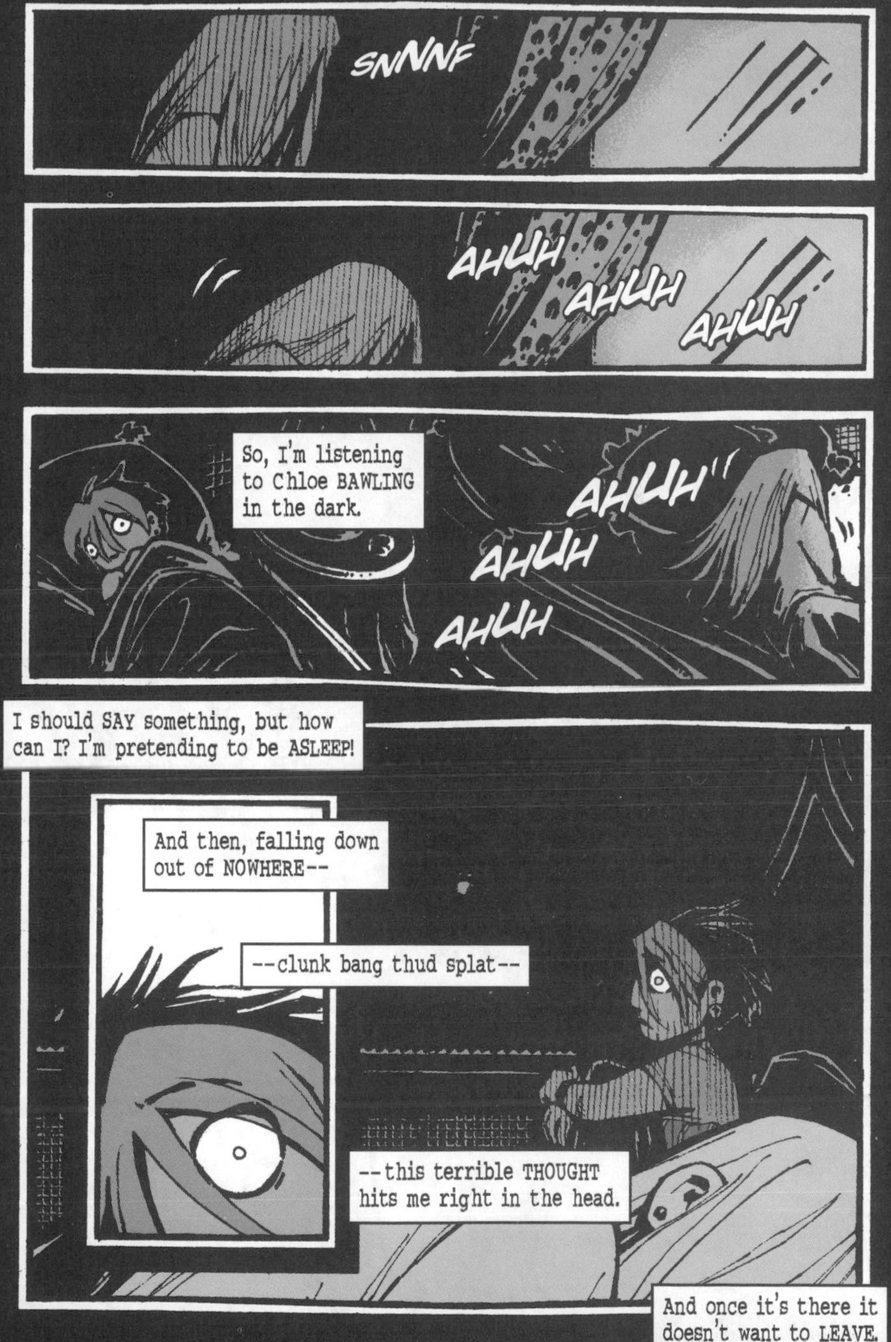
SNNNF
AHUH
AHUH
AHUH
So, I'm listening to Chloe BAWLING in the dark.
AHUH
AHUH
AHUH
I should SAY something, but how can I? I'm pretending to be ASLEEP!
And then, falling down out of NOWHERE--
--clunk bang thud splat--
--this terrible THOUGHT hits me right in the head.
And once it's there it doesn't want to LEAVE.

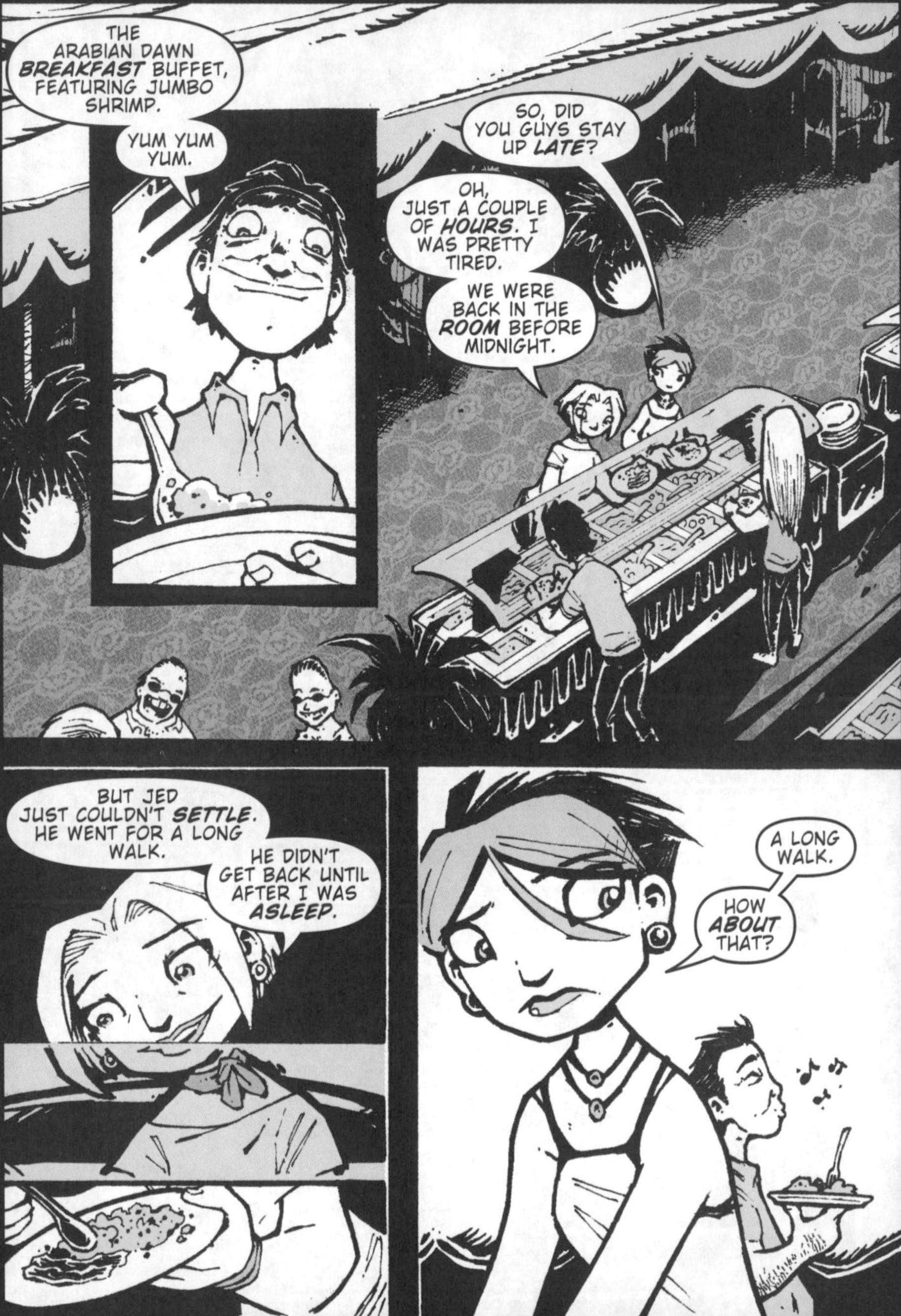
THE ARABIAN DAWN BREAKFAST BUFFET, FEATURING JUMBO SHRIMP.
YUM YUM YUM.
SO, DID YOU GUYS STAY UP LATE?
OH, JUST A COUPLE OF HOURS. I WAS PRETTY TIRED.
WE WERE BACK IN THE ROOM BEFORE MIDNIGHT.
BUT JED JUST COULDN'T SETTLE. HE WENT FOR A LONG WALK.
HE DIDN'T GET BACK UNTIL AFTER I WAS ASLEEP.
A LONG WALK.
HOW ABOUT THAT?

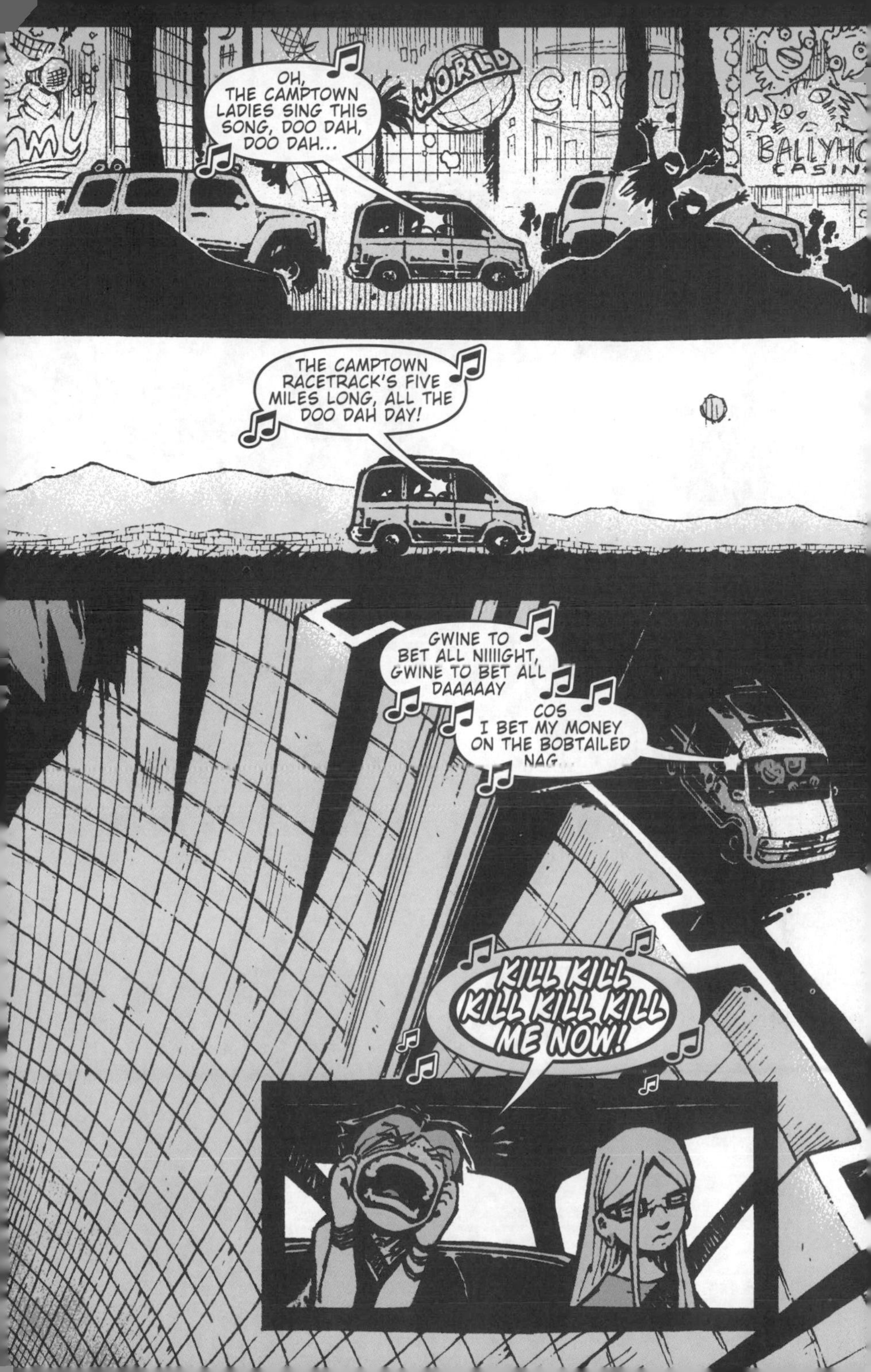
OH, THE CAMPTOWN LADIES SING THIS SONG, DOO DAH, DOO DAH...
WORLD
CIRC
BALLYHO
CASIN
THE CAMPTOWN RACETRACK'S FIVE MILES LONG, ALL THE DOO DAH DAY!
GWINE TO BET ALL NIIIIGHT, GWINE TO BET ALL DAAAAAY
COS I BET MY MONEY ON THE BOBTAILED NAG...
KILL KILL KILL KILL KILL ME NOW!

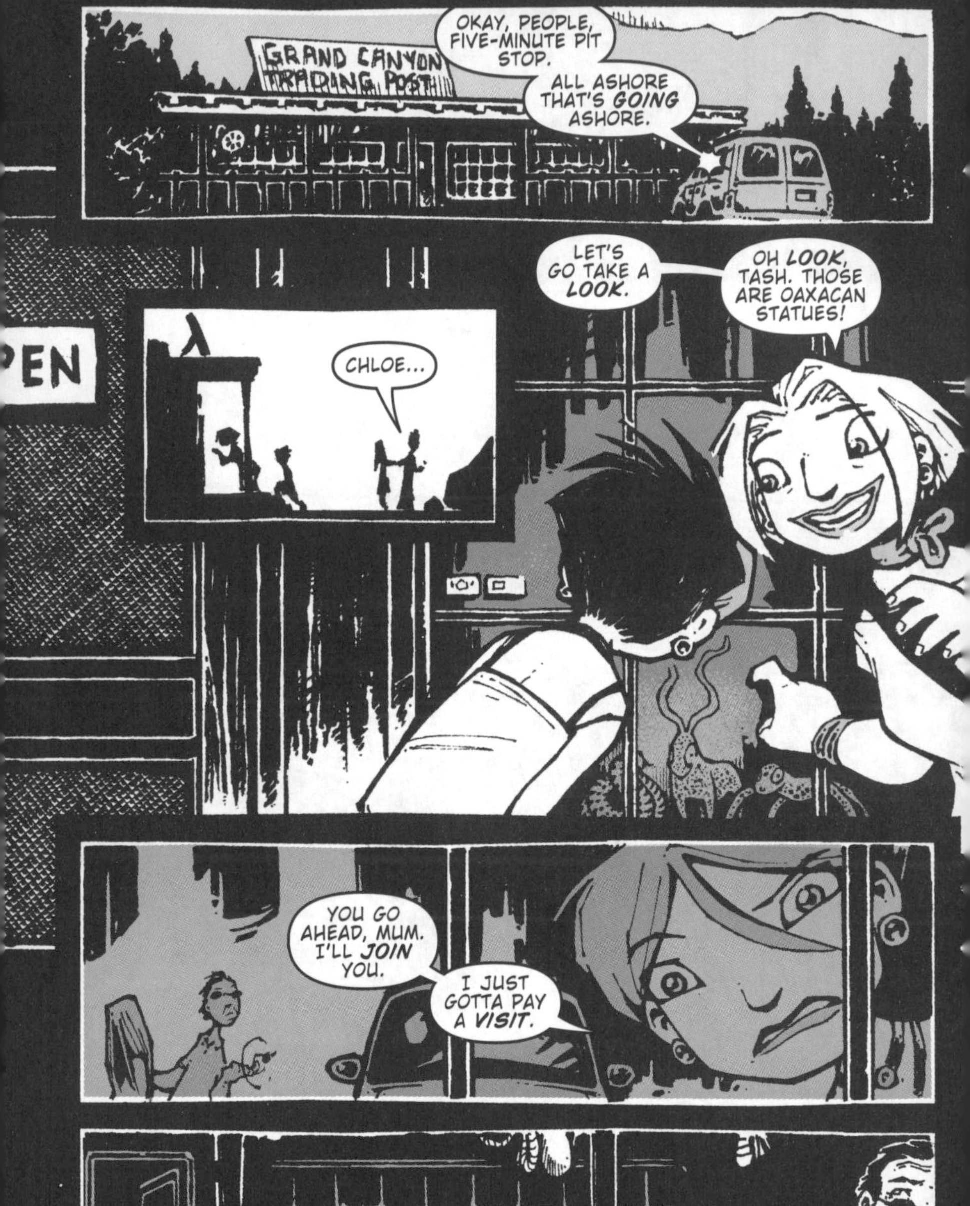
GRAND CANYON TRADING POST
OKAY, PEOPLE, FIVE-MINUTE PIT STOP.
ALL ASHORE THAT'S *GOING* ASHORE.
OH *LOOK*, TASH. THOSE ARE OAXACAN STATUES!
LET'S GO TAKE A *LOOK*.
PEN
CHLOE...
YOU GO AHEAD, MUM. I'LL *JOIN* YOU.
I JUST GOTTA PAY A *VISIT*.

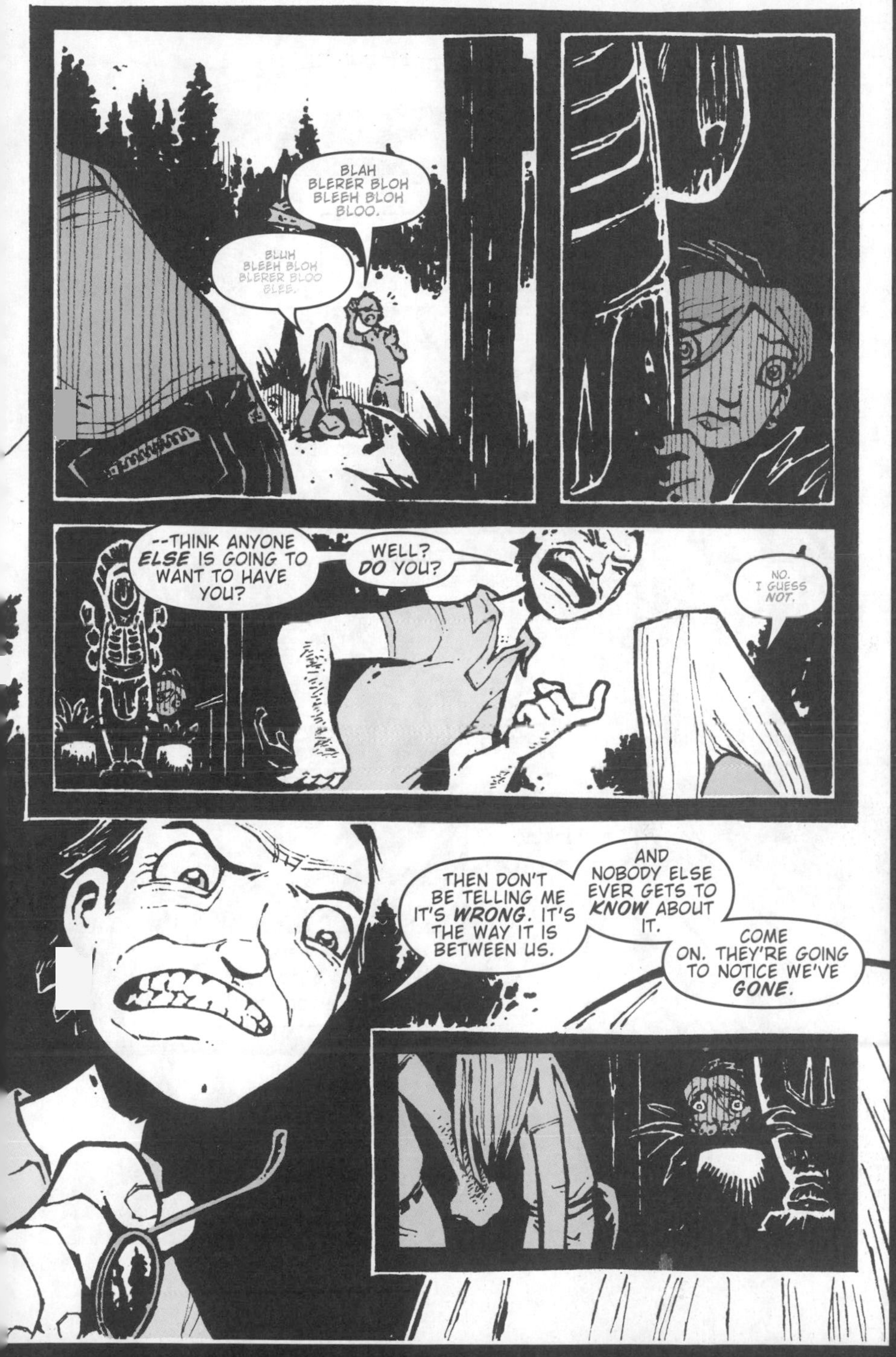
BLAH BLERER BLOH BLEEH BLOH BLOO.
BLUH BLEEH BLOH BLERER BLOO BLEE.
--THINK ANYONE *ELSE* IS GOING TO WANT TO HAVE YOU?
WELL? *DO* YOU?
NO. I GUESS *NOT*.
THEN DON'T BE TELLING ME IT'S *WRONG*. IT'S THE WAY IT IS BETWEEN US.
AND NOBODY ELSE EVER GETS TO *KNOW* ABOUT IT.
COME ON. THEY'RE GOING TO NOTICE WE'VE *GONE*.

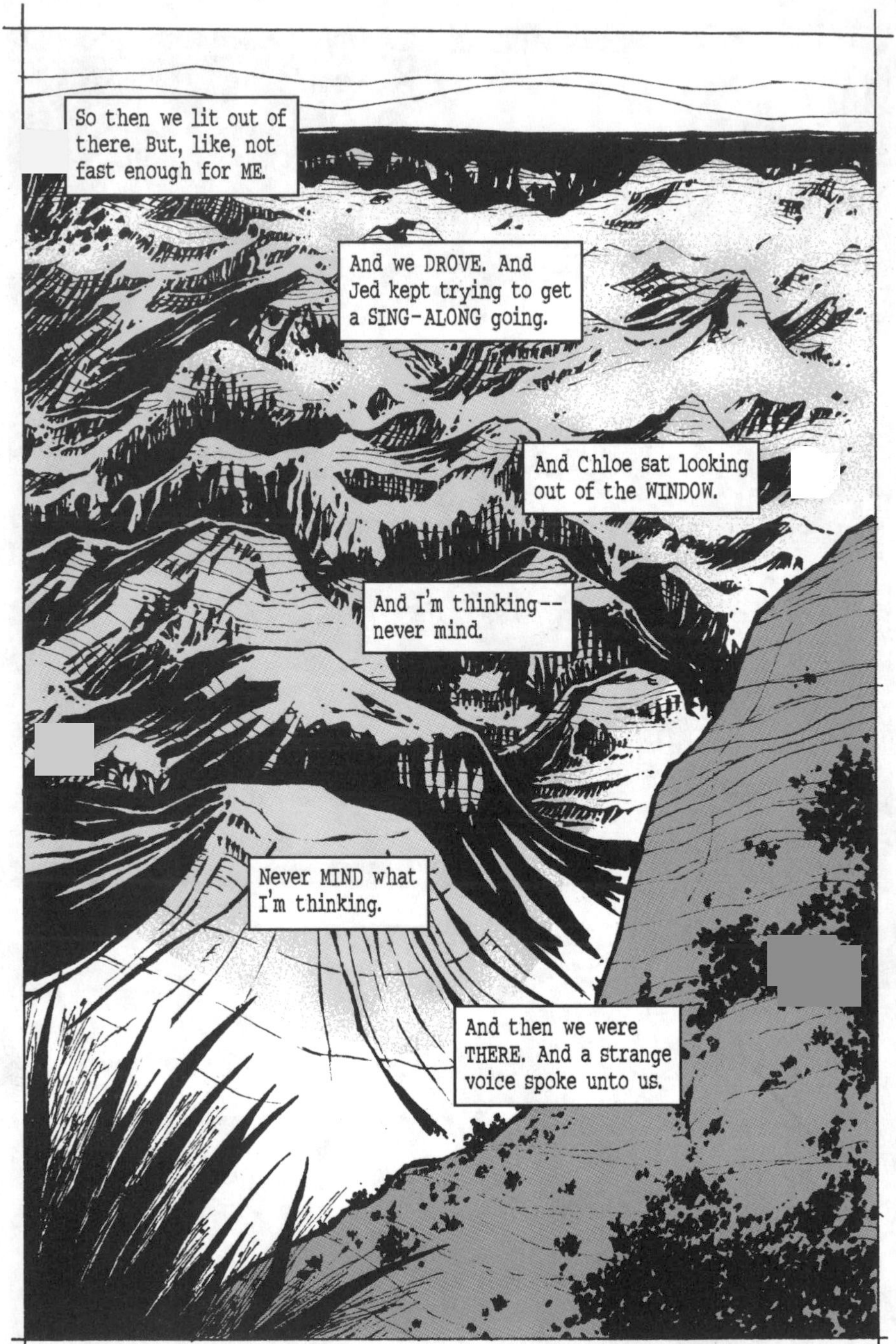
So then we lit out of there. But, like, not fast enough for ME.
And we DROVE. And Jed kept trying to get a SING-ALONG going.
And Chloe sat looking out of the WINDOW.
And I'm thinking-- never mind.
Never MIND what I'm thinking.
And then we were THERE. And a strange voice spoke unto us.

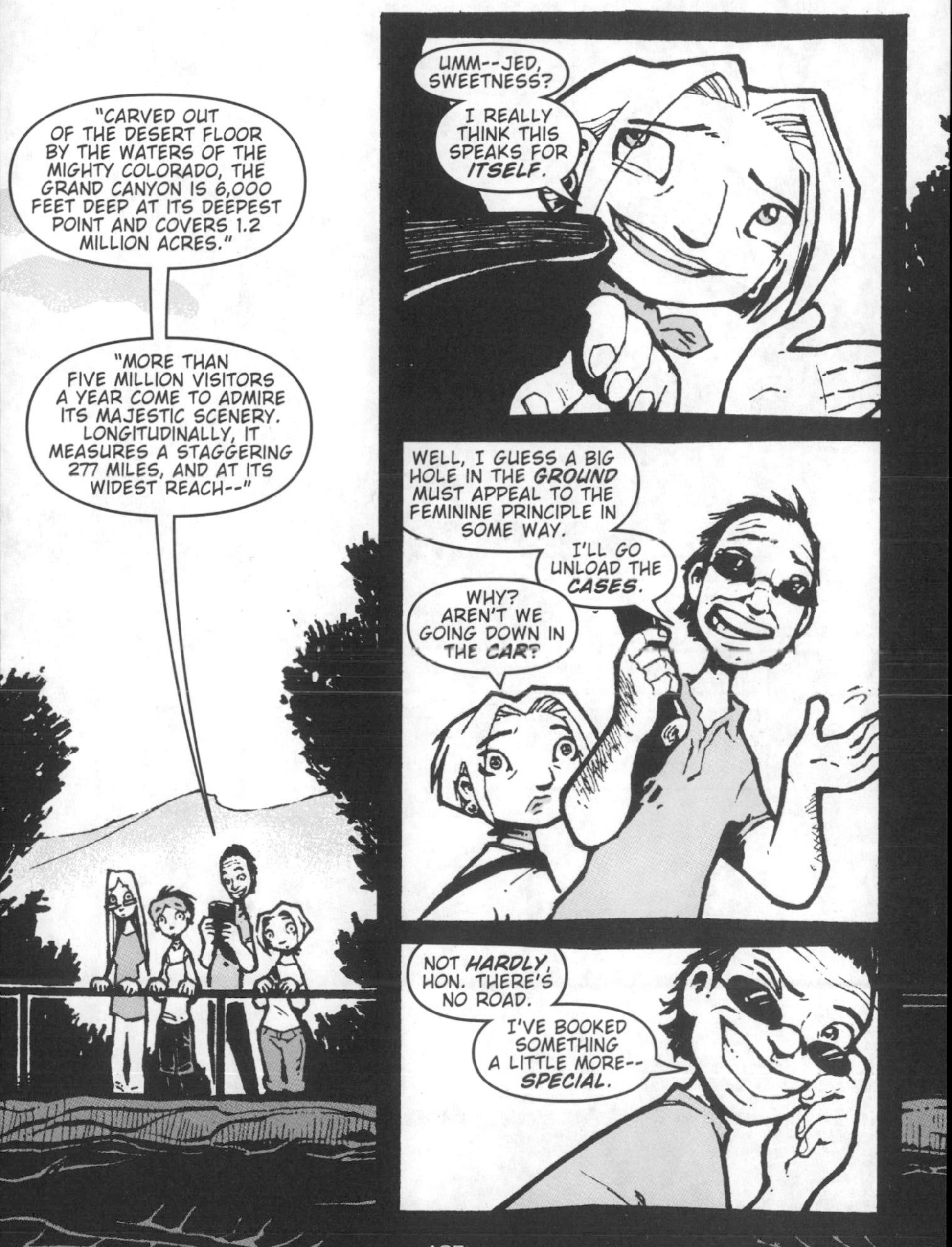
"CARVED OUT OF THE DESERT FLOOR BY THE WATERS OF THE MIGHTY COLORADO, THE GRAND CANYON IS 6,000 FEET DEEP AT ITS DEEPEST POINT AND COVERS 1.2 MILLION ACRES."
"MORE THAN FIVE MILLION VISITORS A YEAR COME TO ADMIRE ITS MAJESTIC SCENERY. LONGITUDINALLY, IT MEASURES A STAGGERING 277 MILES, AND AT ITS WIDEST REACH--"
UMM--JED, SWEETNESS?
I REALLY THINK THIS SPEAKS FOR *ITSELF*.
WELL, I GUESS A BIG HOLE IN THE *GROUND* MUST APPEAL TO THE FEMININE PRINCIPLE IN SOME WAY.
I'LL GO UNLOAD THE *CASES*.
WHY? AREN'T WE GOING DOWN IN THE *CAR*?
NOT *HARDLY*, HON. THERE'S NO ROAD.
I'VE BOOKED SOMETHING A LITTLE MORE-- *SPECIAL*.

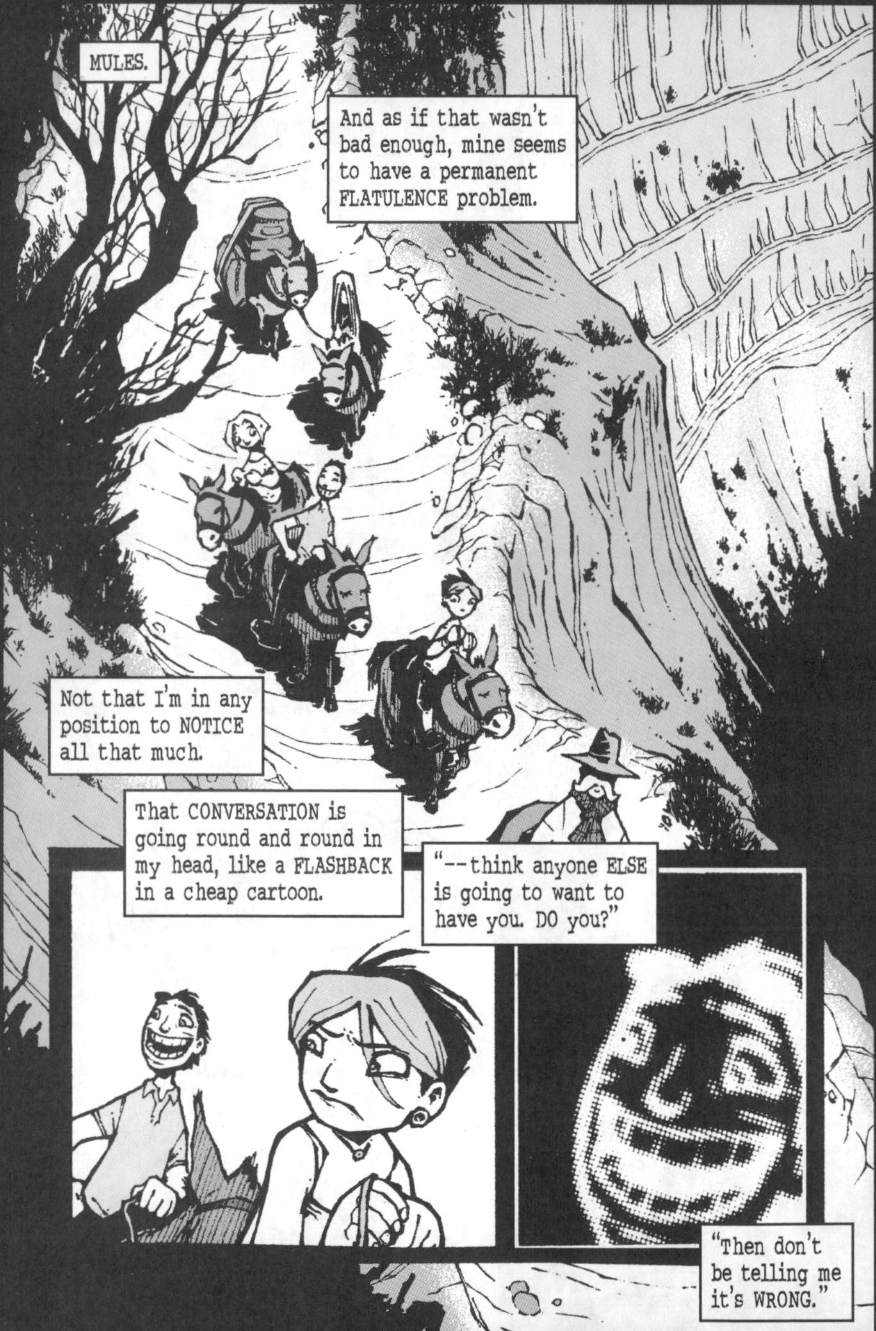
MULES.
And as if that wasn't bad enough, mine seems to have a permanent FLATULENCE problem.
Not that I'm in any position to NOTICE all that much.
That CONVERSATION is going round and round in my head, like a FLASHBACK in a cheap cartoon.
"--think anyone ELSE is going to want to have you. DO you?"
"Then don't be telling me it's WRONG."

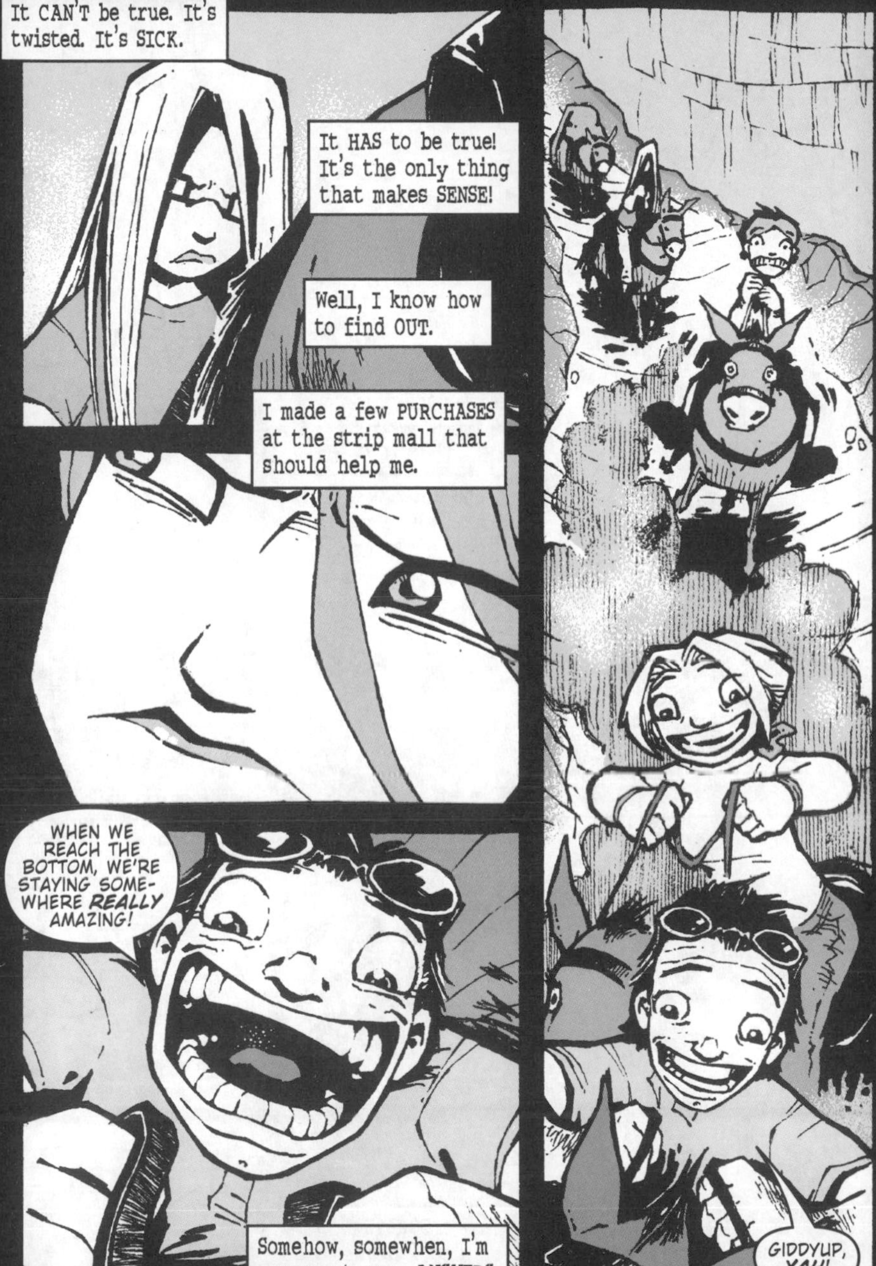
It CAN'T be true. It's twisted. It's SICK.
It HAS to be true! It's the only thing that makes SENSE!
Well, I know how to find OUT.
I made a few PURCHASES at the strip mall that should help me.
WHEN WE REACH THE BOTTOM, WE'RE STAYING SOME-WHERE *REALLY* AMAZING!
Somehow, somewhen, I'm gonna get some ANSWERS.
GIDDYUP, *YAH!*

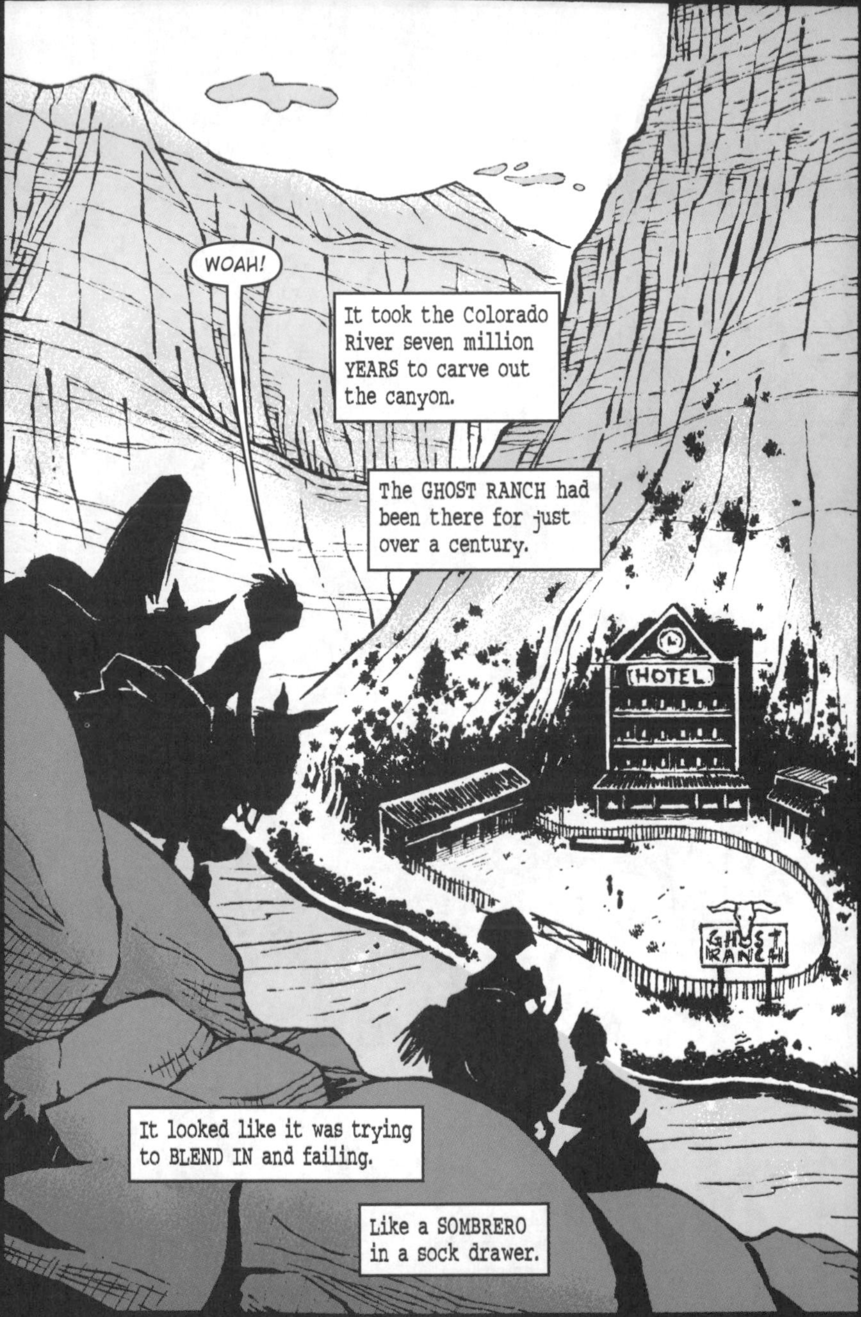
WOAH!
It took the Colorado River seven million YEARS to carve out the canyon.
The GHOST RANCH had been there for just over a century.
HOTEL
GHOST RANCH
It looked like it was trying to BLEND IN and failing.
Like a SOMBRERO in a sock drawer.

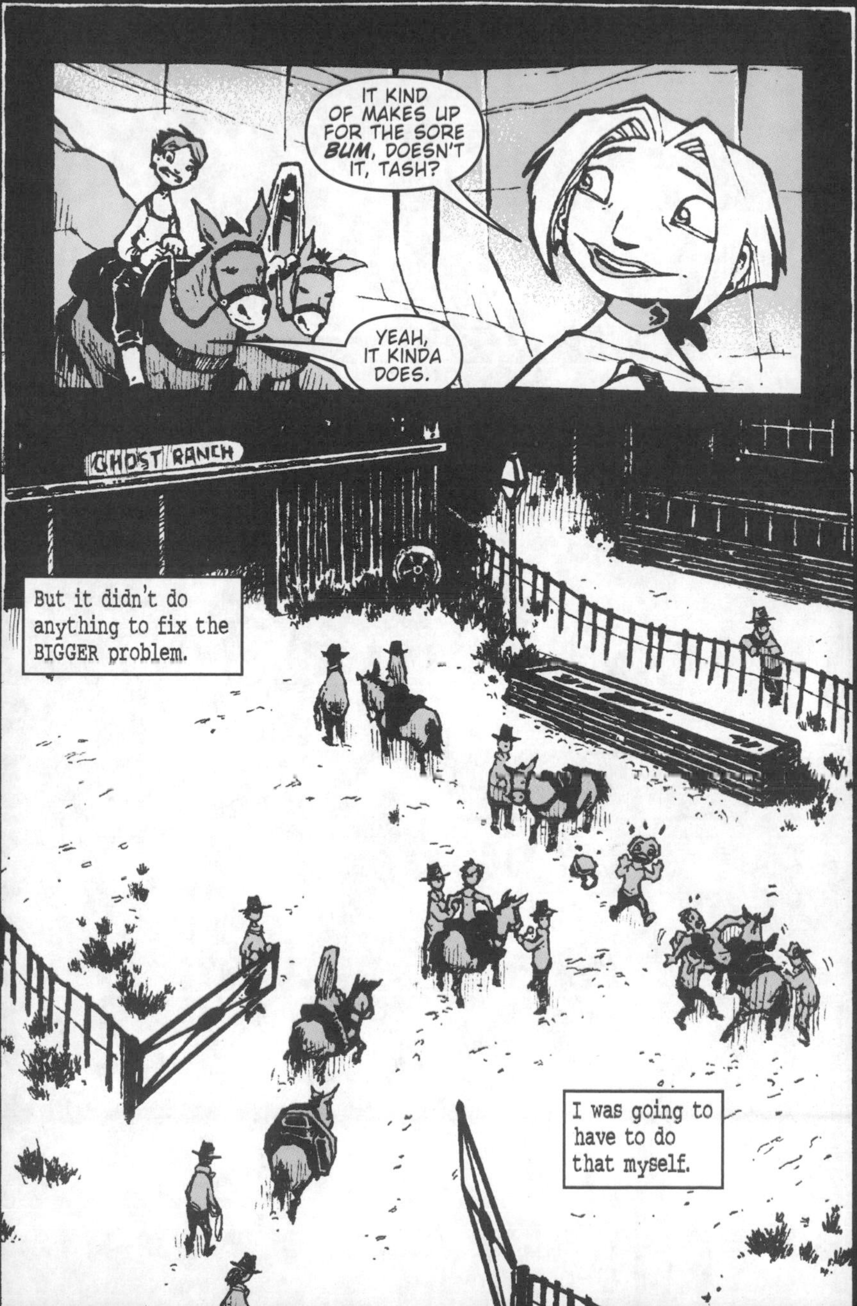
IT KIND OF MAKES UP FOR THE SORE BUM, DOESN'T IT, TASH?
YEAH, IT KINDA DOES.
GHOST RANCH
But it didn't do anything to fix the BIGGER problem.
I was going to have to do that myself.

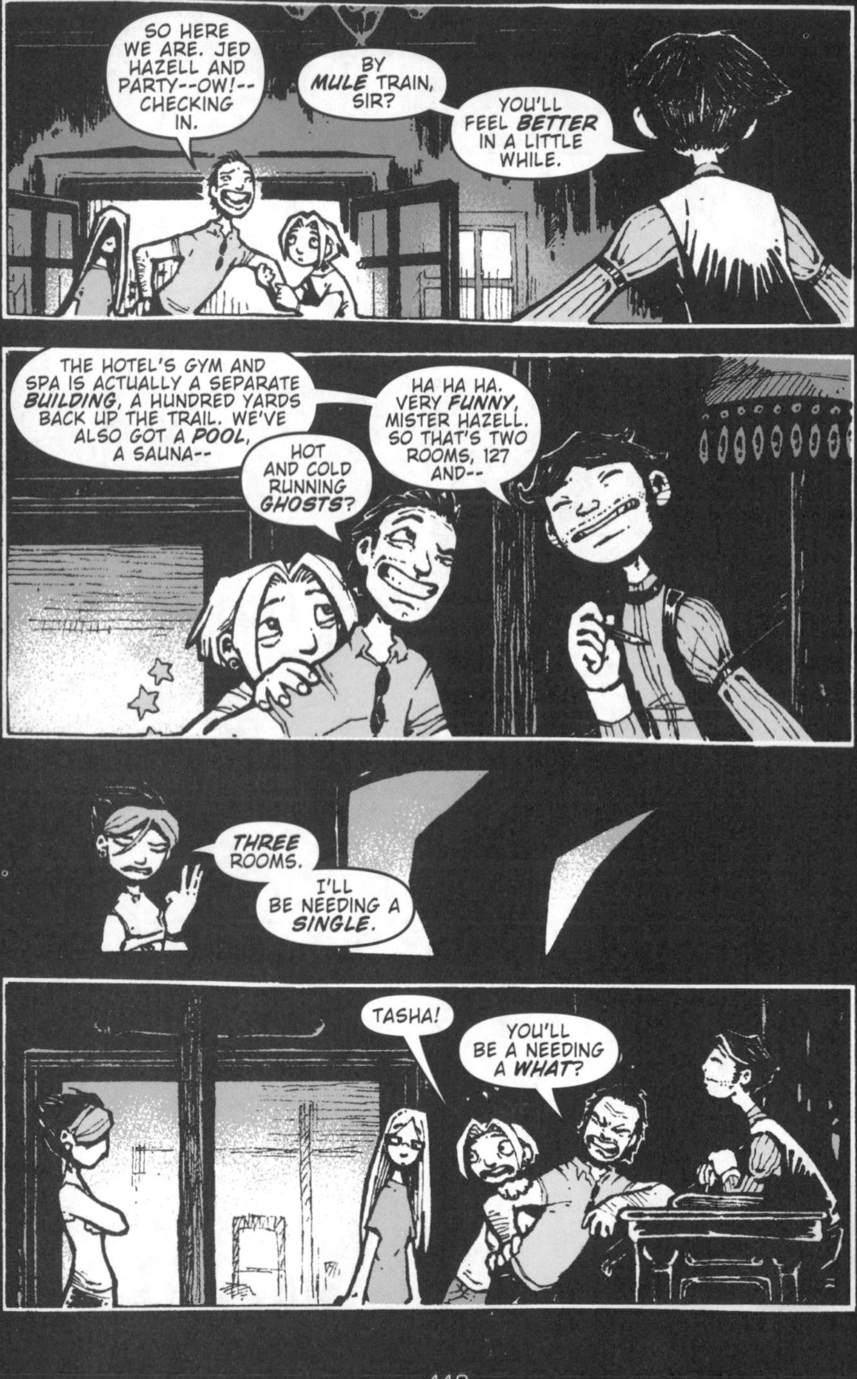
SO HERE WE ARE. JED HAZELL AND PARTY--OW!--CHECKING IN.
BY MULE TRAIN, SIR?
YOU'LL FEEL BETTER IN A LITTLE WHILE.
THE HOTEL'S GYM AND SPA IS ACTUALLY A SEPARATE BUILDING, A HUNDRED YARDS BACK UP THE TRAIL. WE'VE ALSO GOT A POOL, A SAUNA--
HOT AND COLD RUNNING GHOSTS?
HA HA HA. VERY FUNNY, MISTER HAZELL. SO THAT'S TWO ROOMS, 127 AND--
THREE ROOMS.
I'LL BE NEEDING A SINGLE.
TASHA!
YOU'LL BE A NEEDING A WHAT?

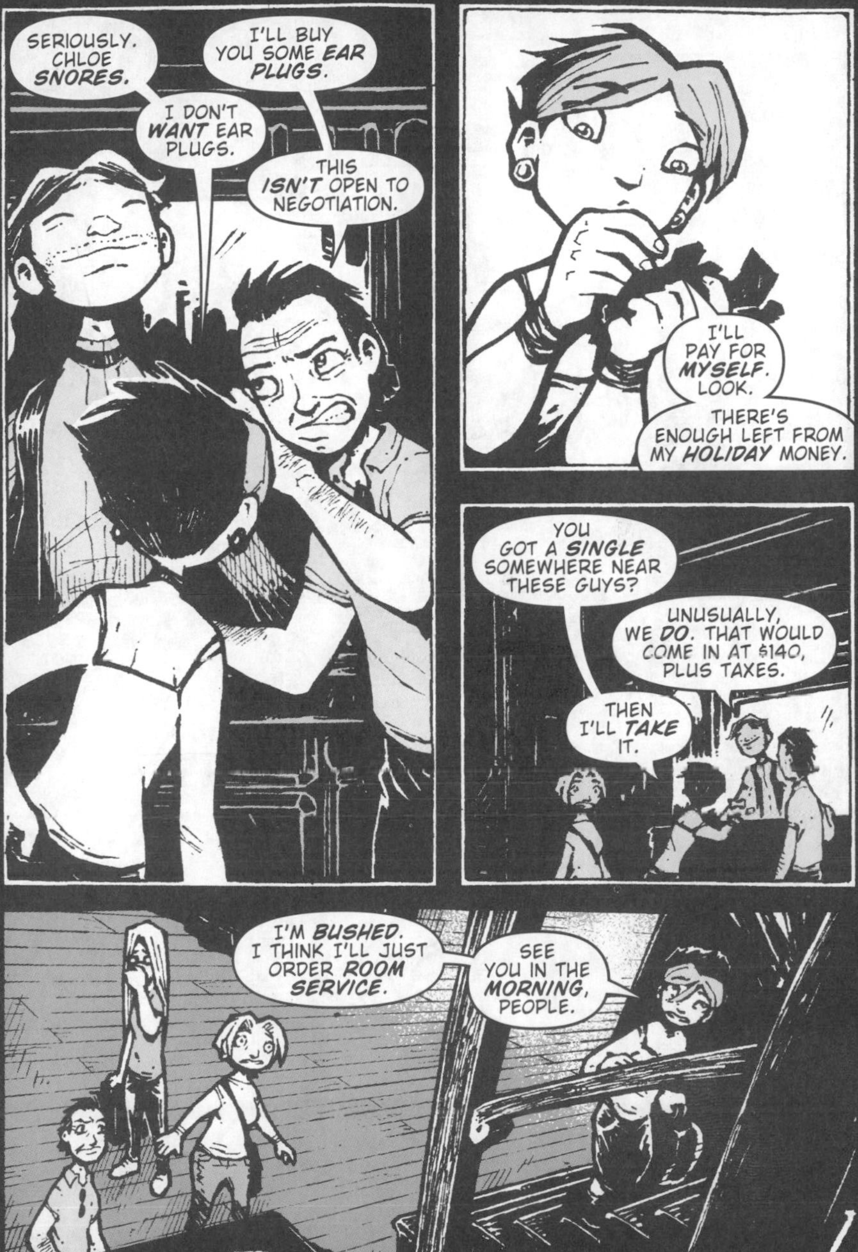
SERIOUSLY. CHLOE SNORES.
I'LL BUY YOU SOME EAR PLUGS.
I DON'T WANT EAR PLUGS.
THIS ISN'T OPEN TO NEGOTIATION.
I'LL PAY FOR MYSELF. LOOK.
THERE'S ENOUGH LEFT FROM MY HOLIDAY MONEY.
YOU GOT A SINGLE SOMEWHERE NEAR THESE GUYS?
UNUSUALLY, WE DO. THAT WOULD COME IN AT $140, PLUS TAXES.
THEN I'LL TAKE IT.
I'M BUSHED. I THINK I'LL JUST ORDER ROOM SERVICE.
SEE YOU IN THE MORNING, PEOPLE.

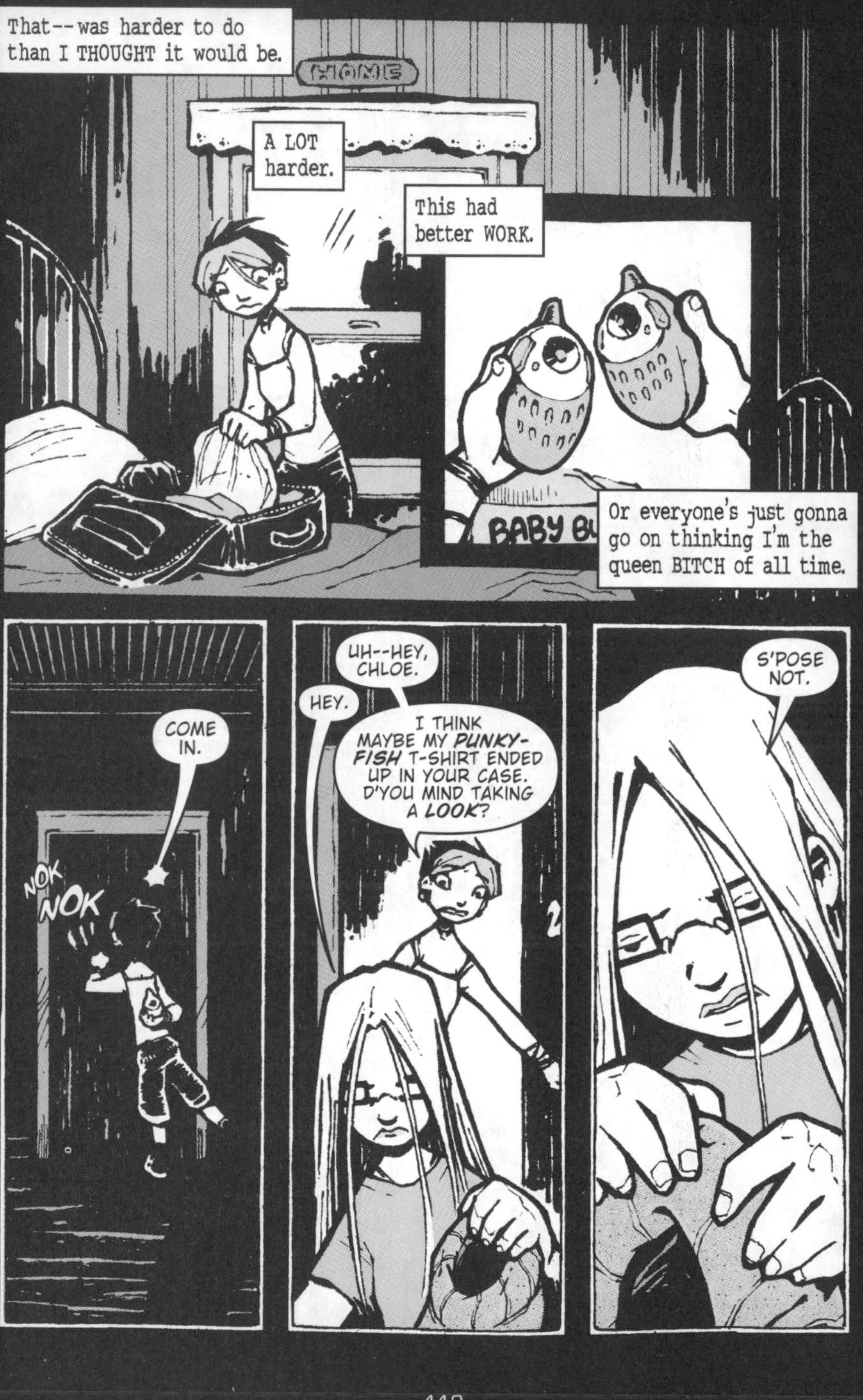
That--was harder to do than I THOUGHT it would be.
HOME
A LOT harder.
This had better WORK.
BABY BU
Or everyone's just gonna go on thinking I'm the queen BITCH of all time.
COME IN.
NOK NOK
UH--HEY, CHLOE.
HEY.
I THINK MAYBE MY PUNKY-FISH T-SHIRT ENDED UP IN YOUR CASE. D'YOU MIND TAKING A LOOK?
S'POSE NOT.

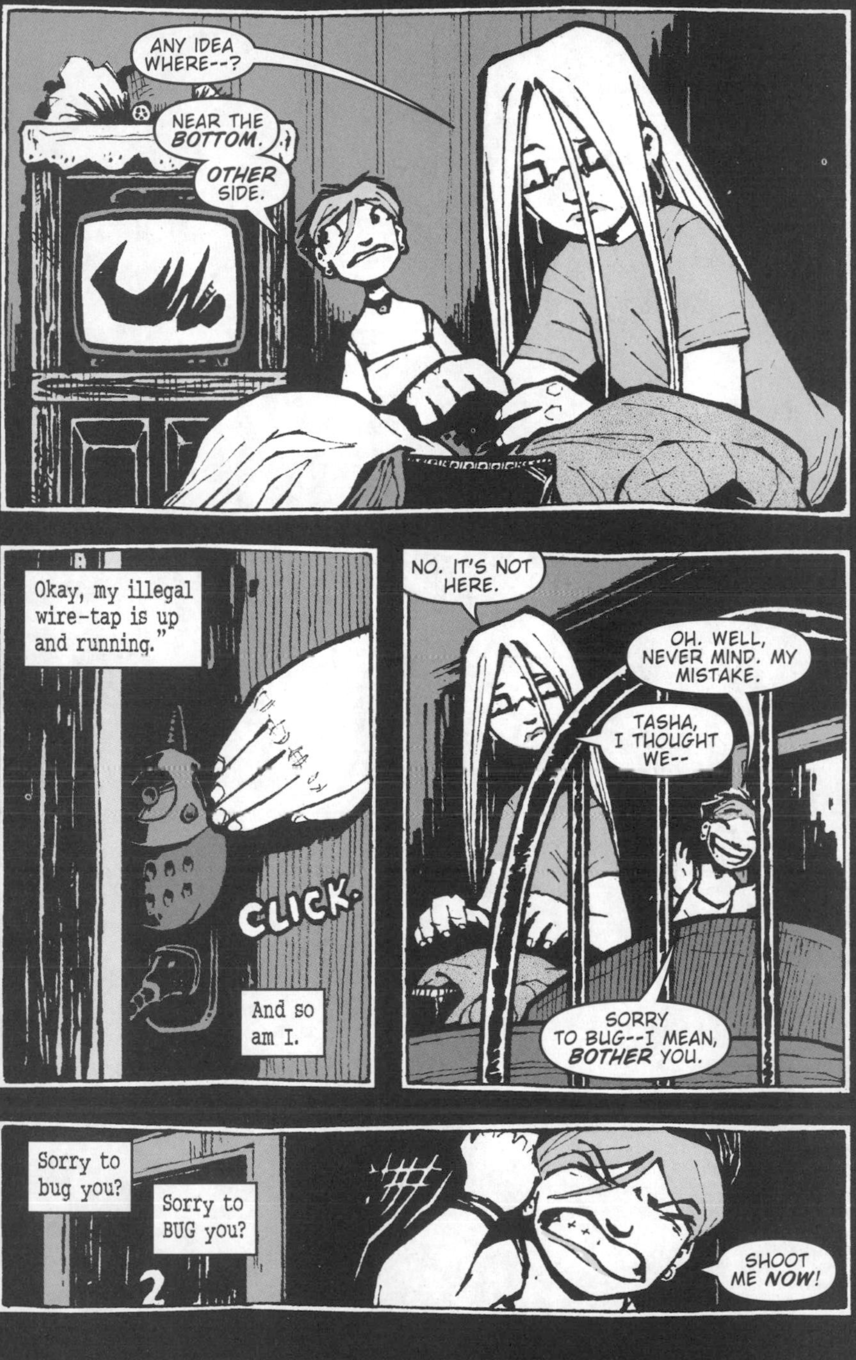
ANY IDEA WHERE--?
NEAR THE BOTTOM.
OTHER SIDE.
Okay, my illegal wire-tap is up and running."
CLICK.
And so am I.
NO. IT'S NOT HERE.
OH. WELL, NEVER MIND. MY MISTAKE.
TASHA, I THOUGHT WE--
SORRY TO BUG--I MEAN, BOTHER YOU.
Sorry to bug you?
Sorry to BUG you?
SHOOT ME NOW!

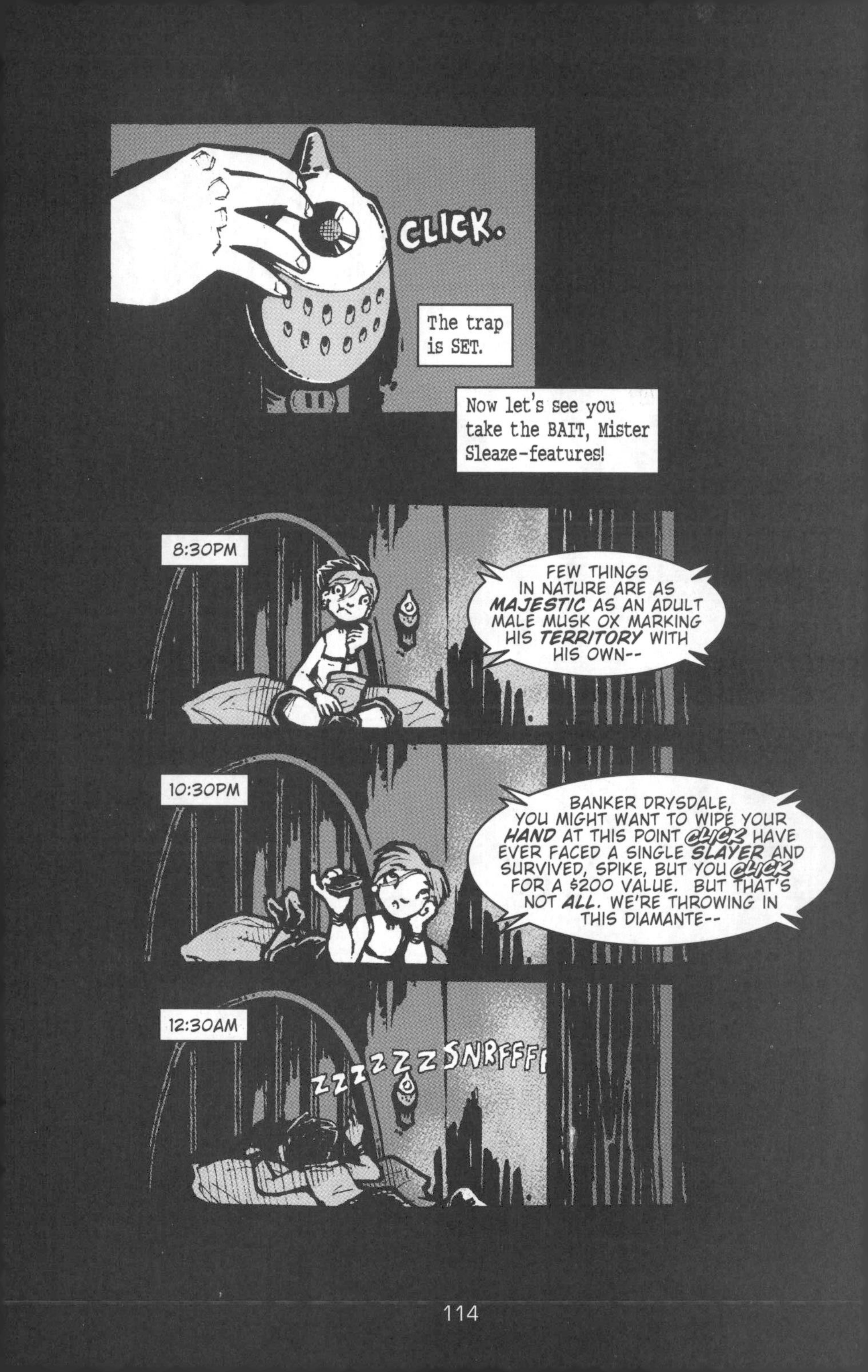

CLICK.
The trap is SET.
Now let's see you take the BAIT, Mister Sleaze-features!
8:30PM
FEW THINGS IN NATURE ARE AS MAJESTIC AS AN ADULT MALE MUSK OX MARKING HIS TERRITORY WITH HIS OWN--
10:30PM
BANKER DRYSDALE, YOU MIGHT WANT TO WIPE YOUR HAND AT THIS POINT CLICK HAVE EVER FACED A SINGLE SLAYER AND SURVIVED, SPIKE, BUT YOU CLICK FOR A $200 VALUE. BUT THAT'S NOT ALL. WE'RE THROWING IN THIS DIAMANTE--
12:30AM
ZZZZZZZSNRFFFF

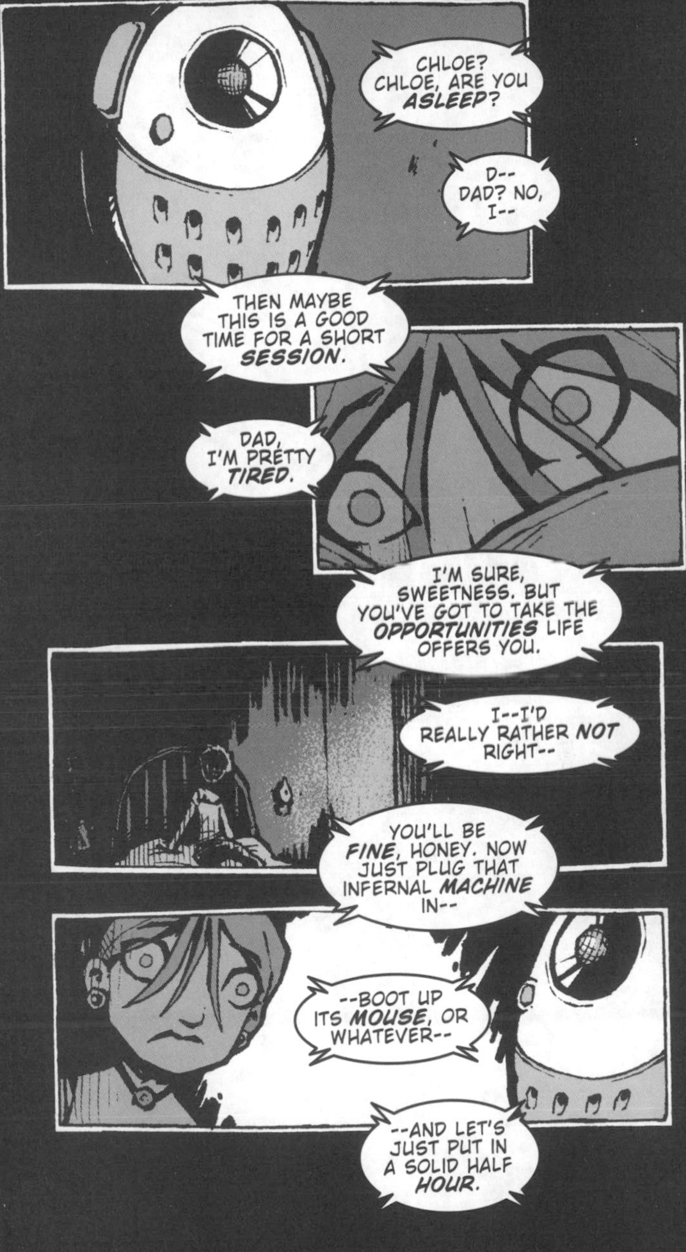
CHLOE? CHLOE, ARE YOU ASLEEP?
D-- DAD? NO, I--
THEN MAYBE THIS IS A GOOD TIME FOR A SHORT SESSION.
DAD, I'M PRETTY TIRED.
I'M SURE, SWEETNESS. BUT YOU'VE GOT TO TAKE THE OPPORTUNITIES LIFE OFFERS YOU.
I--I'D REALLY RATHER NOT RIGHT--
YOU'LL BE FINE, HONEY. NOW JUST PLUG THAT INFERNAL MACHINE IN--
--BOOT UP ITS MOUSE, OR WHATEVER--
--AND LET'S JUST PUT IN A SOLID HALF HOUR.

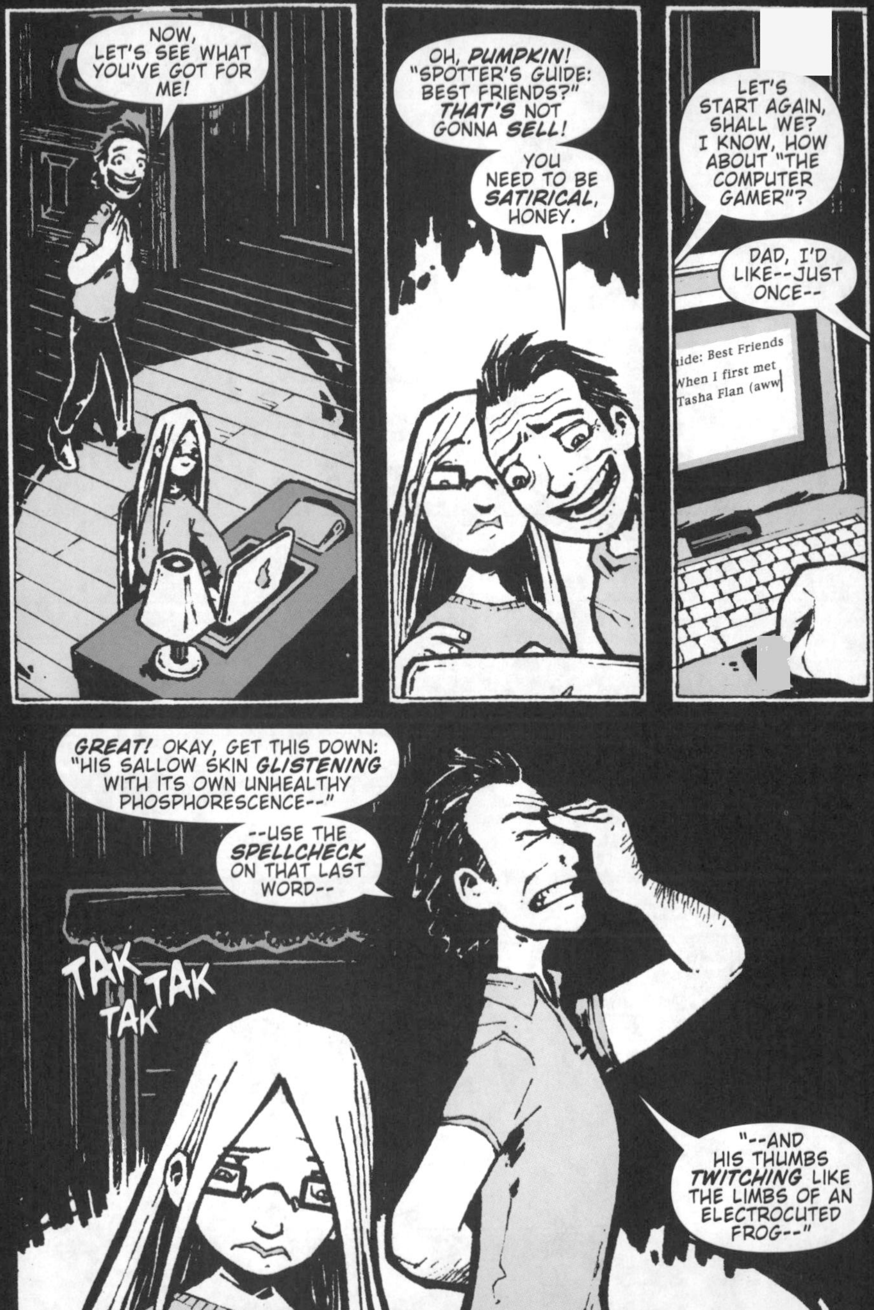
NOW, LET'S SEE WHAT YOU'VE GOT FOR ME!
OH, PUMPKIN! "SPOTTER'S GUIDE: BEST FRIENDS?" THAT'S NOT GONNA SELL!
YOU NEED TO BE SATIRICAL, HONEY.
LET'S START AGAIN, SHALL WE? I KNOW, HOW ABOUT "THE COMPUTER GAMER"?
DAD, I'D LIKE--JUST ONCE--
uide: Best Friends
When I first met
Tasha Flan (aww
GREAT! OKAY, GET THIS DOWN: "HIS SALLOW SKIN GLISTENING WITH ITS OWN UNHEALTHY PHOSPHORESCENCE--"
--USE THE SPELLCHECK ON THAT LAST WORD--
TAK TAK TAK
"--AND HIS THUMBS TWITCHING LIKE THE LIMBS OF AN ELECTROCUTED FROG--"

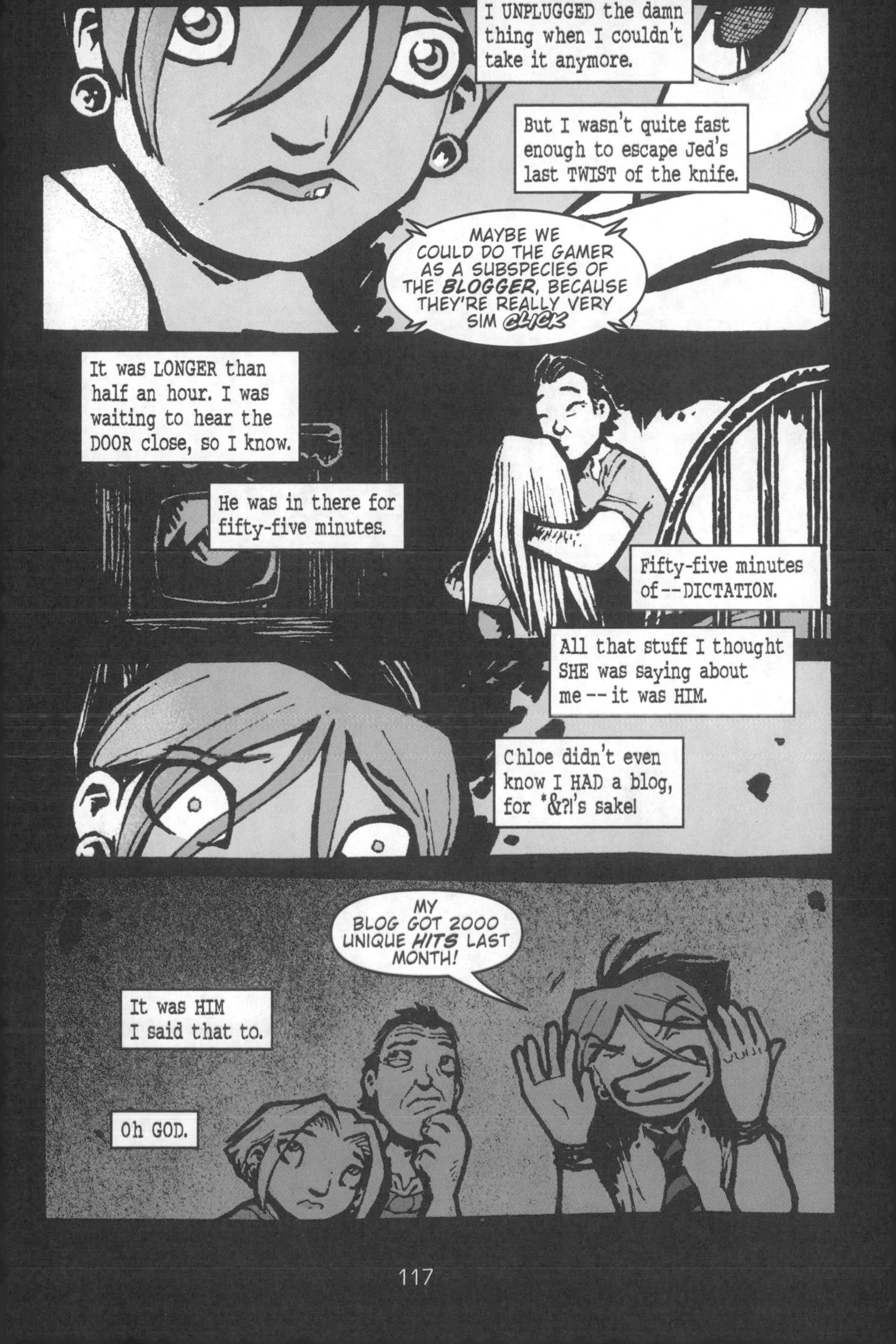

I UNPLUGGED the damn thing when I couldn't take it anymore.
But I wasn't quite fast enough to escape Jed's last TWIST of the knife.
MAYBE WE COULD DO THE GAMER AS A SUBSPECIES OF THE BLOGGER, BECAUSE THEY'RE REALLY VERY SIM CLICK
It was LONGER than half an hour. I was waiting to hear the DOOR close, so I know.
He was in there for fifty-five minutes.
Fifty-five minutes of -- DICTATION.
All that stuff I thought SHE was saying about me -- it was HIM.
Chloe didn't even know I HAD a blog, for *&?!'s sake!
MY BLOG GOT 2000 UNIQUE HITS LAST MONTH!
It was HIM I said that to.
Oh GOD.

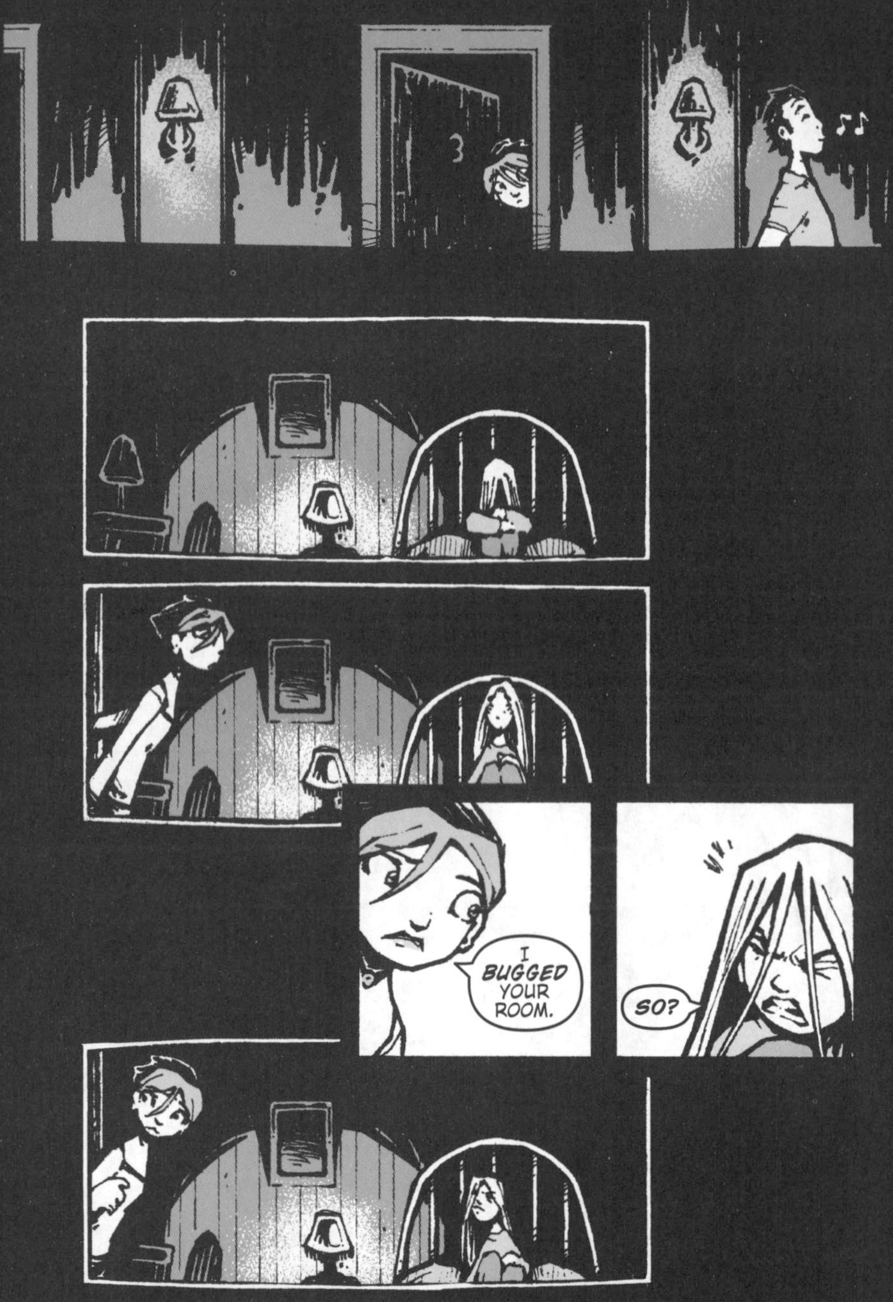
3
I BUGGED YOUR ROOM.
SO?

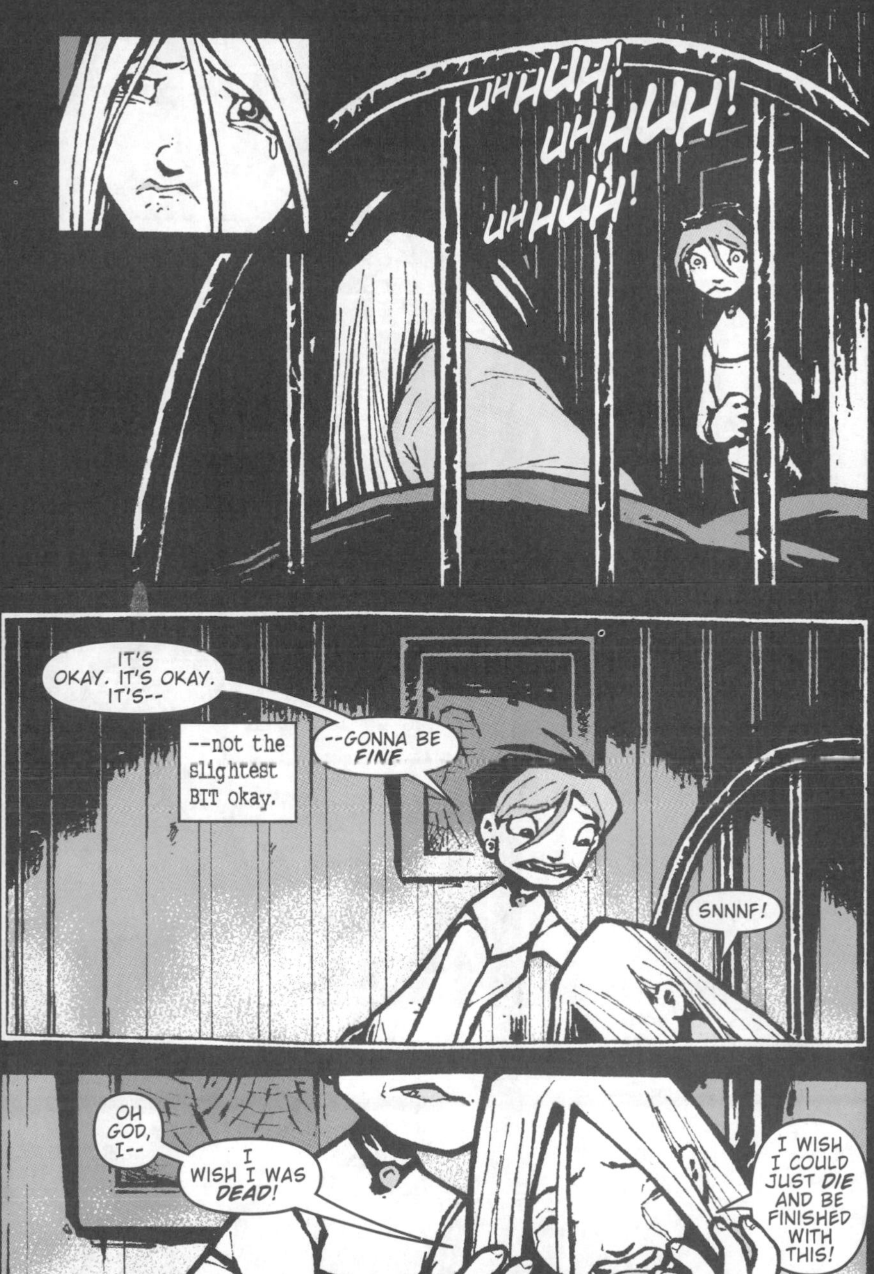
UH HUH! UH HUH! UH HUH!
IT'S OKAY. IT'S OKAY. IT'S--
--not the slightest BIT okay.
--GONNA BE FINE
SNNNF!
OH GOD, I--
I WISH I WAS DEAD!
I WISH I COULD JUST DIE AND BE FINISHED WITH THIS!

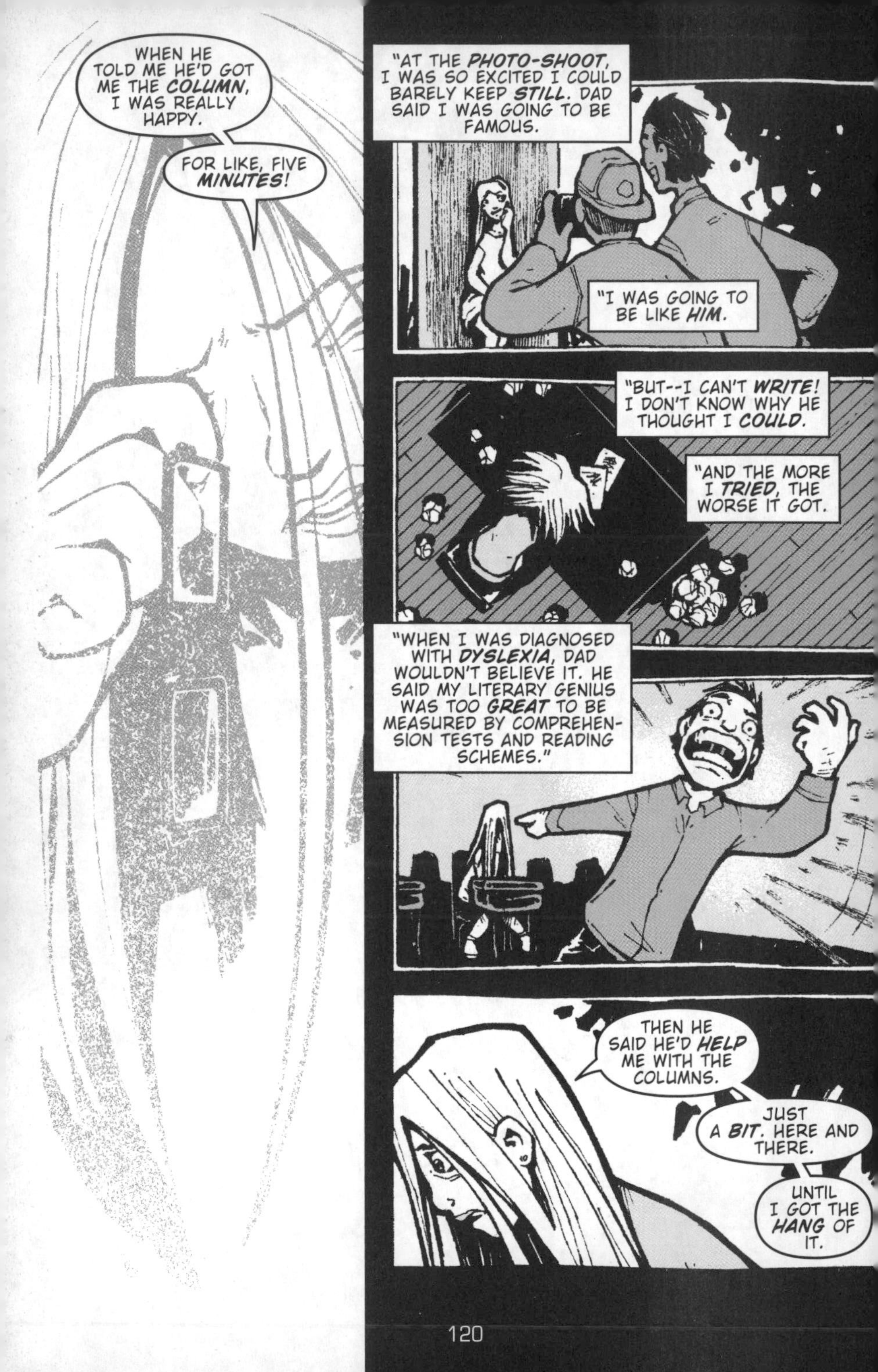
WHEN HE TOLD ME HE'D GOT ME THE COLUMN, I WAS REALLY HAPPY.
FOR LIKE, FIVE MINUTES!
"AT THE PHOTO-SHOOT, I WAS SO EXCITED I COULD BARELY KEEP STILL. DAD SAID I WAS GOING TO BE FAMOUS.
"I WAS GOING TO BE LIKE HIM.
"BUT--I CAN'T WRITE! I DON'T KNOW WHY HE THOUGHT I COULD.
"AND THE MORE I TRIED, THE WORSE IT GOT.
"WHEN I WAS DIAGNOSED WITH DYSLEXIA, DAD WOULDN'T BELIEVE IT. HE SAID MY LITERARY GENIUS WAS TOO GREAT TO BE MEASURED BY COMPREHENSION TESTS AND READING SCHEMES."
THEN HE SAID HE'D HELP ME WITH THE COLUMNS.
JUST A BIT. HERE AND THERE.
UNTIL I GOT THE HANG OF IT.

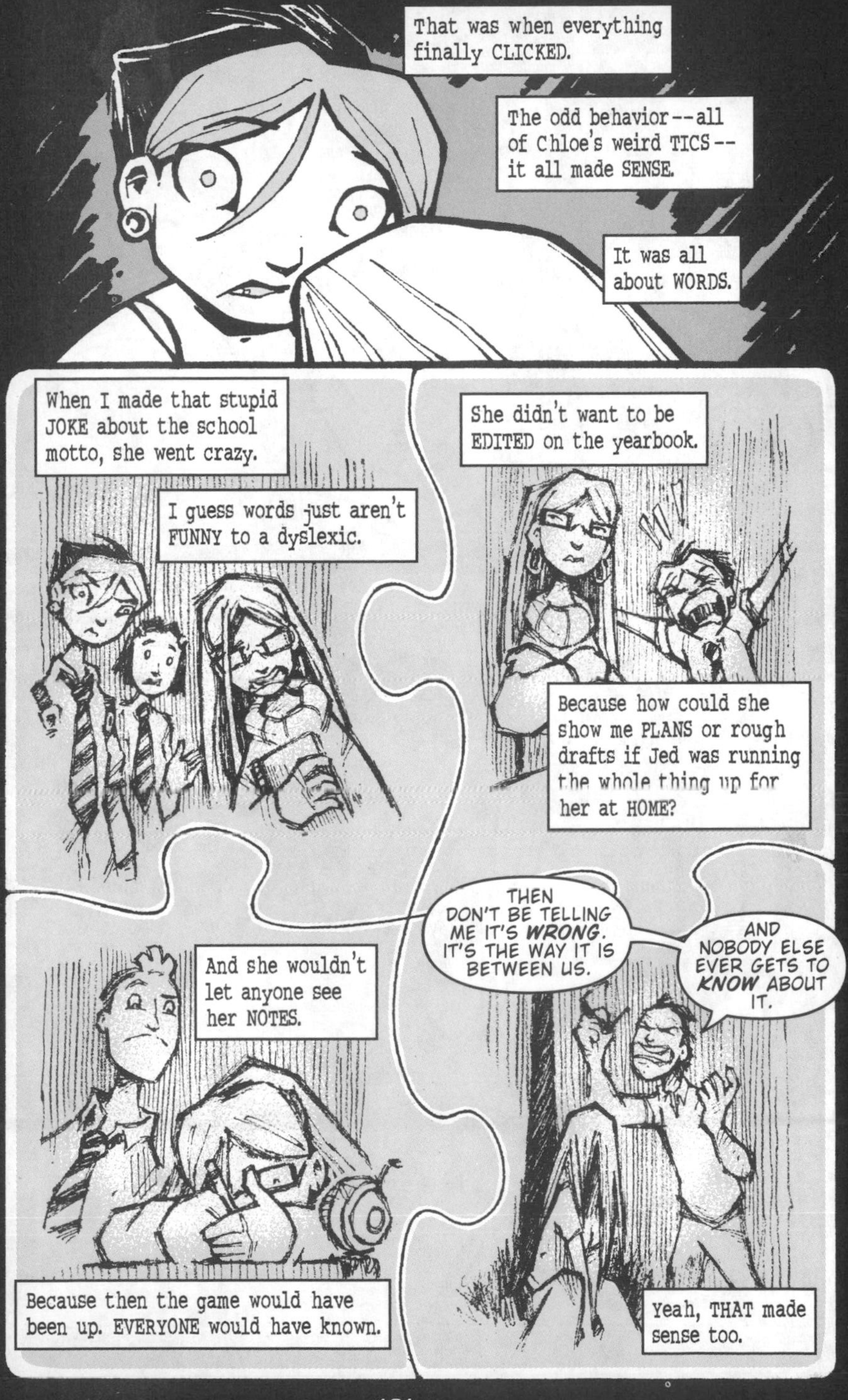
That was when everything finally CLICKED.
The odd behavior--all of Chloe's weird TICS--it all made SENSE.
It was all about WORDS.
When I made that stupid JOKE about the school motto, she went crazy.
I guess words just aren't FUNNY to a dyslexic.
She didn't want to be EDITED on the yearbook.
Because how could she show me PLANS or rough drafts if Jed was running the whole thing up for her at HOME?
And she wouldn't let anyone see her NOTES.
Because then the game would have been up. EVERYONE would have known.
THEN DON'T BE TELLING ME IT'S *WRONG*. IT'S THE WAY IT IS BETWEEN US.
AND NOBODY ELSE EVER GETS TO *KNOW* ABOUT IT.
Yeah, THAT made sense too.

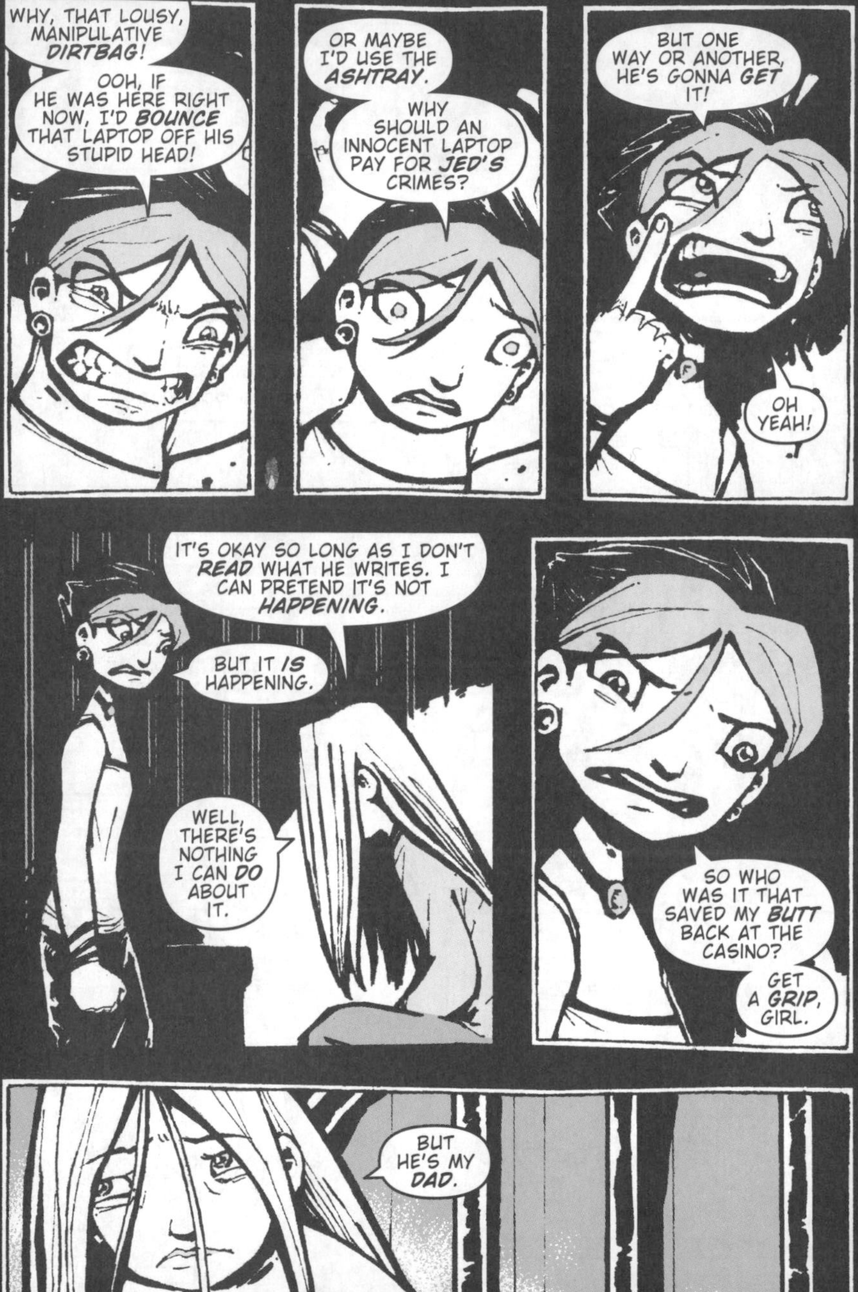
WHY, THAT LOUSY, MANIPULATIVE DIRTBAG!
OOH, IF HE WAS HERE RIGHT NOW, I'D BOUNCE THAT LAPTOP OFF HIS STUPID HEAD!
OR MAYBE I'D USE THE ASHTRAY.
WHY SHOULD AN INNOCENT LAPTOP PAY FOR JED'S CRIMES?
BUT ONE WAY OR ANOTHER, HE'S GONNA GET IT!
OH YEAH!
IT'S OKAY SO LONG AS I DON'T READ WHAT HE WRITES. I CAN PRETEND IT'S NOT HAPPENING.
BUT IT IS HAPPENING.
WELL, THERE'S NOTHING I CAN DO ABOUT IT.
SO WHO WAS IT THAT SAVED MY BUTT BACK AT THE CASINO?
GET A GRIP, GIRL.
BUT HE'S MY DAD.

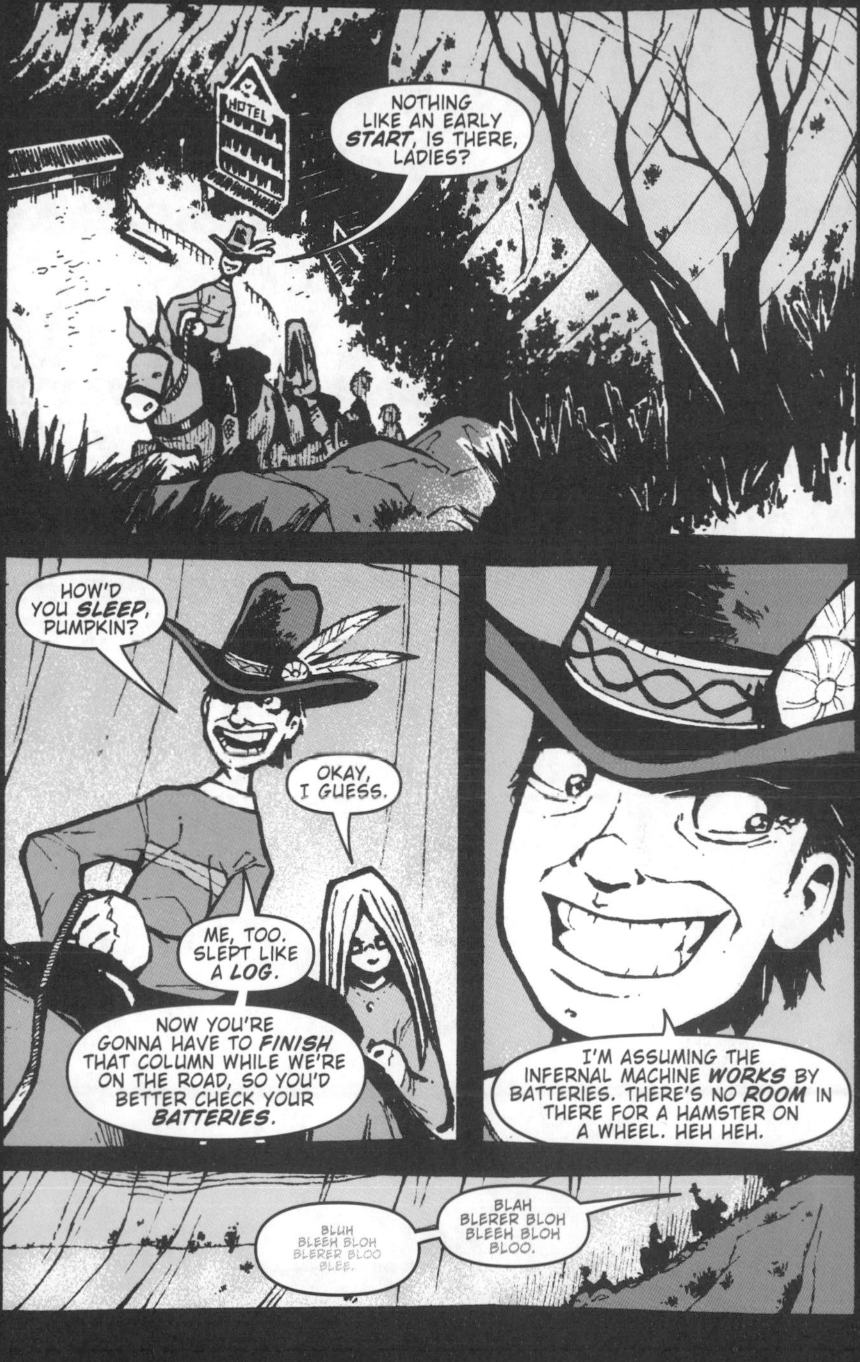
HOTEL
NOTHING LIKE AN EARLY **START**, IS THERE, LADIES?
HOW'D YOU **SLEEP**, PUMPKIN?
OKAY, I GUESS.
ME, TOO. SLEPT LIKE A **LOG**.
NOW YOU'RE GONNA HAVE TO **FINISH** THAT COLUMN WHILE WE'RE ON THE ROAD, SO YOU'D BETTER CHECK YOUR **BATTERIES**.
I'M ASSUMING THE INFERNAL MACHINE **WORKS** BY BATTERIES. THERE'S NO **ROOM** IN THERE FOR A HAMSTER ON A WHEEL. HEH HEH.
BLAH BLERER BLOH BLEEH BLOH BLOO.
BLUH BLEEH BLOH BLERER BLOO BLEE.

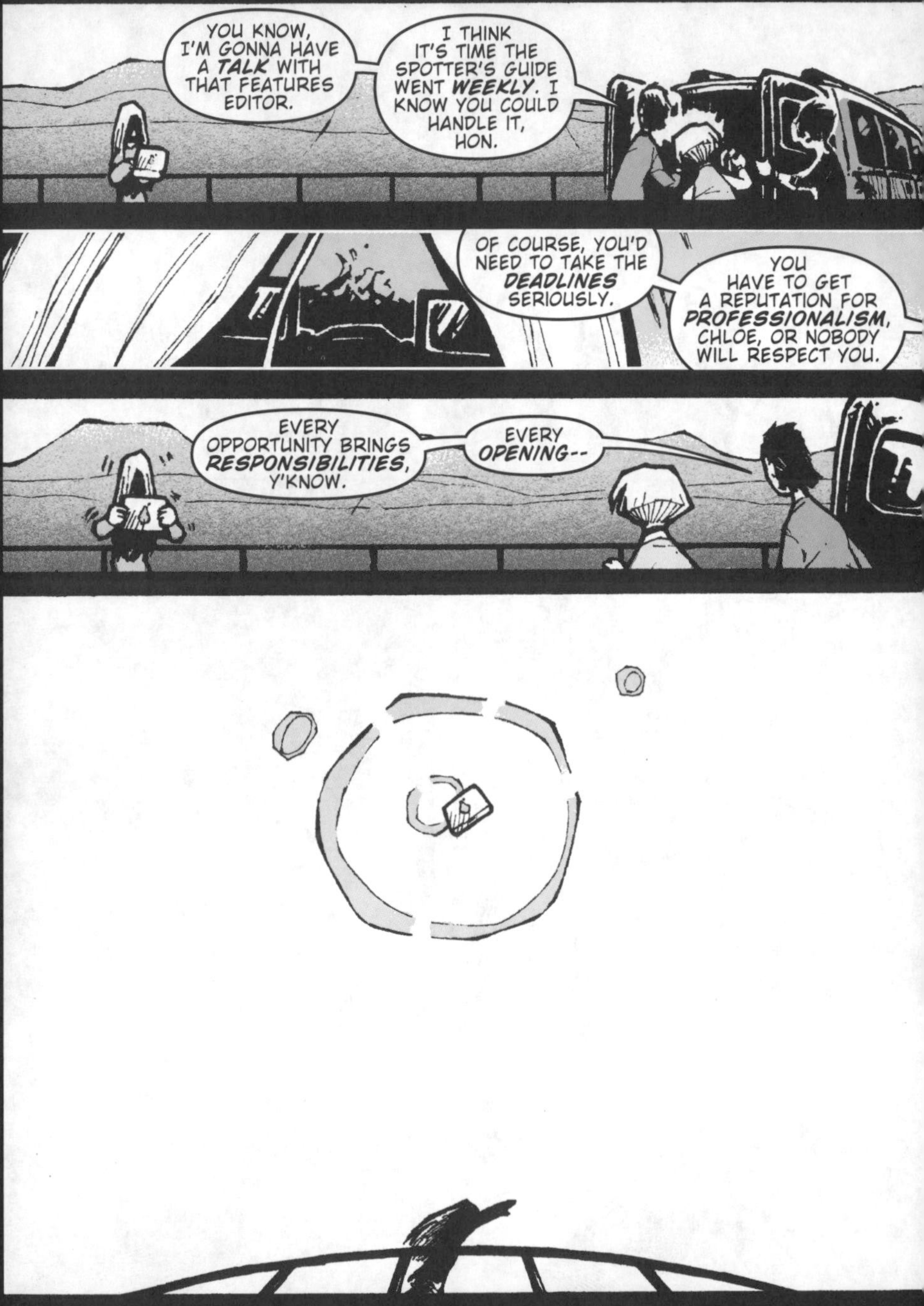
YOU KNOW, I'M GONNA HAVE A TALK WITH THAT FEATURES EDITOR.
I THINK IT'S TIME THE SPOTTER'S GUIDE WENT WEEKLY. I KNOW YOU COULD HANDLE IT, HON.
OF COURSE, YOU'D NEED TO TAKE THE DEADLINES SERIOUSLY.
YOU HAVE TO GET A REPUTATION FOR PROFESSIONALISM, CHLOE, OR NOBODY WILL RESPECT YOU.
EVERY OPPORTUNITY BRINGS RESPONSIBILITIES, Y'KNOW.
EVERY OPENING--

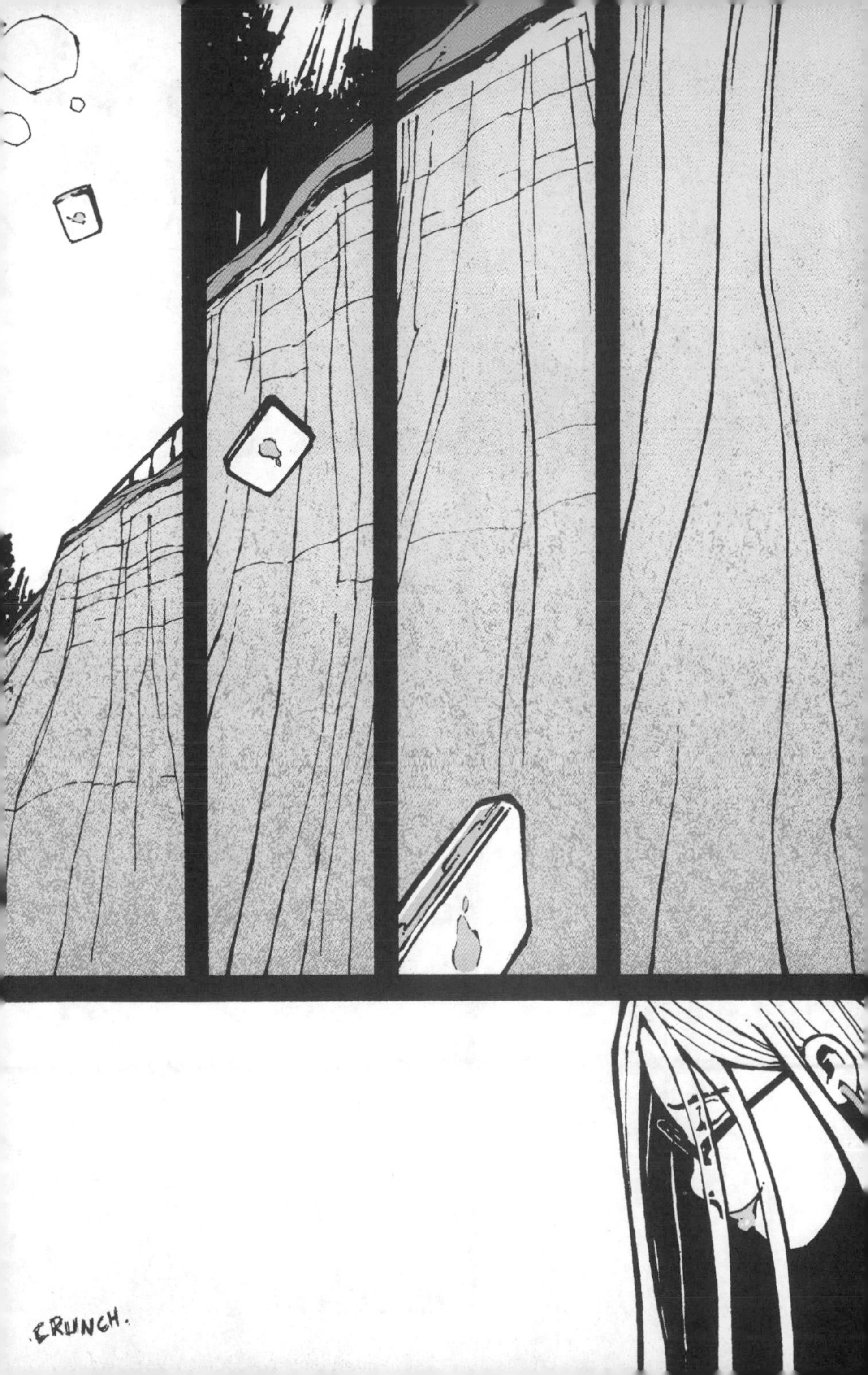
CRUNCH.

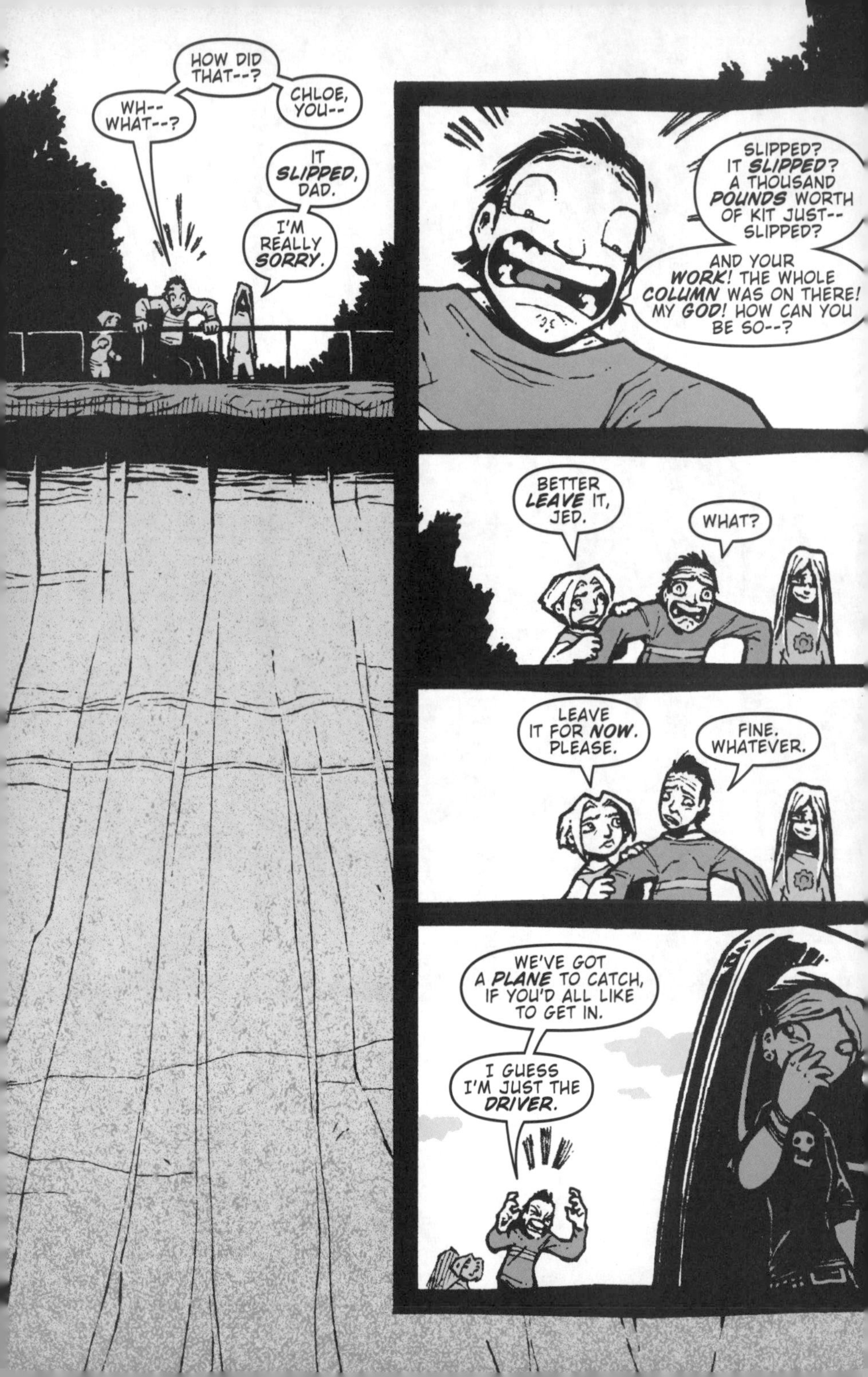

HOW DID THAT--?
WH-- WHAT--?
CHLOE, YOU--
IT SLIPPED, DAD.
I'M REALLY SORRY.
SLIPPED? IT SLIPPED? A THOUSAND POUNDS WORTH OF KIT JUST-- SLIPPED?
AND YOUR WORK! THE WHOLE COLUMN WAS ON THERE! MY GOD! HOW CAN YOU BE SO--?
BETTER LEAVE IT, JED.
WHAT?
LEAVE IT FOR NOW. PLEASE.
FINE. WHATEVER.
WE'VE GOT A PLANE TO CATCH, IF YOU'D ALL LIKE TO GET IN.
I GUESS I'M JUST THE DRIVER.

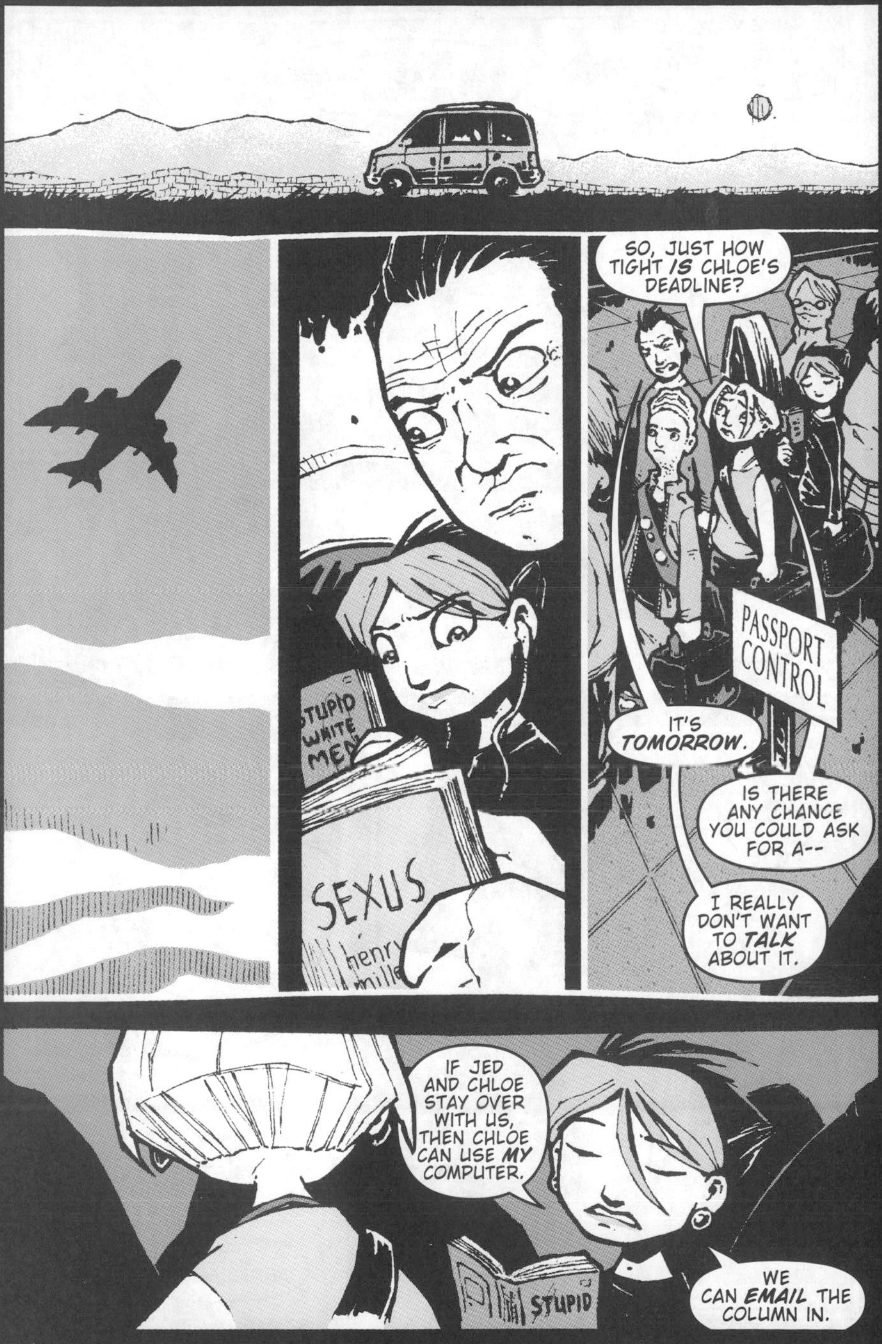
SO, JUST HOW TIGHT IS CHLOE'S DEADLINE?
PASSPORT CONTROL
IT'S TOMORROW.
IS THERE ANY CHANCE YOU COULD ASK FOR A--
I REALLY DON'T WANT TO TALK ABOUT IT.
STUPID WHITE MEN
SEXUS henry miller
IF JED AND CHLOE STAY OVER WITH US, THEN CHLOE CAN USE MY COMPUTER.
STUPID
WE CAN EMAIL THE COLUMN IN.

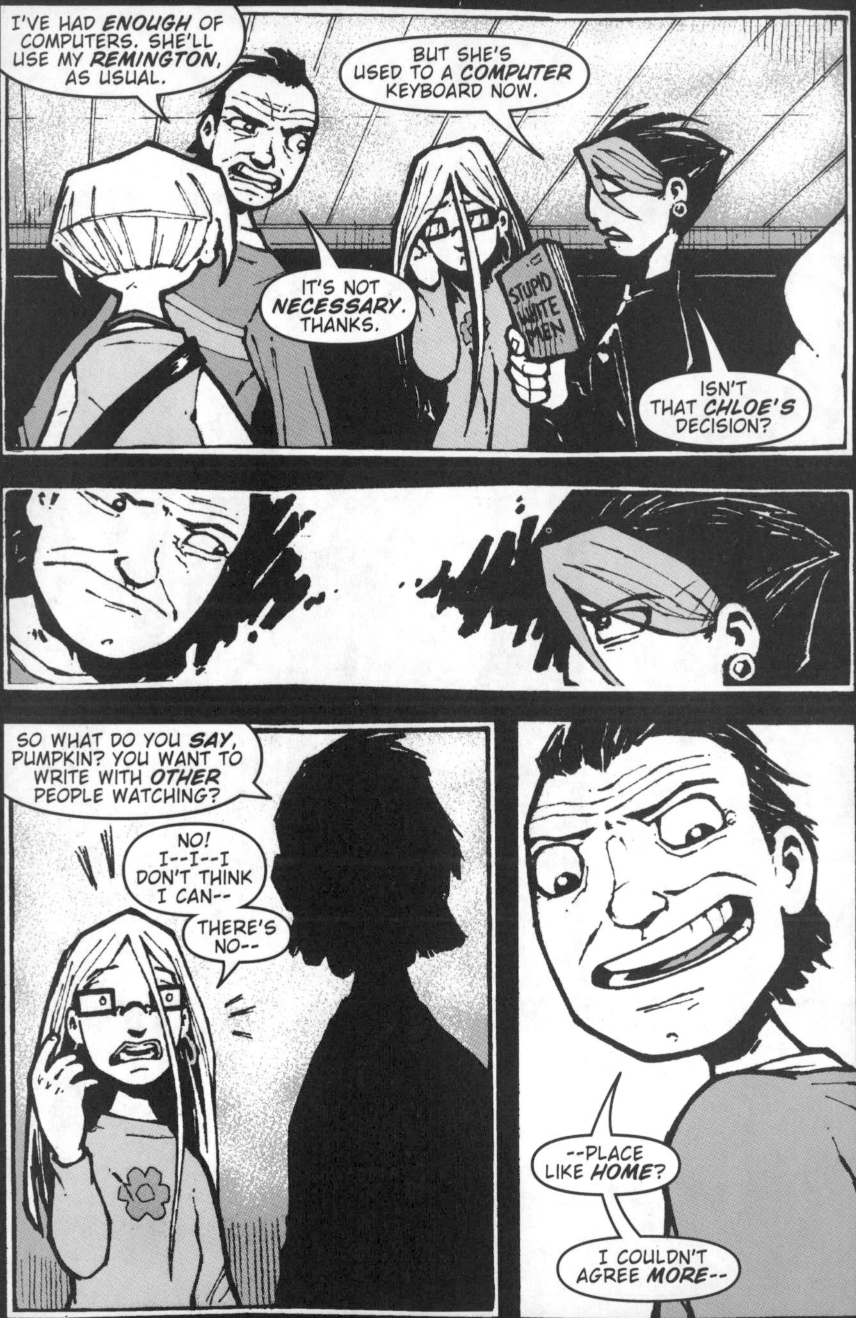
I'VE HAD ENOUGH OF COMPUTERS. SHE'LL USE MY REMINGTON, AS USUAL.
BUT SHE'S USED TO A COMPUTER KEYBOARD NOW.
IT'S NOT NECESSARY. THANKS.
STUPID WHITE MEN
ISN'T THAT CHLOE'S DECISION?
SO WHAT DO YOU SAY, PUMPKIN? YOU WANT TO WRITE WITH OTHER PEOPLE WATCHING?
NO! I--I--I DON'T THINK I CAN--
THERE'S NO--
--PLACE LIKE HOME?
I COULDN'T AGREE MORE--

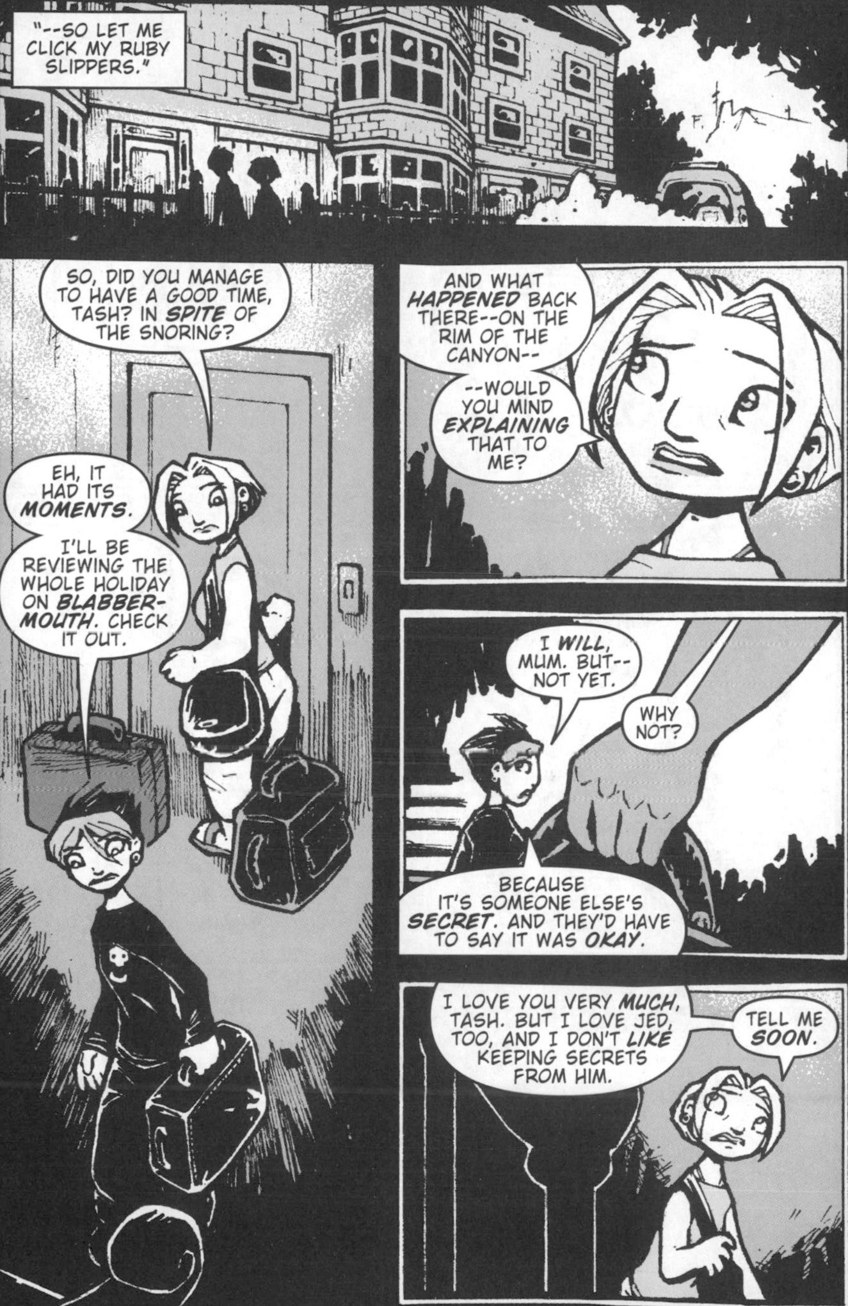
"--SO LET ME CLICK MY RUBY SLIPPERS."
SO, DID YOU MANAGE TO HAVE A GOOD TIME, TASH? IN SPITE OF THE SNORING?
EH, IT HAD ITS MOMENTS.
I'LL BE REVIEWING THE WHOLE HOLIDAY ON BLABBER-MOUTH. CHECK IT OUT.
AND WHAT HAPPENED BACK THERE--ON THE RIM OF THE CANYON--
--WOULD YOU MIND EXPLAINING THAT TO ME?
I WILL, MUM. BUT--NOT YET.
WHY NOT?
BECAUSE IT'S SOMEONE ELSE'S SECRET. AND THEY'D HAVE TO SAY IT WAS OKAY.
I LOVE YOU VERY MUCH, TASH. BUT I LOVE JED, TOO, AND I DON'T LIKE KEEPING SECRETS FROM HIM.
TELL ME SOON.

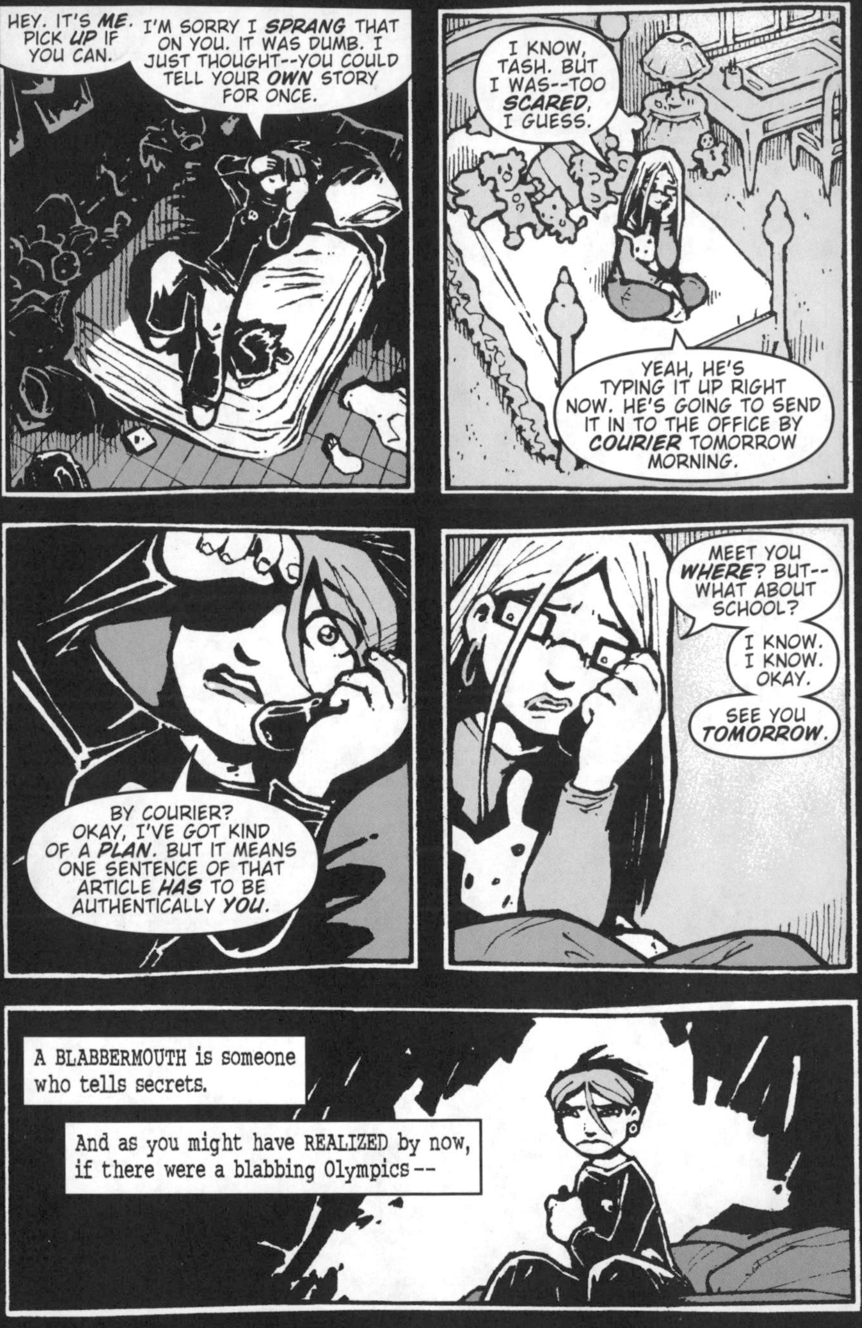
HEY. IT'S ME. PICK UP IF YOU CAN.
I'M SORRY I SPRANG THAT ON YOU. IT WAS DUMB. I JUST THOUGHT--YOU COULD TELL YOUR OWN STORY FOR ONCE.
I KNOW, TASH. BUT I WAS--TOO SCARED, I GUESS.
YEAH, HE'S TYPING IT UP RIGHT NOW. HE'S GOING TO SEND IT IN TO THE OFFICE BY COURIER TOMORROW MORNING.
BY COURIER? OKAY, I'VE GOT KIND OF A PLAN. BUT IT MEANS ONE SENTENCE OF THAT ARTICLE HAS TO BE AUTHENTICALLY YOU.
MEET YOU WHERE? BUT--WHAT ABOUT SCHOOL?
I KNOW. I KNOW. OKAY.
SEE YOU TOMORROW.
A BLABBERMOUTH is someone who tells secrets.
And as you might have REALIZED by now, if there were a blabbing Olympics--

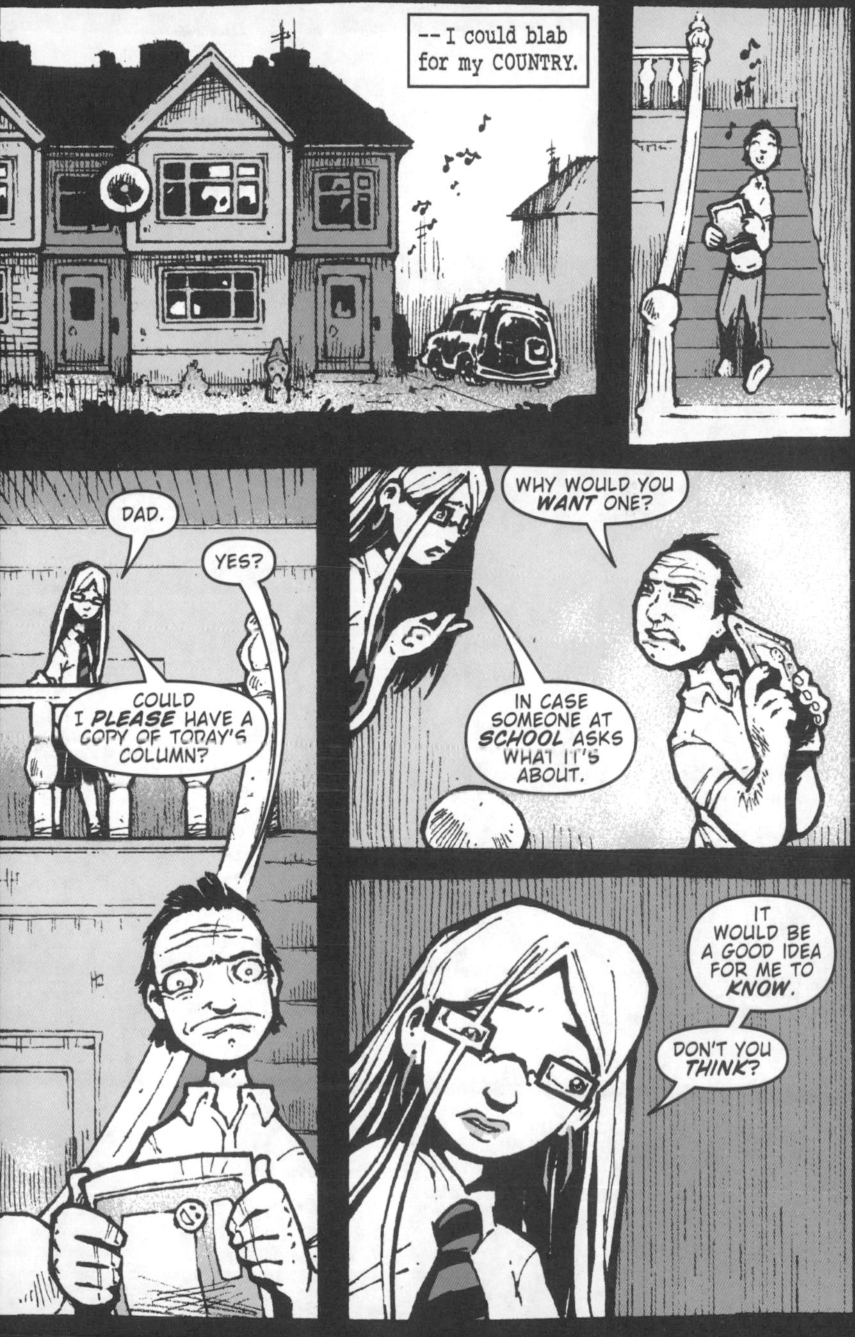

-- I could blab for my COUNTRY.
DAD.
YES?
COULD I PLEASE HAVE A COPY OF TODAY'S COLUMN?
WHY WOULD YOU WANT ONE?
IN CASE SOMEONE AT SCHOOL ASKS WHAT IT'S ABOUT.
IT WOULD BE A GOOD IDEA FOR ME TO KNOW.
DON'T YOU THINK?

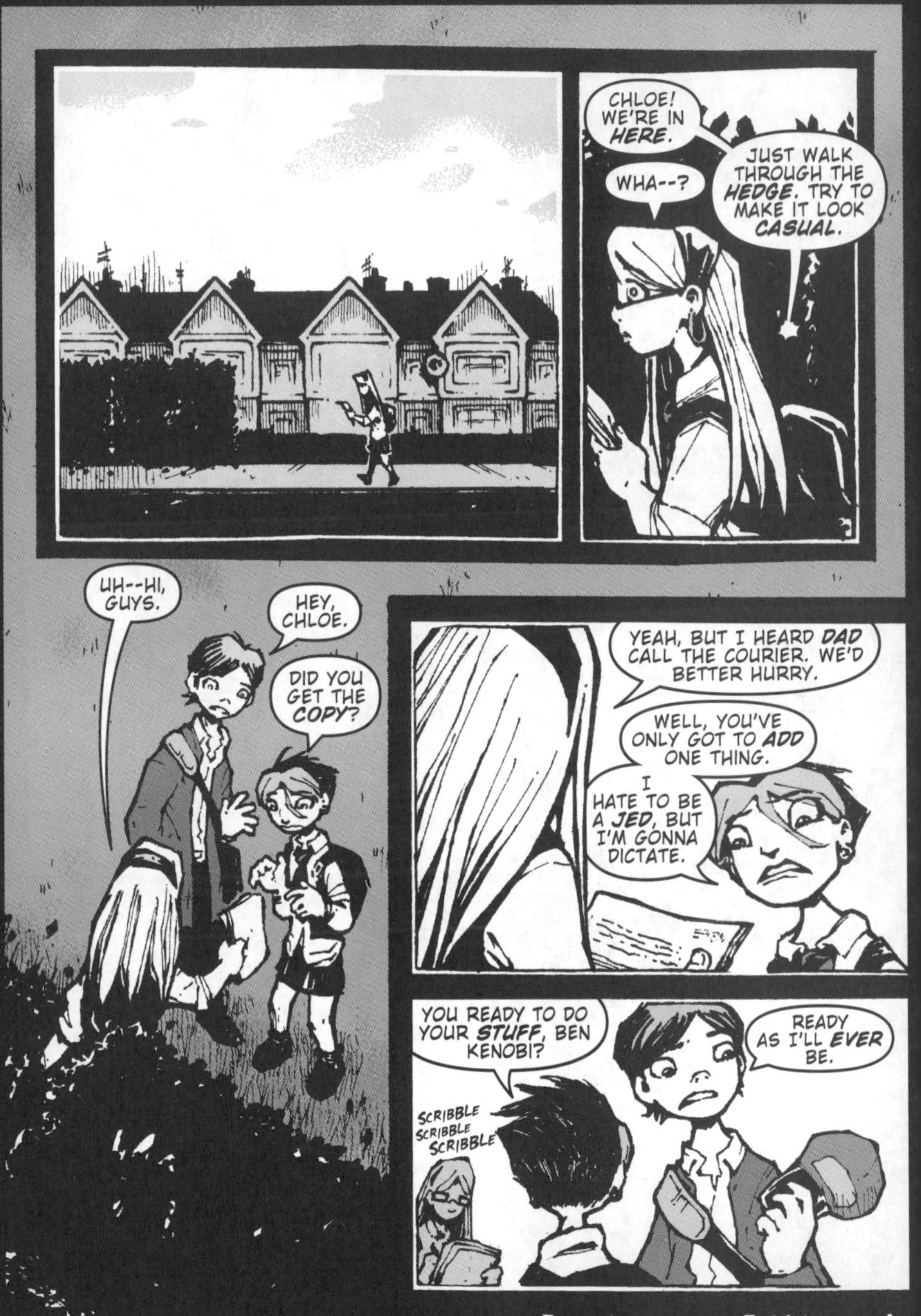
CHLOE! WE'RE IN HERE.
WHA--?
JUST WALK THROUGH THE HEDGE. TRY TO MAKE IT LOOK CASUAL.
UH--HI, GUYS.
HEY, CHLOE.
DID YOU GET THE COPY?
YEAH, BUT I HEARD DAD CALL THE COURIER. WE'D BETTER HURRY.
WELL, YOU'VE ONLY GOT TO ADD ONE THING.
I HATE TO BE A JED, BUT I'M GONNA DICTATE.
YOU READY TO DO YOUR STUFF, BEN KENOBI?
READY AS I'LL EVER BE.
SCRIBBLE SCRIBBLE SCRIBBLE

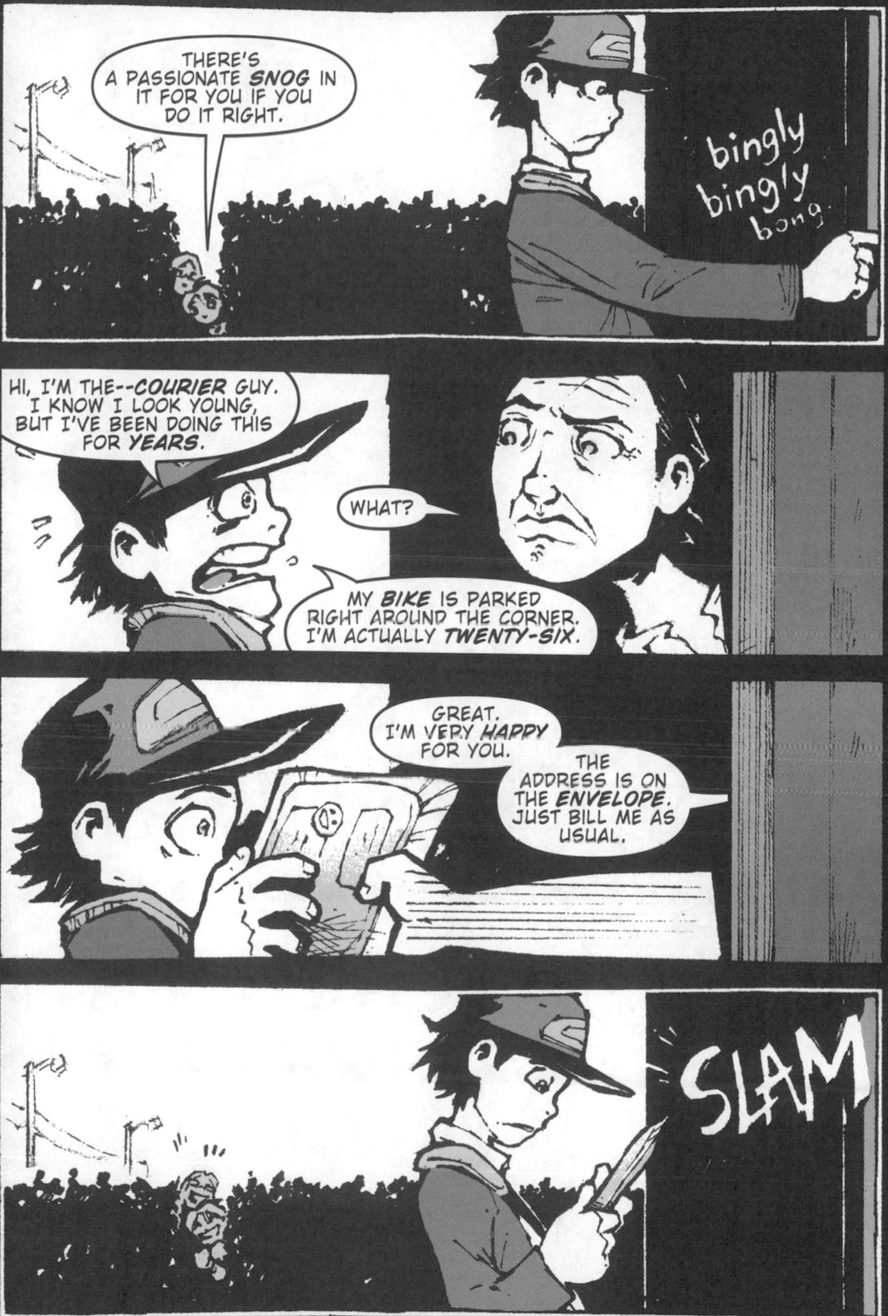
THERE'S A PASSIONATE SNOG IN IT FOR YOU IF YOU DO IT RIGHT.
bingly bingly bong.
HI, I'M THE--COURIER GUY. I KNOW I LOOK YOUNG, BUT I'VE BEEN DOING THIS FOR YEARS.
WHAT?
MY BIKE IS PARKED RIGHT AROUND THE CORNER. I'M ACTUALLY TWENTY-SIX.
GREAT. I'M VERY HAPPY FOR YOU.
THE ADDRESS IS ON THE ENVELOPE. JUST BILL ME AS USUAL.
SLAM

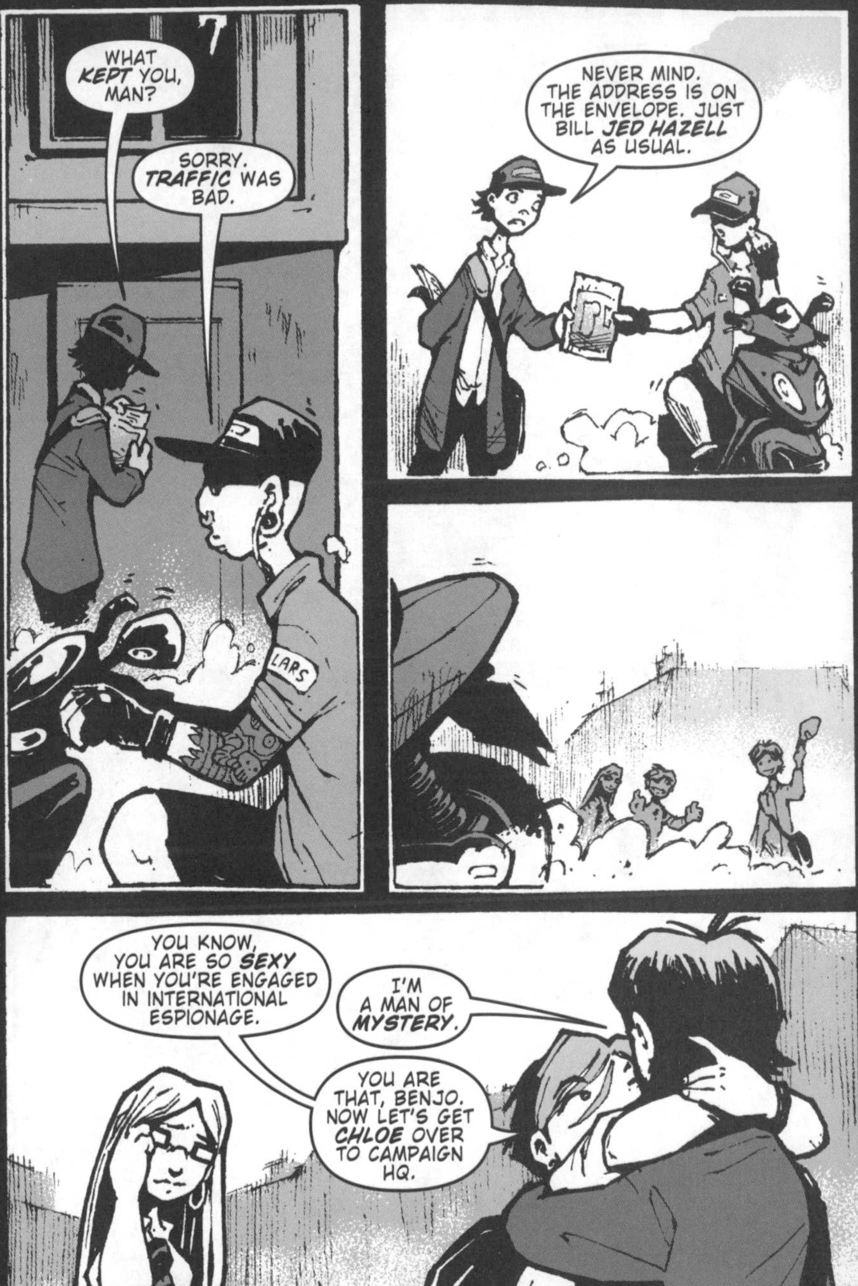
WHAT KEPT YOU, MAN?
SORRY. TRAFFIC WAS BAD.
LARS
NEVER MIND. THE ADDRESS IS ON THE ENVELOPE. JUST BILL JED HAZELL AS USUAL.
YOU KNOW, YOU ARE SO SEXY WHEN YOU'RE ENGAGED IN INTERNATIONAL ESPIONAGE.
I'M A MAN OF MYSTERY.
YOU ARE THAT, BENJO. NOW LET'S GET CHLOE OVER TO CAMPAIGN HQ.

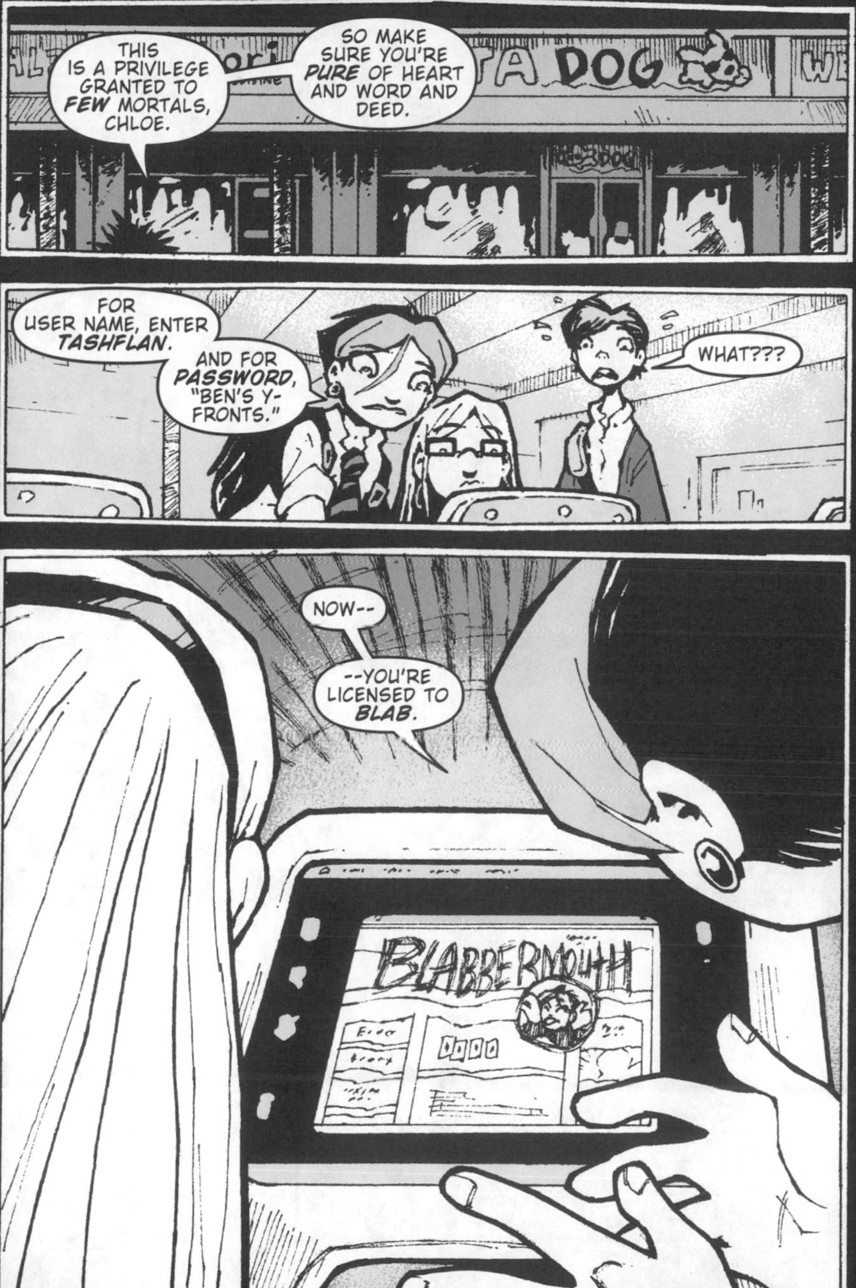
THIS IS A PRIVILEGE GRANTED TO *FEW* MORTALS, CHLOE.
SO MAKE SURE YOU'RE *PURE* OF HEART AND WORD AND DEED.
FOR USER NAME, ENTER *TASHFLAN*.
AND FOR *PASSWORD*, "BEN'S Y-FRONTS."
WHAT???
NOW--
--YOU'RE LICENSED TO *BLAB*.
BLABBERMOUTH

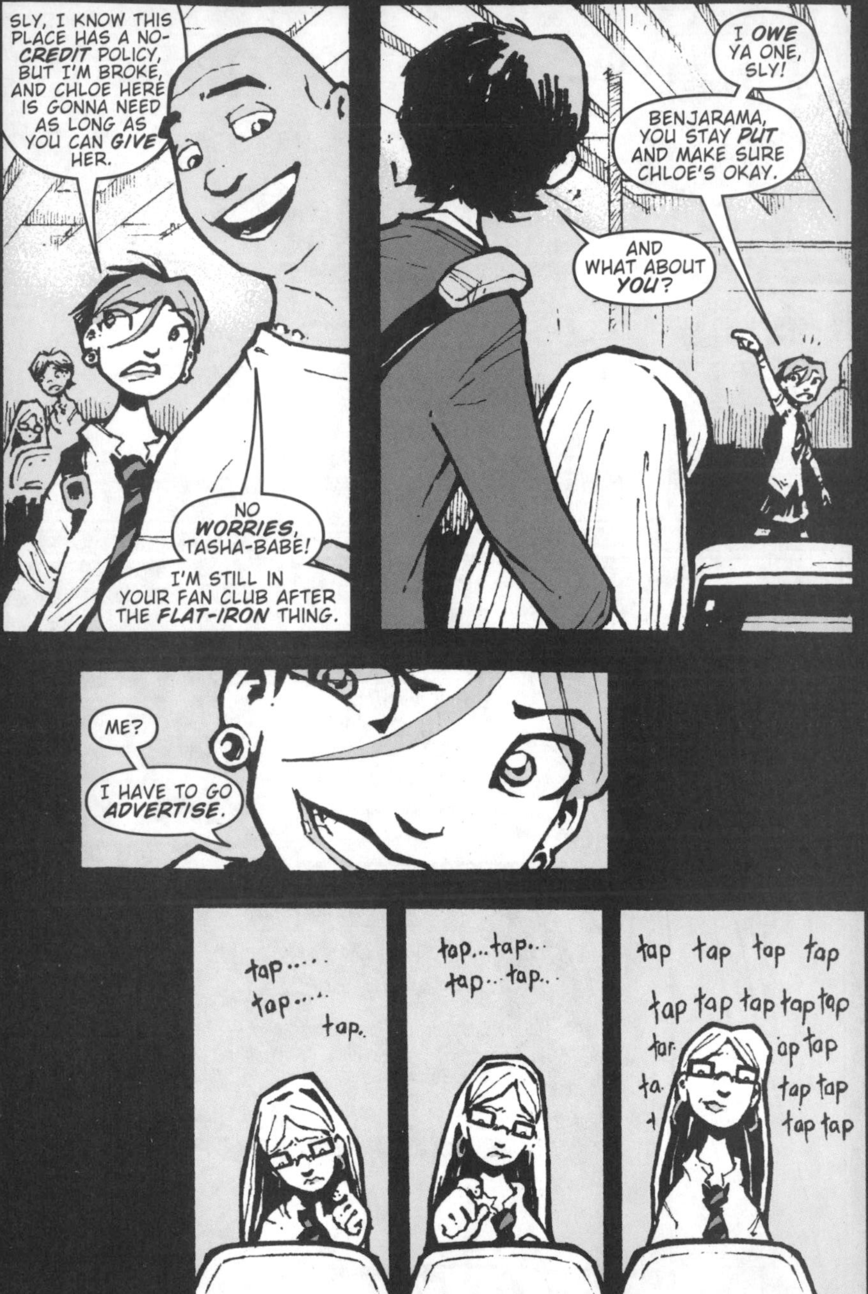
SLY, I KNOW THIS PLACE HAS A NO-CREDIT POLICY, BUT I'M BROKE, AND CHLOE HERE IS GONNA NEED AS LONG AS YOU CAN GIVE HER.
NO WORRIES, TASHA-BABE!
I'M STILL IN YOUR FAN CLUB AFTER THE FLAT-IRON THING.
I OWE YA ONE, SLY!
BENJARAMA, YOU STAY PUT AND MAKE SURE CHLOE'S OKAY.
AND WHAT ABOUT YOU?
ME?
I HAVE TO GO ADVERTISE.
tap..... tap..... tap..
tap...tap... tap...tap..
tap tap tap tap tap tap tap tap tap tap tap tap tap tap tap tap tap

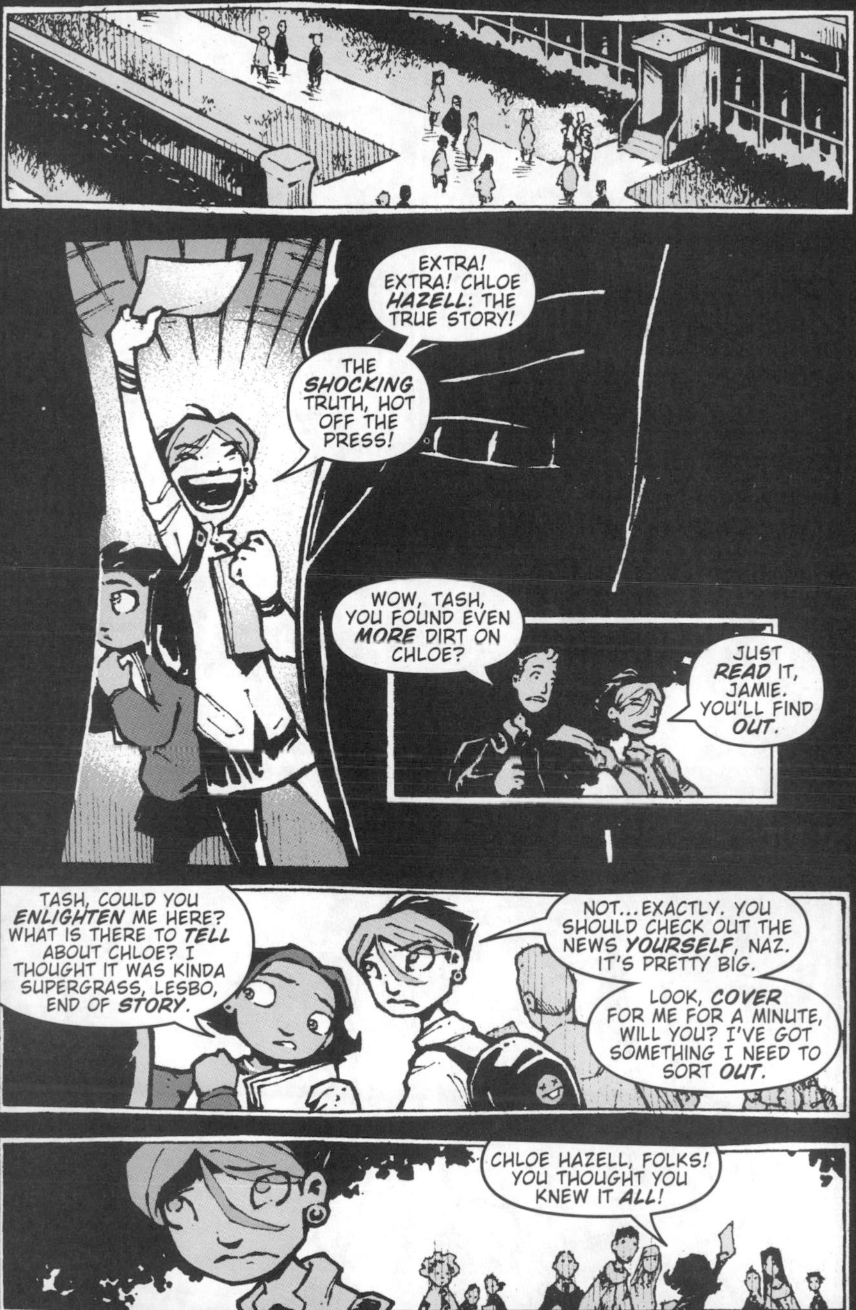
EXTRA! EXTRA! CHLOE HAZELL: THE TRUE STORY!
THE SHOCKING TRUTH, HOT OFF THE PRESS!
WOW, TASH, YOU FOUND EVEN MORE DIRT ON CHLOE?
JUST READ IT, JAMIE. YOU'LL FIND OUT.
TASH, COULD YOU ENLIGHTEN ME HERE? WHAT IS THERE TO TELL ABOUT CHLOE? I THOUGHT IT WAS KINDA SUPERGRASS, LESBO, END OF STORY.
NOT...EXACTLY. YOU SHOULD CHECK OUT THE NEWS YOURSELF, NAZ. IT'S PRETTY BIG.
LOOK, COVER FOR ME FOR A MINUTE, WILL YOU? I'VE GOT SOMETHING I NEED TO SORT OUT.
CHLOE HAZELL, FOLKS! YOU THOUGHT YOU KNEW IT ALL!

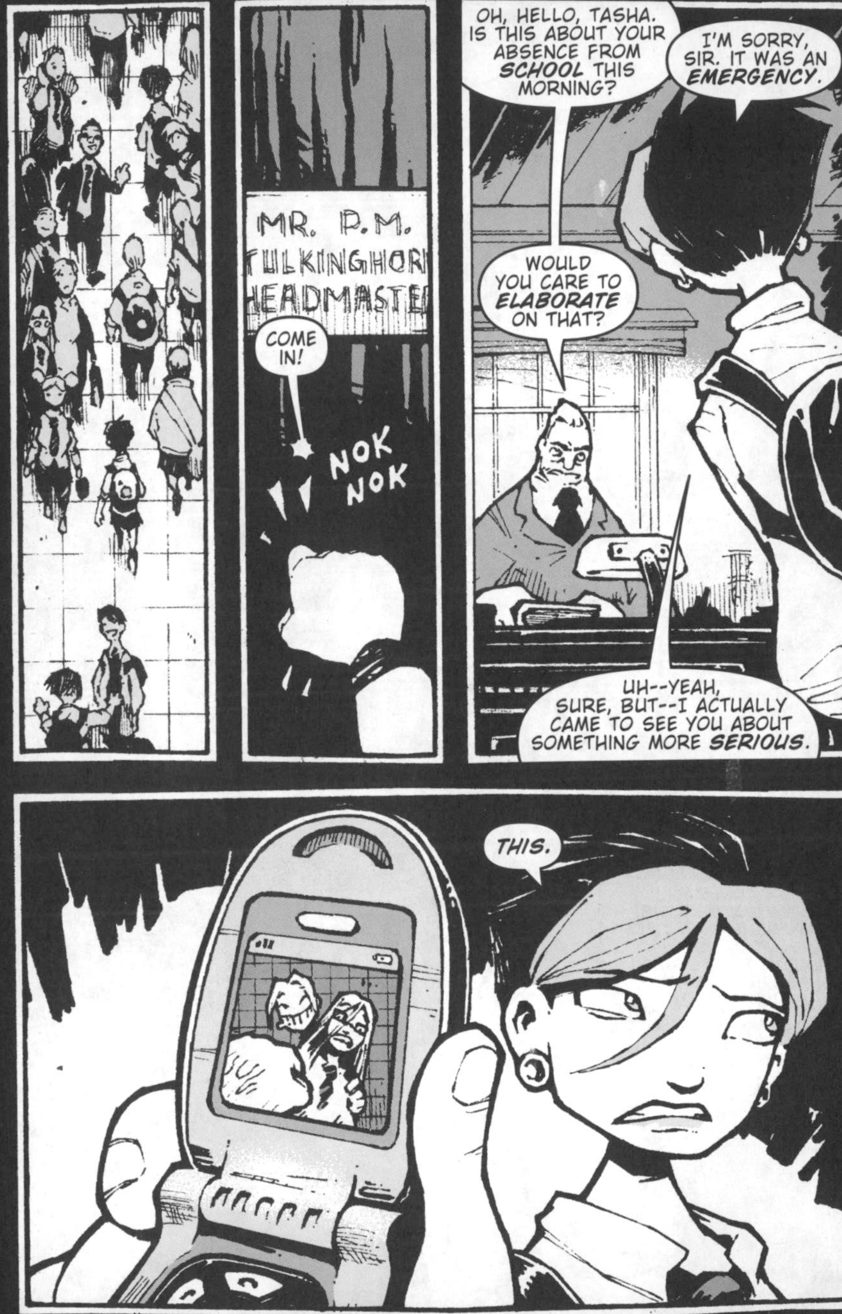
MR. P.M.
TULKINGHOR
HEADMASTE
COME IN!
NOK NOK
OH, HELLO, TASHA. IS THIS ABOUT YOUR ABSENCE FROM SCHOOL THIS MORNING?
I'M SORRY, SIR. IT WAS AN EMERGENCY.
WOULD YOU CARE TO ELABORATE ON THAT?
UH--YEAH, SURE, BUT--I ACTUALLY CAME TO SEE YOU ABOUT SOMETHING MORE SERIOUS.
THIS.

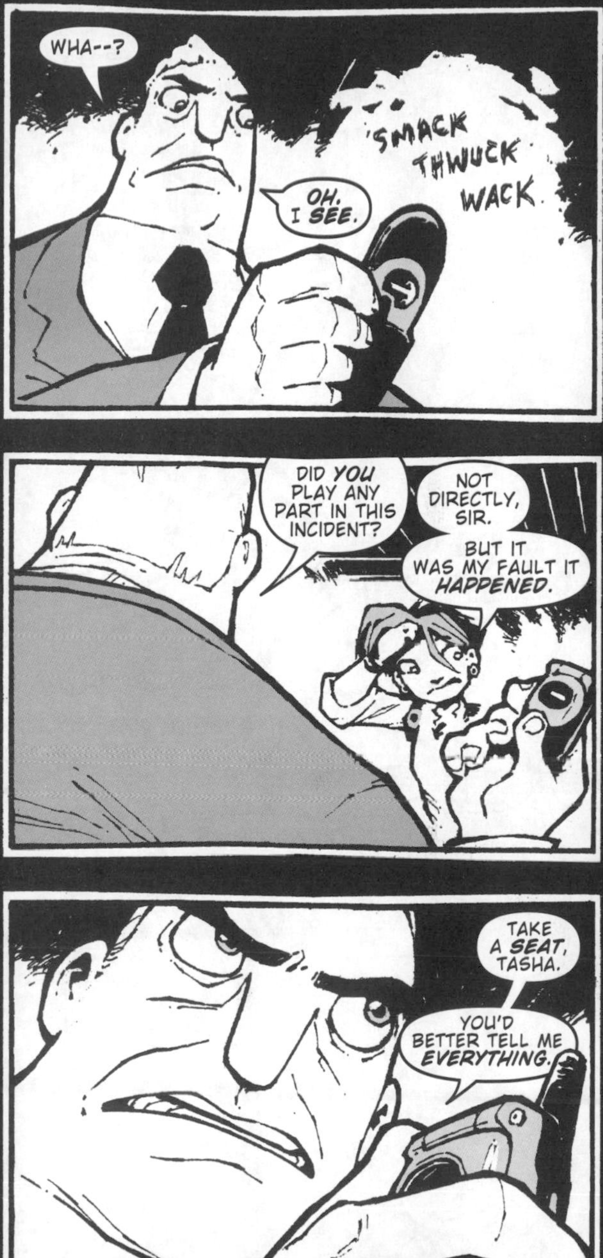
WHA--?
SMACK
THWUCK
WACK
OH. I SEE.
DID YOU PLAY ANY PART IN THIS INCIDENT?
NOT DIRECTLY, SIR.
BUT IT WAS MY FAULT IT HAPPENED.
TAKE A SEAT, TASHA.
YOU'D BETTER TELL ME EVERYTHING.

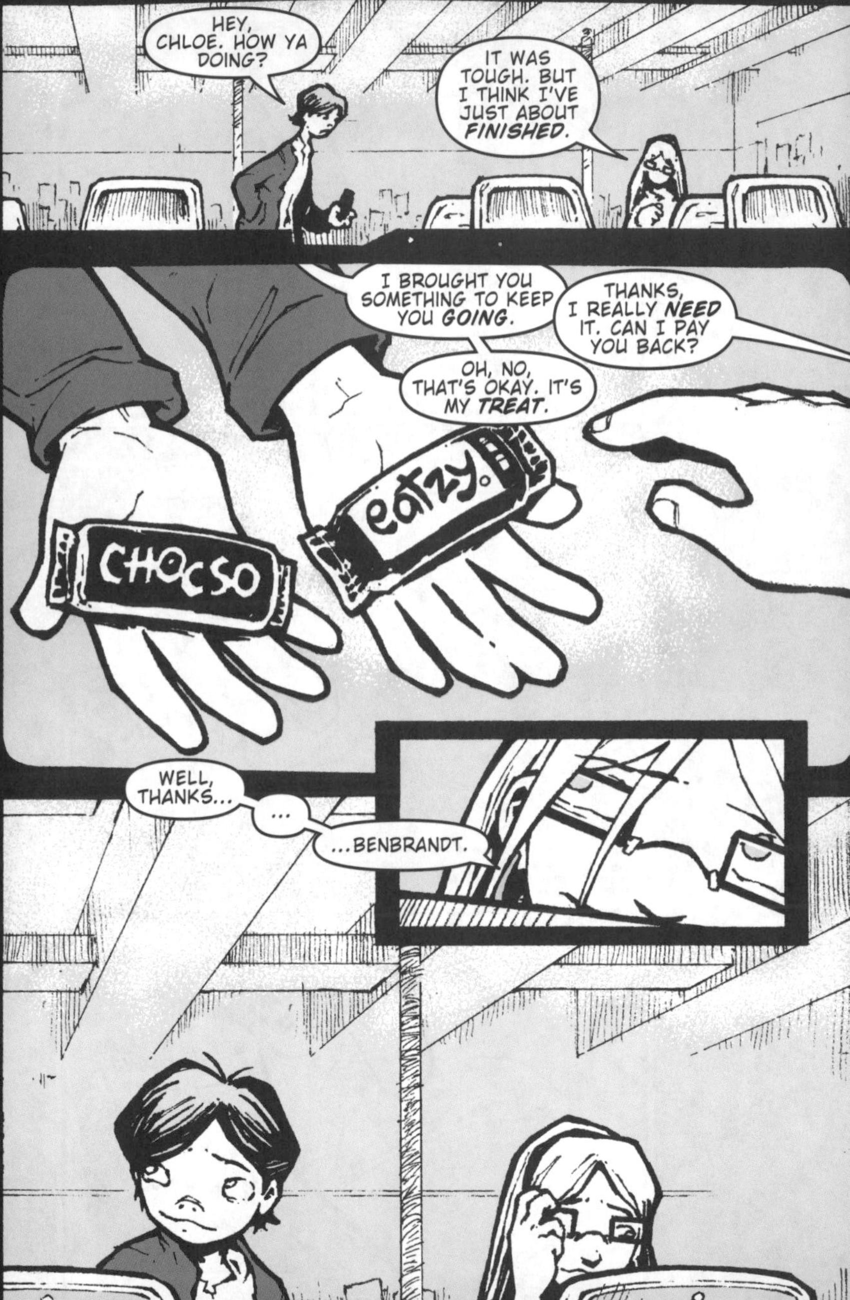
HEY, CHLOE. HOW YA DOING?
IT WAS TOUGH. BUT I THINK I'VE JUST ABOUT FINISHED.
I BROUGHT YOU SOMETHING TO KEEP YOU GOING.
THANKS, I REALLY NEED IT. CAN I PAY YOU BACK?
OH, NO, THAT'S OKAY. IT'S MY TREAT.
CHOCSO
eatzy.
WELL, THANKS...
...
...BENBRANDT.

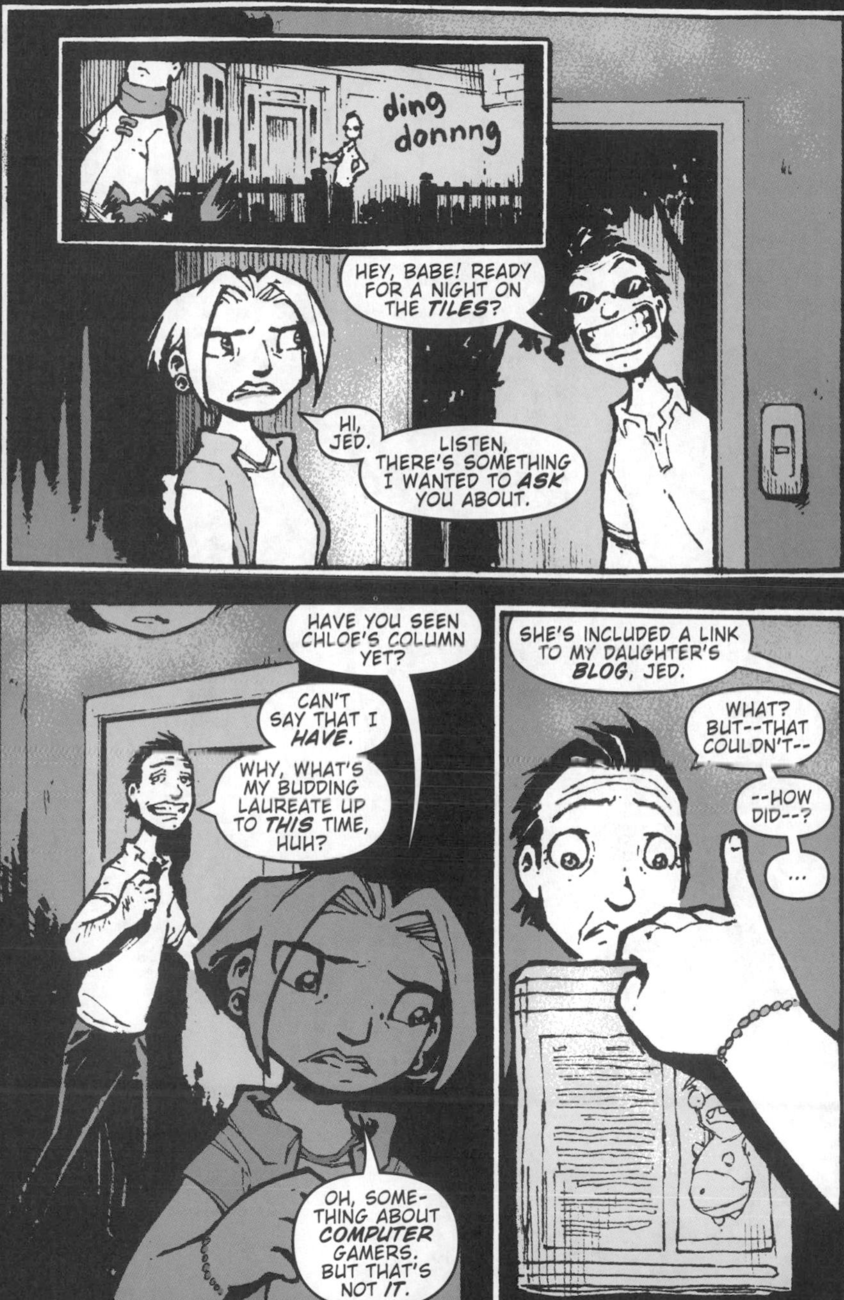
ding donnng
HEY, BABE! READY FOR A NIGHT ON THE *TILES*?
HI, JED.
LISTEN, THERE'S SOMETHING I WANTED TO *ASK* YOU ABOUT.
HAVE YOU SEEN CHLOE'S COLUMN YET?
CAN'T SAY THAT I *HAVE*.
WHY, WHAT'S MY BUDDING LAUREATE UP TO *THIS* TIME, HUH?
OH, SOMETHING ABOUT *COMPUTER* GAMERS. BUT THAT'S NOT *IT*.
SHE'S INCLUDED A LINK TO MY DAUGHTER'S *BLOG*, JED.
WHAT? BUT--THAT COULDN'T--
--HOW DID--?
...

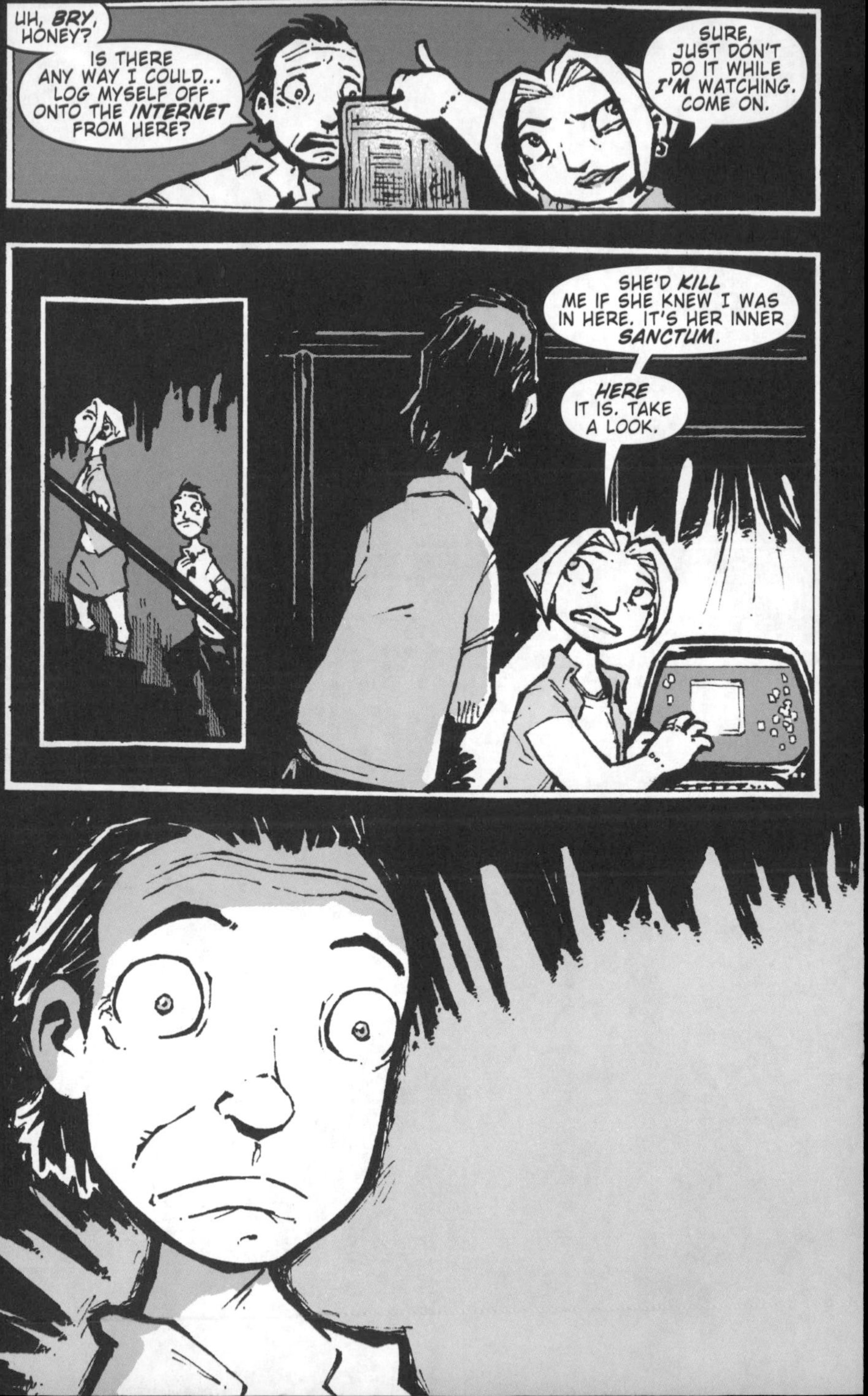
UH, BRY, HONEY?
IS THERE ANY WAY I COULD... LOG MYSELF OFF ONTO THE INTERNET FROM HERE?
SURE, JUST DON'T DO IT WHILE I'M WATCHING. COME ON.
SHE'D KILL ME IF SHE KNEW I WAS IN HERE. IT'S HER INNER SANCTUM.
HERE IT IS. TAKE A LOOK.

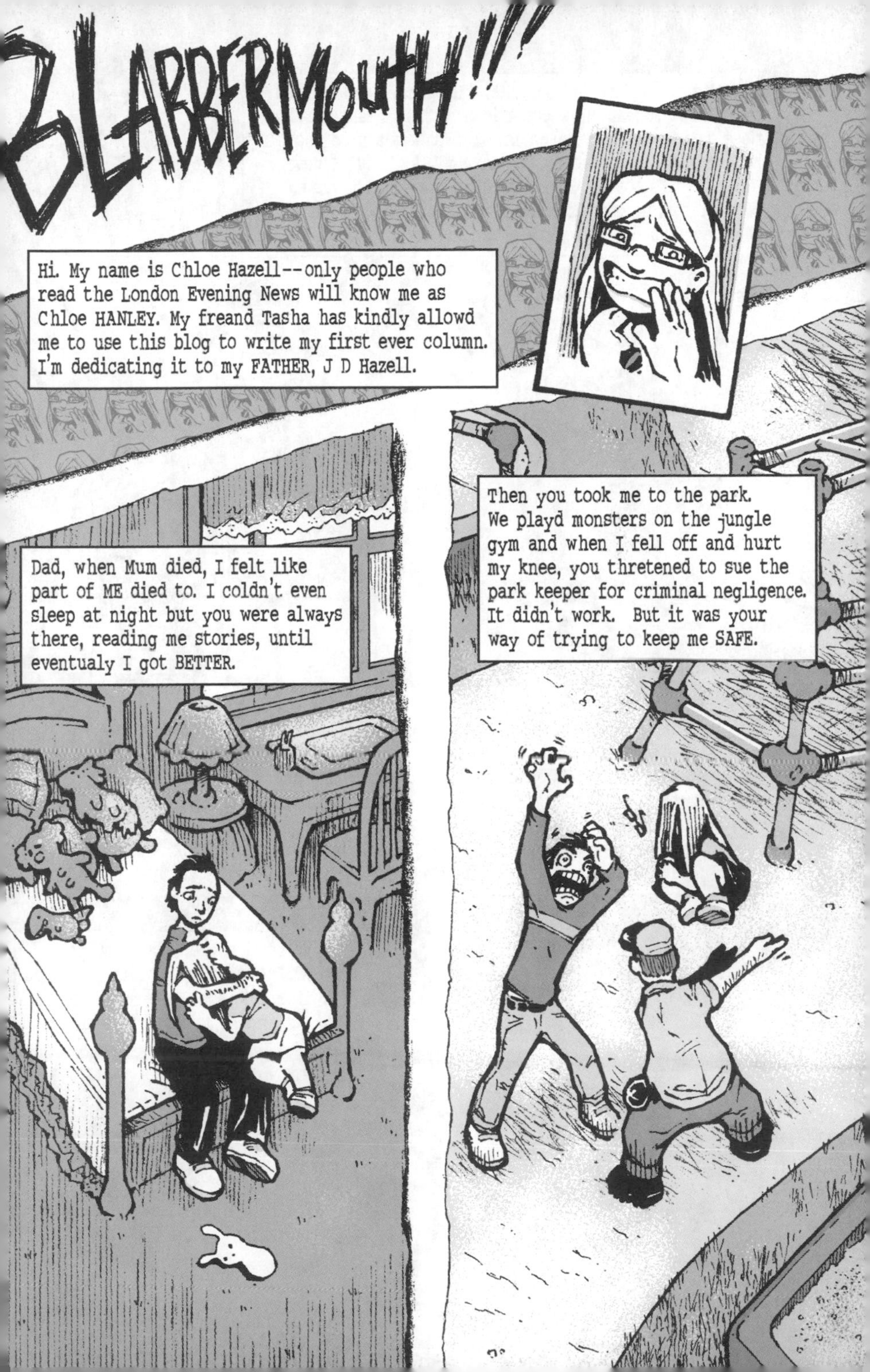
BLABBERMOUTH!!
Hi. My name is Chloe Hazell--only people who read the London Evening News will know me as Chloe HANLEY. My freand Tasha has kindly allowd me to use this blog to write my first ever column. I'm dedicating it to my FATHER, J D Hazell.
Dad, when Mum died, I felt like part of ME died to. I coldn't even sleep at night but you were always there, reading me stories, until eventualy I got BETTER.
Then you took me to the park. We playd monsters on the jungle gym and when I fell off and hurt my knee, you thretened to sue the park keeper for criminal negligence. It didn't work. But it was your way of trying to keep me SAFE.

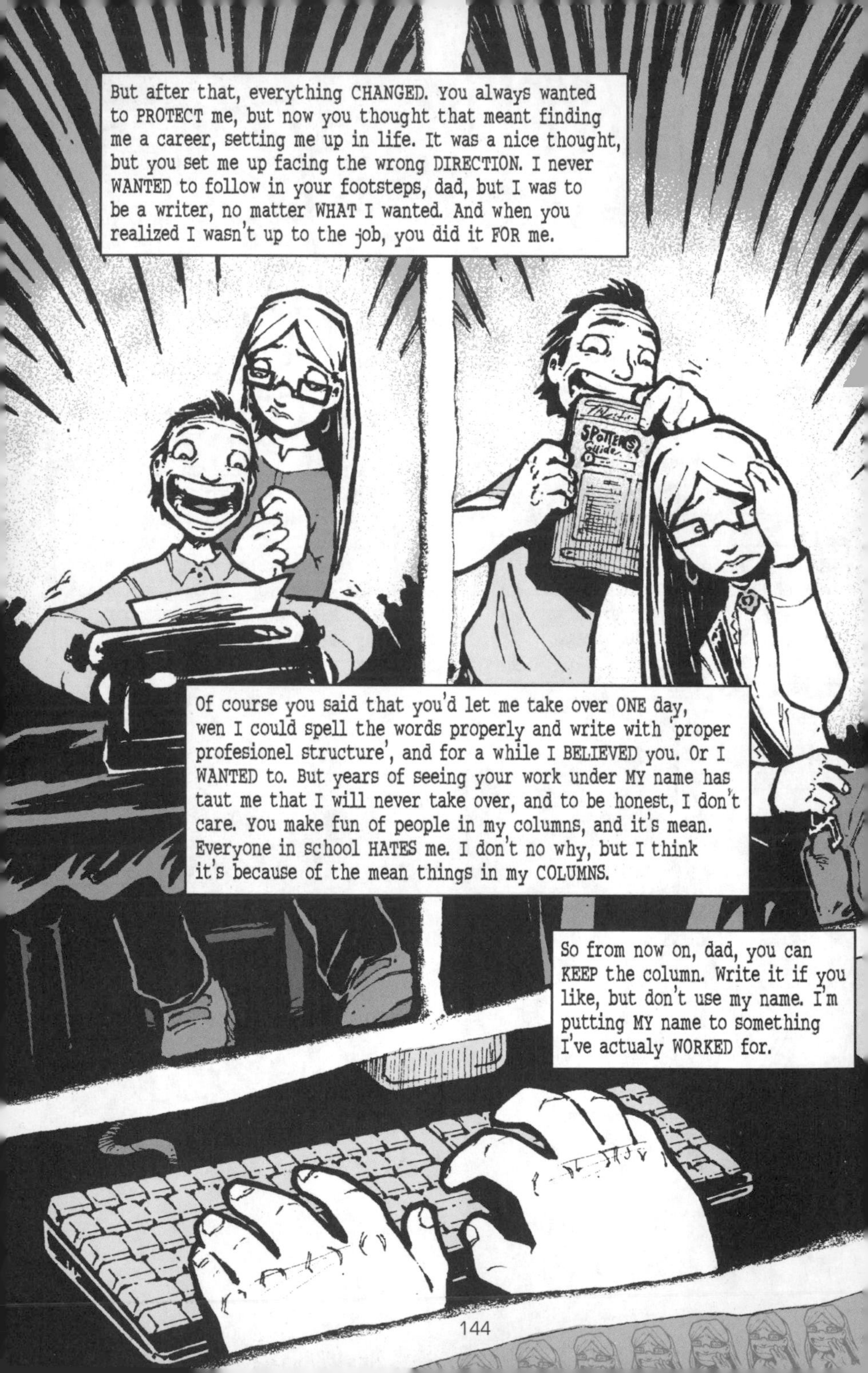
But after that, everything CHANGED. You always wanted to PROTECT me, but now you thought that meant finding me a career, setting me up in life. It was a nice thought, but you set me up facing the wrong DIRECTION. I never WANTED to follow in your footsteps, dad, but I was to be a writer, no matter WHAT I wanted. And when you realized I wasn't up to the job, you did it FOR me.
Of course you said that you'd let me take over ONE day, wen I could spell the words properly and write with 'proper profesionel structure', and for a while I BELIEVED you. Or I WANTED to. But years of seeing your work under MY name has taut me that I will never take over, and to be honest, I don't care. You make fun of people in my columns, and it's mean. Everyone in school HATES me. I don't no why, but I think it's because of the mean things in my COLUMNS.
So from now on, dad, you can KEEP the column. Write it if you like, but don't use my name. I'm putting MY name to something I've actualy WORKED for.

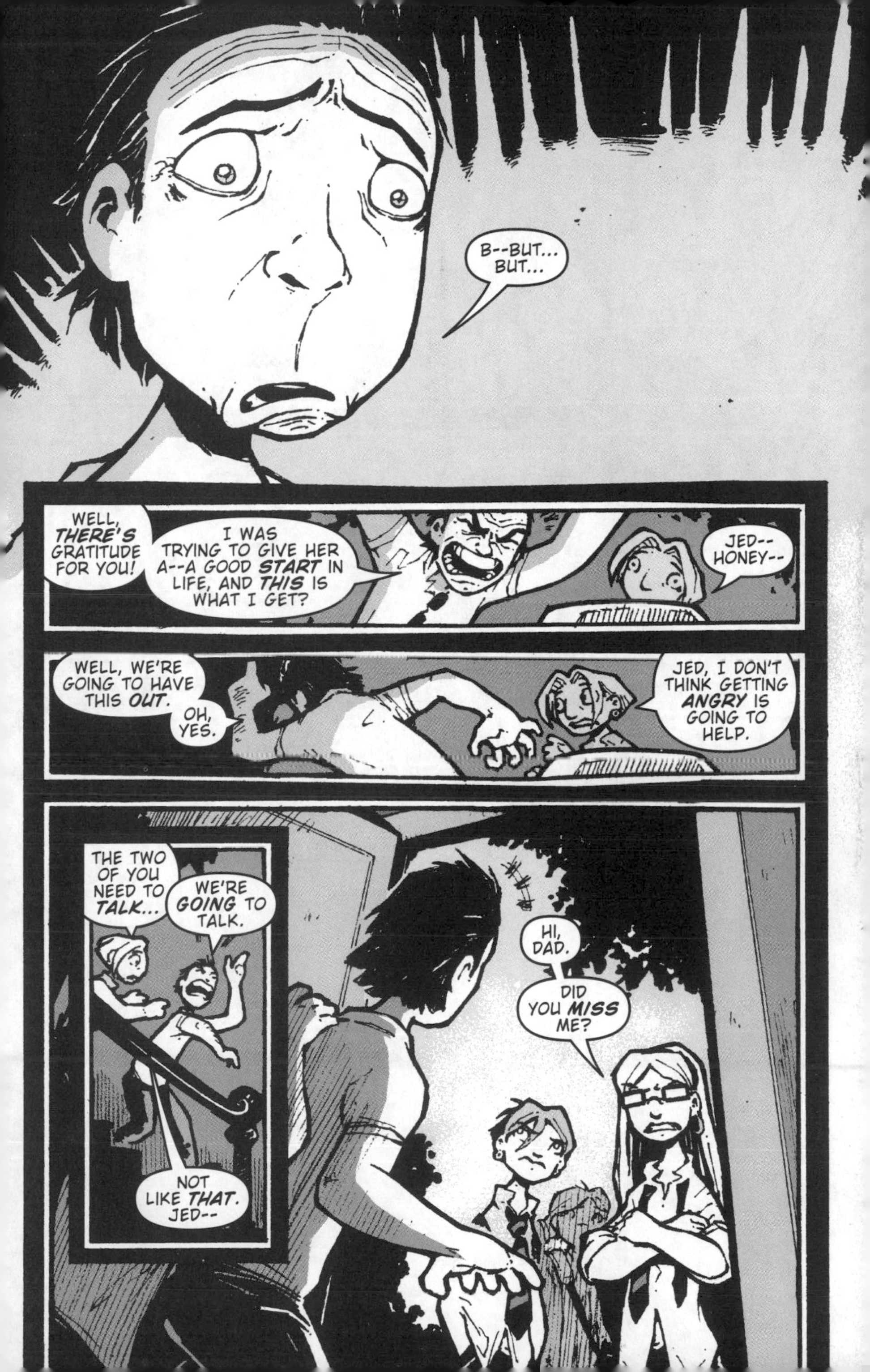
B--BUT... BUT...
WELL, THERE'S GRATITUDE FOR YOU!
I WAS TRYING TO GIVE HER A--A GOOD START IN LIFE, AND THIS IS WHAT I GET?
JED-- HONEY--
WELL, WE'RE GOING TO HAVE THIS OUT.
OH, YES.
JED, I DON'T THINK GETTING ANGRY IS GOING TO HELP.
THE TWO OF YOU NEED TO TALK...
WE'RE GOING TO TALK.
NOT LIKE THAT. JED--
HI, DAD.
DID YOU MISS ME?

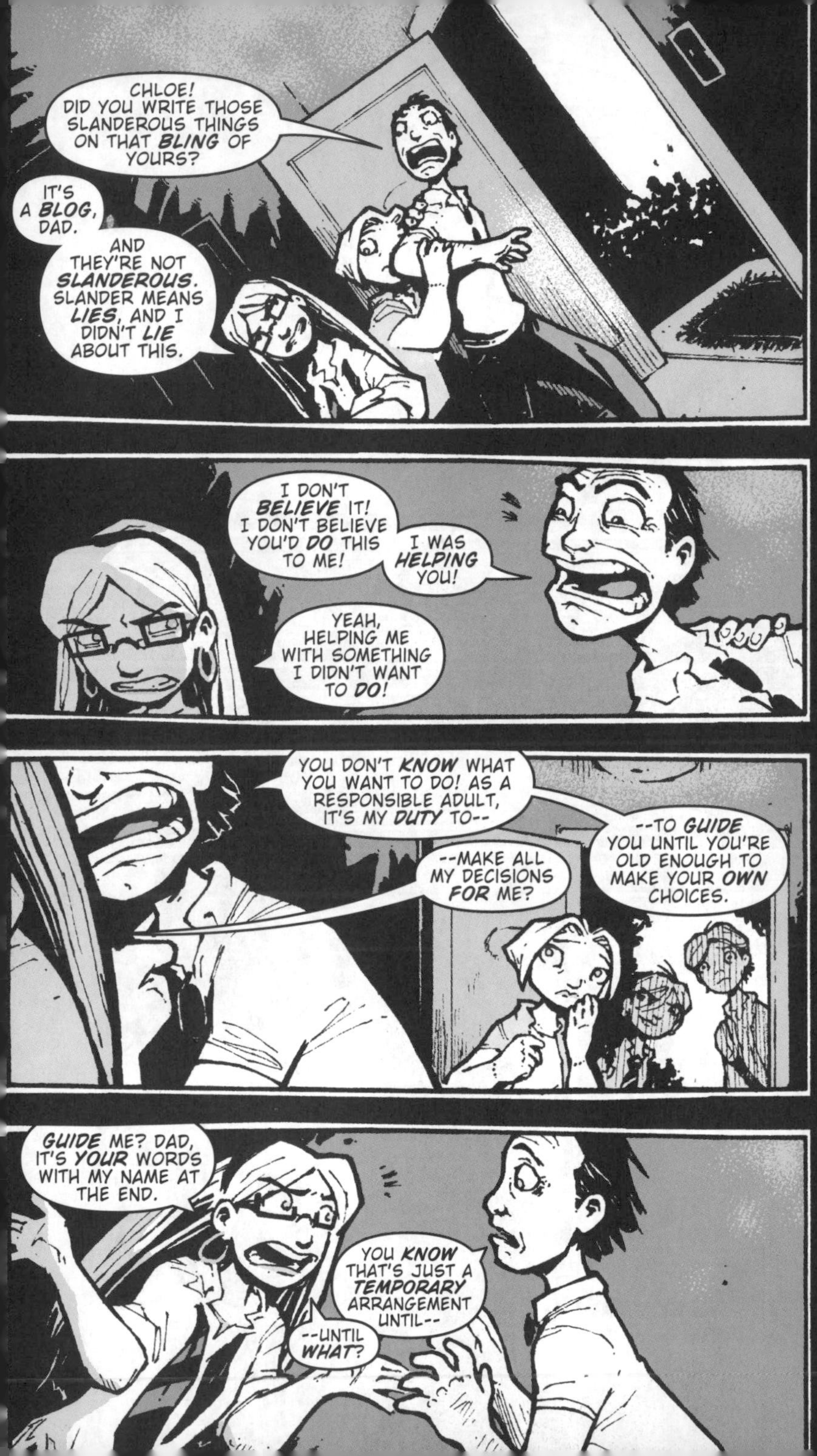
CHLOE! DID YOU WRITE THOSE SLANDEROUS THINGS ON THAT BLING OF YOURS?
IT'S A BLOG, DAD.
AND THEY'RE NOT SLANDEROUS. SLANDER MEANS LIES, AND I DIDN'T LIE ABOUT THIS.
I DON'T BELIEVE IT! I DON'T BELIEVE YOU'D DO THIS TO ME!
I WAS HELPING YOU!
YEAH, HELPING ME WITH SOMETHING I DIDN'T WANT TO DO!
YOU DON'T KNOW WHAT YOU WANT TO DO! AS A RESPONSIBLE ADULT, IT'S MY DUTY TO--
--MAKE ALL MY DECISIONS FOR ME?
--TO GUIDE YOU UNTIL YOU'RE OLD ENOUGH TO MAKE YOUR OWN CHOICES.
GUIDE ME? DAD, IT'S YOUR WORDS WITH MY NAME AT THE END.
YOU KNOW THAT'S JUST A TEMPORARY ARRANGEMENT UNTIL--
--UNTIL WHAT?

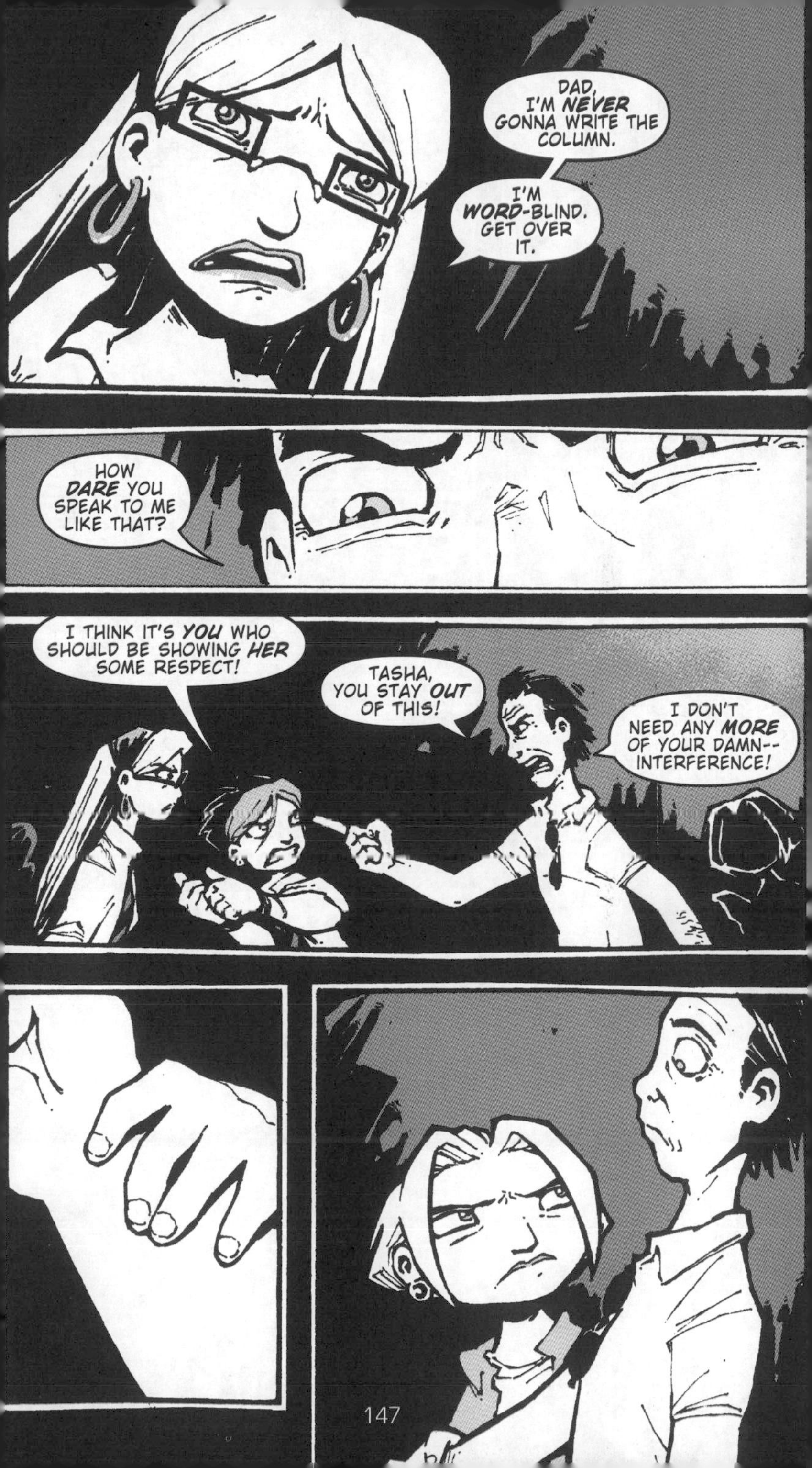
DAD, I'M NEVER GONNA WRITE THE COLUMN.
I'M WORD-BLIND. GET OVER IT.
HOW DARE YOU SPEAK TO ME LIKE THAT?
I THINK IT'S YOU WHO SHOULD BE SHOWING HER SOME RESPECT!
TASHA, YOU STAY OUT OF THIS!
I DON'T NEED ANY MORE OF YOUR DAMN--INTERFERENCE!

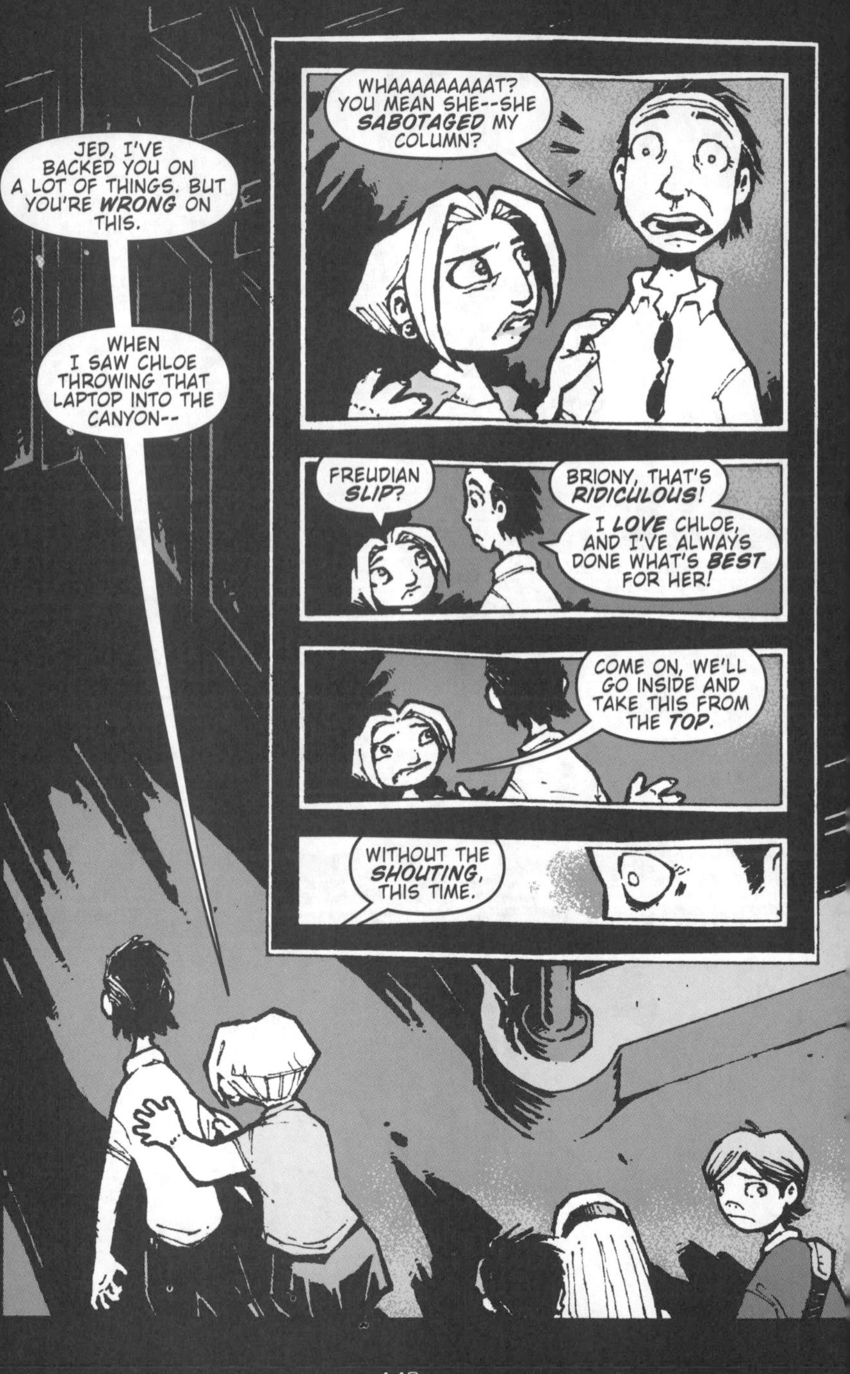
JED, I'VE BACKED YOU ON A LOT OF THINGS. BUT YOU'RE WRONG ON THIS.
WHEN I SAW CHLOE THROWING THAT LAPTOP INTO THE CANYON--
WHAAAAAAAAAT? YOU MEAN SHE--SHE SABOTAGED MY COLUMN?
FREUDIAN SLIP?
BRIONY, THAT'S RIDICULOUS!
I LOVE CHLOE, AND I'VE ALWAYS DONE WHAT'S BEST FOR HER!
COME ON, WE'LL GO INSIDE AND TAKE THIS FROM THE TOP.
WITHOUT THE SHOUTING, THIS TIME.

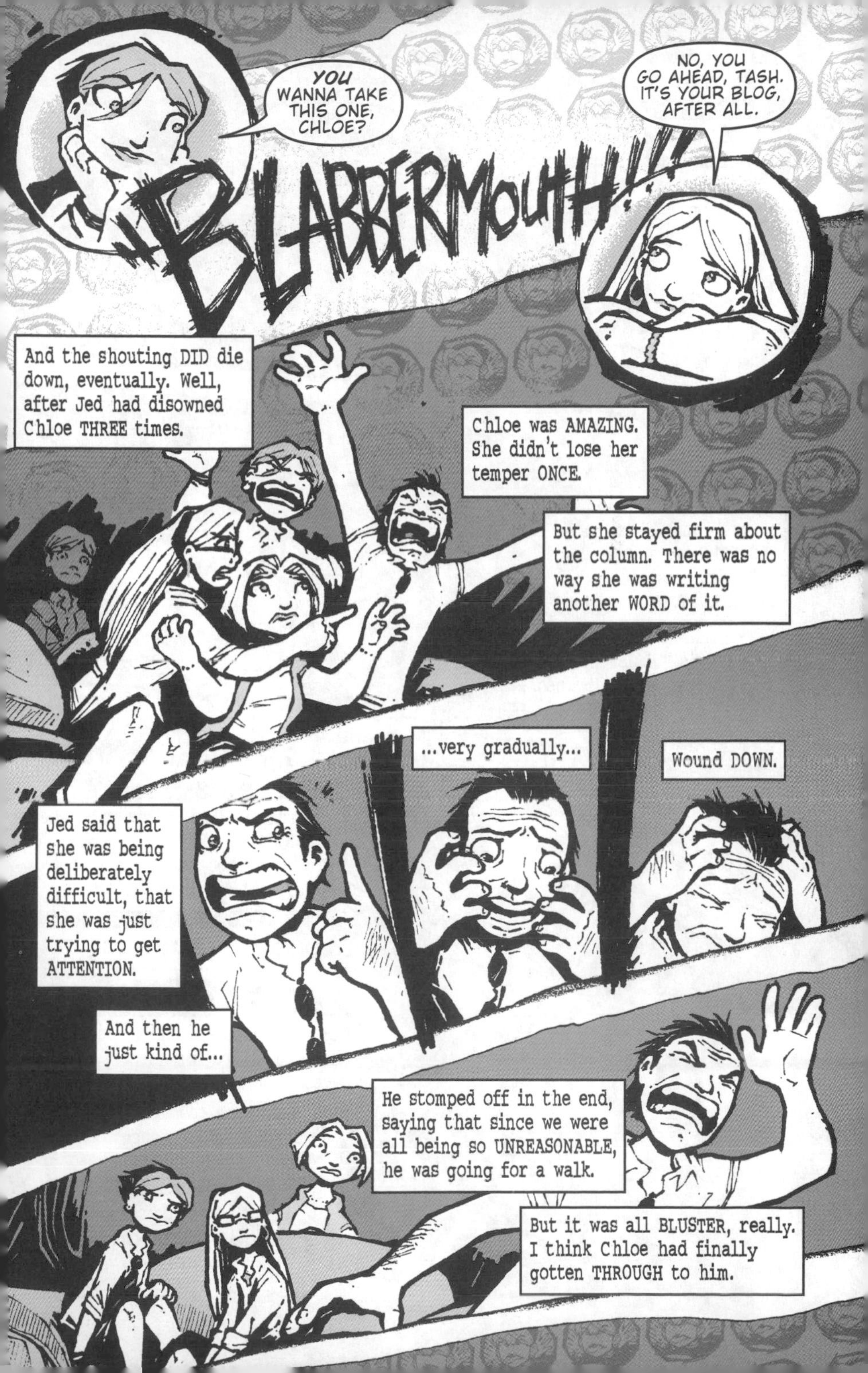
YOU WANNA TAKE THIS ONE, CHLOE?
NO, YOU GO AHEAD, TASH. IT'S YOUR BLOG, AFTER ALL.
BLABBERMOUTH!!!
And the shouting DID die down, eventually. Well, after Jed had disowned Chloe THREE times.
Chloe was AMAZING. She didn't lose her temper ONCE.
But she stayed firm about the column. There was no way she was writing another WORD of it.
Jed said that she was being deliberately difficult, that she was just trying to get ATTENTION.
...very gradually...
Wound DOWN.
And then he just kind of...
He stomped off in the end, saying that since we were all being so UNREASONABLE, he was going for a walk.
But it was all BLUSTER, really. I think Chloe had finally gotten THROUGH to him.

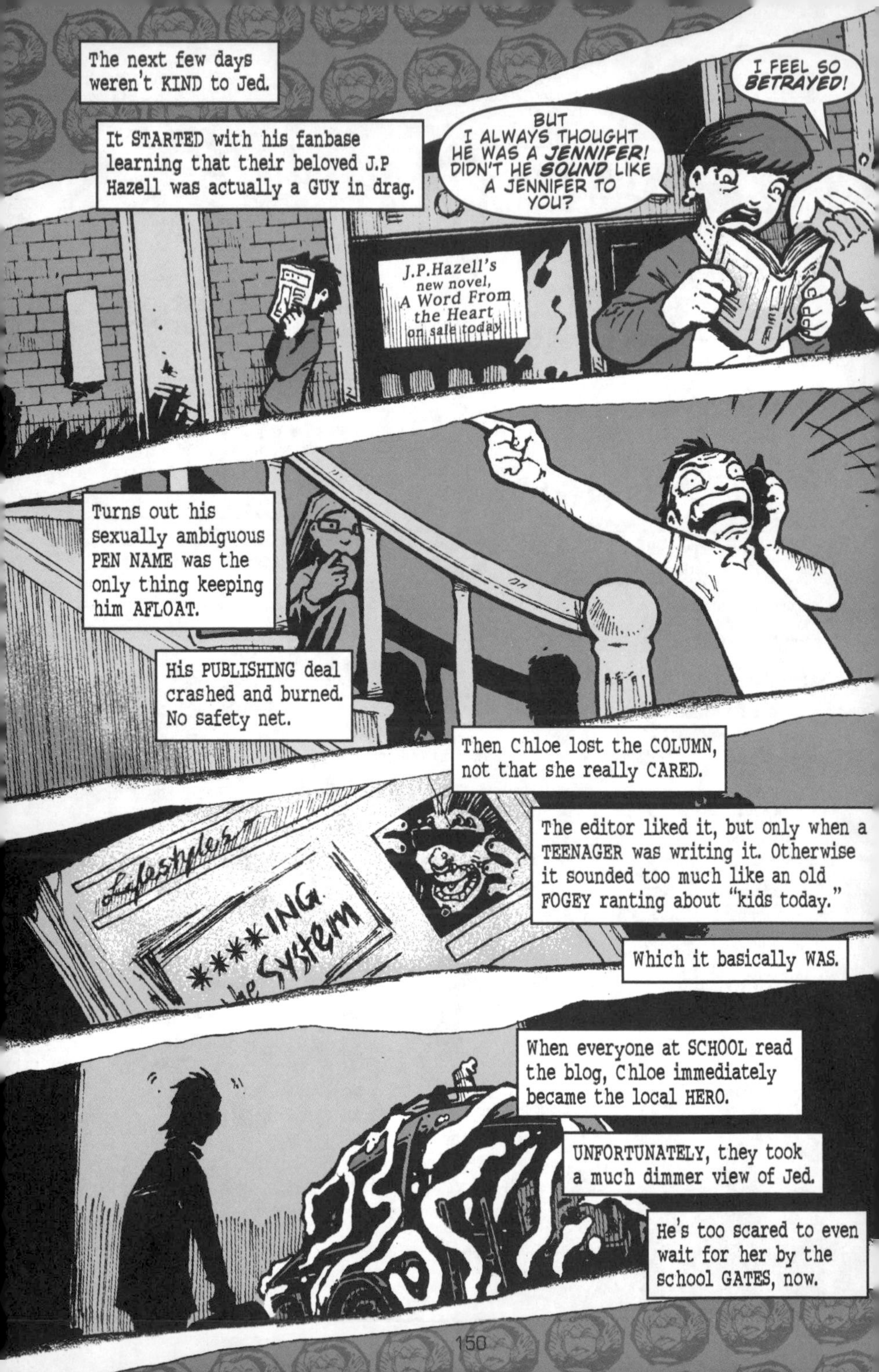

The next few days weren't KIND to Jed.
It STARTED with his fanbase learning that their beloved J.P Hazell was actually a GUY in drag.
BUT I ALWAYS THOUGHT HE WAS A JENNIFER! DIDN'T HE SOUND LIKE A JENNIFER TO YOU?
I FEEL SO BETRAYED!
J.P.Hazell's new novel, A Word From the Heart on sale today
Turns out his sexually ambiguous PEN NAME was the only thing keeping him AFLOAT.
His PUBLISHING deal crashed and burned. No safety net.
Then Chloe lost the COLUMN, not that she really CARED.
Lifestyles
***ING the System
The editor liked it, but only when a TEENAGER was writing it. Otherwise it sounded too much like an old FOGEY ranting about "kids today."
Which it basically WAS.
When everyone at SCHOOL read the blog, Chloe immediately became the local HERO.
UNFORTUNATELY, they took a much dimmer view of Jed.
He's too scared to even wait for her by the school GATES, now.

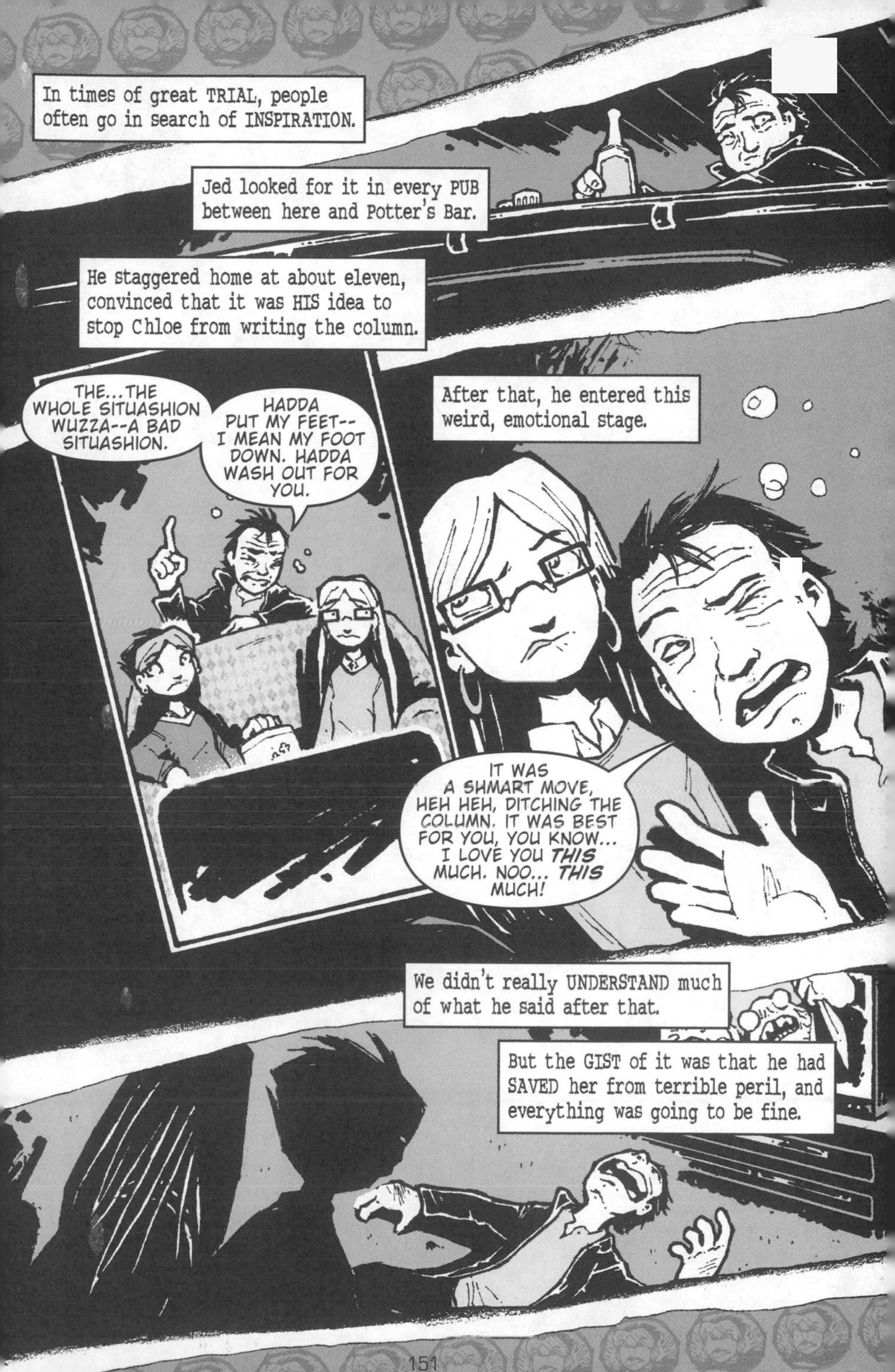

In times of great TRIAL, people often go in search of INSPIRATION.
Jed looked for it in every PUB between here and Potter's Bar.
He staggered home at about eleven, convinced that it was HIS idea to stop Chloe from writing the column.
THE...THE WHOLE SITUASHION WUZZA--A BAD SITUASHION.
HADDA PUT MY FEET-- I MEAN MY FOOT DOWN. HADDA WASH OUT FOR YOU.
After that, he entered this weird, emotional stage.
IT WAS A SHMART MOVE, HEH HEH, DITCHING THE COLUMN. IT WAS BEST FOR YOU, YOU KNOW... I LOVE YOU THIS MUCH. NOO... THIS MUCH!
We didn't really UNDERSTAND much of what he said after that.
But the GIST of it was that he had SAVED her from terrible peril, and everything was going to be fine.

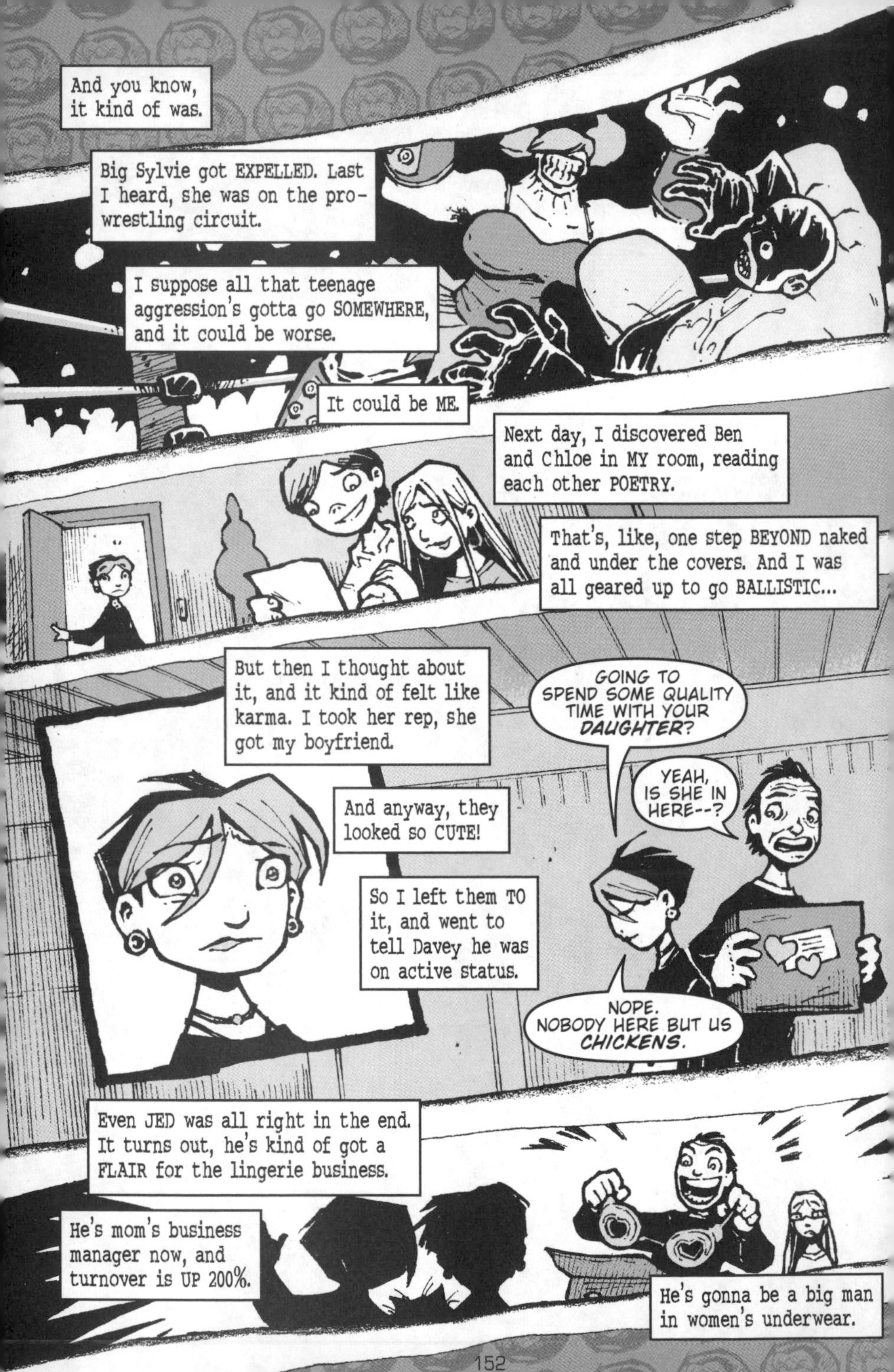

And you know, it kind of was.
Big Sylvie got EXPELLED. Last I heard, she was on the pro-wrestling circuit.
I suppose all that teenage aggression's gotta go SOMEWHERE, and it could be worse.
It could be ME.
Next day, I discovered Ben and Chloe in MY room, reading each other POETRY.
That's, like, one step BEYOND naked and under the covers. And I was all geared up to go BALLISTIC...
But then I thought about it, and it kind of felt like karma. I took her rep, she got my boyfriend.
And anyway, they looked so CUTE!
So I left them TO it, and went to tell Davey he was on active status.
GOING TO SPEND SOME QUALITY TIME WITH YOUR DAUGHTER?
YEAH, IS SHE IN HERE--?
NOPE. NOBODY HERE BUT US CHICKENS.
Even JED was all right in the end. It turns out, he's kind of got a FLAIR for the lingerie business.
He's mom's business manager now, and turnover is UP 200%.
He's gonna be a big man in women's underwear.

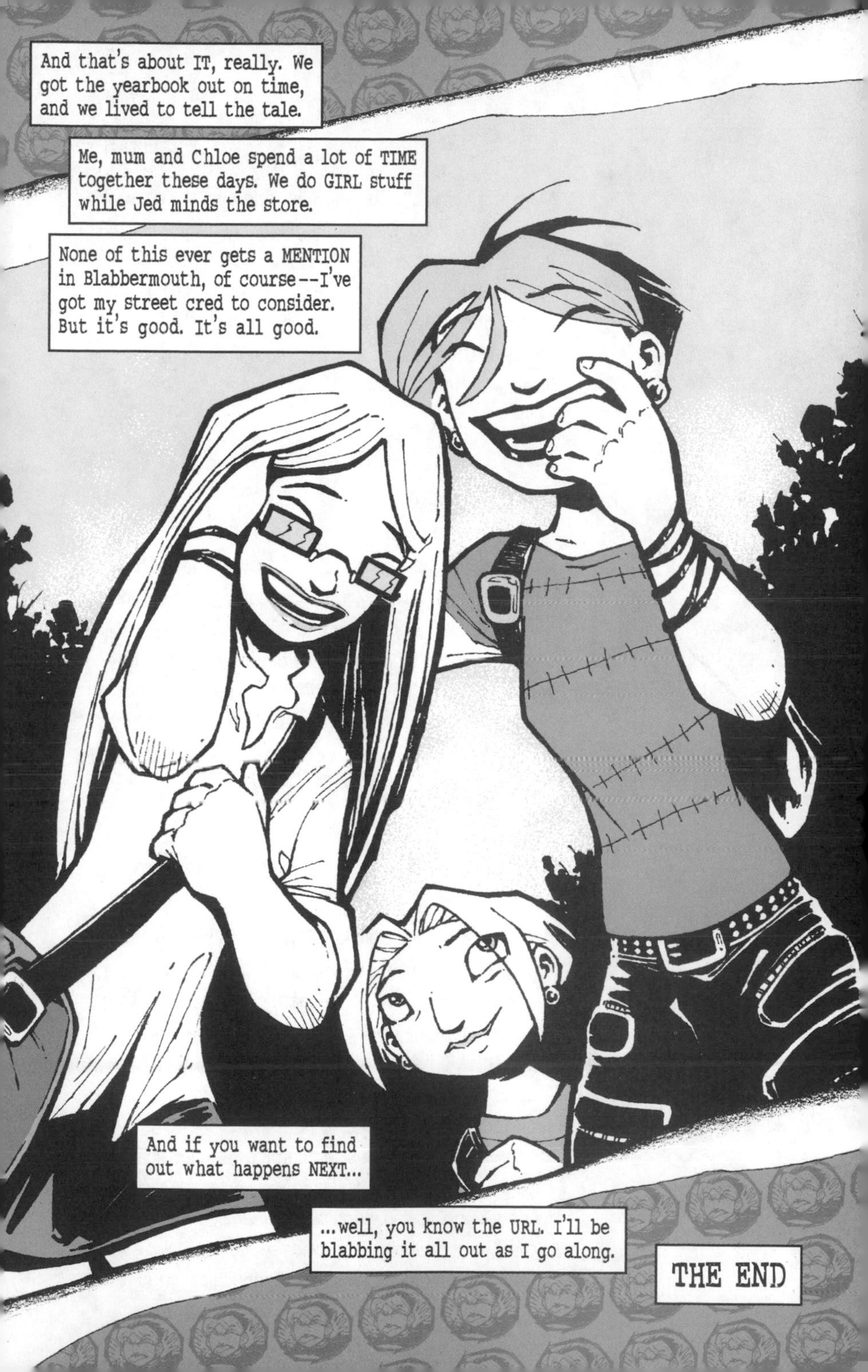
And that's about IT, really. We got the yearbook out on time, and we lived to tell the tale.
Me, mum and Chloe spend a lot of TIME together these days. We do GIRL stuff while Jed minds the store.
None of this ever gets a MENTION in Blabbermouth, of course--I've got my street cred to consider. But it's good. It's all good.
And if you want to find out what happens NEXT...
...well, you know the URL. I'll be blabbing it all out as I go along.
THE END

MIKE CAREY

Mike is a comics writer, novelist and screenwriter who lives and works in London, England. He is best known for his work on the multiple Eisner-nominated LUCIFER series, HELLBLAZER and CROSSING MIDNIGHT. He is the author of the *Felix Castor* novels and the MINX book RE-GIFTERS. His real claim to fame is working with his fifteen-year-old daughter, Louise.

LOUISE CAREY

Mike's fifteen-year-old daughter is the power behind that particular throne and knows a thing or two about Mike's chocolate addiction and his retro-gaming habit. Louise's writing includes the *Diary of a London Schoolgirl* for the website of the London Metropolitan Archive and the novel-in-progress *Bethany's Words*.

AARON ALEXOVICH

Aaron was born in Chicago, Illinois, the year Elvis died but currently sleeps the daylight hours away in Hillsboro, Oregon. After neglecting to graduate from the world-famous California Institute of the Arts, Mr. A. took up space in the animation industry for a little while, contributing character designs to Nickelodeon's *Invader Zim* and *Avatar: The Last Airbender*. He likes making comics way better, though. Aaron's first published work was the critically lauded "spookycute" witch tale *Serenity Rose* for Slave Labor Graphics. His website, which includes a dancing goblin, is at www.heartshapedskull.com.

S P E C I A L   B A C K S T A G E   P A S S :

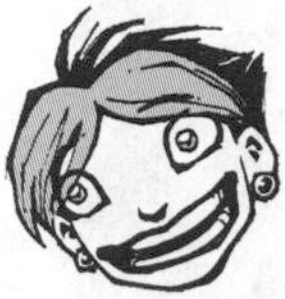

If you liked the story you've just read, fear not: Other MINX books will be available in the months to come. MINX is a line of books that's designed especially for you — someone who's a bit bored with straight fiction and ready for stories that are visually exciting beyond words — literally. In fact, we thought you might like to get in on a secret, behind-the-scenes look at a few of the new MINX titles that will aid in your escape to cool places this fall. So hurry up and turn the page already! And be sure to check out other exclusive material at

minxbooks.net

A Korean-American California girl who's into martial arts learns

that in romance and recycled gifts, what goes around comes around.

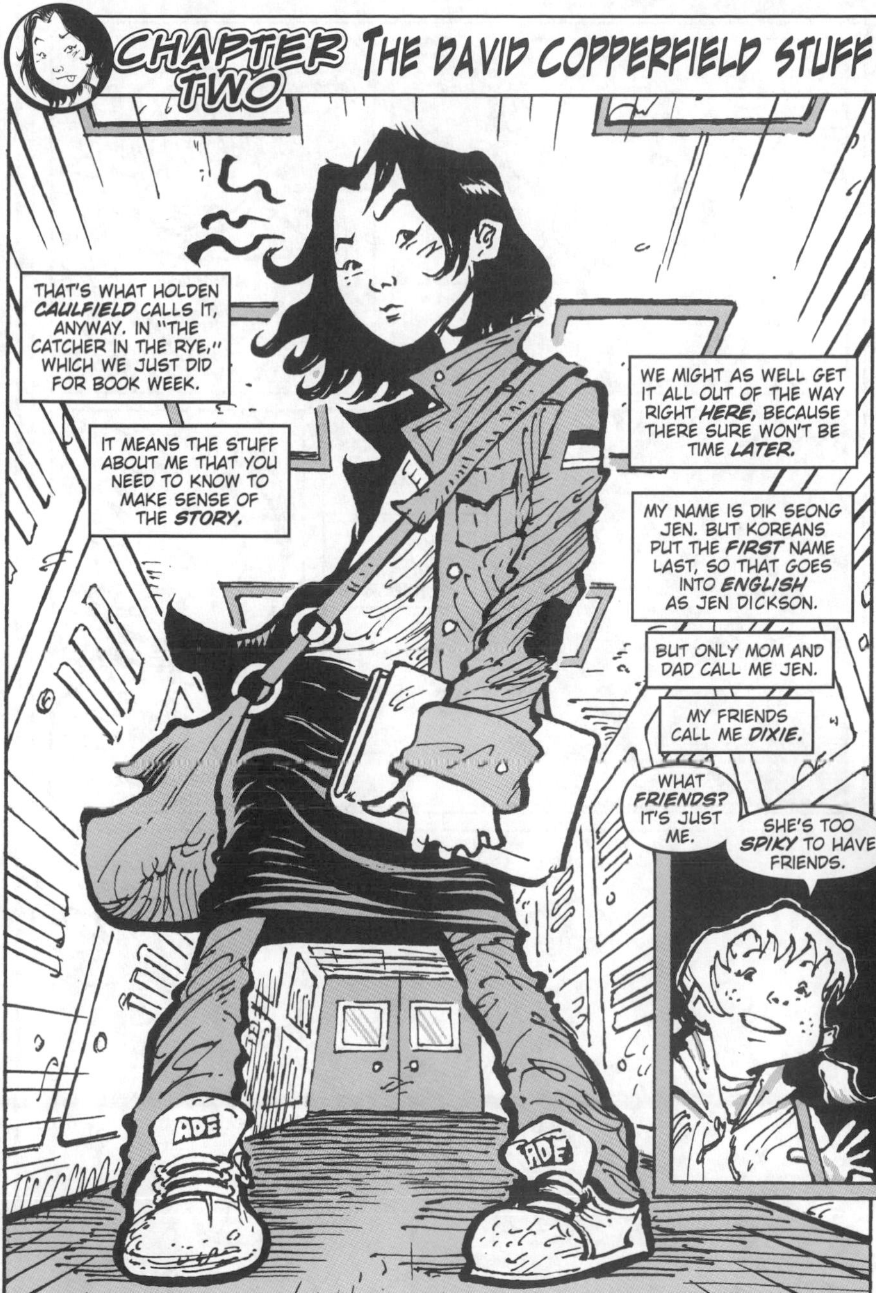
CHAPTER TWO
THE DAVID COPPERFIELD STUFF
THAT'S WHAT HOLDEN CAULFIELD CALLS IT, ANYWAY. IN "THE CATCHER IN THE RYE," WHICH WE JUST DID FOR BOOK WEEK.
IT MEANS THE STUFF ABOUT ME THAT YOU NEED TO KNOW TO MAKE SENSE OF THE STORY.
WE MIGHT AS WELL GET IT ALL OUT OF THE WAY RIGHT HERE, BECAUSE THERE SURE WON'T BE TIME LATER.
MY NAME IS DIK SEONG JEN. BUT KOREANS PUT THE FIRST NAME LAST, SO THAT GOES INTO ENGLISH AS JEN DICKSON.
BUT ONLY MOM AND DAD CALL ME JEN.
MY FRIENDS CALL ME DIXIE.
WHAT FRIENDS? IT'S JUST ME.
SHE'S TOO SPIKY TO HAVE FRIENDS.
ADE
ADE

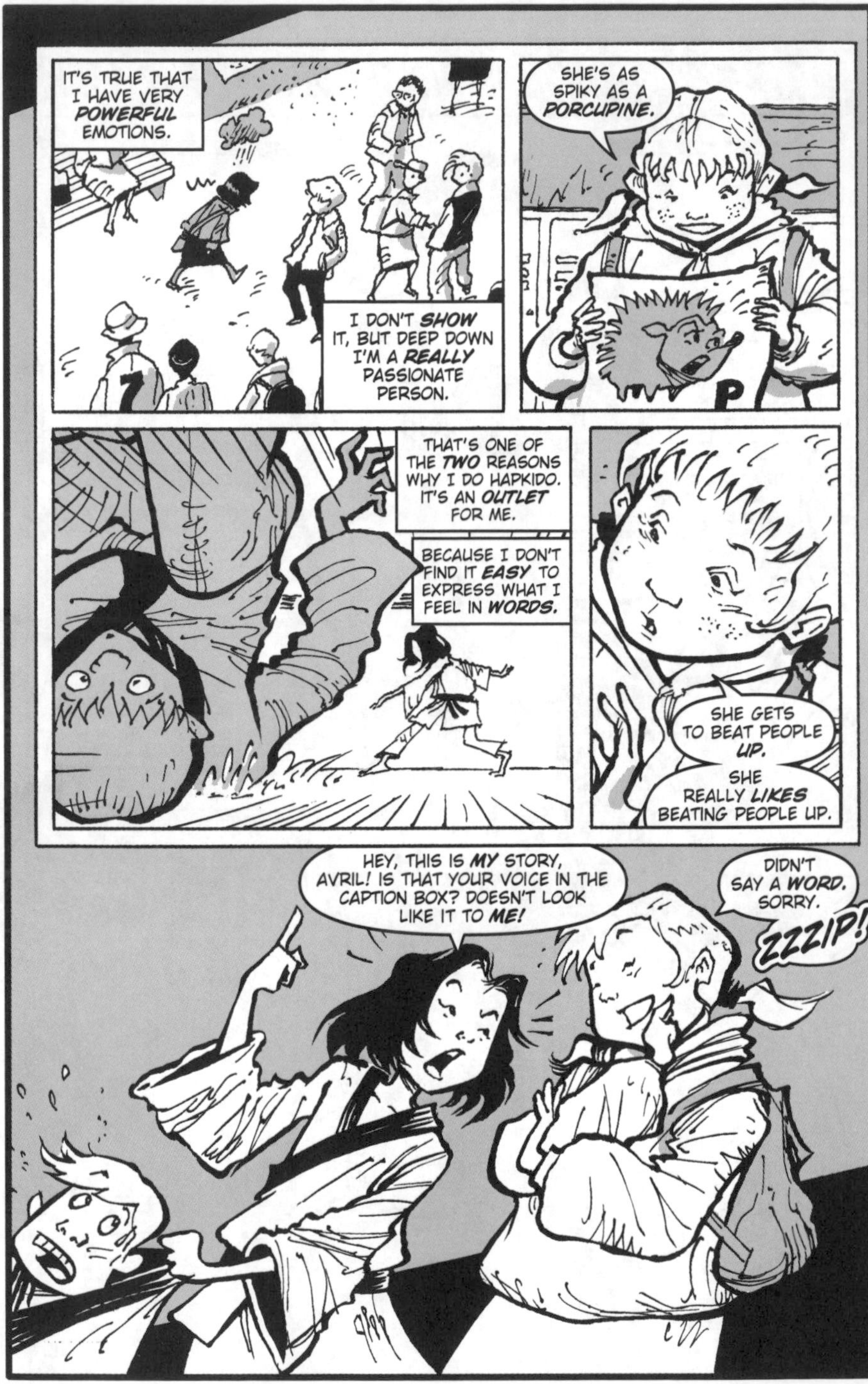
IT'S TRUE THAT I HAVE VERY POWERFUL EMOTIONS.
I DON'T SHOW IT, BUT DEEP DOWN I'M A REALLY PASSIONATE PERSON.
SHE'S AS SPIKY AS A PORCUPINE.
P
7
THAT'S ONE OF THE TWO REASONS WHY I DO HAPKIDO. IT'S AN OUTLET FOR ME.
BECAUSE I DON'T FIND IT EASY TO EXPRESS WHAT I FEEL IN WORDS.
SHE GETS TO BEAT PEOPLE UP.
SHE REALLY LIKES BEATING PEOPLE UP.
HEY, THIS IS MY STORY, AVRIL! IS THAT YOUR VOICE IN THE CAPTION BOX? DOESN'T LOOK LIKE IT TO ME!
DIDN'T SAY A WORD. SORRY.
ZZZIP!

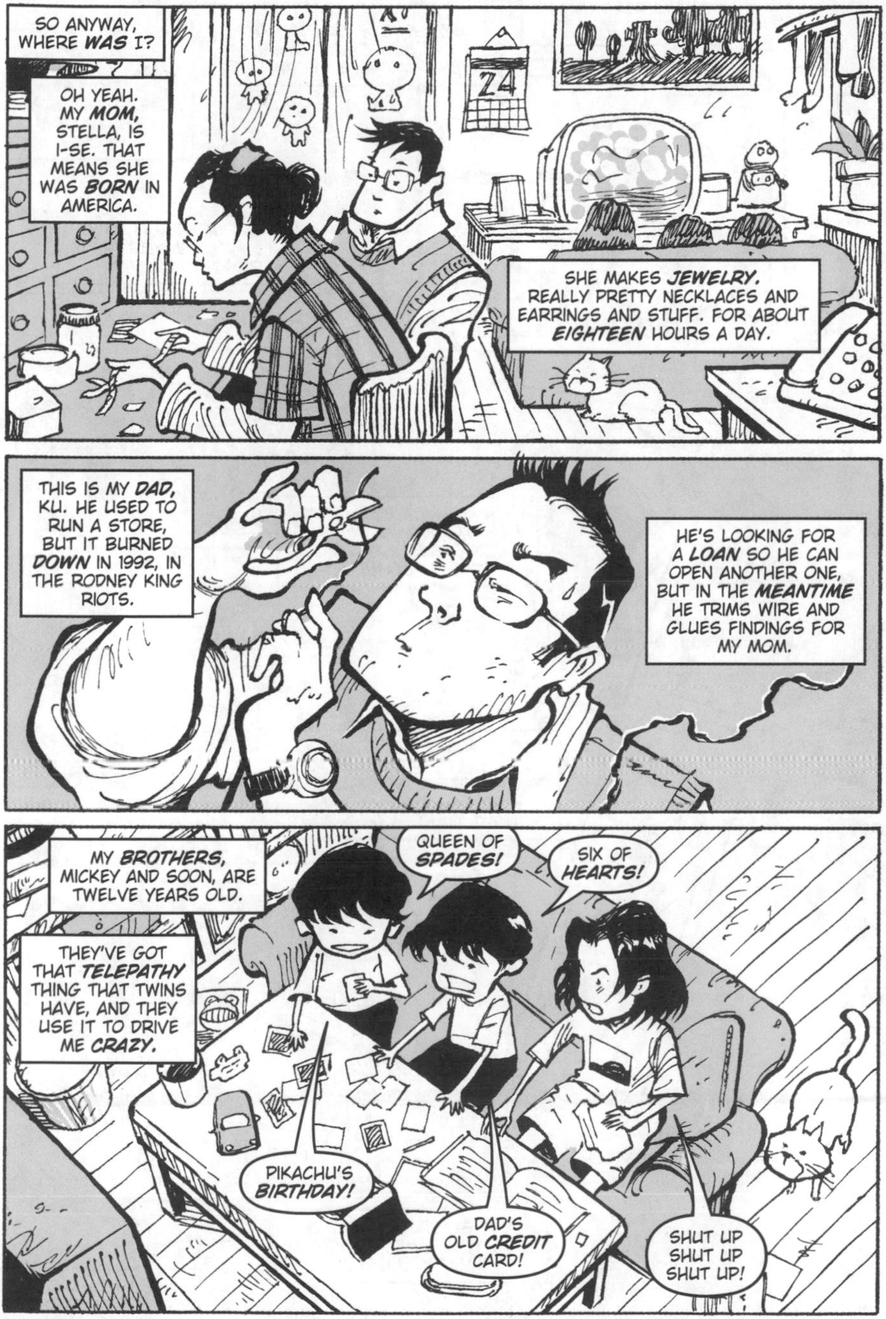
SO ANYWAY, WHERE WAS I?
OH YEAH. MY MOM, STELLA, IS I-SE. THAT MEANS SHE WAS BORN IN AMERICA.
24
SHE MAKES JEWELRY. REALLY PRETTY NECKLACES AND EARRINGS AND STUFF. FOR ABOUT EIGHTEEN HOURS A DAY.
THIS IS MY DAD, KU. HE USED TO RUN A STORE, BUT IT BURNED DOWN IN 1992, IN THE RODNEY KING RIOTS.
HE'S LOOKING FOR A LOAN SO HE CAN OPEN ANOTHER ONE, BUT IN THE MEANTIME HE TRIMS WIRE AND GLUES FINDINGS FOR MY MOM.
MY BROTHERS, MICKEY AND SOON, ARE TWELVE YEARS OLD.
THEY'VE GOT THAT TELEPATHY THING THAT TWINS HAVE, AND THEY USE IT TO DRIVE ME CRAZY.
QUEEN OF SPADES!
SIX OF HEARTS!
PIKACHU'S BIRTHDAY!
DAD'S OLD CREDIT CARD!
SHUT UP SHUT UP SHUT UP!

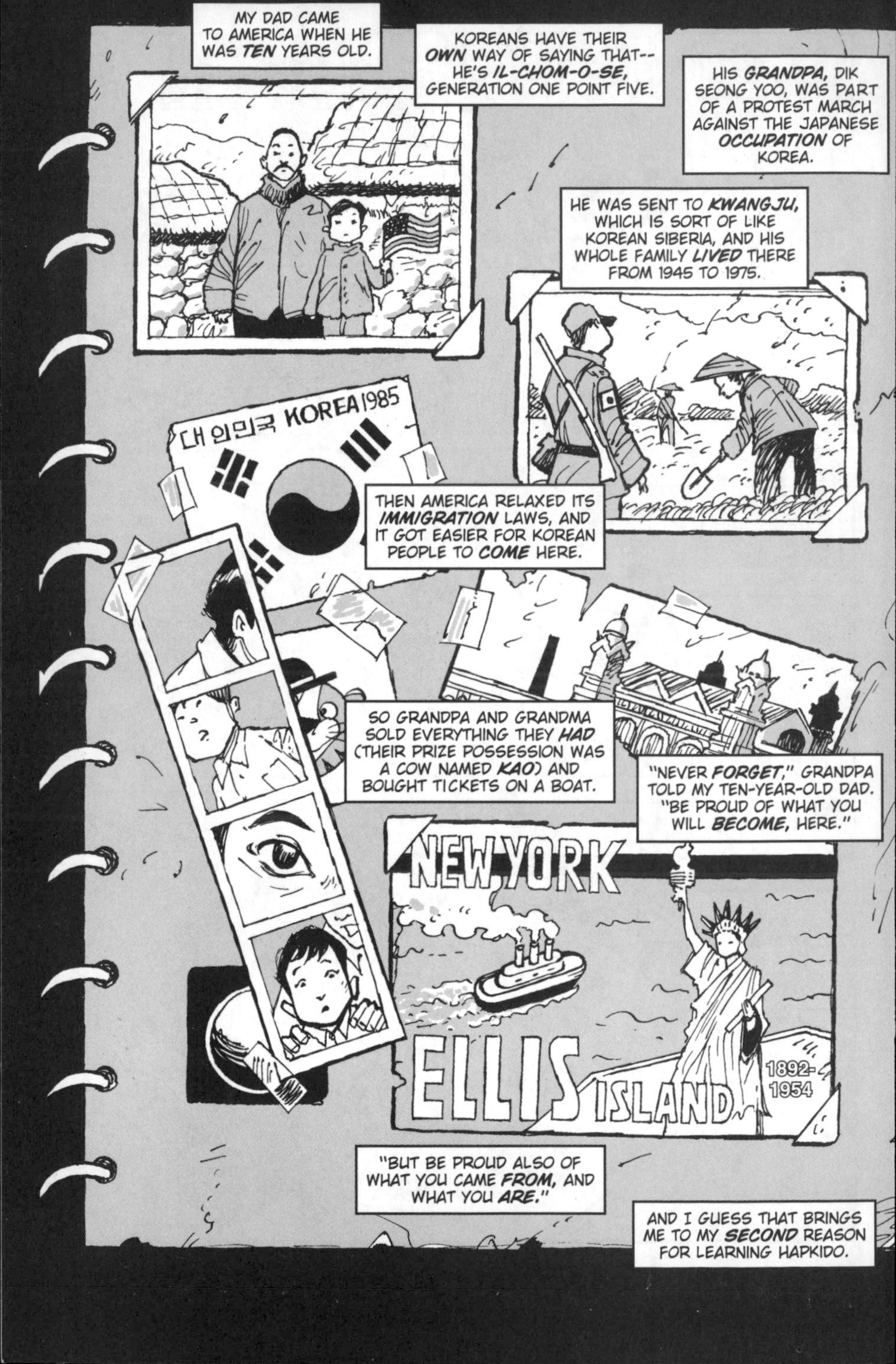
MY DAD CAME TO AMERICA WHEN HE WAS TEN YEARS OLD.
KOREANS HAVE THEIR OWN WAY OF SAYING THAT-- HE'S IL-CHOM-O-SE, GENERATION ONE POINT FIVE.
HIS GRANDPA, DIK SEONG YOO, WAS PART OF A PROTEST MARCH AGAINST THE JAPANESE OCCUPATION OF KOREA.
HE WAS SENT TO KWANGJU, WHICH IS SORT OF LIKE KOREAN SIBERIA, AND HIS WHOLE FAMILY LIVED THERE FROM 1945 TO 1975.
대의민국 KOREA 1985
THEN AMERICA RELAXED ITS IMMIGRATION LAWS, AND IT GOT EASIER FOR KOREAN PEOPLE TO COME HERE.
SO GRANDPA AND GRANDMA SOLD EVERYTHING THEY HAD (THEIR PRIZE POSSESSION WAS A COW NAMED KAO) AND BOUGHT TICKETS ON A BOAT.
"NEVER FORGET," GRANDPA TOLD MY TEN-YEAR-OLD DAD. "BE PROUD OF WHAT YOU WILL BECOME, HERE."
NEW YORK
ELLIS ISLAND
1892-1954
"BUT BE PROUD ALSO OF WHAT YOU CAME FROM, AND WHAT YOU ARE."
AND I GUESS THAT BRINGS ME TO MY SECOND REASON FOR LEARNING HAPKIDO.

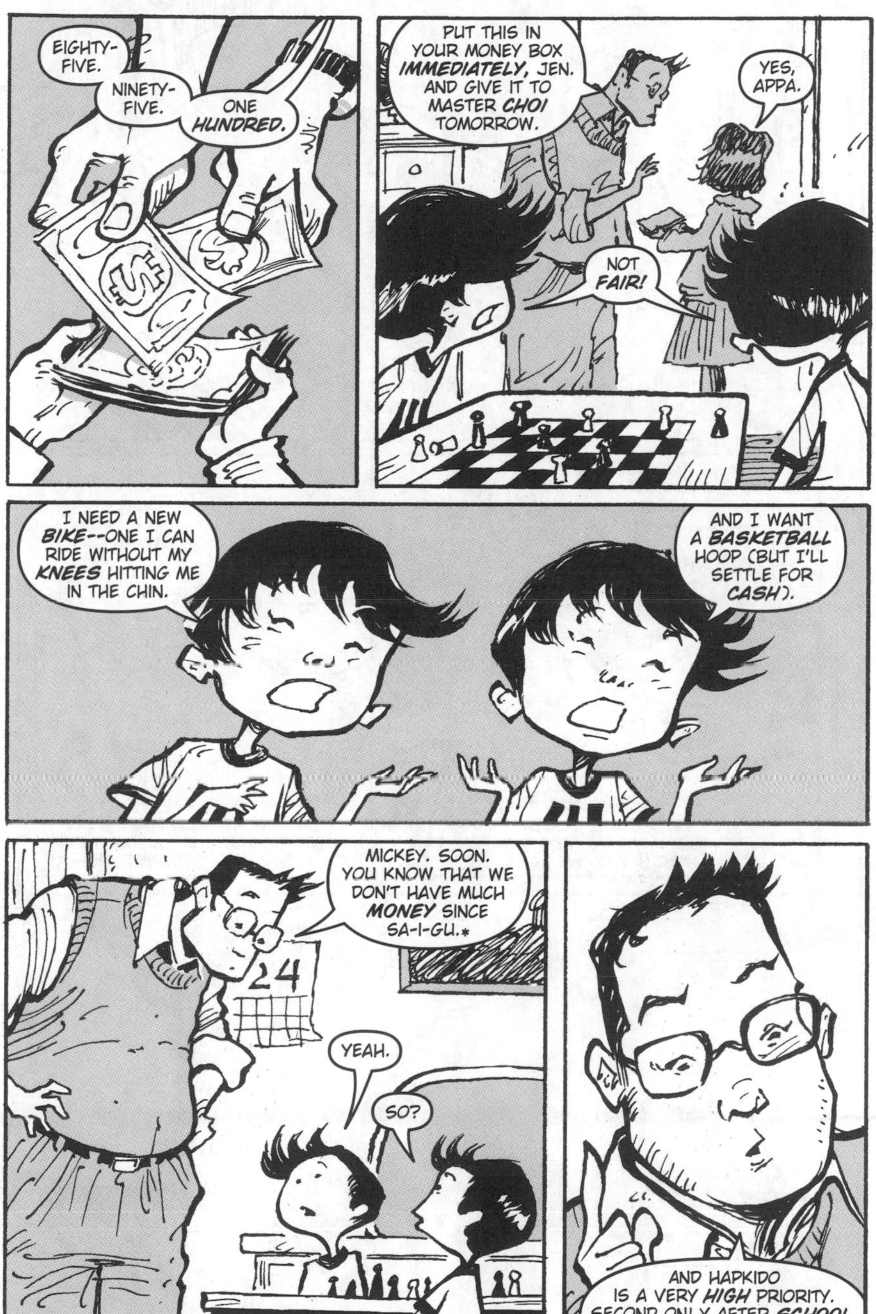
EIGHTY-FIVE.
NINETY-FIVE.
ONE HUNDRED.
PUT THIS IN YOUR MONEY BOX IMMEDIATELY, JEN. AND GIVE IT TO MASTER CHOI TOMORROW.
YES, APPA.
NOT FAIR!
I NEED A NEW BIKE--ONE I CAN RIDE WITHOUT MY KNEES HITTING ME IN THE CHIN.
AND I WANT A BASKETBALL HOOP (BUT I'LL SETTLE FOR CASH).
MICKEY. SOON. YOU KNOW THAT WE DON'T HAVE MUCH MONEY SINCE SA-I-GU.*
24
YEAH.
SO?
AND HAPKIDO IS A VERY HIGH PRIORITY. SECOND ONLY AFTER SCHOOL.

*WHAT KOREANS CALL THE RODNEY KING RIOTS--LITERALLY "APRIL 29TH."

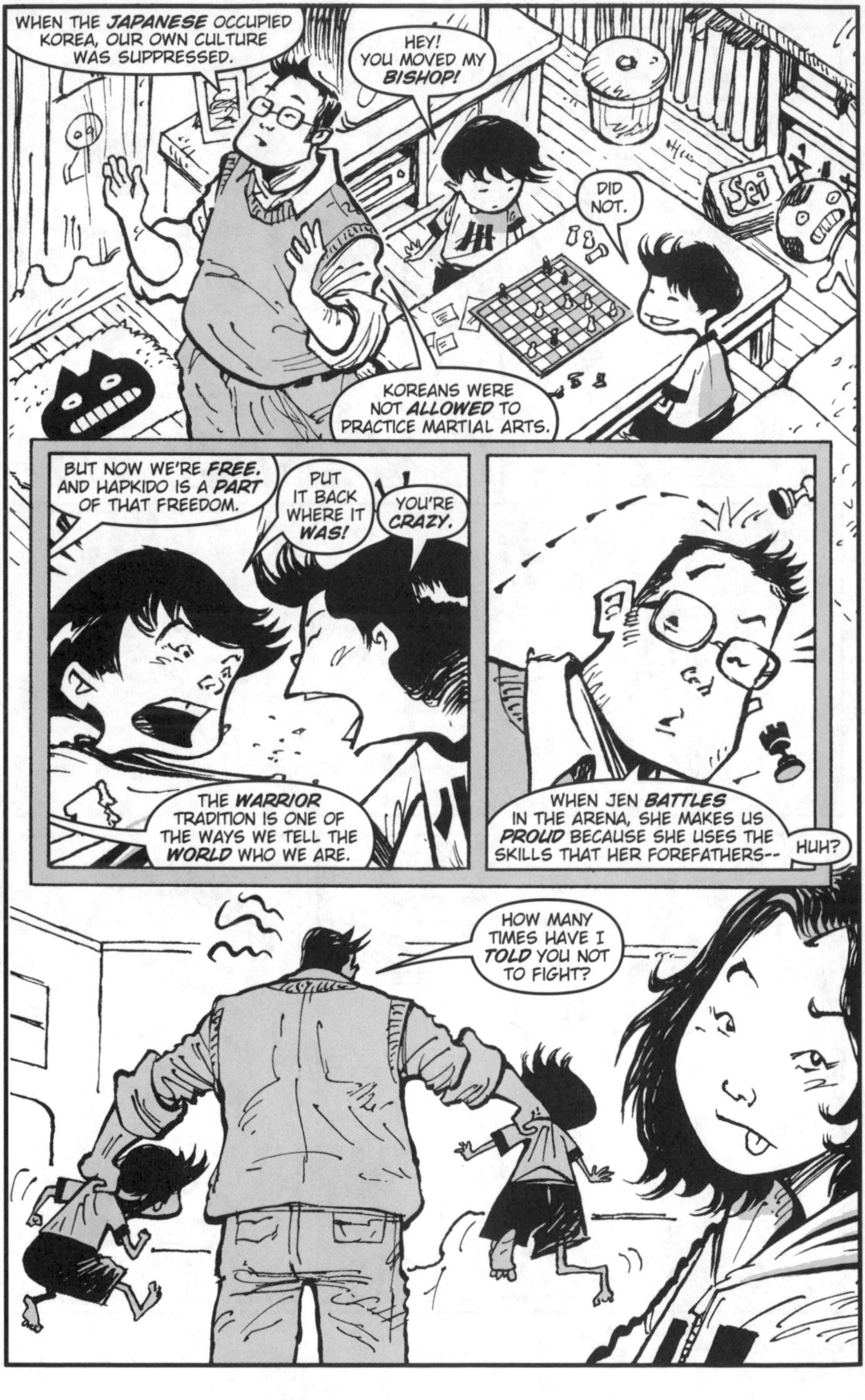
WHEN THE JAPANESE OCCUPIED KOREA, OUR OWN CULTURE WAS SUPPRESSED.
HEY! YOU MOVED MY BISHOP!
DID NOT.
KOREANS WERE NOT ALLOWED TO PRACTICE MARTIAL ARTS.
Sei
BUT NOW WE'RE FREE. AND HAPKIDO IS A PART OF THAT FREEDOM.
PUT IT BACK WHERE IT WAS!
YOU'RE CRAZY.
THE WARRIOR TRADITION IS ONE OF THE WAYS WE TELL THE WORLD WHO WE ARE.
WHEN JEN BATTLES IN THE ARENA, SHE MAKES US PROUD BECAUSE SHE USES THE SKILLS THAT HER FOREFATHERS--
HUH?
HOW MANY TIMES HAVE I TOLD YOU NOT TO FIGHT?

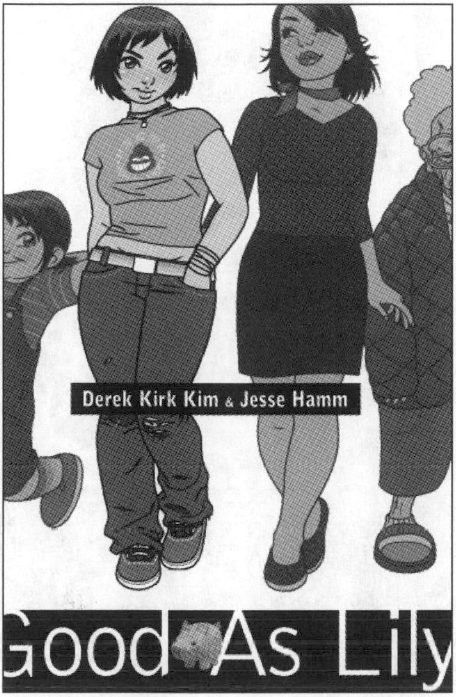
Derek Kirk Kim & Jesse Hamm
Good As Lily

What would you do if versions of yourself at ages 6, 29 and 70

suddenly show up and wreak havoc on your already awkward existence?

AVAILABLE IN AUGUST ■ Read on,

but please note: the following pages are not sequential.

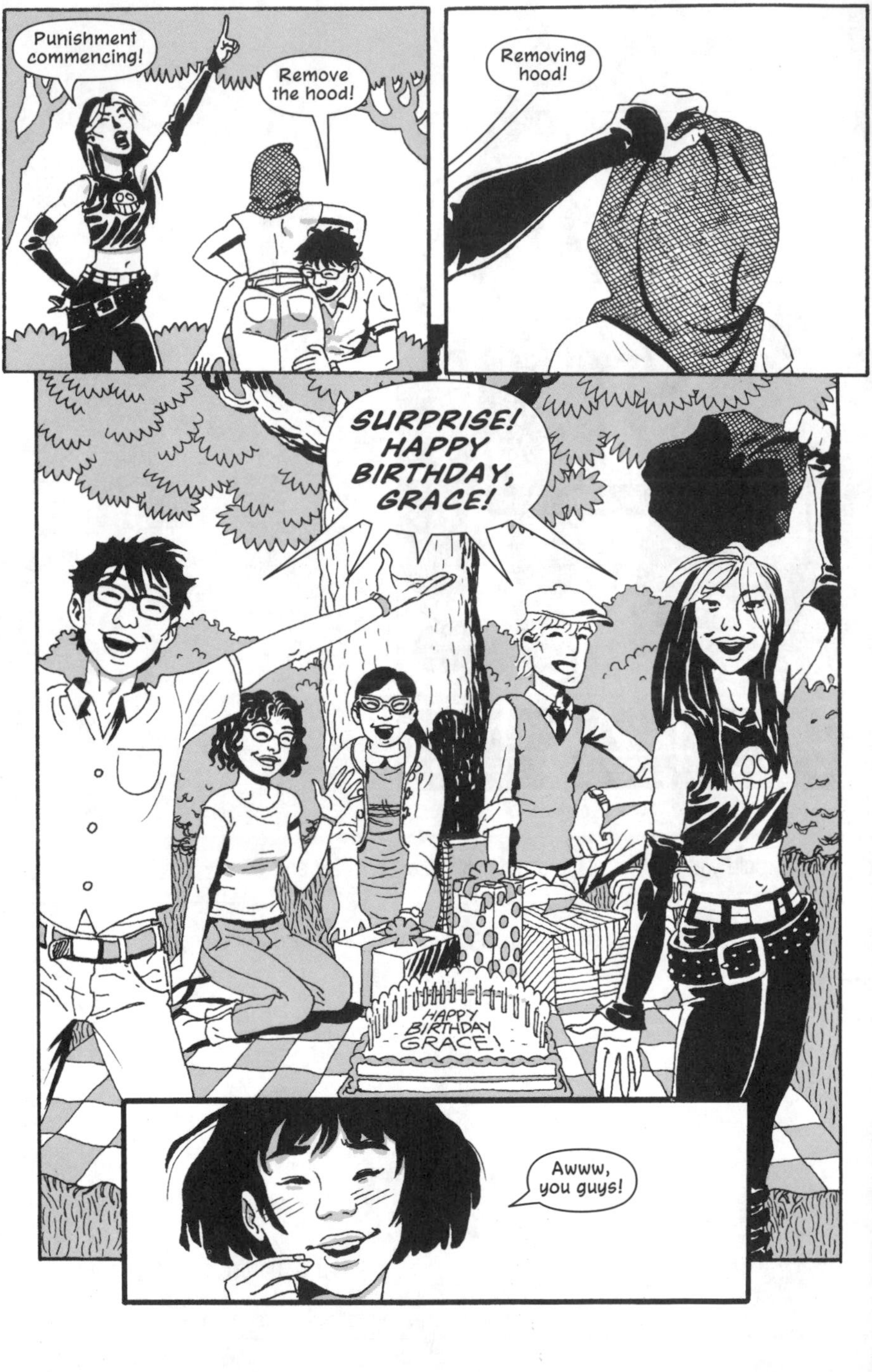
Punishment commencing!
Remove the hood!
Removing hood!
SURPRISE! HAPPY BIRTHDAY, GRACE!
HAPPY BIRTHDAY GRACE!
Awww, you guys!

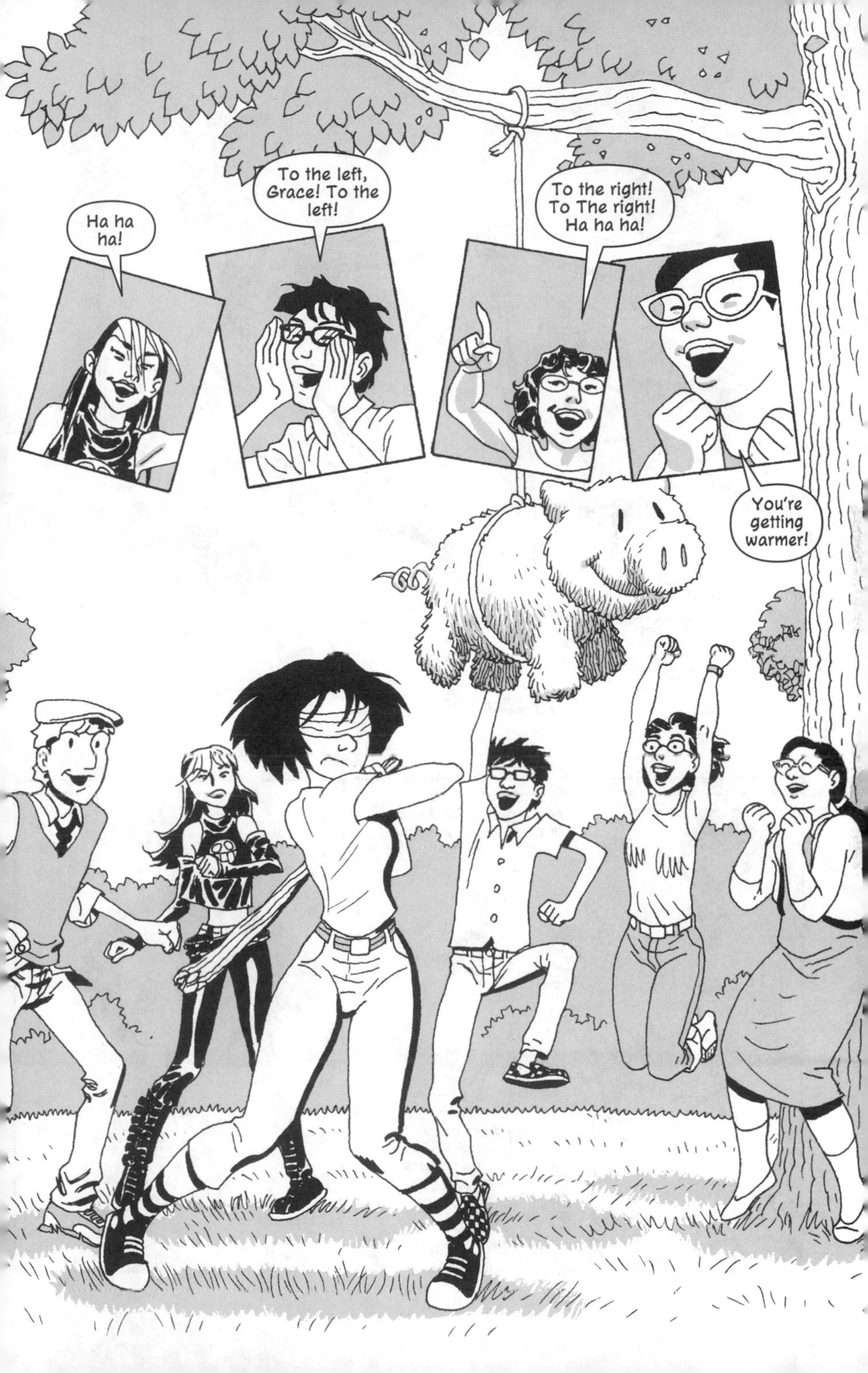
Ha ha ha!
To the left, Grace! To the left!
To the right! To The right! Ha ha ha!
You're getting warmer!

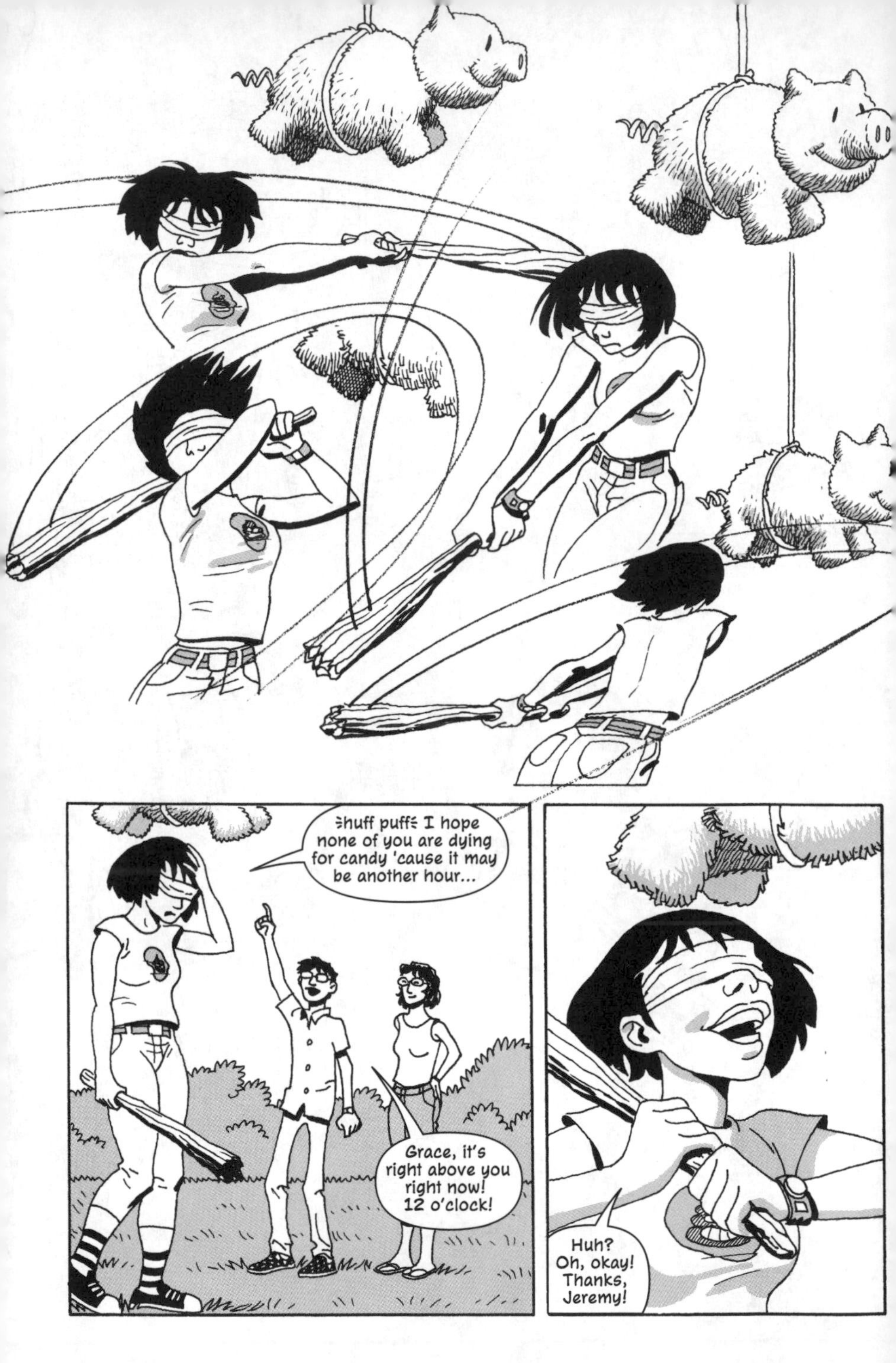
≡huff puff≡ I hope none of you are dying for candy 'cause it may be another hour...
Grace, it's right above you right now! 12 o'clock!
Huh? Oh, okay! Thanks, Jeremy!

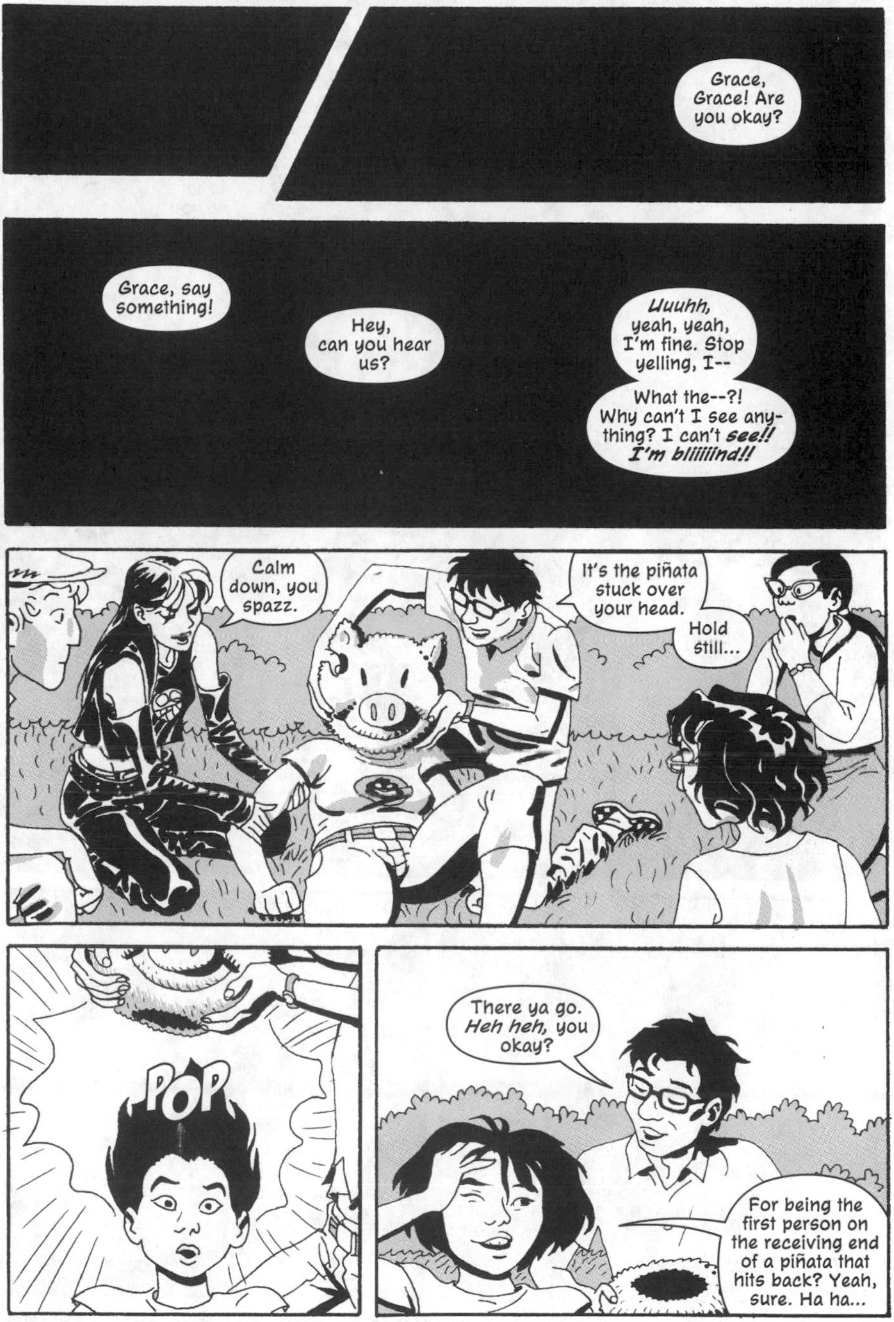
Grace, Grace! Are you okay?
Grace, say something!
Hey, can you hear us?
Uuuhh, yeah, yeah, I'm fine. Stop yelling, I--
What the--?! Why can't I see anything? I can't ***see!! I'm bliiiiind!!***
Calm down, you spazz.
It's the piñata stuck over your head.
Hold still...
POP
There ya go. *Heh heh,* you okay?
For being the first person on the receiving end of a piñata that hits back? Yeah, sure. Ha ha...

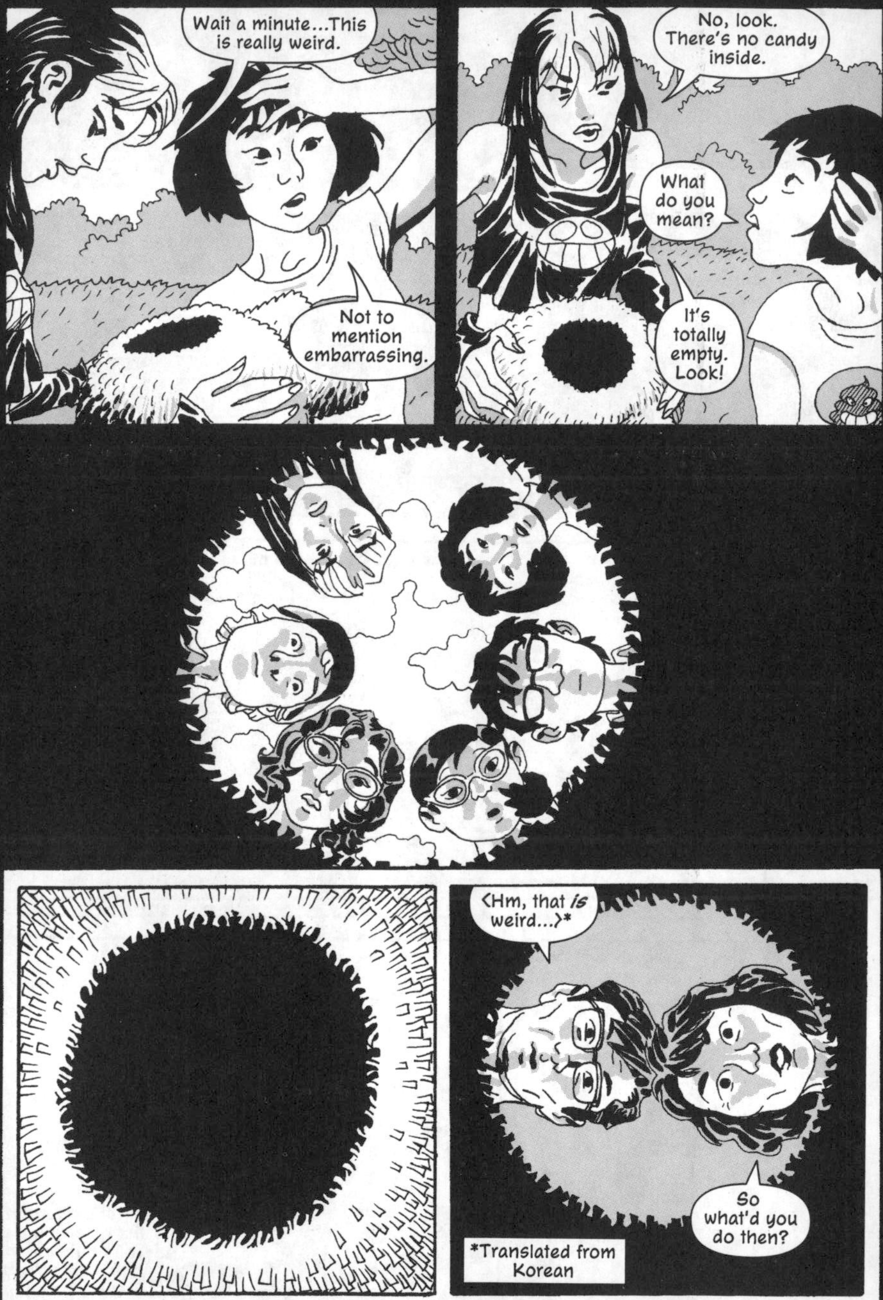

Wait a minute...This is really weird.
Not to mention embarrassing.
No, look. There's no candy inside.
What do you mean?
It's totally empty. Look!
<Hm, that *is* weird...>*
So what'd you do then?
*Translated from Korean

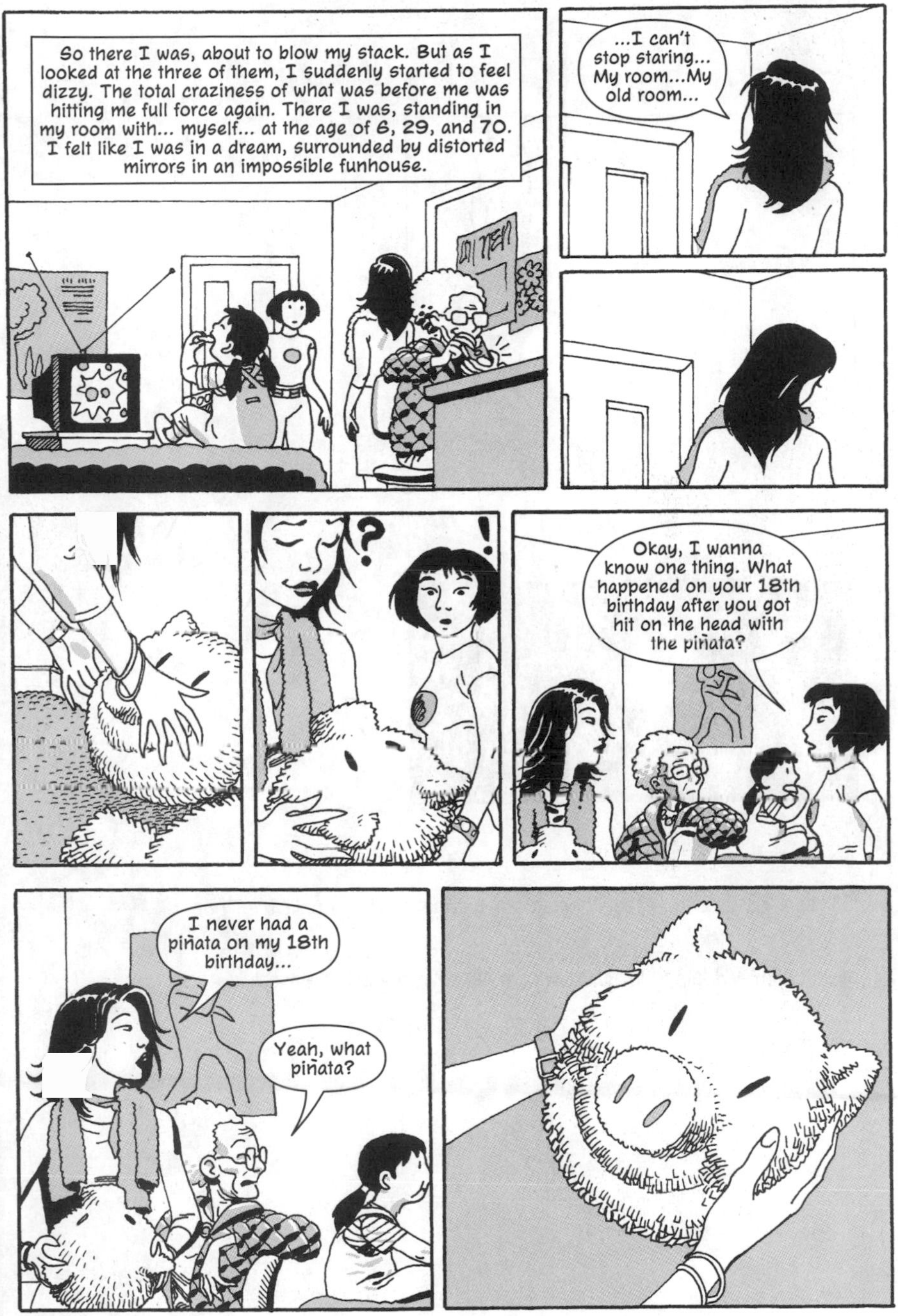

So there I was, about to blow my stack. But as I looked at the three of them, I suddenly started to feel dizzy. The total craziness of what was before me was hitting me full force again. There I was, standing in my room with... myself... at the age of 6, 29, and 70. I felt like I was in a dream, surrounded by distorted mirrors in an impossible funhouse.
...I can't stop staring... My room...My old room...
?
!
Okay, I wanna know one thing. What happened on your 18th birthday after you got hit on the head with the piñata?
I never had a piñata on my 18th birthday...
Yeah, what piñata?

kimmie66
AARON ALEXOVICH

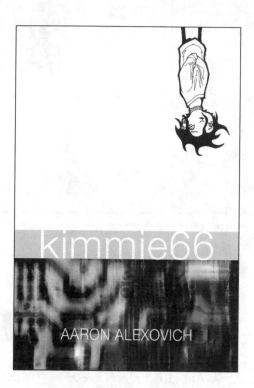

Follow a 23rd century teenager as she navigates the neonlit trenches of an online VR lair to locate the legendary Kimmie66, the world's first digital girl.

COMING IN NOVEMBER 2007

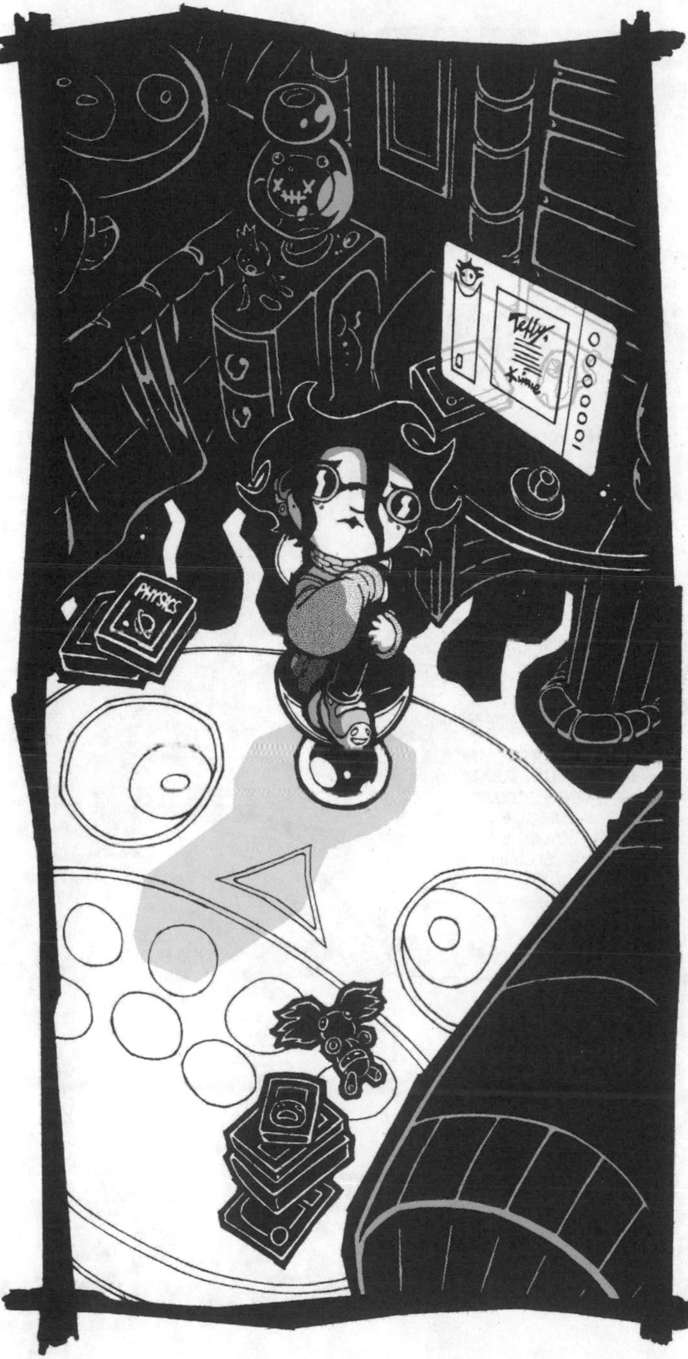
PHYSICS

HOO.

BOY.

IT'S SUCH A PAIN IN THE BUTT WHEN YOU DON'T KNOW YOUR FRIENDS' REAL NAMES. I MEAN, PEOPLE WHO LIVE OUTSIDE THE LAIRS JUST DON'T HAVE PROBLEMS LIKE THIS, DO THEY?

IT'S LIKE... *UM...*

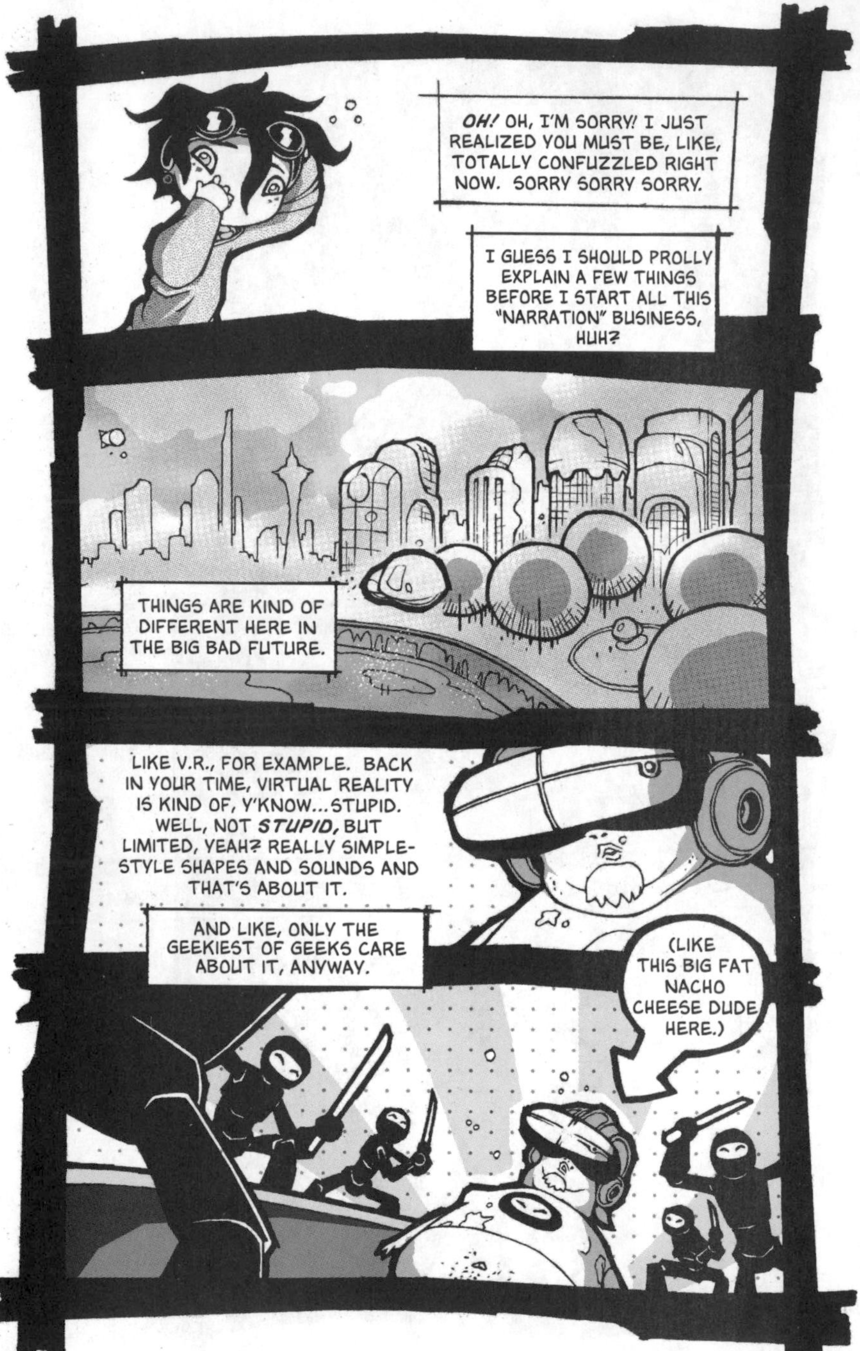
OH! OH, I'M SORRY! I JUST REALIZED YOU MUST BE, LIKE, TOTALLY CONFUZZLED RIGHT NOW. SORRY SORRY SORRY.
I GUESS I SHOULD PROLLY EXPLAIN A FEW THINGS BEFORE I START ALL THIS "NARRATION" BUSINESS, HUH?
THINGS ARE KIND OF DIFFERENT HERE IN THE BIG BAD FUTURE.
LIKE V.R., FOR EXAMPLE. BACK IN YOUR TIME, VIRTUAL REALITY IS KIND OF, Y'KNOW...STUPID. WELL, NOT STUPID, BUT LIMITED, YEAH? REALLY SIMPLE-STYLE SHAPES AND SOUNDS AND THAT'S ABOUT IT.
AND LIKE, ONLY THE GEEKIEST OF GEEKS CARE ABOUT IT, ANYWAY.
(LIKE THIS BIG FAT NACHO CHEESE DUDE HERE.)

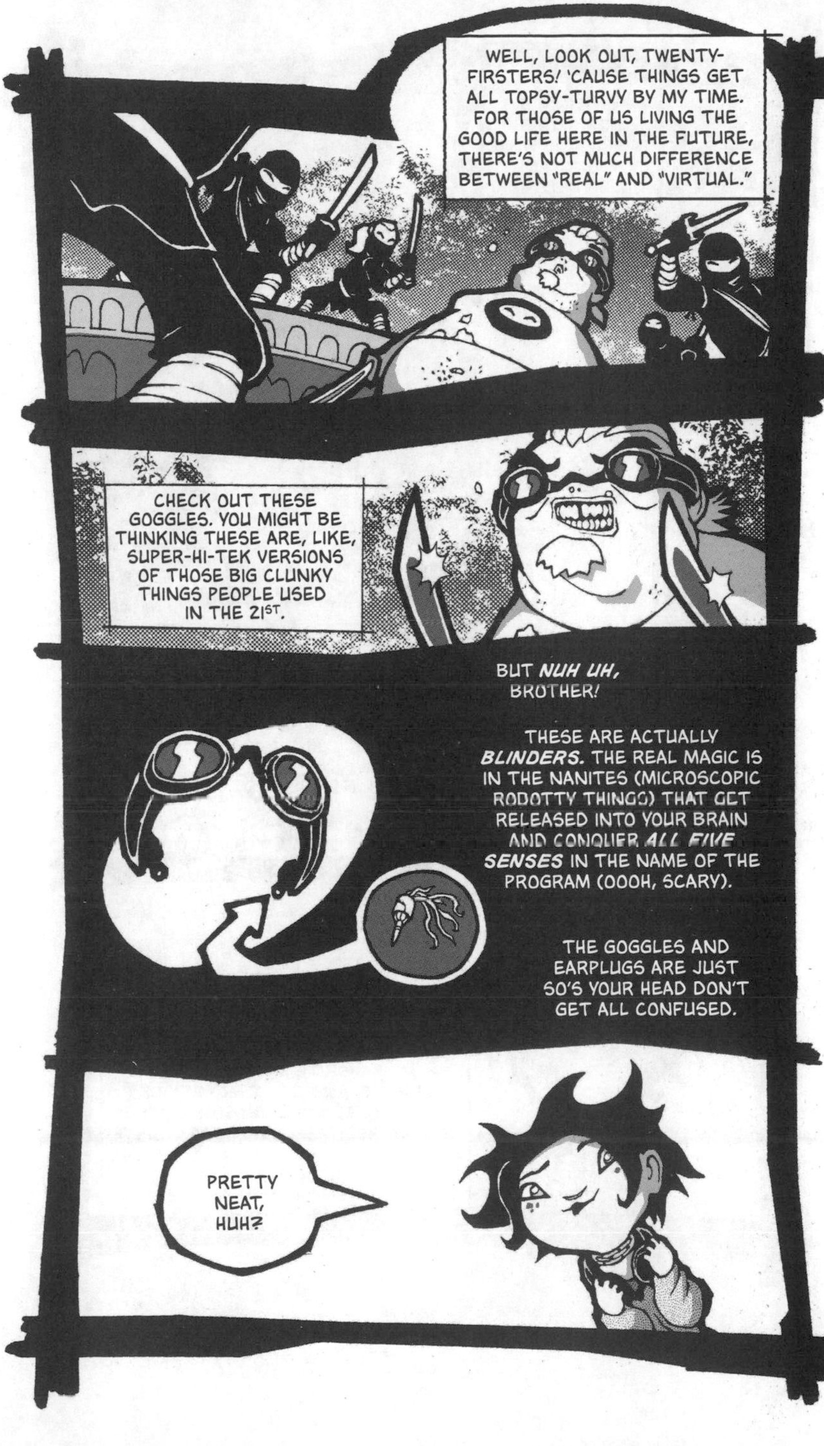
WELL, LOOK OUT, TWENTY-FIRSTERS! 'CAUSE THINGS GET ALL TOPSY-TURVY BY MY TIME. FOR THOSE OF US LIVING THE GOOD LIFE HERE IN THE FUTURE, THERE'S NOT MUCH DIFFERENCE BETWEEN "REAL" AND "VIRTUAL."
CHECK OUT THESE GOGGLES. YOU MIGHT BE THINKING THESE ARE, LIKE, SUPER-HI-TEK VERSIONS OF THOSE BIG CLUNKY THINGS PEOPLE USED IN THE 21ST.
BUT NUH UH, BROTHER!
THESE ARE ACTUALLY BLINDERS. THE REAL MAGIC IS IN THE NANITES (MICROSCOPIC ROBOTTY THINGS) THAT GET RELEASED INTO YOUR BRAIN AND CONQUER ALL FIVE SENSES IN THE NAME OF THE PROGRAM (OOOH, SCARY).
THE GOGGLES AND EARPLUGS ARE JUST SO'S YOUR HEAD DON'T GET ALL CONFUSED.
PRETTY NEAT, HUH?

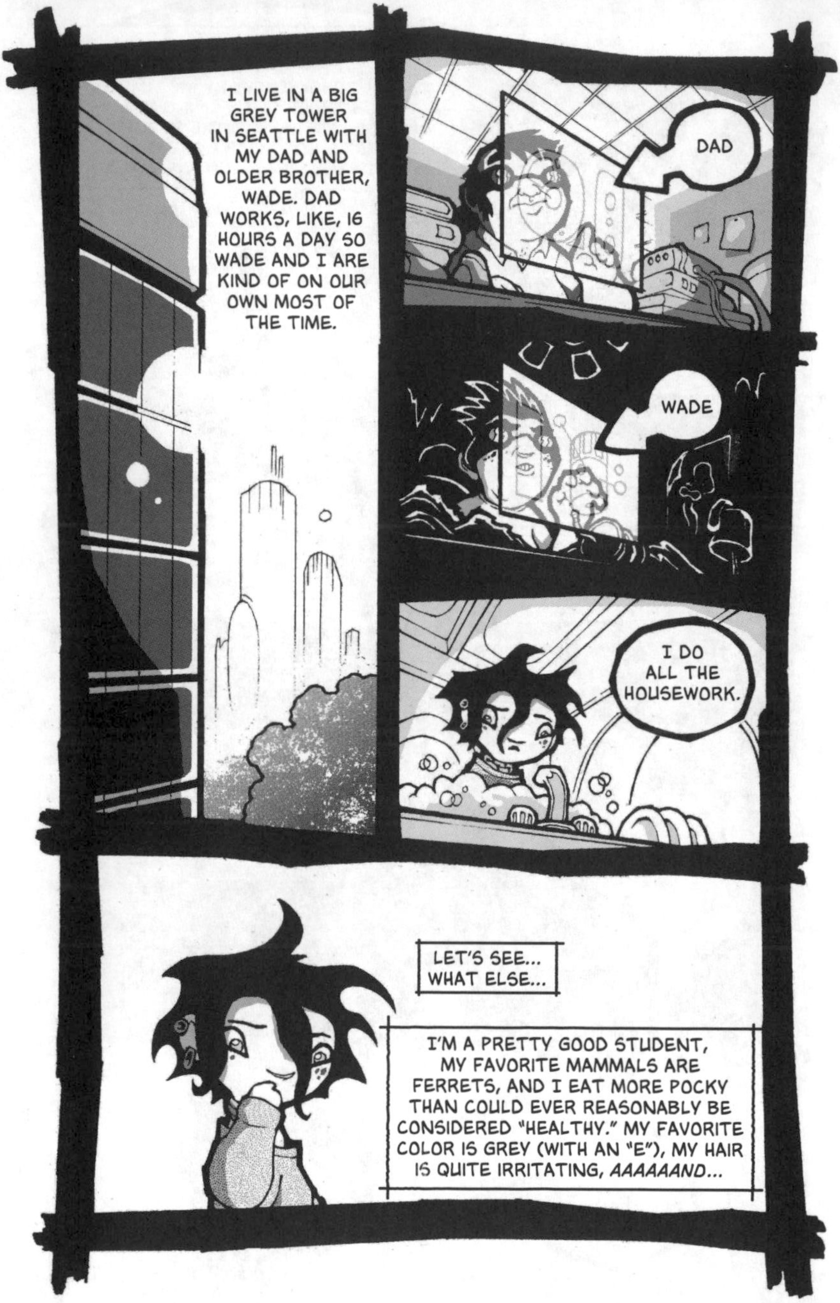
I LIVE IN A BIG GREY TOWER IN SEATTLE WITH MY DAD AND OLDER BROTHER, WADE. DAD WORKS, LIKE, 16 HOURS A DAY SO WADE AND I ARE KIND OF ON OUR OWN MOST OF THE TIME.
DAD
WADE
I DO ALL THE HOUSEWORK.
LET'S SEE... WHAT ELSE...
I'M A PRETTY GOOD STUDENT, MY FAVORITE MAMMALS ARE FERRETS, AND I EAT MORE POCKY THAN COULD EVER REASONABLY BE CONSIDERED "HEALTHY." MY FAVORITE COLOR IS GREY (WITH AN "E"), MY HAIR IS QUITE IRRITATING, *AAAAAAND...*

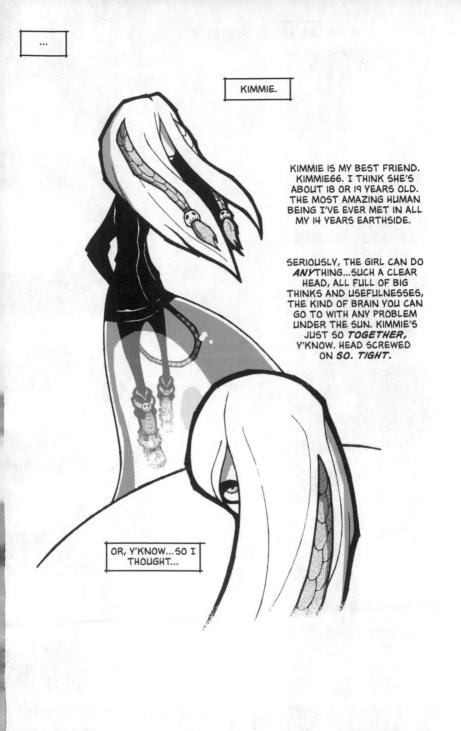

...

KIMMIE.

KIMMIE IS MY BEST FRIEND. KIMMIE66. I THINK SHE'S ABOUT 18 OR 19 YEARS OLD. THE MOST AMAZING HUMAN BEING I'VE EVER MET IN ALL MY 14 YEARS EARTHSIDE.

SERIOUSLY, THE GIRL CAN DO *ANY*THING...SUCH A CLEAR HEAD, ALL FULL OF BIG THINKS AND USEFULNESSES, THE KIND OF BRAIN YOU CAN GO TO WITH ANY PROBLEM UNDER THE SUN. KIMMIE'S JUST SO *TOGETHER*, Y'KNOW. HEAD SCREWED ON *SO. TIGHT.*

OR, Y'KNOW...SO I THOUGHT...